The Third Wave in Science and Technology Studies

David S. Caudill • Shannon N. Conley
Michael E. Gorman • Martin Weinel
Editors

The Third Wave in Science and Technology Studies

Future Research Directions on Expertise
and Experience

Editors
David S. Caudill
Villanova University
Villanova, PA, USA

Shannon N. Conley
James Madison University
Harrisonburg, VA, USA

Michael E. Gorman
University of Virginia
Charlottesville, VA, USA

Martin Weinel
Cardiff University
Cardiff, UK

ISBN 978-3-030-14334-3   ISBN 978-3-030-14335-0   (eBook)
https://doi.org/10.1007/978-3-030-14335-0

This Palgrave Macmillan imprint is published by the registered company Springer Nature Switzerland AG
The registered company address is: Gewerbestrasse 11, 6330 Cham, Switzerland

Foreword

I've spent 40 or more years studying the sociology of gravitational waves, culminating in the acclaimed detection of September 14, 2015. For nearly all of that time, gravitational wave detection was an orphan subject thought by most scientists to be a huge waste of money because of the craziness of the ambition and the near impossibility of success. The sweetness of the eventual success was hugely enhanced by this history of scorn.

What we are engaged in here, in this volume, is not the discovery of gravitational waves, but it has in common the initial rejection followed by growing success. The language of the "Third Wave" began in what Rob Evans and I thought was a modest little paper[1] suggesting that a way out of the logical difficulty of making judgments of competence, from within a social constructivist framework, was to turn attention from the construction of truth to the analysis of expertise: the acquisition of expertise could be observed even if truth was always made by competing parties. We worried that the very notion of expertise would disappear if the democratization of science—making the right to take part in the construction of scientific truth open to anyone—continued to proceed inside Science and Technology Studies (STS). We thought people would look at what we had written, say to us, "Interesting paper," and move on. But to our surprise, we were violently attacked for supposedly re-introducing technocracy and reverting to the bad old days of the 1950s in the social analysis of science.

That is where there is common ground with gravitational wave detection—the sense of "outsiderness," which had very palpable consequences, including marginalization and even non-admission to conferences, and rejection of papers and grants, and the need, at one point, to make a collective decision about whether the professional pressures ought to cause us to abandon the whole thing. On the upside, once the decision to persevere had been made, rejection was energizing, and a whole program has grown out of what would otherwise have been just another paper languishing on a curriculum vitae; instead, that paper has become the second-most cited in the history of the journal, and citations of it together with our book *Rethinking Expertise* (2007) are already well over 4000. The resulting developments include a new understanding of expertise as a social but real, and sometimes ubiquitous, phenomenon; under the SEE (Studies in Expertise and Experience) model, it is no longer hogtied by the criteria of truth and efficacy, and the paradoxes—for example, disagreeing experts and a changing truth—have been dissolved. We have the idea of *interactional expertise*, which seems more and more necessary if the world is to be understood. We have found we can use the Imitation Game to explore these things. And we are learning to unpick the consequences of these things for the understanding and support of democracy. As this history and the contents of this volume make evident, like any good program, this one is still going in unforeseen directions. As with the case of gravitational waves, the pleasure in the growth of these ideas and their diffusion into realms, such as philosophy and psychology, far outside the concerns of STS, is all the greater for that initial negative reaction. My gratitude to the editors and authors of this volume, and my delight and honor at being asked to write this Foreword, is more than I can express.

Cardiff University   Harry Collins
Cardiff, UK

NOTE

1. "The Third Wave of Science Studies: Studies of Expertise and Experience," *Social Studies of Science* 32, no. 2 (2002): 235–296.

Acknowledgments

The editors gratefully acknowledge the administrative assistance of Patricia Trask in the preparation of the manuscript, and the editorial and proof-reading assistance of Christopher Merken, both at Villanova University Charles Widger School of Law. We also thank Palgrave Macmillan editor Rachel Daniel and her editorial assistant Madison Allums for their invaluable help in the successful completion of this project. Finally, the editors thank all those scholars (including those who contributed to this volume) who attended the annual Studies in Expertise and Experience workshops, held in Cardiff and several other locations for the last 13 years, thereby helping to create the intellectual *yet also* convivial community out of which this project grew.

CONTENTS

NOTES ON CONTRIBUTORS

Justus Bauch is a social scientist who received his bachelor's degree in 2018 from the Humboldt-Universität zu Berlin. The main focus of his research is in the field of identity construction in urban areas. He wrote his bachelor's thesis on "The Influence of the Fascination for Football on the Identity Construction of Fans."

Andrew Berardy is a sustainability scientist and a postdoctoral scholar with the Food Systems Transformation Initiative at Arizona State University. His research evaluates all stages of the life cycle of food and assesses potential alternatives or improvements that reduce vulnerability and improve environmental performance. His previous postdoctoral work was an assessment of agricultural vulnerability in central and southern Arizona in the food-energy-water nexus in response to anticipated effects of climate change and identifying strategies for adaptation. His dissertation included the development of a new expertise assessment method.

Celia Bouali is finishing her master's in Social Sciences at Humboldt-Universität zu Berlin, where she also works as a student assistant at the Berlin Institute for Integration and Migration Research (BIM). In 2017, she won the university's Humboldt Award for her Bachelor of Arts thesis on political struggles of South European migrants in Berlin in the context of EU "migration management." Her peer-reviewed article "Facing Precarious Rights and Resisting EU 'Migration Management': South European Migrant Struggles in Berlin" was published in 2018. Her research interests focus on issues around labor, migration, and racism.

Benjamin D. Bowes is a PhD student in Civil and Environmental Engineering at the University of Virginia School of Engineering and Applied Science. His research focus is on the use of machine-learning techniques with applications in hydrology and water resources management. His areas of interests include groundwater table forecasting, flood modeling, and resilience in coastal cities.

David S. Caudill holds the Arthur M. Goldberg Family Chair in Law at Villanova University Charles Widger School of Law in Villanova, Pennsylvania. He is the author of *No Magic Wand: The Idealization of Science in Law* (with L.H. LaRue, 2006) and *Stories About Science in Law: Literary and Historical Images of Acquired Expertise* (2011), as well as numerous articles and book chapters in the fields of legal ethics, law and science, and expert evidence. He is also a senior fellow at the University of Melbourne in Australia, where he teaches Expert Evidence and Entertainment Law in alternate years. Before joining the faculty at Villanova in 2005, Caudill clerked in the U.S. Fifth Circuit Court of Appeals, practiced for seven years with Gray, Cary (San Diego) and Graves, Dougherty (Austin), and taught for 16 years at Washington and Lee University School of Law.

Harry Collins is Distinguished Research Professor and directs the Centre for the Study of Knowledge, Expertise and Science (KES) at Cardiff University, United Kingdom. He is Fellow of the British Academy and winner of the Bernal prize for social studies of science. His 25 books cover sociology of scientific knowledge, artificial intelligence, the nature of expertise, tacit knowledge, technology in sport, the Imitation Game, sociological methodology, and the relationship of science and politics. He is also interested in fringe science, the philosophy of the collectivity, and the relationship between face-to-face and remote communication.

Shannon N. Conley is Assistant Professor of Integrated Science and Technology at James Madison University, and she is the co-director of the James Madison University STS (Science, Technology, and Society) Futures Lab. Her background in political science focused on political theory, public policy, and science and technology studies. She teaches classes on STS, governance, and ethics as well as co-leading the program's junior capstone sequence. She is a member of the Socio-Technical Integration Research (STIR) project, which embeds social scientists and humanities scholars— "embedded humanists"—in laboratories to explore capacities for responsible innovation. Much of her research has focused on the governance of biotechnology and the negotiation of expertise within different political and cultural contexts. She also works on topics related to expertise acquisition, such as T-shaped expertise and the development of interactional competence. She uses case studies to understand and develop the notion of anticipatory governance in connection with political theory.

Lara Danyel is an urban planning student at Technische Universität Berlin. In 2017, she received her first bachelor's degree in Social Sciences from Humboldt-Universität zu Berlin. Her research interests include the dynamics of identity construction and symbolic boundary drawing, qualitative fieldwork, and the academic integration of urban sociology and urban planning.

Deepanwita Dasgupta is Assistant Professor of Philosophy at the University of Texas at El Paso. Her research interests focus on the philosophy of science, especially studying science from a cognitive point of view—exploring the mental models and other embodied practices that scientists use to create new concepts. She is greatly interested in the development of science in the early twentieth-century India, and is writing a book that offers a model of science in such peripheral contexts. She is also interested in understanding the nature of the twenty-first-century science and the possible goals of its transnational scientific community.

Darrin Durant is Lecturer in Science and Technology Studies at the University of Melbourne in Australia. He has published widely on how experts and publics can and should relate to each other in democratic societies. Durant's empirical research focuses on controversies involving nuclear waste management, nuclear power, public policy about energy options, and more recently investigations of climate change policymaking and recycling practices.

Robert Evans is Professor of Sociology in the School of Social Sciences at Cardiff University in Wales. He has worked in the field of science and technology studies for over 20 years, with research projects including sustainable energy, medical genetics, and economic forecasting. In addition to the development of the Imitation Game method, he has also published a number of papers and books developing the "Third Wave of Science Studies," including *Rethinking Expertise* (2007) and *Why Democracies Need Science* (2017), both of which were co-authored with Harry Collins.

Kristina D. Fauss is a fourth-year student at the University of Virginia, finishing her degree in Civil Engineering with a minor in Global Sustainability. Her primary interest is the intersection of natural systems, society, and technology, which she has explored through research with the dMIST project and participation in collaborative design-build projects.

Rob Feick is an associate professor in the School of Planning at the University of Waterloo (Ontario, Canada). His research interests center broadly on methods for using geospatial information technology and data to support decision-making and public participation in land management and planning. His research focuses on data quality and uses of citizen science and volunteered geographic information, methods to extract place-based knowledge from geosocial data streams, and spatial multi-criteria analysis.

Erik Fisher is an associate professor in the School for the Future of Innovation in Society and in the Consortium for Science, Policy and Outcomes at Arizona State University. He studies the governance of emerging technologies from lab to legislature, focusing on policies and practices for socio-technical integration. He developed Socio-Technical Integration Research (STIR), an approach for collaboratively enhancing expert capacities to modulate science and innovation practices in light of societal considerations. To date, STIR has been applied in over 50 laboratories and other organizations around the world. Fisher serves as Editor-in-Chief of the *Journal of Responsible Innovation*.

Michael E. Gorman holds a PhD in Social Psychology (University of New Hampshire, 1981) and does research on collaboration among scientists, engineers, social scientists, and ethicists to both solve pressing problems and create new opportunities. He was an NSF program director (2011–2012). He is Full Professor of Science, Technology and Society at the University of Virginia. His most recent book is *Trading zones and interactional expertise: Creating new kinds of collaboration* (2010).

Martin Hall is a software developer with extensive experience of using and creating distributed and network software in research domains. Examples include remote instrumentation for laboratory devices and remote interactive process control. In the Imitation Game project, Hall created multi-user software using network sockets in web-browsers to monitor and control the status of each participant and enable real-time experiments in geographically distinct areas and is keen to extend use and functionality of this technology. He is working at the University of Winchester, where his role includes data integrations for an attendance-monitoring system.

Nuriani Hamdan is a social scientist with a specialization in social inequality and urban sociology. She studied social sciences at Humboldt-Universität zu Berlin, Sciences Po Paris, and The New School for Social Research, New York. Passionate about qualitative methods as well as postcolonial theories, she aims to look beyond established categories and dichotomies. In her research, she has focused on minorities, particularly Muslim and immigrant groups in the urban context. She is interested in their identity formation, negotiation, and hybridity, especially in the face of experiences of racism and exclusion. Moreover, she is curious about their community organizing and political struggles.

Teresa Hoffmann is a social scientist studying at Humboldt-Universität zu Berlin. She has published on psychosocial influences of soccer on gender in the Palestinian territories in David Becker's book *1:0 für Rafah - Chancen und Herausforderungen psychosozialer Arbeit in Palästina* (2016). She is researching perspectives of German masculinist movements on everyday sexism against women.

Daria Kappel is a social scientist who graduated from Humboldt-Universität zu Berlin in July 2018. She has a special interest in urban studies and qualitative social research and the construction of identities.

Eric B. Kennedy is Assistant Professor of Disaster and Emergency Management in the School of Administrative Studies at York University. His research focuses on understanding and improving decision-making processes within emergency management issues, exploring how these groups handle uncertainty, complex stakeholder relationships, and ever-changing socio-environmental conditions. He works primarily on wildfire management, with secondary emphases on catastrophic flooding, aviation safety, and emergency medical services. He is also the founder and director of the Forum on Science, Policy, and Society, a Canadian not-for-profit organization dedicated to training young leaders to work at the science/policy interface.

Daniel Kubiak is a research associate in the Social Sciences Department at Humboldt-Universität zu Berlin and in his third year of a PhD entitled "Identification and 'Othering' of young East Germans." He has published peer-reviewed articles on social scientific perspectives on East Germany, analogies of Muslims and East Germans, and the generation of post-reunification children. His co-edited volume (with Sandra Matthäus), *Der Osten: Neue sozialwissenschaftliche Perspektiven auf einen komplexen Gegenstand jenseits von Verurteilung und Verklärung*, was published in 2016.

Ida Lübben holds a master's degree in Ideology and Discourse Analysis from the University of Essex, and a bachelor's degree in Social Sciences from Humboldt-Universität zu Berlin. Her research focuses on gender and queer studies. Her recent work has featured such topics as poststructuralist concepts of the subject, heteronormativity, and feminist truth-telling practices.

Yannik Markhof is a Master of Arts student of social sciences at Humboldt-Universität zu Berlin. His research focuses on gendered collective identities and mechanisms of exclusion in Germany.

Bastian Neuhauser studied social sciences at Humboldt-Universität zu Berlin and holds an undergraduate degree with a thesis on LGBT rights in Israel. He is pursuing a graduate degree in cultural policy at Sciences Po Paris.

Hannah O'Mahoney worked on the Imitation Game project at Cardiff University for the final 18 months of its funded lifespan. She has since left the world of academia and holds the position of research officer within the third sector, working for Tenovus Cancer Care based in Cardiff. She remains an honorary research associate at Cardiff University. Her own research interests include environmentalism, volunteering, employment, and well-being.

Ann Potter is Senior Lecturer in Social Work at Manchester Metropolitan University (UK). Prior to taking up her academic role, Potter spent 19 years in social work practice in local authority children and families teams and as a Children's Guardian in the Family Court. Her teaching and research focus on the interface between social work and law, including the communication and evaluation of professional expertise in the Family Court. Potter has presented her work at international conferences and she has also been a guest lecturer at the Judicial College in England.

Colin Robertson is an associate professor in the Department of Geography and Environmental Studies at Wilfrid Laurier University. His research interests include the development and application of spatial analysis and GIS methods, and, increasingly, their application in engaging different communities in monitoring and citizen science projects. His research examines how new geospatial data and technologies can be utilized by communities in Northern Canada to monitor and adapt to environmental change.

Philippe Ross is an associate professor in the Department of Communication, University of Ottawa (Canada). Following a long (if not particularly glamorous) career as an actor in commercials, television and film, he completed a PhD in Communications from the London School of Economics (UK). He likes to think of his research as tackling long-standing problems in media studies through an STS epistemology, and he credits Harry Collins, Rob Evans, Martin Weinel, and their Studies in Expertise and Experience (SEE) collaborators for enabling him to do so in new and exciting ways in recent years.

Bafta Sarbo is a graduate student at the Department for Social Sciences at Humboldt-Universität zu Berlin. She is working on a materialist understanding of racism and the relationship between race and class from a Marxist perspective.

Theresa Schilhab is an associate professor at Aarhus University, Denmark. She holds an MSc in Neurobiology, an MA in Philosophy, a PhD in Philosophy of Science and a senior doctorate in Educational Neuroscience (Dr. paed.). Her research interests embrace the effect of direct experiences on conceptualization and "linguification" processes in a neurobiological and evolutionary perspective. The research corroborating her senior doctorate degree was published as *Derived Embodiment in Abstract Language* (2017), and addresses what defines human learning from the neurobiological, embodied approach given that interactional expertise exists. She manages the Nordea-funded project Natural Technology about children learning with technology in nature.

Laura Schlagheck is a social scientist interested in the discursive formation of national collectives and the consequential production of the *other*. She has, among other things, written on the constitution of the male Muslim *other* through processes of racialization, and gender attribution. She is working on the operating principle and function of antisemitism in German society.

Henrik Schultze is a research associate at the Department of Urban and Regional Studies. He is working in the Collaborative Research Centre 1265 "Re-Figuration of Spaces," Subproject "The World Down My Street: Resources and Networks Used by City Dwellers" funded by the *Deutsche Forschungs gemeinschaft* (German Research Foundation). He completed his PhD on "The role of place within constructions of social and spatial belonging" in 2017 and has published some ideas of this work in edited volumes.

Thomas Seager is an associate professor in the School of Sustainable Engineering and the Built Environment at Arizona State University in Tempe Arizona. Seager leads research teams working at the boundaries of engineering and social science to understand innovation for resilient infrastructure systems, the life-cycle environmental consequences of emerging energy technologies, novel approaches to teamwork and communication in socio-technical integrative settings (including serious play) to teach creativity, and systems thinking in engineering education.

Philip Seitz studied social sciences at Humboldt-Universität zu Berlin and graduated with his bachelor's degree in 2017. The main focus of his research is urban sociology and identity construction. He wrote in his bachelor's thesis about the influence of Berlin-associated narratives on the perception and evaluation of social inequality of young people in Berlin.

Leon Spiegelberg is a social scientist and actor. He graduated with his bachelor's degree in 2016 from the Humboldt-Universität zu Berlin. He wrote his bachelor's thesis on "Psychoanalysis as a capitalistic phenomenon and capitalism's schizophrenic potential." He is studying acting at the Ernst Busch Academy of Dramatic Arts in Berlin and will graduate in 2020.

Martin Weinel is a German sociologist and researcher at the Cardiff School of Social Sciences at Cardiff University. In collaboration with others, most notably Harry Collins, Rob Evans, and Nicky Priaulx, he has written on aspects of expertise, science policy, interdisciplinarity, science communication, and the Imitation Game. He is working on two EU-funded projects exploring the use of new technologies in industrial settings.

Aylin Yavaş is working at ufuq.de, an NGO in Berlin, and is studying social sciences at Humboldt-Universität zu Berlin. Her research interests are postcolonial and Islamic feminisms, as well as intersectionality and anti-Muslim racism.

Zihao Zhang is a PhD candidate in the Constructed Environment at the University of Virginia, School of Architecture. His research offers a critical analysis of the entanglement of technology and nature as well as material agency in the cybernetic environment. Rooted in the discipline of landscape architecture, his research explores concepts from cybernetics such as self-organization, feedback, self-reflexivity, coupling, and so on, in contemporary landscape theories and practices, offering a new understanding of how cybernetics is relevant in today's data-driven paradigm.

Rosa Zylka received her bachelor's degree in Social Sciences at the Humboldt-Universität zu Berlin in May 2018. In her bachelor's thesis, she researched "Gender-Based Street Harassment in Berlin" by interviewing women on the streets in Berlin. Her research interest is focused on qualitative fieldwork. In October 2018, Zylka started studying the Master's Program "Sociocultural Studies" at the Europa-Universität Viadrina in Frankfurt (Oder) and intends to research street harassment from further points of view.

LIST OF FIGURES

LIST OF TABLES

CHAPTER 1

Introduction

David S. Caudill, Shannon N. Conley, Michael E. Gorman, and Martin Weinel

1.1 THE THIRD WAVE OF SCIENCE STUDIES

Just over 35 years ago, Harry Collins, discussing the "new" sociology of scientific knowledge, expressed his disappointment that although "the field has only begun to fulfil its potential, disagreements are now taking up more space than substantive contributions" (Collins 1983, 265). Indeed, the effort "to explain the content of scientific knowledge as far as possible in social terms" invited disagreement, as did "explanations of the outcomes of [scientific controversies] ... by reference to wider social and political

D. S. Caudill (✉)
Villanova University, Villanova, PA, USA
e-mail: caudill@law.villanova.edu

S. N. Conley
James Madison University, Harrisonburg, VA, USA
e-mail: conleysn@jmu.edu

M. E. Gorman
University of Virginia, Charlottesville, VA, USA
e-mail: meg3c@virginia.edu

M. Weinel
Cardiff University, Cardiff, UK
e-mail: WeinelM@Cardiff.ac.uk

© The Author(s) 2019
D. S. Caudill et al. (eds.), *The Third Wave in Science and Technology Studies*, https://doi.org/10.1007/978-3-030-14335-0_1

factors" (272, 275). While the social *aspects* of science are hardly in doubt (there are scientific *communities*, experimental *conventions*, identifiable *cultural* values—e.g., honesty—and so forth), the sociology of scientific knowledge (hereinafter, "SSK") was a challenge to traditional notions that the *content* of science should *not* be affected by society and, consequently, that scientific controversies should be settled by Nature. Reflecting that ideal, the mid-twentieth-century sociology of science associated with Robert K. Merton, now called the "first wave" of science studies, assumed that "sociological accounting had to stop at the door of scientific method and scientific knowledge" (Shapin 1995, 294–295). SSK, having opened that door, is often now referred to as the "second wave" of science studies; it is variously characterized as (1) breaking down the distinction between science and society; (2) highlighting the constitutive, and not merely influential, role of "the social" in the production of scientific knowledge (Shapin 1995, 294–295); and (3) developing a less idealized view of science and scientists— the scientific enterprise is part of, and not above, culture.

A feature of the latter ("second wave") development—the argument for a more modest view of science—was the proposal that ordinary citizens could and should play a role in scientific decision-making—for example, an *elite* scientist helping a community suffering from an environmental crisis may not know as much about the problem (and workable solutions) as a local farmer (Wynne 1989). It is this phenomenon—this proposal to increase citizen participation in science—which in large part inspired the so-called Third Wave of science studies—indeed, the Third Wave was a reaction *against* a broad notion of "citizen scientists":

> Though science studies has [shown] that the basis of technical decision-making can and should be widened beyond the core of certified experts, it has failed to [answer the question:] "How far should participation in technical decision-making extend?" In other words, science studies has shown that there is more to scientific and technical expertise than is encompassed in the work of formally accredited scientists and technologists, but it has not told us how much more. (Collins and Evans 2002, 237)

This reaction is relevant in numerous contemporary debates, including concerns about a "post-truth" era, populism, and, for example, anti-vaccine movements. And it is of particular relevance to the ongoing criticism of forensic science in legal settings, as the Third Wave project is in part focused on who should participate in scientific decision-making, which becomes a question of who is a credible trial expert (see Chap. 2 in this volume). More broadly, who is a credible expert in policy settings that require scientific input (see Chaps. 3 and 4 in this volume)? Briefly, in Third Wave terminology, experts include (1) those who are trained and credentialed in the consensus science of the relevant field, *as well as* (2) those who have sufficient experience (even without formal training) in the field to interact productively with trained experts and thereby contribute to the task at hand. While an "ordinary" citizen has no business influencing scientific decisions, an experienced farmer (and therefore not an "ordinary" citizen, with respect to farming) without scientific training can help a trained scientist (with no farming experience) understand and solve a problem.

1.2   FOCUSING ON EXPERTISE AND EXPERIENCE

The usual marker of expertise is a credential, perhaps a certificate indicating a proficiency of some type; but to the extent that many types of expertise are not associated with an external credentialing entity, credentials cannot serve as the standard for expertise.

> A criterion that does seem to set the boundary in a better place is experience in a [technical] domain. [Without] experience at judging the products of a technical domain, there is no specialist expertise. (Collins and Evans 2007, 67–68)

In 2007, Harry Collins and Robert Evans published *Rethinking Expertise*, an attempt to invent a sociology not of science but of expertise. The authors even constructed a taxonomy of expertise, beginning with *ubiquitous expertises* that everybody has in order to live in society—"a huge body of tacit knowledge"—and then moving to *specialist expertises*, the three lower levels of which "are better described as levels of [ubiquitous tacit] knowledge"—(1) "beer-mat knowledge",[1] (2) popular understanding of science, and (3) primary source knowledge (e.g., literature and the internet) (Collins and Evans 2007, 13–14). The higher levels of specialist expertise (or "specialist tacit knowledge"), requiring more than ubiquitous expertise, are, for example, most relevant to science that is appropriated in legal and policy settings: *contributory* expertise, "which is what you need to do an activity with competence", and *interactional* expertise, "which is the ability to master the language of the specialist domain in the absence of professional competence" (Collins and Evans

2007, 14). The latter category, "a new concept" and the focus of much of *Rethinking Expertise*, is important because it captures the genuine expertise of a non-scientist (i.e., without formal training or credentials) who, through experience in a scientific community, knows what he or she is talking about when there is a scientific controversy (Collins and Evans 2007, 14).

Finishing out the taxonomy, there are five *meta*-expertises, including (1) ubiquitous discrimination (evaluating, e.g., "the experts' demeanor [or] the internal consistency of their remarks"); (2) local discrimination, both of which involve judges who are not experts but who make judgments about experts; (3) technical connoisseurship (the expertise of an art critic who is not an artist); (4) downward discrimination, when a specialist judges a lesser expert; and (5) referred expertise, when an expert moves to a new domain and applies his or her expertise from an earlier domain (Collins and Evans 2007, 15). The primary focus of this book is on the two highest levels of specialist expertises: contributory and interactional expertises, but readers will find other categories of expertise (in the taxonomy summarized above) discussed in various chapters of this volume.

In distinguishing these two higher levels of specialized expertise, Collins and Evans (2007) note that the "first three categories of expertise, beer-mat knowledge, public understanding, and primary source knowledge, might be said hardly to enter the category of specialist expertise at all", since they do not require mastery of a domain and basically involve

> reading rather than immersion in the specialist culture. "Enculturation" is the only way to master an expertise which is deeply laden with tacit knowledge because it is only through common practice with others that the rules that cannot be written down can come to be understood. (24)

Much of the catalyzing work on interactional expertise, enculturation, and immersion can be attributed to Collins' own self-study on the topic as he immersed himself in an expert community comprised of gravitational wave physicists (Collins 2017). During this decade-plus-long immersion, Collins, a sociologist and outsider to the specialist community of scientists, slowly learned the language of gravitational wave physics and spent time with members of the community in both formal and informal spaces (Collins 2017, 313). He gained both formalized and tacit knowledge through this experience, and was able to pick up on slight linguistic nuances in expert conversation, and importantly came to understand and even make inside jokes. Although he could not "do" the science in the sense of being a contributory expert, he could fluently engage with the expert community, even going so far as to pass a Turing-test-like experiment in which he managed to convince an expert judge that he was an actual gravitational wave physicist, and not the "pretender" or outsider (Davies 2006).

After defining expertise as immersion in a specialist "culture", Collins and Evans *divide* those with expertise between contributory and interactional experts.[2] As to contributory experts, which is the conventionally recognized type of expert, they begin as novices and advance through the stages of advanced beginner, competence, proficiency, and finally, expertise (Collins and Evans 2007, 24–27). Interactional experts, a new category proposed by Collins and Evans (2007), do not go through the stages required to become an expert; instead, by immersion in an expertise community, they learn enough of the expert's language to carry on intelligent, thoughtful conversations about (1) the nature of the community, (2) the key programs and players, and (3) cutting-edge issues—they can even tell the sorts of jokes that would only seem funny to (or even be understood by) an expert in the field.

According to Collins and Evans, "mastery of any language, naturally occurring or specialist, requires enculturation within a linguistic community" (Collins and Evans 2007, 30). Interactional expertise therefore can be acquired only by immersion in a language community. Collins' work therefore challenges both (1) the view that *full* immersion in a domain is necessary to master a language and (2) the view that mastering a domain's language requires *only* "the acquisition of propositional knowledge—a set of formal rules and facts gained through reading and instruction" (Collins and Evans 2007, 29).

> The idea of interactional expertise implies that complete fluency in the language of a specialist domain can be acquired in the *absence* of full-blown physical immersion …, [and] the level of fluency … that can be attained by … an interactional expert is indistinguishable from that [of] a full-blown contributory expert. (Collins and Evans 2007, 30–31)

The significance of this analysis is that an expert in a scientific field, for example, need not be a scientist who "contributes" to that field—examples offered by Collins and Evans (2007) include "activists," seemingly mere members of the public, who actually *know* enough to interact successfully (i.e., they "possess interactive ability") with scientists (32). More importantly, the interactional expert is often one who communicates to the general public, such as a sociologist of science who publishes a study of a scientific domain, or a science journalist who reports on a scientific controversy (Collins and Evans 2007, 31–32).

Collins and Evans (2007) even raise the question whether an interactional expert could be admitted as an expert witness in courts of law, since (in their view) "interactional expertise is just as good in forums that work through the medium of language as contributory expertise" (42). The example offered by Collins and Evans (2007) is Simon Cole, in his role as an expert in criminal prosecutions involving fingerprint evidence—although he has studied the profession, he has been attacked on cross-examination (as a junk scientist) because he is not (and has no experience as) a fingerprint examiner:

> What we would like to bring about is the establishment of a discourse that would enable Cole ... under cross-examination [to respond] with a confident: "I do not have contributory expertise in the matter of fingerprint identification but I do have interactional expertise in the domain.... (72)

Of course, the category of contributory experts in science is not limited to the core set of trained scientists, because Collins and Evans (2007) talk of the possibility of specialist *contributory* "experts without formal qualifications," who have "no paper qualifications" (49).[3] Cole, however, had neither formal training nor experience as a fingerprint examiner, so his expertise was interactional. Given that Collins and Evans believe that an interactional expert (unlike a mere member of the public) has the legitimacy to participate in scientific decision-making, it is not surprising that they believe an interactional expert should be able to testify as an expert witness.

The final piece of this focus on expertise is the problem of pseudo-science, but Third Wave theory does not really distinguish between the status of expertise *as expertise* (1) in fields such as witchcraft or astrology (experts in those practices do exist), on the one hand, and (2) in what we might call "efficacious" expertise (associated with successful scientists), on the other. Collins and Evans (2007) do, however, address the problem of allowing extrinsic influences to distort the results of tests, studies, or experiments—here they can only rely on the protection of consensus where it exists, such that when genuine scientists propose a new theory based on new findings:

[T]he scientists pushing forward in the new direction have the intention to change as little as possible consistent with their new theories and findings. They do not want to overthrow the scientific method, nor the greater body of scientific findings, nor the major social institutions of science, nor the existing data of science. (130)

Science as we know involves "the elimination of personal bias" and the preservation of "continuity between a new approach and the main body of science" (Collins and Evans 2007, 130, 132).

1.3   IMITATION GAMES

The Imitation Game, inspired by Alan Turing's (1950) proposals to test the intelligence of computers, is a new social science research method that seeks to "measure" interactional expertise qualitatively and quantitatively. The fact that interactional expertise—the ability to talk fluently about a practice without necessarily being able to perform the practice—is one of the central concepts of the Third Wave program, turns the Imitation Games method into a central element of this research program.

Unlike the concept of expertise that underpins the Third Wave approach, which is a recent development within Science & Technology Studies (Collins and Evans 2002, 2007), the idea of the imitation game as a "method" to systematically explore expertise can be traced back to Alan Turing's attempt to devise a test that was able to resolve the question whether "machines can think" (Turing 1950, 433). Turing himself drew upon a much older parlor version of the imitation game, the principles of which he succinctly explained as follows:

> It is played with three people, a man (A), a woman (B), and an interrogator (C) who may be of either sex. The interrogator stays in a room apart from the other two. The object of the game for the interrogator is to determine which of the other two is the man and which is the woman. He knows them by labels X and Y, and at the end of the game he says either "X is A and Y is B" or "X is B and Y is A". (Turing 1950, 433)

To achieve the aim of the game, the interrogator—referred to as Judge in the context of Imitation Game research—is allowed to put testing questions, one at a time, to the two respondents who answer according to their roles in the game. The respondent of the same sex as the interrogator—

the Non-Pretender—answers naturally, while the respondent of the differ-ent sex—the Pretender—has to answer the question as if she or he shares the same sex with the interrogator.

The famous Turing test adapts the parlor game by shifting the focus of the game from gender toward "human intelligence," and by replacing one of the human respondents with a machine. For the purpose of the modern sociological Imitation Game (we capitalize when referring to the socio-logical variant, and not the parlor game), we replace Turing's machine with a human, which means we can involve members of different social groups or categories, and we shift our interest from "thinking" to "exper-tise." The same principles of the imitation game—dialogical interaction and the physical separation of players which affords a narrow focus on linguistic ability—which according to Turing makes it ideal for the pur-pose of testing a machine's ability to think, turn it also into an ideal method to explore expertise in general and interactional expertise in particular.

> The question and answer method seems to be suitable for introducing almost any one of the fields of human endeavor that we wish to include. We do not wish to penalise the machine for its inability to shine in beauty com-petitions, nor to penalise a man for losing in a race against an aeroplane. The conditions of our game make these disabilities irrelevant. The "witnesses" can brag, if they consider it advisable, as much as they please about their charms, strength or heroism, but the interrogator cannot demand practical demonstrations. (Turing 1950, 435)

First, the dialogical nature of the interaction enables the exploration of any topic. Over the last several years, Imitation Games have been played on topics such as gravitational wave physics (Giles 2006), gender (Evans et al. 2019), visual impairment, perfect pitch, color perception (Collins et al. 2006), sexuality, religiosity (Collins et al. 2017), national and regional identities (e.g., Kubiak and Weinel 2016; Collins et al. and Kubiak, Chaps. 7 and 9 in this volume), sub-cultural identities (Ross and Bauch et al., Chaps. 8 and 10 in this volume; Segersven et al., unpublished manuscript), and chronic illnesses (Wehrens 2015; Evans and Crocker 2013). Second, the disconnect between the linguistic ability to describe a practice, and the physical ability to demonstrate, which the imitation game supports through the physical separation and electronic communication, makes it an ideal method to explore interactional expertise. The very point of interactional expertise is the ability to talk about a domain without being able to perform the practice that is the subject of the conversation.

The Imitation Game contributes in two principal ways—one intended and anticipated, the other surprising—to the Third Wave program. First, the Imitation Game has been specifically and intentionally used as an ingenious quasi-experimental method to test the interactional expertise concept (see Chaps. 7, 8, 9, and 10 of this volume). By the time Collins and Evans proposed the Third Wave program in 2002, Collins had already played Imitation Games since the 1990s. It did not take Collins and Evans long to recognize the potential of the Imitation Game to test empirically whether interactional expertise exists or not. Between 2004 and 2008, a series of small-scale proof-of-concept Imitation Games was played that lend credence to the idea of interactional expertise. Second, and often surprisingly, playing Imitation Games for the purpose of testing the interactional expertise concept has generated new empirical data and material that contributes to the further theorizing of the Third Wave, and opened up new and different uses for the Imitation Game. With regard to the latter, Imitation Games have been used as a "can opener" (or ice breaker) for subsequent focus groups (Wehrens 2015, 2016), or as a potential training tool for medical staff dealing with chronic patients (Evans and Crocker 2013). With regard to the former, a shift of focus from the performance of the Pretender to the Non-Pretender, who belongs to the same social category or group as the Judge, has spurred new research into the nature of social groups (Arminen et al. 2019).

1.4   INTERACTIONAL EXPERTISE AND THE PROBLEM OF INCOMMENSURABILITY

If two fields are incommensurable from a Kuhnian perspective (Kuhn 1970), how could someone from one field gain interactional expertise in another? Peter Galison's solution is trading zones (Galison 2010), which he developed from a case study of the development of radar. Multiple apparently incommensurable expertises had to be combined to reach a solution—the experts and the military organizations they were serving had to develop a trading zone, where they could exchange ideas and solutions without any party having to understand the other's paradigm. Consider also the development of a new expertise like biochemistry, the name of which shows that it emerged out of the collaboration between biology and chemistry. That new expertise likely began with trading zones in order to solve problems where the biology and the chemistry were tightly coupled.

Galison noted that these kinds of exchanges occur all the time in the sorts of trading zones that develop in port cities and across borders between cultures and countries. The key is the development of a creole, or reduced common language, sufficient to trade. If the trades lead to cooperation on a new technology, as in the case of radar, or a new expertise, as in biochemistry, the creole might begin to become its own specialist language and a new expertise might emerge (see Chaps. 14 and 15 in this volume). Collins and the gravitational wave physicists, mentioned above, were not on a mission to combine elements of gravitational wave physics and sociology; so for Collins, interactional expertise was sufficient. In cases where a trading zone is necessary, however, interactional experts can become translators, facilitating initial exchanges (see Chap. 15 in this volume).

1.5   The Purpose and Organization of This Volume

The editors of, and contributors to, this volume intend to confirm the significance of the theoretical framework known as the Third Wave in Science and Technology Studies by demonstrating its analytical utility in numerous and varied contexts. The chapters that follow have been divided into four parts, each with its own introduction to the chapters within that part. In the first part, we highlight the applicability of Third Wave approaches in contemporary legal and policy settings where science is appropriated and evaluated. In the second part, we discuss representative Imitation Games research, both to enhance readers' understanding of Third Wave theory and to demonstrate how Imitation Games can enhance sociological analysis. The third part explores the paramount concept of interactional expertise in various practical settings, offering examples to enrich that foundational category. Finally, the fourth part reaches beyond the conventional conceptions associated with Third Wave research to identify several recent theoretical developments. The extensive variation in terms of topics and arguments in this volume is intentional—we want to overcome any presumption that the Third Wave in Science Studies is a narrow field with limited application. Consequently, in our view, this volume is not in any sense exhaustive in terms of the potential of Third Wave theory. Quite the contrary, we hope that the present studies will inspire further engagement with the field.

NOTES

1. The reference to beer-mat (i.e., the cardboard coasters placed under beer glasses on a bar) knowledge comes from the phenomenon of printing statements or questions of general knowledge (e.g., distance to the moon, the country with the largest population) on beer-mats, sometimes constituting a quiz, perhaps with the answer on the opposite side. An example is a beer-mat with a definition of a hologram, thereby delivering knowledge to the reader:

   > The words on the beer mat are not simply nonsense nor could they be taken to be, say, a riddle or a joke. Presumably there are people … who have studied the beer mat and, if asked: "Do you know how a hologram works?" would reply: "Yes". (Collins and Evans 2007, 18)

   Notably, acquisition of the three low levels of expertise "rests on the prior acquisition of a vast, but generally unnoticed, foundation of ubiquitous expertise" (Collins and Evans 2007, 14).

2. It bears mention that since 2007, Collins and Evans (2015) have continued to refine the concept of interactional expertise, and Collins et al. (2016) have also reflected further on the concept of contributory expertise.

3. Collins and Evans (2007) offer the example of "expert" farmers in Brian Wynne's study of the effect of the Chernobyl disaster on Cumbrian sheep (Wynne 1989) "after radioactive fallout contaminated their pastures"—the "sheep farmers have specialist contributory expertise" (48–49). Collins and Evans (2007) have therefore constructed "a wider envelope of experts … in that anyone with the right kind of experience, whether they have scientific training or not, has a potential place inside it" (114).

REFERENCES

Arminen, Ilkka, Otto Segersven, and Mika Simonen. 2019. Active and Latent Social Groups and Their Interactional Expertise. *Acta Sociologica*. https://doi.org/10.1177/0001699318786361.

Collins, H.M. 1983. The Sociology of Scientific Knowledge: Studies of Contemporary Science. *Annual Review of Sociology* 9: 265–285.

———. 2017. *Gravity's Kiss: The Detection of Gravitational Waves*. Cambridge, MA: The MIT Press.

Collins, H.M., and R. Evans. 2002. The Third Wave of Science Studies: Studies of Expertise and Experience. *Social Studies of Science* 32 (2): 235–296. https://doi.org/10.1177/0306312702032002003.

———. 2007. *Rethinking Expertise*. Chicago, IL: University of Chicago Press.

————. 2015. Expertise Revisited, Part I—Interactional Expertise. *Studies in the History and Philosophy of Science, Part A* 54: 113–123.

Collins, Harry M., Robert Evans, Rodrigo Ribeiro, and Martin Hall. 2006. Experiments with Interactional Expertise. *Studies in History and Philosophy of Science Part A* 37 (4): 656–674.

Collins, H.M., R. Evans, and M. Weinel. 2016. Expertise Revisited, Part II—Contributory Expertise. *Studies in the History and Philosophy of Science, Part A* 56: 103–110.

Collins, Harry M., Robert Evans, Martin Weinel, Jennifer Lyttleton-Smith, Andrew Bartlett, and Martin Hall. 2017. The Imitation Game and the Nature of Mixed Methods. *Journal of Mixed Methods Research* 11 (4): 510–527.

Davies, D. 2006. Faking the Physics: If a Sociologist Can Convince a Jury of Physicists That He Is an Expert on Gravity Waves, Doesn't That Mean He Is One? *The Guardian*, October 10. www.theguardian.com/commentisfree/2006/oct/10/fakingthephysics.

Evans, Robert, and Helen Crocker. 2013. The Imitation Game as a Method for Exploring Knowledge(s) of Chronic Illness. *Methodological Innovations Online* 8 (1): 34–52.

Evans, Robert, Harry M. Collins, Martin Weinel, Jennifer Lyttleton-Smith, Hannah O'Mahoney, and Willow Leonard-Clarke. 2019. Groups and Individuals: Conformity and Diversity in the Performance of Gendered Identities. *British Journal of Sociology*. https://doi.org/10.1111/1468-4446.12507.

Galison, P. 2010. Trading with the Enemy. In *Trading Zones and Interactional Expertise*, ed. M.E. Gorman, 25–52. Cambridge, MA: MIT Press.

Giles, Jim. 2006. Sociologist Fools Physics Judges. *Nature* 442 (7098): 8.

Kubiak, Daniel, and Martin Weinel. 2016. DDR-Generationen revisited—Gibt es einen Generationszusammenhang der 'Wendekinder'? In *Die Generation der Wendekinder*, ed. Adriana Lettrari, Christian Nestler, and Nadja Troi-Boeck, 107–129. Wiesbaden: Springer Fachmedien Wiesbaden. https://doi.org/10.1007/978-3-658-11480-0_8.

Kuhn, T.S. 1970. *The Structure of Scientific Revolutions.* 2nd ed. Chicago, IL: University of Chicago Press.

Segersven, Otto, Ilkka Arminen, and Mika Simonen. Exploring Groupness: A Mixed Methods Imitation Game Enquiry (unpublished manuscript).

Shapin, S. 1995. Here and Everywhere: Sociology of Scientific Knowledge. *Annual Review of Sociology* 21: 289–321.

Turing, Alan. 1950. Computing Machinery and Intelligence. *Mind* 59 (236): 433–460. https://doi.org/10.1093/mind/LIX.236.433.

Wehrens, Rik. 2015. The Potential of the Imitation Game Method in Exploring Healthcare Professionals' Understanding of the Lived Experiences and Practical Challenges of Chronically Ill Patients. *Health Care Analysis* 23 (3): 253–271. https://doi.org/10.1007/s10728-014-0273-8.

———. 2016. De Imitation Game als blikopener: Praktijkervaringen met patiënten met eetstoornissen en hun behandelaren. *KWALON: Tijdschrift voor Kwalitatief Onderzoek in Nederland* 21 (2): 31–37.

Wynne, B. 1989. Sheep Farming After Chernobyl: A Case Study in Communicating Scientific Information. *Environment* 31 (2): 10–39.

Law and Policy Studies in Expertise

David S. Caudill

1.1   INTRODUCTION TO PART I

The need for expertise in scientific decision-making is especially evident in each nation's legal system—that is, where courts of law adjudicate litigated disputes, many of which involve scientific or technical matters. Even more evident, however, is the need for expertise in policy contexts, where governments seek to improve the health and welfare of its citizens, for example, through administrative regulations and statutory law. This opening part—of a volume intended to demonstrate the utility of the "Third Wave" in science and technology studies—presents five studies concerning expertise in legal and policy contexts.

Chapter 2, "Twenty-five Years of Opposing Trends," highlights both (1) the turn in the US legal system from an idealistic view of science, on the part of judges and law professors, toward skepticism, as conventional forensic identification techniques have been discredited, and (2) the turn in the sociology of science, from the emphasis in the "Second Wave" upon deconstructing the determinative social aspects of science, toward more normative concerns, such as evaluating expertise, in the "Third Wave." Neither turn is complete—scientific and technical evidence remains highly valued in law, and the "Third Wave" focus on identifying expertise is not a rejection of the "Second Wave" focus on the social aspects of science. In fact, there is greater balance in both law and in science studies between the extremes of idealizing science and the relativism associated with social constructivism, which makes the sociology of science more relevant for law—opening the door for new appropriations of (formerly non-existent) science studies in law.

Chapter 3, "Ignoring Experts," takes up the controversy over climate science in governmental contexts. When experts are constructed as undemocratic authority figures, there is a risk that they will be ignored, as demonstrated when the electrical grid failed in Australia in 2016—good technical advice was ignored due to partisan politics. This chapter provides a reaction to the call for citizen science—often arising from an emphasis on democratic decision-making—which can devolve into an argument against expertise. Along the way, this chapter responds to critics of the Third Wave, including Wynne and Jasanoff.

Chapter 4, "Recognizing Counterfeit Scientific Controversies in Science Policy Contexts," discusses the phenomenon of expert disagreement—sometimes genuine, but sometimes "counterfeit," that is, wholly constructed to create uncertainty and hide consensus. Distinguishing between the two is crucial, as illustrated in the South African controversy over azidothymine, a drug that reduces mother-to-child transmission of HIV during pregnancy and childbirth. The South African government identified and publicized a scientific controversy where none existed, leading to poor policy. The author offers four criteria to demarcate genuine from counterfeit scientific controversies, and claims an important role for science and technology studies in these types of policy disputes.

Chapter 5, "Judging Social Work Expertise in Care Proceedings," returns to the legal system with a focus on British proceedings where state-employed social workers apply to family courts to remove a child from his or her family, to prevent harm. The author reports on a study exploring how judges evaluate social work evidence, with a focus on expertise as a process involving socialization to enable meaningful communication. That study applied Collins and Evans' work identifying categories of expertise, and also demonstrated potential applications of that work in other interdisciplinary processes that involve communication, presentation, and evaluation of professional knowledge across disciplinary boundaries.

Finally, Chap. 6, "Geographical Expertise," addresses the diminishing trust, in our time, on conventional knowledge holders. Citizen scientists, with new resources and involvement in scientific research and decision-making, can challenge the authority of experts. The authors suggest that geographic expertise provides a case study to link traditional categories of expertise to local, experience-based knowledge. "Third Wave" language and theory offer a set of tools to operationalize the integration of local experts in applied environmental management.

CHAPTER 2

Twenty-Five Years of Opposing Trends: The Demystification of Science in Law, and the Waning Relativism in the Sociology of Science

David S. Caudill

2.1   INTRODUCTION

My purpose is to identify two opposing trends—reverse trajectories—over the past 25 years: one in US legal contexts with respect to admissibility of scientific expertise and the other in the sub-discipline (or interdiscipline) of sociology known alternatively as (1) the sociology of scientific knowledge (SSK), (2) science and technology studies (STS), (3) the sociology of science, or simply (4) "science studies." As to law, I will argue that there has been a shift, or trend, away from an idealistic view of science to a skepticism of sorts toward science. Moreover, I believe that the shift or trend in law, with respect to how science is viewed or theorized, is the opposite of what has happened in science studies, insofar as that field of inquiry—called the "second wave" of science studies—was based (at least after Merton's "first wave" norms for science were rejected[1]) upon a skeptical

D. S. Caudill (✉)
Villanova University, Villanova, PA, USA
e-mail: caudill@law.villanova.edu

© The Author(s) 2019
D. S. Caudill et al. (eds.), *The Third Wave in Science and Technology Studies*, https://doi.org/10.1007/978-3-030-14335-0_2

view of science that both (1) challenged the notion that science and culture were separable and (2) highlighted the arguably determinable social aspects, perhaps even social construction, of scientific facts and theories. Finally, I conclude that these trends bode well for the future of science in law, insofar as the field of US law will hereafter (because of these trends) benefit from an engagement with the discipline of science studies.

I concede at the outset that I am of course speaking in generalities. Every discipline is riven with disagreements, such that perspectives on science, whether in law or in science studies, have always varied, and they continue to vary—there were scholarly disagreements in 1993, in US legal contexts and in science studies, respectively, about the nature of science, and there are debates in both disciplines today—but at any point in time, some perspectives likely dominate the field. My point is that in law, the idealism reflected in *Daubert v. Merrell Dow Pharmaceuticals* (Daubert) in 1993 (a US Supreme Court opinion that set new standards for expertise offered as evidence in trials) has been slowly losing dominance to skeptics in the field of law, just as the social constructivists of 1993, in science studies contexts, have been losing ground over the years to those who, we might say, have a more idealized view of science, or at least more trust or belief in its stability and progress.

Around 1993, when judges, evidence scholars, and lawyers were starting to pay attention to the history and philosophy of science (in order to identify the essential characteristics of science, by which the reliability of expert scientific testimony could be evaluated), the phenomenon known as the "science wars," as well as the growing field of science studies (not only the history and philosophy, but also the *sociology*, of science), likely went unnoticed by most in the field of law. The "wars" resulted as a backlash against the emphasis in science studies on the social, and not merely natural, influences on the results of scientific activities. That is, some science studies scholars had engaged in ethnographic, almost anthropological research (in laboratories) that revealed the cultural aspects of scientific practice (e.g., its economic interests, funding bias, theoretical preferences, institutional gatekeeping, and negotiation and consensus-building). In reaction, some conventional philosophers of science, and some scientists, criticized science studies scholars as antiscientific, insofar as sociologists of science "seemed to argue [in the jargon of postmodernism] that language, politics, and interests, rather than objective reality, determine the nature of scientific knowledge"[2] (Labinger and Collins 2001, 1).

The science wars arguably began in 1992, the year before *Daubert* appeared, with the publication of Lewis Wolpert's *The Unnatural Nature of Science* and Steven Weinberg's *Dreams of a Final Theory*, both of which attacked science studies; and the "wars" were still going on in 1994, the year after *Daubert*, when Paul Gross and Norman Levitt identified science studies as an attack on science itself in *Higher Superstition: The Academic Left and its Quarrels with Science*. I would characterize these *critics* of science studies as having an idealized view of science, and I believe that *Daubert* supported that perspective.

2.2   Science in Law

The appearance of the US Supreme Court's *Daubert* opinion in 1993 marked that year as a watershed moment in the US law of evidence—the Court created an unexpected set of rules concerning admissibility of expert evidence in court. While the lawsuit against Merrell Dow Pharmaceuticals, the manufacturer of Bendectin, a morning sickness drug, alleged that the drug caused birth defects, the Court's opinion focused primarily on establishing a new evidentiary regime, and a new judicial role, for evaluating scientific testimony. One explanation for the Court's endeavor is that there had been growing concerns in the 1980s, among manufacturing companies and liability insurers, that plaintiffs' attorneys were using charlatan experts and junk science in the courtroom to convince juries, for example, that workplace injuries were caused by exposure to certain chemicals, even in the absence of good epidemiological evidence. There were also related concerns over inconsistent verdicts concerning liability arising from exposure to the *same* chemical (or use of the *same* allegedly dangerous drug). So the Court, in *Daubert*, heard an appeal of the trial court's judgment rejecting the plaintiff's experts, and in the process clarified (and seemingly raised) the standard for admissible expertise, to ensure that courtroom expertise was actually based on reliable scientific methodology.

That focus on reliability in science, on the part of the *Daubert* Court, led the justices (against Justice Rehnquist's warning that "definitions of scientific knowledge, scientific method, scientific validity, and peer review [are] matters far afield from the expertise of judges" (Daubert, 599)) to venture "into the treacherous crosscurrents of the philosophy of science" (Goodstein 2000, 92)—a sub-discipline with a substantial literature and a history of controversy.[3] The Justices' research (or that of their clerks) seemed to reveal that Karl Popper and Carl Hempel were the leading, authoritative philosophers of science (a highly questionable conclusion), and therefore that the law should appropriate their views. In Susan Haack's assessment, the Court, after mistakenly (1) equating "reliable" with "scientific," (2) assuming that there is a singular practice identifiable as "scientific 'methodology' which, faithfully followed, guarantees reliable results," and (3)

> casting about for a philosophy of science to fit this demanding bill, the *Daubert* Court settled on an unstable amalgam of Popper's and Hempel's very different approaches—neither of which, however, is suitable to the task at hand. (Haack 2008, 163)

In any event, the Court cobbled together a particular vision of science, then gave all federal judges the authority to decide which experts were reliable, in accordance with some standards, like (1) falsifiability or testability, (2) a low error rate, (3) peer-reviewed publications, and (4) general acceptance in the relevant scientific community (Daubert, 593–594).

L.H. LaRue and I, in *No Magic Wand: The Idealization of Science in Law* (2006), argued that *Daubert* (and its application in subsequent cases) resulted in a romanticized or idealized image of science in law, particularly because the Court, in its focus on methodology, ignored the social, institutional, and rhetorical aspects of science—in short, the Court was oblivious to the field of science studies.[4] Briefly, we identified two types of "idealization" errors on the part of trial judges evaluating experts. On the one hand, some judges were too strict due to a failure to understand (1) that medical diagnosis often involves *subjective* patient reports (not objective measurement); (2) that science involves teamwork, uncertainty, disagreements between credible scientists, alternative explanatory models, and probabilistic decision-making; (3) that not all scientific knowledge is peer-reviewed and published; and (4) that the limitations of social scientific research do not render it unscientific (Caudill and LaRue 2006, 18–23). On the other hand, some judges were (paradoxically) too lenient because they deferred too quickly to the social authority—the "cloak" and "mantle"—of expertise that a scientist might have even in the absence of methodological reliability (Caudill and LaRue 2006, 36–41).

By 2010 that situation had somewhat changed. The 2009 report from the National Academy of Sciences rejected most of the forensic identification techniques that had been used for decades to convict suspects of crime (Nat'l Res. Council 2009), and in 2010, at a conference in Washington, DC, on the role of the court with respect to experts, Judge Harry Edwards announced that he had become a skeptic toward forensics:

I started the [National Academy of Science] project with no skepticism regarding the forensic science community. Rather, I assumed, as I suspect many of my judicial colleagues do, that the forensic disciplines are well grounded in scientific methodology and that crime laboratories follow proven practices that ensure the validity and reliability of forensic evidence offered in court. I was surprisingly mistaken in what I assumed. (Edwards 2010)

Almost every judge is now skeptical of bite mark evidence, hair sample analysts, even fingerprint analysis, notwithstanding the fact that FBI analysts have years of experience and great credentials (Kennedy and Merrill 2003, 33–34). Judges should likewise be skeptical of alcohol blackout experts (Pressman and Caudill 2013), and also of many arson experts, who have lately been found to be very unscientific—basically peddling mythologies about fire origins (Lentini 2006). Judges continue to appreciate genuine science, such that DNA, as well as toxicology,[5] are easily admitted into court; but there is a spirit, a mood, of skepticism—mere credentials will not work, and there is more appreciation of scientific uncertainties, of multiple or alternative explanations, and of biases or interests and their effects on laboratory results. Even the results of DNA or toxicological analyses need to be scrutinized for human error. Judges are becoming more realistic about what the scientists who appear in court can offer.

During the same 25-year trend in law away from idealizing science and toward a healthy skepticism about experts, the trend has been the opposite in science studies.

2.3   SCIENCE STUDIES

In 1979, Bruno Latour and Steve Woolgar, in *Laboratory Life: The Social Construction of Scientific Facts*, opened the black box of the laboratory and popularized the ethnographic method in science studies. Like anthropologists visiting a foreign culture, sociologists of science might visit laboratories and observe how scientific knowledge is produced, or rather, co-produced, because a great deal is going on besides listening to Nature "speak." There are institutions, authority structures, influential theories, methodological preferences, specialized languages (and governing metaphors), experimental conventions (limited by measurement and instrument technologies), consensus-building strategies, and even negotiated scientific papers. So much going on, indeed, that it was tempting in science studies circles to say that scientific knowledge is actually *socially* con-structed—that science is not *above* culture but part of it.

And yet in 1993, the year that *Daubert* appeared, Bruno Latour's *We Have Never Been Modern* appeared in English, with his famous warning against reductionism in science studies:

> Yes, the scientific facts are indeed constructed but they cannot be reduced to the social dimension because this dimension is populated by objects mobi-lized to construct it.... The ozone hole is too social and too narrated to be truly natural; the strategy of industrial firms and heads of state is too full of chemical reactions to be reduced to power and interest; the discourse of the exosphere is too real and too social to boil down to meaning effects. Is it our fault if the networks are simultaneously real, like nature, narrated, like dis-course, and collective, like society? (Latour 1993, 6)

Scholars in science studies had already, in 1993, experienced a series of analytical or disciplinary "turns," two of which are exemplified in the above quotation from Latour. First, there was a turn away from theory-driven science, from Kuhnian paradigms to a focus on science as experi-ment, that is, to an engagement with laboratories—not only with their methodologies, but with their negotiations and power structures and funding; it was Latour and Woolgar who took that turn in *Laboratory Life* (1979).[6] And second, when you view science as a (cultural) practice, then it is a short step to *cultural studies*, and we can identify the "semiotic" turn in science studies whereby science is reconfigured as a discursive practice, with rhetoric and metaphors in the very substance of scientific practice—here, language is material and not simply symbolic. Beyond those two turns (to science as practice, then to science as language), Latour was also anticipating the *naturalist* turn in science studies, which is the beginning of the end of skepticism. For Latour, there are quasi-objects in the world, not of our own making, which brings an end to the science wars because very few people are willing to take either of the extreme positions carica-tured in those wars—who wants to argue for a strong version of social construction, and who wants to argue that social aspects are always exter-nal to and negligible with respect to scientific practice?

By the time we get to 2010, the year that Judge Harry Edwards became a skeptic with respect to science in the courtroom, the naturalist turn has a firm foothold in science studies. This could be due to the fact that science studies scholars want to take normative positions in debates over climate change or creationism, or to identify distortion of lab results due to financial bias; and it is disheartening when climate change deniers, critics of evolution, or pharmaceutical companies appropriate the language of social constructivism to claim there is little scientific certainty about so many things. More importantly, there is now the designation of a *third wave* in science studies, the subject of this volume—the first wave being the era of Merton's norms (which were *not* oriented to identifying the social determinants of scientific knowledge), and the second wave breaking down the boundary between science and society (revealing the inevitability of cultural interests and rhetorical forces inside science itself). In 2002, however, Harry Collins and Robert Evans published their highly influential article entitled *The Third Wave of Science Studies: Studies of Expertise and Experience*. Without denying the importance of the "second wave"—the need to identify the social aspects of science—Collins and Evans suggested that science studies should be in the business of identifying reliable expertise, including identifying those social or political influences that distort scientific results (Collins and Evans 2002). In 2007, Collins and Evans wrote *Rethinking Expertise*, in an effort to develop the Third Wave emphasis on reliable expertise (Collins and Evans 2007).

Then, in 2010, at the annual meeting of the Society for the Social Studies of Science in Tokyo, Harry Collins was on a plenary panel with Brian Wynne, who had argued for the need for citizen participation in scientific decision-making, based on his famous study of Cumbrian sheep farmers whose sheep suffered from fallout from the Chernobyl disaster (Wynne 1989, 1996a, b). The sheep farmers knew more about how sheep walk around the pasture than the scientific experts studying the fallout and issuing a report—the "experts" made mistakes because they did not know enough about the behaviors of sheep. Wynne used that situation to argue for citizen participation, to which Collins replied, roughly, that "those were not ordinary citizens—those farmers were experts!" That is, expertise does not require graduate degrees. Conversely, since we need experts (on the basis of formal training *or* relevant experience) participating in scientific decision-making, citizens who are not experts in the relevant scientific field (in any public or regulatory debate) not only should be excluded but also should be identified as illegitimate, external, and political influences that should be resisted.

Collins and Evans knew they would be criticized for being old-fashioned realists,[7] but they made it clear that they were not rejecting wave two:

Wave Three ... does not show that Wave Two is intellectually bankrupt. In this strange sea, Wave Two continues to roll on, even as Wave Three builds up. Wave Three is one of the ways in which Wave Two can be applied to a set of problems that Wave Two alone cannot handle in an intellectually coherent way. Wave Three involves finding a special rationale for science and technology even while we accept the findings of Wave Two—that science and technology are much more ordinary than we once thought. [Our] aim ... is to hammer a piton into the ice wall of relativism with enough delicacy not to shatter the whole edifice (the destruction that so many critics [of science studies] believe is the only solution). (Collins and Evans 2002, 240)

In the next section, I offer a few other examples to support my reverse trajectories thesis, to show that what was happening (with respect to science) in 1993, in US legal contexts, appears to be the opposite of what was happening in the science studies community in 1993; and nowadays, likewise, the trends in legal contexts (with respect to the acquisition and evaluation of science in court) are roughly the opposite of trends in science studies.

2.4   REVERSE TRAJECTORIES

In *Daubert*, the US Supreme Court published its foray into the philosophy of science and offered its guidelines to help judges discern reliable scientific expertise, without really making any decision as to the quality of the trial experts, in the actual *Daubert* case, on each side of the Bendectin controversy. The case was sent back to the Ninth Circuit Court of Appeals, where Judge Kozinski evaluated the expertise offered in the lawsuit. His commentary on scientific expertise could not have been more oblivious to science studies. When Judge Kozinski looked at the expertise offered by the defendant, Merrell Dow Pharmaceuticals, which consisted of earlier epidemiological studies done in pharmaceutical labs, and compared it to the expertise of the plaintiff, which had all being prepared after the trial began (i.e., the plaintiff's expert had performed some medical procedures and also some re-analyses of the defendant's epidemiological studies), he decided that a fifth factor was needed (to add to the four *Daubert* guidelines, namely testability, error rate, publications, and general acceptance) to evaluate scientific expertise:

That an expert testifies for money does not necessarily cast doubt on the reliability of his testimony.... [But testimony] based on research he has conducted independent of the litigation provides important, objective proof that the research comports with the dictates of good science.... [E]xperts whose findings flow from existing research are less likely to be biased toward a particular conclusion by the promise of renumeration.... (Daubert on Remand, 1317)

Judge Kozinski seemed oblivious to the problem, identified frequently in science studies, of the risks of bias due to corporate funding (Krimsky 2013; McGarrity and Wagner 2008). Moreover, in his idealization of pharmaceutical research prepared before trial, Judge Kozinski unwittingly condemned law enforcement forensic science, which is "developed ... principally for purposes of litigation." However, instead of following his principle, he caught himself condemning (accidentally) forensic science, and oddly concluded that the litigation-driven nature of *forensic* science "will obviously not be a substantial consideration" (Daubert on Remand, 1317 n.5). The 2009 National Academy of Sciences report would later discredit Judge Kozinsky's evaluation when it called for independent forensic laboratories—there are all sorts of reasons to doubt the validity of almost all forensic identification techniques (Nat'l Res. Council 2009). In 1995, however, when science studies scholars were revealing social influences on the internal workings of laboratory science, including financial bias due to corporate or law enforcement funding, the judiciary was paying no attention.

When we move to 2010, the situation is arguably reversed, with skeptical judges leading the charge to discredit forensic science, while the formerly skeptical science studies community had become comfortable with Michel Callon's notion that corporate funding of university laboratories is not necessarily a bad thing!—the old boundaries between academic and commercial pursuits, between public and private, give way to beneficial hybrids and networks, and to the end of the knee-jerk reaction to all funding as leading to bias (Callon 2002, 279–280).

As I conceded at the outset, I recognize that not everyone follows the trends I have identified, and that my "reverse trajectories" are not *complete* reversals. Even as Latour and his followers moved from laboratory studies to network-building and quasi-objects, and along the way rejected the social explanation genre in favor of co-production of objects and social relations (Callon and Latour 1992), there are critics in science studies like Steve Fuller who hold on to second-wave sociology of science—who claim that Latour is a realist who has become a quite conventional historian of science, explaining scientific discoveries by granting agency to *things* (Fuller 1999). Indeed, Fuller holds Latour responsible for the decline of science studies, for its loss of any normative critique of science (Fuller 1999, 6). Similarly, the debate between Harry Collins and Brian Wynne betrays diversity within the science studies community. Nevertheless, there are identifiable trends. Among law professors, in 1993, the sociology of science was either unknown or considered too fanatical for appropriation into law (Risinger 2007, 682); but nowadays in both the committees criticizing forensic science and in evidence symposia, science studies scholars like Gary Edmond at the University of New South Wales, or Simon Cole at University of California-Irvine, are welcomed in as participants. By contrast, at the annual meetings of the Society for the Social Studies of Science, 25 years ago, a panelist would have been viewed as naïve if he or she went outside the social explanation genre; but nowadays at those meetings there is plenty of room for both Latourian "actor network theory" (which grants agency to objects) and, apropos to this volume, Third Wave studies of expertise.

2.5   Conclusion: These Are Good Trends

I consider these reverse trajectories to be good things. There are many trends in the United States over the last 25 years that one might not celebrate, but the openness in law to a certain level of skepticism about scientific expertise, and the openness in science studies to a normative theory of expertise, seems to result in a balanced perspective toward science. It could also result in fewer stereotypes and better communication than were present during the science wars.

For example, in 1999, there appeared a particularly sneering critique of science studies, by physicist David Goodstein and philosopher James Woodward (1999), who (1) basically mocked the "fashion" of ethnographic sociologists who "visit the strange continent of Science and send back reports on the natives," (2) remarked that the science wars were "becoming amusing," and (3) arrogantly suggested that it might be "useful" for someone to describe science from the *inside*—that latter quip was a slight to the outsider status of social scientists in the world of natural science (Goodstein and Woodward 1999, 83). A science studies scholar familiar with the science wars would have thought, "Here we go again; I know what is coming—something like 'there are no social or cultural influences that affect the content, the substance, of scientific knowledge'...." But then Goodstein and Woodward explained that since the seventeenth century, science has been about admiration and esteem, in order to gain the power to join the Authority Structure—it has been a race for prestige, reputation, financial support, and invitations to speak—to get ahead, one should become a professor at an elite institution, get research support, get published, get noticed, get more funding, get appointed to boards and win prizes (Goodstein and Woodward 1999, 84–88). This description of the scientific community is strangely parallel to the one in Latour and Woolgar's *Laboratory Life*, where science is a *social* quest for credibility and career strategies, in which it is important to accumulate credentials, get invited to meetings, get noticed, get prestige, get published, and get positions of power (Latour and Woolgar 1979, 187–233). Latour and Woolgar's revelation of the social aspects of science appears to be cheerfully conceded by Goodstein and Woodward—they even say that the reward system in science "beggar[s] the etiquette of a medieval royal court," that you need to be "in the right place at the right time," and that the layers of influence are subtle (Goodstein and Woodward 1999, 84–85, 88). So there is less to fight about when highly conventional commentators like Goodstein and Woodward are basically quasi-Latourian co-productionists, celebrating the social relations that mediate Nature's brute facts.

And on the *other* side of the science wars, on the side of science studies, we have Latour wondering how he got to be the whipping boy for social constructivism (Berreby 1994). He is being criticized by Steve Fuller for being a neo-liberal, even while (1) he has rejected social constructivism for merely replacing Nature with Society, and (2) he has taken the naturalist turn while keeping discourse and society in play—but *then* he gets accused of debunking science (Latour 2004, 232). Twelve books criticizing social reductionism, yet Latour is the poster child for social reductionism! (Latour 2004, 232). That simply shows how ridiculous the science wars were.

I see the trend away from skepticism in science studies, especially the Third Wave in science and technology studies, as a new opportunity to engage law and legal processes. And I see the trend in law, away from idealizing science, as creating a new receptivity to sociological approaches. These two trends seem to have resulted in a more balanced perspective among judges and among science studies scholars. And this new opportunity to work together bodes well for science in law over the next 25 years.

NOTES

1. Sociologist Robert K. Merton was known for articulating four "norms" that ensure good science, namely "communism" (by which he meant collective availability of knowledge), universalism, disinterestedness, and scrutiny through organized skepticism (Cole 2010, 441; Merton 1949). By the 1970s, Merton's norms were seen as an idealization of science by most science studies scholars, since

   > Merton's norms appear to function more as ideals to which to aspire than as determinants of actual behavior. Indeed, one particularly well-known empirical study of a set of actual (normal, respectable, non-deviant) scientists involved in a scientific controversy found that, rather than behaving according to Merton's norms, they behaved in precisely the opposite fashion.... (Cole 2010, 443; Mitroff 1974, 587–589)

   Later in this chapter, I refer to Merton's influence as "Wave One," or the first wave of science studies—the second wave is the relativistic approach which I am identifying as dominant in science studies around 1993.

2. The quote is actually a reference to what Alan Sokol "seemed to argue" in an article (Sokol 1996a) which was published before the editors of SOCIAL TEXT realized it was a *parody* of science studies—it was a hoax that Sokol immediately revealed in another article (Sokol 1996b) arguing that cultural studies scholars could not tell the difference between scholarship and nonsense.

3. Goodstein believes that the Court made a "respectable stab at showing" how to recognize real science, and that the Court "emerged with at least their dignity intact" (Goodstein 2000, 79, 82), but others might disagree.

4. Sheila Jasanoff (1992) had made that same argument just prior to *Daubert*, but I do not believe very many judges or lawyers paid attention to her "brief" on behalf of science studies.

5. However, I offered an account (Caudill 2009, 27–29) of the Cindy Sommers prosecution, in San Diego, for arsenic poisoning, which case was later dismissed due to *faulty* toxicological tests.

6. The title *Laboratory Life: The Social Construction of Scientific Facts* (1979) was changed in 1986, in the second edition, to remove the word "social," which removal suggests a shift toward non-human actors, perhaps a turn to naturalism or at least co-production.

7. "We have [been] and will be said to be putting forward a pro-science view redolent of the 1950s," as we have "a preference for the norms and culture of evidence-based scientific argument" (Collins and Evans 2007, 10–11).

REFERENCES

Berreby, David. 1994. ...That Damned Elusive Bruno Latour. *Lingua Franca*, September/October.

Callon, Michel. 2002. From Science as an Economic Activity to Socioeconomics of Scientific Research. In *Science Bought and Sold*, ed. Philip Mirowski and Esther-Mirjam Sent. Chicago: University of Chicago Press.

Callon, Michel, and Bruno Latour. 1992. Don't Throw the Baby Out with the Bath School: A Reply to Collins and Yearley. In *Science as Practice and Culture*, ed. Andrew Pickering. Chicago: University of Chicago Press.

Caudill, David S. 2009. Arsenic and Old Chemistry: Images of Mad Alchemists, Experts Attacking Experts, and the Crisis in Forensic Science. *Boston University Journal of Science & Technology* 15: 1–33.

Caudill, David S., and L.H. LaRue. 2006. *No Magic Wand: The Idealization of Science in Law*. Lanham, MD: Rowman & Littlefield.

Cole, Simon A. 2010. Acculturating Forensic Science: What Is 'Scientific Culture,' and How Can Forensic Science Adopt It? *Fordham Urban Law Journal* 38: 435–472.

Collins, H.M., and Robert Evans. 2002. The Third Wave of Science Studies: Studies of Expertise and Experience. *Social Studies of Science* 32 (2): 235–296.

———. 2007. *Rethinking Expertise*. Chicago: University of Chicago Press.

Daubert v. Merrell Dow Pharmaceuticals On Remand, 43 F.3d 1311 (9th Cir. 1995).

Daubert v. Merrell Dow Pharmaceuticals, 509 U.S. 579 (1993).

Edwards, Harry T. 2010. *The National Academy of Sciences Report on Forensic Sciences: What It Means for the Bench and Bar* (Presentation at the Superior Court of the District of Columbia, Conference on the Role of the Court in an Age of Developing Science and Technology, Washington, DC, May 6, 2010). https://www.cadc.uscourts.gov/internet/home.nsf/AttachmentsByTitle/NAS+Report+on+Forensic+Science/$FILE/Edwards,+The+NAS+Report+on+Forensic+Science.pdf.

Fuller, Steve. 1999. Why Science Studies Has Never Been Critical of Science: Some Recent Lessons on How to Be a Helpful Nuisance and a Harmless Radical. *Philosophy of Social Science* 30: 5–32.

Goodstein, David. 2000. How Science Works. In *Reference Manual on Scientific Evidence*. Washington, DC: Federal Judicial Center.

Goodstein, David, and James Woodward. 1999. Inside Science. *American Scholar* 68: 83–90.

Haack, Susan. 2008. *Putting Philosophy to Work: Inquiry and Its Place in Culture—Essays on Science, Religion, Law, Literature, and Life*. Amherst, NY: Prometheus Books.

Jasanoff, Sheila. 1992. What Judges Should Know About the Sociology of Science. *Jurimetrics Journal* 32: 345–359.

Kennedy, Donald, and Richard A. Merrill. Fall 2003. Assessing Forensic Science. *Issues in Science and Technology*. http://www.issues.org/20.1/kennedy.html.

Krimsky, Sheldon. 2013. Do Financial Conflicts of Interest Bias Research? An Inquiry into the 'Funding Effect' Hypothesis. *Science, Technology & Human Values* 38 (4): 566–587.

Labinger, Jay A., and Harry Collins. 2001. Introduction. In *The One Culture? A Conversation About Science*, ed. J.A. Labinger and H. Collins. Chicago: University of Chicago Press.

Latour, Bruno. 1993. *We Have Never Been Modern*. Translated by C. Porter. Cambridge, MA: Harvard University Press.

———. 2004. Why Has Critique Run Out of Steam? From Matters of Fact to Matters of Concern. *Critical Inquiry* 30: 225–248.

Latour, Bruno, and Steve Woolgar. 1979. *Laboratory Life: The Social Construction of Scientific Facts*. Los Angeles: Sage; title changed in 1986, in the Second Edition (Princeton, NJ: Princeton University Press), to remove the word "Social" in the title.

Lentini, John J. 2006. The Mythology of Arson Investigation. In *Scientific Protocols for Fire Investigation*. New York: CRC Press. http://firescientist.com/Documents/The%20Mythology%20of%20Arson%20Investigation.pdf.

McGarrity, Thomas O., and Wendy E. Wagner. 2008. *Bending Science: How Special Interests Corrupt Public Health Research*. Cambridge, MA: Harvard University Press.

Merton, Robert K. 1949. *Social Theory and Social Structure: Toward the Codification of Theory and Research*. New York: The Free Press, Simon & Schuster.

Mitroff, Ian I. 1974. Norms and Counter-Norms in a Select Group of the Apollo Moon Scientists: A Case Study of the Ambivalence of Scientists. *American Sociological Review* 39: 579–595.

Nat'l Res. Council. 2009. *Strengthening Forensic Science in the United States: A Path Forward*. Washington, DC: National Academy of Science.

Pressman, Mark, and David S. Caudill. 2013. Alcohol-Induced Blackout as a Criminal Defense of Mitigating Factor: An Evidence-Based Review and Admissibility as Scientific Evidence. *Journal of Forensic Science* 58 (4): 932–940.

Risinger, Michael D. 2007. The Irrelevance, and Central Relevance, of the Boundary Between Science and Non-Science in the Evaluation of Expert Witness Reliability. *Villanova Law Review* 52: 679–722.

Sokol, Alan D. 1996a. Transgressing the Boundaries: Toward a Transformative Hermeneutics of Quantum Gravity. *Social Text* 46/47: 217–252.

———. 1996b. A Physicist Experiments with Cultural Studies. *Lingua Franca*, May/June.

Wynne, Brian. 1989. Sheep Farming After Chernobyl: A Case Study in Communicating Scientific Information. *Environment Science and Policy for Sustainable Development* 31 (2): 10–39.

———. 1996a. May the Sheep Safely Graze? A Reflexive View of the Expert-Lay Knowledge Divide. In *Risk, Environment and Modernity*, ed. Scott Lash, Bronislaw Szerszynski, and Brian Wynne. London: Sage.

———. 1996b. Misunderstood Misunderstandings: Social Identities and Public Uptake of Science. In *Misunderstanding Science? The Public Reconstruction of Science and Technology*, ed. Alan Irvin and Brian Wynne. Cambridge: Cambridge University Press.

CHAPTER 3

Ignoring Experts

Darrin Durant

3.1 INTRODUCTION

Experts will always be potentially problematic for democracy, because experts complicate the ideal of government by discussion. Yet while we can all find our own *particular* cases that warrant ignoring experts, this does not warrant a *general* case for ignoring experts. In this chapter, I criticize two general arguments for ignoring experts—the "robotic experts" and "dangerous experts" arguments. My point is that some general arguments for ignoring experts create more problems for democracy than they solve. When experts are constructed as mechanically reflecting instrumental reason, as robotic experts, expert judgment is misrepresented and deference relations mischaracterized. To dispute the argument that experts are robotic, I draw upon interviews with climate scientists in Australia. I show how these climate scientists are not as unreflexive as they need to be to warrant painting them as robots to whom deference would be inhuman. And when experts are constructed as undemocratic authorities, as dangerous experts, that image is reasonable in mild form but normatively disabling in its more radical version. To dispute the argument that experts are dangerous, I reflect on the political response to a major failure of the electrical grid in Australia in 2016. I show that good technical

D. Durant (✉)
University of Melbourne, Melbourne, VIC, Australia
e-mail: ddurant@unimelb.edu.au

© The Author(s) 2019
D. S. Caudill et al. (eds.), *The Third Wave in Science and Technology Studies*, https://doi.org/10.1007/978-3-030-14335-0_3

advice was ignored, with partisan politics treating expertise as superfluous to democratic deliberation.

Given the way this chapter owes much to the work of Harry Collins and Robert Evans (2007, 2017) on expertise and democracy, and because I have said I will be criticizing general arguments for ignoring experts, does my argument amount to giving experts a democratic free pass? Such might be expected, if we take critics of Collins and Evans at their word, for critics claim Collins and Evans are closet technocrats (cf. Wynne 2003, 402; Fischer 2009, 159). Yet the critics have mistaken a project of asking how experts can help democracy, with a project of turning democracy over to experts. In my estimation, the critics often adopt politically narrow conceptions of the democracy they defend and an implicitly ambiguous stance about the experts they critique (Durant 2011, 2016). Hence, to be clear, there are indeed ample grounds for being vigilant about the scope of expert power and sanguine about expert utility. Expert contributions to governance are often diverse and contradictory, exacerbating the problem of how to "discriminate among or organize the mass of truths scientists create" (Sarewitz 2016, 28). When experts illicitly treat as a technical problem what is also a political problem, they can underwrite an "enforcement of control, through the medium of science" (Wynne 2016, 101), effectively short-circuiting democratic deliberation. And because non-experts typically cannot judge expert claims, genuinely mutual discussion within our liberal democracies is imperiled (Turner 2003). Expert input into democratic deliberation and decision-making can also be wrong, unhelpful and capable of misleading about what is at stake. Experts do not always enhance democratic discussion.

For instance, in Australia high profile scientific and engineering bodies (ANSTO 2009, 2014; ATSE 2013, 2014) have argued Australia should "go nuclear." Using the rhetoric that climate change is so serious that "all options should be on the table," these experts argue that Australia should build either large nuclear reactors (1000 MW Gen-III) or Small Modular Reactors (less than 300 MW). This "go nuclear" judgment based on an "all options" rationale is a bad idea. More reflective judgments demonstrate that the global nuclear industry is already a failed project (Schneider and Froggatt 2017), while the arguments for small modular reactors are characterized by group-fantasies that erase environmental and economic problems (Sovacool and Ramana 2015). But also, the "all options" rationale enhances democracy only if you limit democracy to a system for keeping issues open and complex. Such limited conceptions of democracy provide little defense against failed, poorly conceived or strategically unproductive options over-burdening the deliberative process by their continual resuscitation. Democracy is also an institutional means for bringing divisive issues to a peaceful resolution (Durant 2018). Whether experts help or hinder such resolutions is a contingent matter, so our own *particular* cases for warranting the ignoring of experts do not warrant a *general* case for ignoring experts. To sustain a useful role for experts in democracy, we must do more than pay lip service to such roles. For instance, within an otherwise denunciatory treatment of experts, Brian Wynne claims "not to oppose the legitimate, if always questionable, authority of relevant scientific experts *over relevant propositional questions* in their field" (2014, 62). Yet Wynne does almost nothing to help identify what might count as not respecting that legitimate authority. In this chapter, I aim to illuminate when we might be unjustly ignoring experts, by illuminating some weaknesses in general arguments against experts.

3.2   Robotic Experts

The first way in which experts are ignored is that experts are constructed as icons of instrumental reason rather than as socially situated actors like the rest of us. This way of ignoring experts is evident in accounts of expertise that construct experts as prone to dogmatism and authoritarianism, and generally to have little capacity to be reflexive about their underlying practices and roles. Experts are depicted as mechanically reproducing their scientific programming. The most cited scholar for such treatments of experts is Wynne, who has been propagating images of unreflexive experts and alienated publics for a generation (1992, 2016). But accounts of experts as unreflexive often contain an ironic implication. The depiction of experts as robotic can quickly replicate the error at the heart of deficit models of science communication, of judging a social actor by what they lack not by what they possess. Expert judgments are thereby potentially misconstrued just as much as public judgments are misconstrued in deficit models of communication. Based upon interviews with politically engaged climate change experts in Australia, I suggest that constructing experts as unreflexive may of course be true in some cases, but if deployed as a general thesis, it runs the risk of misconstruing expert judgment by ignoring the socially and politically situated life of being an expert.

3.2.1 Theorizing Robotic Experts: Or, Reflexive Chickens

Of what relevance is the deficit model of science communication to an understanding of accounts of experts as robots? Unsurprisingly, because deficit models underplay the potential role of lay publics in deliberation about issues involving technical claims and overplay the role of experts, critics of deficit models are often also critics of experts. But the two need not go hand-in-hand. The surprising relevance is that critics of deficit models of science communication successfully illuminate two pieces of methodological wisdom in their critiques of deficit models and apply that methodological wisdom to their treatment of lay public members. Yet those same critics then fail to adequately heed that methodological wisdom in their treatment of experts. The result is that experts are depicted as robots.

To unpack that argument we should clarify that, in deficit models of science communication, it is assumed that filling the demonstrable gap in information and understanding between experts and lay publics will ease public anxieties about science. The deficit model of science communication rests on at least three incorrect assumptions. First, that public misgivings about science are due to cognitive deficiencies on the part of publics. In fact, public misgivings are grounded in social experiences and trust relations. Second, that downloading information to publics will alleviate public concerns about the trajectories of techno-scientific research or the import of uncertainty and ignorance within science. In fact, public concerns are partly reacting to the presumptuous dependency relationship itself. Third, that because science has authority over what an issue means, communication can be a one-way street from experts to publics. In fact, science assuming the role of de facto author of public meanings and proper concerns is the route to alienating publics. Wynne (2006) contains a more elaborated discussion of the deficit model of science communication, including the way the model has been continually reinvented by adding alibis and evasions. Scientific institutions, argues Wynne, have responded to science being increasingly pressed into corporate and government service by projecting onto others the responsibility for public disaffection.

Critiques of deficit models contain two pieces of methodological wisdom. The first is the colloquial observation that if you wish to understand a social actor, it pays to focus on what they possess rather than what they lack. Deficit models of science communication focus on that which members of the lay public lack, such as a scientific or engineering body of knowledge, and thus it makes sense within the orbit of deficit model thinking to try to fill the lay public up with facts. If the lay public lacking facts is the cause of their dissent from scientific advice, so the deficit model argument goes, then filling publics up with facts should breed appreciation for science. Yet as critiques of the deficit model make clear, members of the lay public possess their own meanings and concerns with regard to policy issues involving expert knowledge. When publics experience those meanings and concerns not being taken seriously, public mistrust of science can result. The second piece of methodological wisdom is the analytic observation that we should reject "the convenient use" of whatever a social actor lacks "as the supposed explanation" (Wynne 2006, 213) of how that actor behaves and makes judgments. Applied to public opposition to policy commitments justified in the name of science, the analytic observation implies we should reject convenient recourse to public deficits in information as explanations of public opposition.

Unfortunately, many who criticize deficit models of publics forget—when they turn to theorizing experts—the two pieces of methodological wisdom that ground that critique. A useful analogy here is to recall Harry Collins and Steven Yearley's (1992) critique of Actor-Network Theory (ANT) for being epistemological chickens. ANT was said to have given up on a thoroughly social analysis of scientific knowledge by letting the material world re-enter explanations in prosaic ways. Just as there can be epistemological chickens, there can also be reflexive chickens. Accounts of experts as robotic tend to give up on a thoroughly reflexive analysis, failing to attribute the same capacity for reflexive curiosity to an expert that was attributed to lay publics. Recall that for Wynne, reflexivity refers to the capacity to explore the prior commitments framing knowledge (1993). It appears easy to over-cook this reflexivity thesis. Wynne thus depicts science as manifesting an "idolatrous attribution of self-unfolding deterministic power," and scientists as purveyors of "dogmatic, anti-democratic political presumption" (2014, 62), while "this evident lack of reflexivity" manifests itself as "scientific denial [or] dishonesty" (2016, 106). Overall, Wynne depicts experts as deeply disconnected from their surrounding political culture.

Wynne's work is central for understanding the image of experts as robots because Wynne is a very clear exponent of the contrastive analytic that grounds the mechanical image. In Wynne's account of the differences between lay publics and scientists, lay publics are pictured as autonomous agents engaged in active and interpretive work; by contrast, scientists are attacked as a kind of rigid failure and are pictured as cultural dopes under the sway of their socialization (Durant 2008, 11–12). Wynne makes this clear by describing scientists as "expressing and reproducing their intellectual-administrative framework of prediction, standardization and control" (1992, 258), and as "inadvertent agents of the reproduction of an established set of institutional reflexes" (2006, 217). Critics of experts who adopt Wynne's contrastive style follow suit. For instance, Frank Fischer (2009) depicts lay publics as practicing a socially sensitive form of flexible and adaptable reasoning (see below); by contrast, experts are depicted in mechanical terms. Values are something expert reasoning "takes for granted" (Fischer 2009, 156) and criteria or standards are also "taken as given" (156), while expert reasoning works best on the "hard or fixed" and is "governed by calculation" (157). While it is true that humans are capable of working in routine and habitual ways that suggest the capacity to be mechanical, Fischer's imagery explicitly reduces experts to that of robots carrying out externally provided programming.

The general point here is that depicting experts as unreflexive robots tends to rely upon a contrastive strategy *vis-à-vis* the supposed reflexivity of lay publics and lack of reflexivity of experts. Yet depicting experts as robots implicitly replicates the very methodological sins of the deficit model of science communication. Only now, instead of repudiating those sins for their inability to grasp the life-world of lay publics, those sins are applied to experts as if they capture the life-world of experts. Applied to experts, the focus is on what experts lack rather than what experts possess, coupled with a tendency to make convenient use of expert deficits as explanations of expert engagements with publics. The reflexive chicken will attempt to head off this critical reading. It will be admitted that scientists have the capacity to be reflexive, but such capacities depend upon whether they are subjected to criticism and feel a little insecure; and thus the extent of reflexivity amongst scientists is empirically contingent (cf. Wynne 1992, 301). The reflexive chicken might even build that empirical conjecture into a "law of reflexivity," whereby "reflexivity is inversely proportional to power" (Wynne 1993, 337). Yet that posited socio-structural grounding for reflexive capacity sits uncomfortably with the way the "social identities" of publics are typically offered as the "more fundamental concept" for how to understand reflexive publics (Wynne 1992, 300). Our reflexive chicken will attempt to have an each-way bet, eliding the distinction between social identities and socio-structural relations to smuggle in a picture of lay publics as uniquely reflexive, while trying to mask the asymmetric depiction of experts as slaves to their structurally programmed deficits (Durant 2008). Yet the normative case for being wary of experts because of their lack of reflexivity is weakened if we find experts being more reflexive than the "robotic experts" image imagines.

3.2.2   A Case: Australian Climate Change Experts

Like the rest of the planet, research and discussion in Australia about climate change is highly politicized and science advice about climate policy has a tempestuous relationship with government. In Australia, this is signaled by the roller-coaster on which climate advisory bodies have ridden, especially since 2010. In February 2011 the (Left-wing) Labor Government of Prime Minister (PM) Julia Gillard—who had ousted her own sitting PM Kevin Rudd in a leadership spill in June 2010—established the Climate Commission as an independent body to provide authoritative and reliable information about climate change. In July 2012 Gillard also established the Climate Change Authority (as a statutory agency) to provide independent advice to the government on carbon pricing and emissions reductions targets. Yet after the Labor government was destabilized via another leadership spill in June 2013 (Rudd replacing Gillard), and the (Right-wing) Liberal party was subsequently elected in September 2013, Prime Minister Tony Abbott set about dismantling these advisory bodies. Abbott "sacked" the Climate Commission almost immediately in September 2013, though the former commission members immediately formed the Climate Council as a non-profit organization for distributing reliable information about climate change. Abbott also sought to axe the Climate Change Authority, but was unable to secure cross-bench support in Parliament to repeal the relevant legislation, and so instead began the process of appointing members supporting climate inaction rather than climate action (Readfearn 2017). When Abbott himself was deposed in September 2015 by yet another leadership spill—Malcolm Turnbull became PM—the process of undermining the Climate Change Authority continued. Turnbull embraced the idea of "clean coal," so that by July 2017 the last climate scientist had resigned in protest. Australia's climate rollercoaster would continue, though, as Scott Morrison would depose Turnbull in yet another leadership spill in August 2018. Morrison is famous for having brought a lump of coal into Parliamentary question time in February 2017, telling all not to be afraid of coal.

Based on interviews with past and present members of the Climate Council and the Climate Change Authority, which commenced in 2015 and with the help of snowball sampling has yielded dozens of interviews to date, I have not found the relevant experts to be as unreflexive as the image of experts as robots require. If experts are robotic, we should expect them to delete or fail to acknowledge scientific uncertainty and to display a strong tendency toward scientism. Yet along both those dimensions the climate scientists I interviewed defied the pessimistic predictions. Wynne's argument is that robotic experts either delete or fail to acknowledge the natural uncertainties and contingencies of science (1992, 298; 2016, 106). But the fallibility and contingency of science was a common theme in interviews: "the science is never settled" (D. Karoly, Climate Change Authority, 18 August 2015); "there will always be more to find out" (L. Hughes, Climate Council, 31 August 2015); "there is a lot of uncertainty [i.e.: about Australian water cycle effects; the tipping points of polar ice sheets]" (W. Steffen, Climate Council, 13 August 2015). Of course, even robots can say the right words in response to stimuli and that does not necessarily imply understanding, as John Searle (1980) argued in suggesting the Turing test was not a good measure of artificial intelligence. Wynne's test of reflexivity is thus a better measure, and Wynne claims publics are more reflexive than robotic because publics understand the natural uncertainties and contingencies of science in relation to a broad context of "issue over-spills" (1992, 298; 2016, 114). Yet such issue overspills were a prominent theme for climate scientists: "Obviously there are still many uncertainties and climate science will continue to evolve … [but] it's just so obvious that any apparent crack will be, you know, the deniers will stick a crowbar in it and attempt to widen it into … a fatal fracture" (C. Hamilton, Climate Change Authority, 13 August 2015). Climate scientists can thus display a reflexive attention to issue overspill and an implicit understanding of the way uncertainty arguments are strategic resources (Campbell 1985).

Yet are experts still prone to scientism, defined analytically as the belief that broad social values "should not be considered in decisions about science and technology" (Kleinman and Kinchy 2003, 379); or, more politically, as a form of dogma by which "public concerns … can only be about the 'science' [and] any other concerns are illegitimate 'hidden interests' and 'anti-scientific'" (Wynne 2014, 63). In opposition to such scientism, the need for a broad framing of the climate change issue was a common theme in the interviews: "I don't see a single frame around climate change" (D. Karoly, Climate Change Authority, 18 August 2015); "climate change is as much a moral issue as a physical one … [T]he role of civil society is so important" (L. Hughes, Climate Council, 31 August 2015); "[Science] let's you do more but it doesn't tell you whether doing more is right or wrong" (I. Chubb, Climate Change Authority (and Australia's former Chief Scientist), 17 August 2015). Moreover, forming judgments about the climate change issue was admitted to be "a complex process of forming judgments [out of the mix of input from civil society, NGO's and other experts]" (C. Hamilton, Climate Change Authority, 13 August 2015), in part because of the necessary role of "values when we are talking about interpreting data and consequences" (D. Karoly, 18 August 2015). If the height of scientism is to appoint oneself the "*de facto* authors of public meanings" (Wynne 2014, 62), by contrast I found a recoiling from such quasi-dictator public roles. Interviewees typically said it was "quixotic … to think that you can set policy" (C. Hamilton, Climate Change Authority, 13 August 2015), because few respond well to "being told on the soap box what they should do" (I. Chubb, Climate Change Authority, 21 September 2015).

Just as publics are said to be reflexive because of their "awareness of unpredicted future consequences" (Wynne 2006, 216), I found climate scientists worrying about how that domain of unpredictability is created in the first place. For instance, projections of temperature rise often favor the most confident estimate at the expense of "lower probability but higher consequence [projections]" (D. Karoly, Climate Change Authority, 18 August 2015). Overall, treating experts as robots disposes the analyst to *not* seek the interplay between institutional and social identity factors when explaining experts—the very interplay demanded when explaining publics. Wynne thus dismisses a scientist's motivations, even if "as pure as the driven snow" (2014, 217), in favor of the doctrinaire depiction of experts as dopes of institutional arrangements. Such mechanical framings of experts amount to ignoring the lived experience of experts, limiting the factors deemed relevant to understanding technical judgment and policy advice. For instance, what place in a robotic image exists for the climate scientist who reports "growing up angry," surrounded by socio-economic inequality, gender discrimination and unchecked urban-industrial waste; and who later realizes that "social setting kind of manifested itself in so many ways" (V. Sahajwalla, Climate Council, 1 September 2015)? When real human experts are replaced in social critique by robotic experts, technical judgment is inevitably misconstrued, because the human making the judgment is misconstrued. Moreover, to misconstrue the human making the expert judgment also means misconstruing any acts of public deference to or acceptance of expert claims. This is so because, on a fully democratic model of authority relations, deference relations involve judgments of claims themselves, the sources of any claims, and the authority relation itself (Moore 2017, 59–67). Because authority depends on the judgment of those under it and those judgments are conditioned by shared beliefs, values and judgments, to think of experts as robots is to undermine the possibility of anything shared between experts and lay publics by definitional fiat. At that point, it is easy to misread public agreement, even if you have understood public dissent.

3.3   DANGEROUS EXPERTS

The second way in which experts are ignored is that experts are constructed as a danger to democracy that must be corralled into servitude. This way of ignoring experts has a mild and a radical version. Conceptions of experts as mildly dangerous can be found in calls for experts to be considered "delegates," and this version has a lot to recommend it from the perspective of fair and legitimate democratic procedure. The radical version of the argument that experts are dangerous incorporates the conception of experts as delegates and the notion that experts lack reflexivity, but radicalizes both ideas via two additional arguments. One, a *picture* of experts as prone to infecting any communicative exchange into which they enter over-plays the contrast between experts and lay publics. Two, this picture of experts is then taken to warrant a watertight compartmentalization between authority structures and citizens. This radical account is doubly deficient, undermining even the limited expert power implicit in treating experts as delegates and also replicating the worst feature of political populism, which is the anti-pluralist delegitimizing of independent institutions. Suitably radicalized, the dangerous experts account acts as a white ant to the capacity of experts to address the pernicious effects of "epistemic rift" (Hess 2016, 52–58), thinning out any liberal-democratic objections to the way partisan politics can display a callous disregard for technical advice. I illustrate the perils of the radical version of the dangerous experts account by reflecting upon political responses to an electricity supply blackout event in Australia in 2016.

3.3.1   *Theorizing Dangerous Experts: Mild and Radical*

Experts can be dangerous in the general sense that the autonomy that conditions their utility can also be the conditions for exercising social power (Pels 2003). In democracies, because the exercising of any power must be justified, it is quite reasonable to attempt to limit the power of experts just as you would limit the power of any person, group or institution. A good example of such mild accounts is Sheila Jasanoff's work on the politics of expertise. Jasanoff writes that the expanding role of science advisers in modern democracies makes experts a kind of fifth branch of government (1990), but because democracies limit all forms of power it is normatively best to view experts as "a form of delegated authority" (2003, 158). Jasanoff seeks to broaden the role of lay publics in debating and deciding contentious policy issues that involve technical claims, but she also specifies that "expertise, like other forms of democratically delegated power, is entitled to respect only when it conforms to norms of transparency and deliberative adequacy" (160). Experts can thus be dangerous if they act outside of the "scope of their delegation" (Jasanoff 2003, 158), constructed as speaking only "on matters requiring specialized judgment" (158). Public input is necessary because "expert judgment needs to be supplemented by other inputs under conditions of uncertainty" (Jasanoff 2003, 160).

Delegate conceptions of experts thus acknowledge the ambiguous character of experts. Experts hold a limited form of power due to their utility value and ability to shape the meaning of issues, but that power needs to be kept in check if democracy is to retain its integrity. This mild version, that experts are *potentially* dangerous if not democratically restrained, has many good arguments for it. One, there is the danger of the scientization of politics. Expert assessment can narrow the scope of democratic discussion by dominating agendas and social choices, thereby threatening to make political decision-makers the mere agent of a scientific intelligentsia (Habermas 1971). Two, there is the danger of subtle co-option of the grounds of political discussion. This can occur because control over "the real" is now disproportionately enjoyed by experts (Ezrahi 1990). Three, there is the problem of information asymmetry between experts and non-experts. Democratic civility is compromised by experts persuading non-experts while non-experts have less capacity and/or success persuading experts (Turner 2003). Four, there are the distortions imminent in our modern excess of objectivity. Science can become so balkanized that it becomes capable of supporting radically divergent and politically partisan causes, turning policy deliberation into a game of "who has the most/right facts" rather than a broad discussion about social values and trajectories (Sarewitz 2000). The *potential* for democratically unconstrained expertise to be dangerous characterizes the mild version of the dangerous experts account, but in the mild version the utility value of expertise is tacitly and sometimes explicitly admitted. Thus, the democratic value of experts sometimes involves "narrowing the range of options" to help resolve intransigent value conflicts (Jasanoff 2008, 242), and experts are envisioned as performing the roles of both diagnosis (helping alert us to problems) and assessment (guiding action after political consensus) (Sarewitz 2000, 93).

In summary, the mild version of the dangerous experts account embraces the contestation of expertise because of its democratic effects: the articulation of issues, meanings and identities; the enabling of oversight; and the creation of forms of preventive power that can demand justifications from authorities (cf. Moore 2017, 95–111). A more radical version of the dangerous experts account incorporates such virtues of contesting expertise, but continues by greatly heightening the contrast between experts and lay publics. Experts are made part of a "tortured and alienated" institution beset by "dogmatic, anti-democratic political presumption" (Wynne 2014, 67, 62), that manifests as "scientific denial, or dishonesty" (Wynne 2016, 106). Wynne's work is central here because Wynne makes explicit the mechanisms shifting the "dangerous experts" account from mild to radical, beginning with the idea that alienated science insults publics even if it does not realize it is doing so. The individually robotic (unreflexive) expert is converted at the level of the social institution to that of a maniacal artificial intelligence harming people in the name of their best interests. Science as a social institution is thus envisioned as akin to HAL 9000 from *A Space Odyssey* or Skynet from *Terminator*. Experts and citizens can then be represented as occupying poles on a spectrum of reasoning, for instance from technical to sociocultural. Experts are confined to one of the poles.

Wynne's classic case study of the Cumbria sheep farmers dealing with the radioactive fallout from Chernobyl in 1986, and the erroneous assurances of nuclear experts about the nature and extent of the risks faced by sheep farmers, displayed the contrastive style that generates pictures of experts as a kind of "disease of the body politic." Wynne (1992) discussed the "baleful succession of blows to their cultural and social identity" (298) experienced by farmers at the hands of the scientists: "the farmers experienced the scientists as denying, and thus threatening, their social identity by ignoring the farmers' specialist knowledge and farming practices, including their adaptive decision-making idiom" (258). The farmers were also said to have experienced scientists as engaged in a conspiracy with the government, a fear that was historically grounded in distrust stemming from skepticism about official denials of radioactive contamination following the 1957 "Windscale" fire at a nuclear fuels reprocessing center. By contrast, scientists "were expressing and reproducing their intellectual-administrative framework of prediction, standardization and control" (Wynne 1992, 298); they also "deleted" uncertainties, "black boxed" the farmers and their farms, and "suppressed" any "private awareness" of "the cultural limits and precommitments of their science" (298). When Wynne (2016, 110) reflected on that Cumbria sheep farmer case study, he noted the way the representations of the farmers were presented to the farmers and farmers were asked if they recognized themselves. Affording the scientists the same opportunity to comment upon how scientists were represented is curiously absent from this reflective practice. Yet it is not hard to imagine scientists finding their robotic representations to be a species of the very "entrenched presumption" (Wynne 2016, 116) Wynne takes himself to be interrogating.

The radical version of the dangerous experts account thus starts to undermine even the limited form of power afforded to experts in the mild version, because of the insinuation that experts will contaminate the possibility of reasonable discussion. Fischer thus claims to "take seriously [Collins and Evans'] concern about losing the technical contribution to public policymaking" (2009, 138). Yet having endorsed Wynne's public alienation thesis (Fischer 2009, 148–149), Fischer moves swiftly to suggest experts and citizens utilize two different forms of reason and "technical and social criteria confront each other without a common metric" (155). Fischer suggests there is a form of practical discourse found in normative policymaking and deliberation that operates "in the pragmatic intersection between technical and cultural reason" (156). But it turns out that practical discourse is characterized by adopting the sociocultural reason of lay citizens *in opposition to* the technical reason of experts. Table 3.1 captures the contrast Fischer (2009, Chap. 5) draws between citizens and experts respectively.

The problem with this schema of reason is two-fold. First, the critique of "robotic experts" should cast doubt on the ability to sustain the strong contrast for any given social actor or institution. Second, we are being asked to imagine that sociocultural reason is protected to the extent it is able to stand *in opposition to* technical reason. The expert is made not just a servant of democracy, but radically subservient, and the route to political populism has been laid down.

The political populism lurking in the radical version of the dangerous experts account becomes clear when we consider the typical distinction between democracy and liberal democracy. Political theorists who analyze

Table 3.1 Two dogmas of human reason

Sociocultural reason	*Technical reason*
1. Is geared to social processes	1. Scientific method
2. Social knowledge gained from social experiences (personal or otherwise)	2. Logical consistency
	3. Empirical outcomes
3. Draws upon traditional social and peer groups	4. Generalizability of findings
4. Attends to unanticipated consequences of decisions	5. Privileges expert judgments
5. Trusts process over predictive outcomes	6. Depersonalized calculations
6. Pays attention to the circumstances under which judgments are made (such as the standing and interests of the claimant)	7. Statistical probabilities
	8. Risk-benefit ratios
	9. Causal relations and outcomes
7. Existing social values and previous social experiences are relevant to assessments	10. Standards are treated as a given
8. Concerned with impacts and intrusions	11. Values are taken for granted (they are not part of the analytic assessment)
9. Standards arrived at by deliberation (what justifies their use?)	

political populism (cf. Judis 2016; Mudde and Kaltwasser 2017; Müller 2017) distinguish between the principles of popular sovereignty and majority rule that comprise democracy and liberal democracy, which includes those two principles but also includes provisions for independent institutions (like the judiciary and the free press) and the protection of rights (be they civil, economic or cultural). Political populism can be characterized as an anti-elitist and anti-pluralist appeal to the general will of the people, usually via a thin-centered ideology that is parasitic on more specific policy proposals. Populism tends to be practiced a little differently in Left-wing (dyadic; the people versus elites) versus Right-wing form (triadic; the people versus elites but with an out-group the people claim are coddled by the elites). The crucial aspect of populism that ought to worry liberal democrats is the anti-pluralism, which manifests as a strong challenge to independent institutions within democracy because they are claimed to be not representative of either the real people at the level of citizenry or true representatives at the level of formal politics. The radical version of the dangerous experts account replicates the anti-pluralism of populist politics, because the strong contrast between expert and lay public reason situates experts as like a class of political actor prone to infecting the communicative exchanges into which they enter. Just as political populism is wary of power drifting away from "the people" and so advises a watertight compartmentalization between the authority structures of independent institutions and what governs the people (Pettit 1997, 177–180), the radical version of the dangerous experts account replicates that desired watertight compartmentalization at the level of normative politics.

Here we have to be sensitive to the slippage between a descriptive effort to display the fluidity and socially negotiated character of "boundaries," such as those between science and politics, and an underlying normative preference about the policing of those boundaries. The radical version of the dangerous experts account trades on the political image of the need to police the influence of experts, and implicitly posits a desire for a watertight compartmentalization between expertise as an institution and the deliberative forums of democracy. Such normative preferences usually manifest in the form of strong critiques of instances of "leakage" in which experts over-stepped their authority, usually at the expense of public meanings, issues or identities. The mild version of a dangerous experts account talks of policing experts in the name of securing broad public participation. The radical version evinces a straight claim that experts will pollute democracy by naturally insulting and crowding out publics. The subsequent normative talk is of isolating experts in as exact a fashion as possible. It is that *exactness of intent* that replicates the political populism of aiming for a watertight compartmentalization in the distribution of powers between independent institutions and citizens. To the extent the institution of expertise is a fifth branch of government, as the mild version of the dangerous experts account holds and which the radical version assumes by making experts a target in the name of democracy, a radical version of the dangerous experts account becomes anti-pluralist in the style of political populists. Liberal democrats should think twice before blithely replicating direct attacks on the independent institutions within liberal democracies.

3.3.2   A Case: The Lights Go Out in South Australia

What can happen if the legitimacy of expertise as an independent institution is brought into doubt? The first casualty is going to be that partisan politics can be set adrift from the ability of expert claims to act as a check against not just contentiously grounded but completely ungrounded policy claims.

A case in point is the responses to a State-wide blackout in South Australia on 28 September 2016, following a fierce storm that blew over in excess of twenty high voltage power poles and transmission towers and three major transmission lines. In South Australia, the share of renewables (wind and solar) in the electricity supply mix already exceeds fifty percent. Australia's (conservative) Liberal-National coalition government swiftly blamed renewable energy for the blackout, with conservative parliamentarians blanketing the media with claims the blackout was due to the State's over-reliance on wind power. As shown in detail elsewhere (Farrell 2016; Lucas 2017; Durant 2018) it was claimed that: "the generators don't work when the wind is blowing too hard" (Senator Nick Xenophon); "[the country should] urgently exit all climate change policies that are the direct cause of this huge mess in SA" (Senator Malcolm Roberts); "the virtue of the increasing amount of renewables … does raise questions for the stability of the system" (Josh Frydenberg, Minister for the Environment and Energy); "[Wind power] wasn't working too well last night, because they had a blackout" (Barnaby Joyce, Deputy Prime Minister); "the South Australian blackout [is a] wake-up call [to focus on] energy security [and move away from] ideological [renewable energy targets]" (Malcolm Turnbull, Prime Minister). The only problem with this "the wind did it" theory is that it was not remotely true *and* the conservative politicians knew it. We now know that all those conservative parliamentarians who blamed wind power for the blackout had in fact been advised by the Australian Electricity Market Operator (AEMO) that the problem was not wind power (Hutchens 2017). The final AEMO report would later confirm that advice, explaining the blackout as a complicated affair tied to the severity of the storm, transmission tower loss, voltage settings in the electricity network and even market dynamics (AEMO 2017).

While it is true that competing expert assessments sought to disabuse the public of the simple idea that wind power equates to blackouts (Durant 2018), in our digital age memes die hard. Partisan misrepresentations about the causes of the blackout contributed significantly to the construction of a political fact about "energy security": that it requires less renewable power and more fossil-fuel-based power (Lucas 2017). Radical versions of the dangerous expert account do not *cause* expert input to be ignored in cases like the partisan response to the blackout. But radical versions of the dangerous expert account participate in the same valorization of anti-pluralism found in political populism, and thus participate in a form of politics that makes the (unwarranted) ignoring of experts plausible, acceptable and increasingly more difficult to socially sanction.

3.4   Conclusion

Where does this analysis leave us? It should leave us thinking there are poor theoretical grounds for *generally* assuming experts are unreflexive. We may even view with suspicion the attempted face-saving empirical bet that the less powerful publics are more often reflexive than the experts. Wynne makes that empirical bet (1992, 298) but also clouds it in caveats: the law of reflexivity was "only half in jest", and "all else equal (*which it is not*) … typical publics are more reflexive than … scientists" (2016, 115; emphasis added). The metaphor of the empirical bet suggests we can consider this kind of theorizing about reflexivity as akin to an argument "off the bit," which in horse racing refers to a horse being ridden on a loose rein to allow it to gallop freely. An early gallop is great except if the horse is quite a distance from the finish line and will probably tire and fade from the lead. Similarly, the assumption that experts lack reflexivity helps generate an initially plausible account of experts as robotic. But the argument is off the bit, and as we actually approach the empirical finishing line, we often find the robotic picture fading in plausibility. The conditions said to give rise to reflexivity amongst lay publics, such as lay public members placing themselves into questioning with others or the powerless and vulnerable being forced to reflect on their situation (Wynne 2006, 219; 2016, 115), can exist for experts too. However, treating experts as robotic licenses the ignoring of experts by in effect licensing an inattention to the political field in which the expert perceives themselves to reside or in which the expert resides regardless of their grasp of its intricacies.

While the treatment of experts as robotic can thus misconstrue (and ignore) expert judgment, by implicitly treating experts as either dopes of their intellectual-political fields or simply diverting attention from the fields in which experts intervene, the dangerous experts account ignores experts wherever it devolves into anti-pluralist political populism. The radical version of the dangerous experts account leaves the social analyst with little grounds for objecting to the straight ignoring of technical advice in a contested policy debate. When expertise as an independent institution is presented as threatening to pollute sociocultural and even practical reason with the pernicious limitations of technical reason, the legitimacy of the independence of the institution of expertise is under fire, thereby replicating the anti-pluralism of populist politics. The concept of "epistemic rift" (Hess 2016, 52–58) captures the political problem made worse by participating in the implicit denigration of independent institutions within liberal democracies. An epistemic rift occurs when there is a breakdown of the circulation between technical advice and political deliberation and decision-making. Such breakdowns go beyond failing to act on some specific technical claim, and extend to a strategy by government or industry to deny consensus, politicize whole fields of research unjustly, and build publics through echo chambers in the media. For the moment, imagine expertise as an independent institution "one might hope" could be capable of performing the role of a "neutral court" or "source of arbitration" (Hess 2016, 53). None of the potential problems with that role—usefully flagged in the worries that experts can be robotic and are best treated as delegates—outweighs the problems you invite by destabilizing the basic legitimacy of that hope. Epistemic rifts are breakdowns in our liberal-democratic orders and radical versions of the dangerous experts account participate in giving oxygen to the anti-pluralism of our populist political age.

References

AEMO. 2017. Australian Electricity Market Operator. *Black System South Australia 28 September 2016*. Final Report, March 28. AEMO Limited. Accessed June 10, 2017. http://www.aemo.com.au/Media-Centre/AEMO-publishes-final-report-into-the-South-Australian-state-wide-power-outage.

ANSTO. 2009. Australian Nuclear Science and Technology Organization. *The Nuclear Option as Part of a Diverse Energy Mix*. Submission to Energy White Paper. Accessed April 10, 2018. http://www.ansto.gov.au/__data/assets/pdf_file/0004/42385/ANSTO_Submission_to_Energy_White_Paper.pdf.

———. 2014. Australian Nuclear Science and Technology Organization. Paterson, A., M. Ho & G. Storr, *New to Nuclear Countries: Considerations for Adoption of Small Modular Reactors – A Guide to Future Adopters*. Conference Paper Presented to the 19th Pacific Basin Nuclear Conference, Vancouver, Canada, August 24–28, 2014. Accessed April 10, 2018. http://www.nuclearaustralia.org.au/wp-content/uploads/2015/04/PBNC2014-Paterson-et-al.-paper.pdf.

ATSE. 2013. Australian Academy of Technological Sciences and Engineering. *Nuclear Energy for Australia? Conference Report*. Accessed April 10, 2018. https://www.atse.org.au/atse/content/publications/reports/energy/nuclear-energy-australia.aspx.

———. 2014. Australian Academy of Technological Sciences and Engineering. *Nuclear Energy Is an Option*. Accessed April 10, 2018. https://www.atse.org.au/atse/content/publications/policy/nuclear-energy-is-an-option.aspx.

Campbell, Brian. 1985. Uncertainty as Symbolic Action in Disputes Among Experts. *Social Studies of Science* 15 (3): 429–453.

Collins, Harry M., and Robert Evans. 2007. *Rethinking Expertise*. Chicago: University of Chicago Press.

———. 2017. *Why Democracies Need Science*. Cambridge: Polity Press.

Collins, Harry M., and Steven Yearley. 1992. Epistemological Chicken. In *Science as Practice and Culture*, ed. Andy Pickering, 301–326. Chicago: University of Chicago Press.

Durant, Darrin. 2008. Accounting for Expertise: Wynne and the Autonomy of the Lay Public Actor. *Public Understanding of Science* 17 (1): 5–20.

———. 2011. Models of Democracy in Social Studies of Science. *Social Studies of Science* 41 (5): 691–714.

———. 2016. The Undead Linear Model of Expertise. In *Political Legitimacy, Science and Social Authority: Knowledge and Action in Liberal Democracies*, ed. M. Heazle and J. Kane, 17–37. London: Routledge.

———. 2018. Servant or Partner? The Role of Expertise and Knowledge in Democracy. *The Conversation*, March 9. https://theconversation.com/servant-or-partner-the-role-of-expertise-and-knowledge-in-democracy-92026.

Ezrahi, Yaron. 1990. *The Descent of Icarus: Science and the Transformation of Contemporary Democracy*. Cambridge, MA: Harvard University Press.

Farrell, Paul. 2016. South Australia Weather: 80,000 People Still Without Power in Adelaide. *The Guardian*, September 29. Accessed June 10, 2017. https://www.theguardian.com/australia-news/2016/sep/29/south-australia-storms-frydenberg-adelaide-renewable-energy-weatherill.

Fischer, Frank. 2009. *Democracy and Expertise: Reorienting Policy Inquiry*. Oxford: Oxford University Press.

Habermas, Jurgen. 1971. *Toward a Rational Society: Student Protest, Science, and Politics*. Boston: Beacon Press.

Hess, David J. 2016. *Undone Science: Social Movements, Mobilized Publics, and Industrial Transitions*. Cambridge, MA: MIT Press.

Hutchens, Gareth. 2017. Turnbull Ignored Advice That Renewable Energy Not to Blame for SA Blackouts. *The Guardian*, February 13. Accessed July 20, 2017. https://www.theguardian.com/australia-news/2017/feb/13/turnbull-ignored-advice-that-renewable-energy-not-to-blame-for-sa-blackouts.

Jasanoff, Sheila. 1990. *The Fifth Branch: Science Advisers as Policymakers*. Cambridge, MA: Harvard University Press.

———. 2003. (No?) Accounting for Expertise. *Science and Public Policy* 30 (3): 157–162.

———. 2008. "Speaking Honestly to Power." Review of *The Honest Broker*, by Roger Pielke, Jr. *American Scientist* 3 (96): 240–243.

Judis, John B. 2016. *The Populist Explosion: How the Great Recession Transformed American and European Politics*. New York: Columbia Global Reports.

Kleinman, Daniel L., and Abby Kinchy. 2003. Why Ban Bovine Growth Hormone? Science, Social Welfare, and the Divergent Biotech Policy Landscape in Europe and the United States. *Science as Culture* 12 (3): 375–414.

Lucas, Adam. 2017. Confected Conflict in the Wake of the South Australian Blackout: Diversionary Strategies and Policy Failure in Australia's Energy Sector. *Energy Research & Social Science* 29 (July): 149–159.

Moore, Alfred. 2017. *Critical Elitism: Deliberation, Democracy and the Problem of Expertise*. Cambridge: Cambridge University Press.

Mudde, Cas, and Cristobal Rovira Kaltwasser. 2017. *Populism: A Very Short Introduction*. New York: Oxford University Press.

Müller, Jan-Werner. 2017. *What Is Populism?* London: Penguin Books.

Pels, Dick. 2003. *Unhastening Science: Autonomy and Reflexivity in the Social Theory of Knowledge*. Liverpool: Liverpool University Press.

Pettit, Philip. 1997. *Republicanism: A Theory of Freedom and Government*. Oxford: Oxford University Press.

Readfearn, Graham. 2017. Climate Change Authority Loses Last Climate Scientist. *The Guardian*, July 5. Accessed May 5, 2018. https://www.theguardian.com/environment/planet-oz/2017/jul/05/climate-change-authority-loses-last-climate-scientist.

Sarewitz, Daniel. 2000. Science and Environmental Policy: An Excess of Objectivity. In *Earth Matters: The Earth Sciences, Philosophy, and the Claims of Community*, ed. R. Frodeman, 79–89. Upper Saddle River, NJ: Prentice Hall.

———. 2016. Saving Science. *New Atlantis* 49 (Spring/Summer): 5–40.

Schneider, Mycal, and Antony Froggatt. 2017. *The World Nuclear Industry Status Report 2017*. Accessed April 10, 2017. https://www.worldnuclearreport.org/.

Searle, John R. 1980. Minds, Brains, and Programs. *Behavioral and Brain Sciences* 3 (3): 417–457.

Sovacool, Benjamin K., and M.V. Ramana. 2015. Back to the Future: Small Modular Reactors, Nuclear Fantasies, and Symbolic Convergence. *Science, Technology & Human Values* 40 (1): 96–125.

Turner, Stephen. 2003. *Liberal Democracy 3.0: Civil Society in an Age of Experts*. London: SAGE.

Wynne, Brian. 1992. Misunderstood Misunderstanding: Social Identities and Public Uptake of Science. *Public Understanding of Science* 1 (3): 281–304.

———. 1993. Public Uptake of Science: A Case for Institutional Reflexivity. *Public Understanding of Science* 2 (4): 321–337.

———. 2003. Seasick on the Third Wave: Subverting the Hegemony of Propositionalism. *Social Studies of Science* 33 (3): 401–417.

———. 2006. Public Engagement as a Means of Restoring Public Trust in Science – Hitting the Notes, but Missing the Music. *Community Genetics* 9 (3): 211–220.

———. 2014. Further Disorientation in the Hall of Mirrors. *Public Understanding of Science* 23 (1): 60–70.

———. 2016. Ghosts in the Machine: Publics, Meanings and a Social Science in a Time of Expert Dogma in Denial. In *Remaking Participation: Science, Environment and Emergent Public*, ed. Jason Chilvers and Matthew Kearnes, 99–120. New York: Routledge.

CHAPTER 4

Recognizing Counterfeit Scientific Controversies in Science Policy Contexts: A Criteria-Based Approach

Martin Weinel

4.1 Introduction

A popular myth about science holds that "experts can be expected to agree" (Collingridge and Reeve 1986). Dispelling this myth has been integral part of early work in the sociology of scientific knowledge (Collins 1981; Nelkin 1979), leading authors such as Collingridge and Reeve (1986, 16–19) to emphasize that the "reality of science" is that experts can indeed be expected to disagree (Goldman 2001; Martin and Bammer 1996). Furthermore, they and others (Jasanoff 1990, 1991) argue that

This chapter is based on ideas developed between 2006 and 2010. An earlier version was presented to SEESHOP in 2008 and has been publicly available as a Cardiff School of Social Science working paper. I'm indebted to Harry Collins and Rob Evans, to SEESHOP participants, and to members of the Knowledge Expertise Science (KES) group at the Cardiff School of Social Sciences.

M. Weinel (✉)
Cardiff University, Cardiff, UK
e-mail: WeinelM@Cardiff.ac.uk

© The Author(s) 2019
D. S. Caudill et al. (eds.), *The Third Wave in Science and Technology Studies*, https://doi.org/10.1007/978-3-030-14335-0_4

expert disagreements will become even fiercer if the contested issue is of import to science policy-making.[1] The reasons for expert disagreements are manifold; they might be caused, for example, by differences in values and interests held by experts, or by different methods to generate facts, or they might come about as a result of diverse framings of issues (Jasanoff 1990; Lindblom and Woodhouse 1993; Rushefsky 1982; Stirling 2008).

While this body of work shows that genuine expert disagreement is part and parcel of science—whether it has policy-relevance or not—there is another kind of "expert disagreement." Unlike genuine expert disagreements, this other kind of disagreement does not really exist within expert communities, but is specifically and deliberately manufactured to create a public perception of prevailing uncertainty and controversy within those communities and to disguise relative certainty and consensus that might exist in expert communities. The tobacco industry, for example, has mastered the art of "manufacturing doubt," but so have other actors, most notably oil companies with respect to global warming and climate change (Michaels 2008; Ceccarelli 2011; Oreskes 2004; Oreskes and Conway 2010; Weinel 2011).

Thus, when scientific or technical claims become relevant for policy-making and science, policy-makers are confronted with expert disagreement; one key task is to assess whether the degree of publicly visible disagreement about some scientific fact accurately represents the uncertainty in the expert community, or whether the controversy has been artificially created to serve other ends. Distinguishing between the two in science policy contexts is important: if there is real scientific controversy, then science policy-makers need to be careful as to how science enters a policy decision; if, however, the controversy is "counterfeit" or "manufactured" then claims that the science is "not settled" or "uncertain" should not have any effect on the policy process.[2]

4.2   The South African AZT Controversy[3]

In 1994, the outcomes of clinical trial ACTG076 were published in the *New England Journal of Medicine* (Connor et al. 1994). The results showed that administering AZT (azidothymidine) reduced the risk of mother-to-child transmission (MTCT) of HIV during pregnancy and childbirth by about 50 per cent. In the following years, more clinical trials confirmed the effectiveness of AZT in the prevention of mother-to-child transmission (PMTCT) (Dabis et al. 1999; Shaffer et al. 1999; Wiktor et al. 1999). The US American Food and Drug Agency (FDA) licensed AZT for PMTCT in 1994 and the drug has been approved for this use by regulatory bodies around the world, including the South African Medicines Control Council (MCC). As a result, AZT is used in numerous countries for PMTCT.

In South Africa, various institutions and actors, including the ANC-led government, have been considering whether and how to make AZT available throughout the public health sector since the mid-1990s. Plans to introduce pilot sites in every province were about to be implemented in late 1998 when the government decided to shelve those plans on financial grounds. The government argued that scarce resources would be better spent on programmes that focus on education and information that would prevent people from becoming infected with HIV in the first place. One year later, however, President Thabo Mbeki said that the government could not provide AZT for PMTCT because the drug is too toxic.[4] He made the following comment at the end of his inaugural speech to the National Council of Provinces, the second chamber of parliament on 28 October 1999:

> There ... exists a large volume of scientific literature alleging that, among other things, the toxicity of this drug [AZT] is such that it is in fact a danger to health. These are matters of great concern to the Government as it would be irresponsible for us not to head [sic] the dire warnings which medical researchers have been making. I have therefore asked the Minister of Health, as a matter of urgency, to go into all these matters so that, to the extent that is possible, we ourselves, including our country's medical authorities, are certain of where the truth lies. To understand this matter better, I would urge the Honourable Members of the National Council to access the huge volume of literature on this matter available on the Internet, so that all of us can approach this issue from the same base of information. (Mbeki 1999, ¶¶ 59–63)

The speech marked the beginning of a heated public policy disagreement in South Africa about the safety of AZT and similar drugs that paralysed policy-making for four years. In 2003, the courts forced the government to introduce AZT for PMTCT. The government repeatedly justified the delay in decision-making regarding the provision of these drugs for PMTCT by claiming the existence of an ongoing scientific controversy. The question asked and answered here is: was it a genuine scientific controversy?

I argue that science and technology studies (STS) insights can help to make judgements about the authenticity of scientific controversies in "real policy time."[5] In this chapter, I propose a criteria-based approach that draws on insights generated by both the sociology of scientific knowledge (SSK) and studies in expertise and experience (SEE). As with any demarcation exercise there will be "borderline cases" where the judgement is difficult or impossible, but there will also be cases that are more clear-cut and afford a judgement. Another problem with this kind of criteria-based demarcation exercise is that the criteria, just like any other rules, do not contain the rules for their application. There is a tendency in science and technology studies to assume that, because rules do not contain the rules for their own application and because there are always exceptions, formulating rules is a deeply flawed activity. But everyone follows rules all the time, which is why we can tell when mistakes are made, and all social institutions rely on rules. The challenge, therefore, is to help develop rules that go wrong less often and in less damaging ways.[6] Progress is been made if the method of making such decisions is worked out for a few extreme cases even if it will not yet work for every case. In sum, this chapter is looking for practical ways to conduct demarcation work in an explicit manner by identifying possible criteria, which can then structure judgements that demarcate genuine from counterfeit scientific controversies.

The four criteria, which will be discussed and justified in greater detail, are as follows:

1. conceptual continuity with science
2. expertise of claim-maker
3. explicit argument within relevant expert communities
4. constitutive work.

The first criterion checks whether controversial claims are conceptually continuous with science or, put differently, whether controversial claims are "scientific." The second criterion checks whether an actor has the appropriate expertise to make a particular claim or answer a propositional question. The third criterion checks whether the claim is supported by some kind evidence or "constitutive work." The fourth checks whether a claim is still subject of an explicit argument or whether it has yet reached the stage of implicit rejection.

I assert that if a single criterion is not met then a controversy should be classified as "counterfeit." The four criteria can be read as a decision tree:

the "scientificness" of a controversy increases from stage to stage, but only if a controversy satisfies all four criteria can it be judged to be a genuine scientific controversy.

4.3   FIRST CRITERION: CONCEPTUAL CONTINUITY WITH SCIENCE

The first criterion, "conceptual continuity with science," sounds abstract, but the idea behind it is readily intelligible: if a technical claim does not reflect any intention to be part of the domain of science, there is no reason to assume that a *scientific* controversy can be caused by it. For example, the claim in *Genesis* that God created the earth in just seven days (if the day of rest is included) is regarded by some as a statement of fact, since this is stated in the Bible. This is, however, a claim that belongs to the realm of religion and usually there is no intent to make it continuous with science. Such a claim ought not to have any impact on, say, paleontological archaeology, which, according to literal believers of the Bible, ought not to exist.

The underlying argument is that if a claim, however, controversial, is outside the realm of science it cannot be part of a genuine scientific controversy. We can call this criterion "conceptual continuity with science" and its absence is characterized by what Collins and Evans (2007, 126) call a "lack of intention to make a body of work [or a specific] claim fit with the existing body of science." Note that this formulation does not imply that a claim has to be accepted by mainstream science. In other words, it allows *Denkstil* (style-of-thought) changes in a Fleckian sense to occur (Fleck 1979).[7] Thus, while a body of work might be "revolutionary," it retains "conceptual continuity" so long as the intention is to keep as much as possible of existing science in place making revolutionary changes only as necessary.[8] As long as this is the case, a body of work or a particular claim can be said to be part of science. But if a body of work or a claim is too far removed from science so that there appears to be no intent to make it part of science, it cannot be said to be part of a scientific controversy.[9]

Applying this criterion to the publicly visible disagreement about the safety of AZT set out in the case study introduced above does not suggest it to be a counterfeit scientific controversy. As there is virtually no drug that does not have some unwanted side-effects, assessing whether such side-effects outweigh the benefits of a certain drug regime is a routine process in medicine. The claim that AZT might be too toxic to be used for PMTCT is therefore conceptually continuous with science.

However, another example from South Africa illustrates what a claim that is not continuous with existing science might look like. In September 2000, the media reported widely that the South African Minister of Health received a letter containing a book chapter written by one William Cooper (MacGregor 2000). In the book chapter, Cooper explains that HIV was developed by a coalition of Illuminati, aliens, the Central Intelligence Agency (CIA) and a few other organizations. HIV was then introduced to Africa through smallpox vaccines in the 1970s with the aim of reducing the world population. This account differs markedly from contemporary textbook accounts of the origins of HIV, which describe HIV as originating from a virus found in chimpanzees (Whiteside 2008). Moreover, neither Illuminati nor aliens nor any of the other leading characters of the conspiracy narrative play roles in scientific theories nor are they likely to do so in the foreseeable future. Unperturbed by this aspect of the claims, the then Minister of Health sent copies of the book chapter to all provincial Departments of Health, expecting that it would inform provincial decision-makers' views on HIV/AIDS. An explanation of the South African HIV/AIDS problem that causally involves imagined entities such as aliens and Illuminati is so far removed from accepted scientific explanations that it should not count as an element in any scientific controversy about the origins of HIV/AIDS in Africa.

4.4   Second Criterion: Expertise of the Protagonists

The second criterion, "expertise of claim-maker," asserts that those who make claims that challenge a consensus or contribute to one or the other side in a supposedly scientific disagreement should possess relevant technical expertise. This is, for example, the reason why PR companies, which write articles and letters containing technical claims attempting to shed doubt on the scientific consensus that smoking is dangerous on behalf of tobacco companies, pay scientists for their signature (Michaels 2008). If these documents were clearly marked as written by a PR company, no one would take them seriously.

To demarcate genuine from counterfeit scientific controversies therefore requires an analysis of expertise of protagonists in a visible disagreement about science. The suitability of a potential controversy originator can be discussed in the light of the Periodic Table of Expertises proposed by Collins and Evans as part of their new theory of expertise (2007, 14). Their re-definition of expertise centred on the acquisition of tacit knowledge. Deep understanding of any form of life—reflected in the ability of an actor to be able to "go on" (or "to know what to do next") in a situation—requires the acquisition of the relevant tacit knowledge related to the domain in question.[10] Collins and Evans (2002, 2007) argued that the only way for an actor to acquire the necessary domain-specific tacit knowledge is through social immersion into those collectives that already hold and maintain this tacit knowledge. In this case, the criterion can be operationalized by examining the social networks in which the person making the claims is embedded. To the extent that these include networks of relevant experts, then there are grounds for believing the person making the claim might know what she or he is talking about. If, however, there is no evidence of such interaction, then it is hard to see why the person should be trusted as an expert (Goldman 2001; Hardwig 1985).

In the South African case, it can be argued that Mbeki was initially not a protagonist in the controversy about the safety of AZT even though he was publicly urging other politicians to pay attention to a body of supposedly scientific literature critical about AZT found on the Internet. At the very least, he became a key protagonist shortly afterwards, however, after rejecting the findings of a technical report by the Medicines Control Council (MCC), the official regulatory agency concerned with the safety of drugs, issued in February 2000 that concluded that there is no evidence to suggest that AZT is not safe when used for PMTCT.[11] As I have demonstrated elsewhere (Weinel 2007, 2011), Mbeki's expertise on matters of drug safety, pharmacology, toxicology, and other related domains amounted, at best, to primary source knowledge (PSK). The analysis of Mbeki's interactions suggests that he had minimal contact with members of relevant expert communities and acquired almost all of his knowledge about AZT and its supposed effects from reading literature that he either found on the Internet or that he had been sent or given by various people who were also not experts on the matter.[12] Given Mbeki's isolated knowledge acquisition and the absence of any evidence indicating that Mbeki had any prolonged social interaction with any experts on the safety of AZT suggests that he did not acquire the relevant bodies of tacit knowledge that characterize expertise in a specialist domain.

4.5   THIRD CRITERION: CONSTITUTIVE WORK

The third criterion, "constitutive work," is based on the insight that nobody would accept a controversial technical claim that is not based on some sort of scientific activity. While experts might dream just as much anyone else, one should not take a scientific claim seriously if a scientific expert insists that the content of the claim occurred to her/him in a dream.[13] The purpose of the criterion is to distinguish between "baseless" claims—speculations—and claims that have at least the chance to be based on more than just "mere, unsubstantiated belief."

The term "constitutive work" draws on the idea of a "constitutive forum," a concept that has been developed by Collins and Pinch (1979). Collins and Pinch (1979, 239–240) define the constitutive forum as an abstract "space" which comprises "scientific theorising, and experiment … [with or without] corresponding publication and criticism in the learned journals and, perhaps, in the formal conference setting." The abstract space of the constitutive forum is bounded by what are generally considered to be the set of activities that constitute science as a distinctive form-of-life. This contrasts with the "contingent forum" which is the abstract space of activities carried out by scientists which are not generally considered legitimate contributions to scientific knowledge creation. Sociologists of scientific knowledge have shown that there is no epistemological distinction between the two for a, but the sociological distinction remains clear and must remain clear if we want to continue to demarcate science as a distinctive activity. It is important to bear in mind the constitutive work is operationalized in practice by evidence of systematic data collection, observation, and reflection. While the traditional format is the peer-reviewed paper, a broader definition of expertise allows that constitutive work can also be done by the scientifically unqualified outside of official scientific institutions.

In the South African case, the government never publicly revealed the basis of their concerns about AZT. One of the sources inspiring Mbeki was a paper written by three well-known Australian AIDS denialists which suggested that AZT cannot possibly work as it is not metabolized in such a way that would create the chemicals needed to successfully fight HIV (Papadopulos-Eleopulos et al. 1999). The paper contained no new research and the claims were based on a review of relatively dated literature. It appeared in a fringe journal and the editor later admitted having published it on the back of mixed reviews in the hope to create some impact in the wider community. The other main source for Mbeki's scepticism about the safety of AZT is a booklet entitled *Debating AZT* (Brink 2001) which has been written by Anthony Brink, a South African lawyer and "AIDS activist." It is a partial review of mainstream scientific literature although Brink manages to convey a picture of AZT as dangerous and toxic drug by quoting the reviewed literature in a highly selective and decontextualized way (Weinel 2011). In contrast, the scientific mainstream can point to numerous clinical trials and to the fact that not a single drug regulating agency anywhere in the world has raised safety concerns about AZT when used for PMTCT. Moreover, AZT has been successfully used to reduce the risk of MTCT around the world since the mid-1990s.

In sum, the visible disagreement in South Africa about the safety of AZT appears to fail the test set by the criterion that claims must be supported by constitutive work. Applying the criterion suggests that the disagreement is a manufactured scientific controversy as there was no evidence to suggests that it was too toxic to be considered safe.

4.6 Fourth Criterion: Ongoing Argument

A fourth proposed criterion suggests that publicly visible disagreements must reflect an ongoing disagreement within the relevant expert communities to count as genuine scientific controversies. This is necessary because one common tactic of those on the losing side of a scientific argument is to shift their attempts of persuasion from those within their expert communities to outside audiences. For example, the debate whether HIV causes AIDS was, for all practical purposes, resolved in the mid-1980s. While the claims of the AIDS sceptics have not been taken seriously within the scientific community since then, these sceptics have from time to time managed to create episodes of visible disagreement on the issue by persuading journalists or, as in the case of Mbeki, politicians to promulgate their views in public.[14] Given that a scientific consensus is something that usually develops over time also suggests that consensus might be preceded by times of heightened uncertainty and controversy. The difficulty for outsiders is to judge whether controversial technical claims indicate an ongoing scientific disagreement or whether these claims are considered to be past their sell-by date within the scientific community.[15]

While assessing whether a particular argument is ongoing or not is difficult, there is evidence that it can be done in practice. Shwed and Bearman (2010), for example, did this by analysing complete sets of published scientific literature on supposedly controversial issues. Their externalist and quantitative analysis revealed patterns in the published scientific discourse that can be taken to indicate periods of consensus and controversy. For example, their analysis of the scientific discourse around the aetiology of AIDS confirmed that disagreement about the causes of AIDS had largely disappeared from the written scientific discourse by the late 1980s. Collins (2004), in contrast, used quasi-ethnographic qualitative techniques of deep social immersion into an expert community to, among other things, inform judgements on the existence of explicit arguments around a range of issues. For example, Collins (2004) described how Joe Weber, one of the pioneers of gravitational wave detection, time and again tried to convince his colleagues during conferences that his sensitivity calculations for bar detectors were correct, although no one in the community believed Weber. While Weber's claims were repeatedly heard during those conferences, Collins' deep understanding of the expert community allowed him to conclude that this visible disagreement should not be interpreted as an explicit argument among scientists about some fact or issue.

As the discussion of the previous criterion has already indicated, there simply was no real argument—ongoing or past its sell-by date—about the safety of AZT. Since the original findings in 1994 that short courses of AZT can significantly reduce the risk of MTCT, no subsequent research has indicated that these findings were flawed even though new and better drug-based preventative approaches have been developed (e.g. Nattrass 2008).

4.7   CONCLUSION

The main aim of this chapter has been to start thinking about ways that STS can contribute to policy-making. One way to do this is to find criteria that might help science policy-makers to demarcate between genuine and counterfeit scientific controversies when they are confronted with expert disagreement. The South African AZT controversy is, admittedly, an "extreme" case which has been analysed retrospectively. There is, however, nothing in the nature of the criteria that would prevent them from being applied to ongoing controversies and, all being well, future work will turn to the examination of contemporary cases.

I have gone on to show that it is possible to draw on sociological expertise on scientific controversies to find criteria to guide the analyst in the demarcation process. Four criteria for distinguishing between genuine and counterfeit scientific controversies have been proposed and tested: conceptual continuity, expertise, constitutive work, and ongoing argument. These have been tested using a historic case study from South Africa where the safety of AZT when used for PMTCT was the subject of a visible disagreement. The government claimed that AZT could not be made available in the public health sector because of an ongoing scientific controversy about the safety of the drug.

The criteria-led analysis shows that the South African case fails the test of being a genuine scientific controversy. While the claims that a drug, however effective, might be too toxic to be regarded as beneficial are not unscientific per se, the counterfeit character of the controversy is revealed by showing that the main protagonists did not possess the relevant expertise to make any technical claims about the safety or toxicity of AZT. Moreover, the critics of AZT also failed to present any convincing evidence to back up the claims that AZT is too toxic when used for PMTCT. As the unsupported claims about AZT were made by non-experts, it also meant that there simply was no ongoing scientific argument about this issue in the relevant expert communities.

The possible contribution to policy-making that follows from the four sociological criteria is to reduce the effect of counterfeit scientific controversies on science policy-making. By delaying policy decisions on the provision of AZT to reduce the risk of MTCT with reference to the alleged ongoing scientific controversy about AZT's safety for more than three years, it is very likely that tens of thousands of babies have been unnecessarily infected with HIV.[16] Without any chance of getting long-term treatment to slow down the progression to AIDS, survival rates for infected children in South Africa (and elsewhere) are virtually zero after only a few years.

While the intervention in the science policy process proposed in this chapter can be described as an exercise in "policing," such policing is restricted to technical aspects of controversies. Collins and Evans (2002, 2007) introduced a distinction between what they call a "political" and a "technical phase" (Evans and Plows 2007, 833–835). In these terms, the proposed criteria would only impact on the technical phase which deals with narrowly framed propositional questions—for example: Does AZT meet certain safety benchmarks and is it therefore safe to be used for particular purposes in a public health sector? The political phase deals with the much wider question of preferences, for example: Do we want to spend taxpayer money on drug-based HIV/AIDS prevention programmes or do we want to spend it on something else? All that is argued here is that it should not be possible for politicians like Thabo Mbeki or capitalist enterprises like the tobacco industry or oil companies or anyone else for that matter to use counterfeit scientific controversies to influence policy-making.

The example of the AZT controversy illustrates the point about the relationship between the technical and political phases with clarity. It shows that it is possible to criticize Thabo Mbeki's decision not to provide AZT on the ground that he misread the technical literature on AZT's toxicity and apparently based his decision against AZT on this misreading. But with the analytic tools proposed in this chapter it would not be possible to criticize Mbeki if, for example, he had said that he did not like the idea of being dependent on foreign pharmaceutical companies or that he preferred to spend taxpayer money elsewhere. These imagined decisions would be open to political debate—which is (hopefully) open, inclusive, and fair. But the critical point is that if the illegitimate framing of the debate as scientific controversy is not challenged, then the political process is disempowered as political decisions are taken by default as a result of the apparently unfolding scientific investigation. It is only by recognizing the controversy as a fake controversy—something STS with its expertise in the social analysis of science is uniquely well-placed to do—that the proper political process can be allowed to take place.[17]

NOTES

1. The term "science policy" (or "science in policy") is adopted from Harvey Brooks (1964, 76) and refers to "matters that are basically political or administrative but are significantly dependent upon technical factors—such as the nuclear test ban, disarmament policy, or the use of science in international relations."
2. Similar criteria-based approaches to make potentially policy-relevant distinctions between legitimate and illegitimate contributions have been advanced by Collins and Weinel (2011) and, more recently, by Collins et al. (2017). The former paper proposes a range of criteria to help non-experts to distinguish between genuine and fake experts, while the latter proposes criteria to distinguish between mainstream and fringe approaches to physics.
3. This chapter is based on my long-term research on issues around HIV/AIDS in South Africa and fieldwork done in the country in 2008. For ethical reasons, some interviewees have to remain anonymous.

4. No attempt was made to explain why Thabo Mbeki questioned the safety of AZT. I consider this question beyond the reach of sociological investigation as a considerable "forensic effort" would be needed to find out what was going on in Thabo Mbeki's head. Some researchers have, however, tried to tackle the question. For me, the best explanation to date was provided by James Myburgh (2007, 2009), whose forensic investigation of the so-called Virodene affair showed that while the government was publicly doubting the safety of AZT as well as the causal relationship between HIV and AIDS, it spent millions of Rand until 2002 trying to prove that Virodene was working and was not just an industrial solvent as the Medicines Control Council suggested after an initial investigation in 1998. If Myburgh is correct, it can be argued that Mbeki and his helpers in government manufactured a scientific controversy to gain time allowing them to develop an African alternative to Western AIDS drugs. Other explanations are summarized in the works of Nattrass (2007), Coovadia and Coovadia (2008) and Whiteside (2008).

5. The problem for science policy-makers to choose between conflicting expert opinions is specific instance of the problem that Goldman (2001, 90) calls "novice/2-expert problem." In his interesting discussion of this problem, Goldman (p. 93) suggests five sources of evidence that might help novices or lay persons to find out which of the disagreeing expert opinions to believe: (1) arguments presented by the contending experts to support their own views and critique their rivals' views; (2) agreement from additional putative experts on one side or other of the subject in question; (3) appraisals by 'meta-experts' of the experts' expertise; (4) evidence of the experts' interests and biases *vis-à-vis* the question at issue; and (5) evidence of the experts' past "track-record." Goldman's assessment of the usefulness of these sources to lay persons is not gloomy but also not overly optimistic. Part of the problem is that Goldman seems to be too ambitious. In contrast, I limit the task for lay persons to assess whether a scientific controversy they are presented with is "genuine" or "counterfeit." I do not claim that the criteria I'm going to propose can possibly tell a lay person which side of an argument to believe when they are confronted with a "genuine scientific controversy."

6. I'm grateful to Rob Evans for making this point.

7. Fleck's early ideas about styles of thoughts were later popularized by Kuhn (1962) under the heading "paradigm shifts." I prefer to refer to Fleck rather than to Kuhn, since Fleck's ideas preceded those of Kuhn by about 30 years.

8. Collins and Evans (2007, 128) put this in the following rule, which they call the "family resemblance rule": "Except where specific new findings demand a break, the intentional stance of a science must be to maintain continuity as far as possible with the existing science."

9. Lack of conceptual continuity may have to do with content—let us imagine it has to do with magic—or method—let us say the claim is based on the discovery of some ancient manuscript or on divination—or both.

10. Accordingly, reading scientific literature in isolation—acquiring primary source knowledge without any further social immersion into the relevant epistemic community—does not afford the acquisition of tacit knowledge. For more extensive, empirically informed expositions of this argument, see Weinel (2007) and Priaulx and Weinel (2014).

11. The report, incidentally, was published in response to Mbeki's speech in October 1999. A South African scientist, who asked to remain anonymous, told me in 2008 that Mbeki consulted a small group of scientists from the Medical University of South Africa two or three months before making the speech, but the contact was brief and he only sustained contact with those scientists of the group who supported the claim that AZT was too toxic to be used. The low intensity and short duration of these contacts, however, would not have enabled Mbeki to develop an appropriate level of interactional expertise.

12. Weinel (2011) and others (Geffen 2010; Myburgh 2009; Nattrass 2007) show that Mbeki's initial exposure to AIDS denialist literature have come from people without deep expertise on the issue. One was a lawyer who persistently misrepresents established scientific literature through selective quoting. Another one was Ziggy Visser who, together with his wife, claimed to have discovered a cure for HIV/AIDS, a compound called Virodene, in 1997.

13. There are, of course, cultures in which the content of dreams is not regarded as "baseless," but is taken very seriously. While this might be so, it is clear that "dreaming" is not an acceptable base for causal claim in a scientific form-of-life as it clashes with the formative intentions of the scientific culture. Scientists in modern societies might get ideas from dreams, but they must not invoke dreams as a justification for certain belief.

14. Of course, one problem that lends complexity to this issue is that both "consensus" and "scientific community" are inextricably intertwined and co-produced. The scientific community forming around the issue of AIDS would look very different if the argument that AIDS is a disease caused by certain lifestyle choices had won the day in the mid-1980s.

15. The Studies of Expertise and Experience (SEE) approach suggests that the difficulty for outsiders wanting to make a judgement about whether the existence of certain claims really represents genuine disagreement within the expert community is that the "locus of legitimate interpretation" rests within an expert community (Collins and Evans 2007; Collins et al. 2016). The difficulty for outsiders to make such judgements arises out of the necessity to understand what is going on inside the expert community.

16. The rough calculation goes like this: the South African government estimated that in the late 1990s about 70,000 babies were infected through MTCT. It is assumed here that this number remains constant. At this point in time, no drug-based MTCT prevention programme was in place in the public sector. Such a programme, if the results of the drug trials are extrapolated, has the potential to reduce the transmission rate by about 50 per cent. Given all this, over the course of three years 105,000 babies could have been saved from getting infected with HIV, had there been a countrywide PMTCT programme in place from 1999 onwards. See also Chigwedere et al. (2008) and Nattrass (2008) for estimates concerning the overall implications of bad policy-making around HIV/AIDS that characterized South Africa between 1999 and 2005.

17. In principle, the four criteria aid a process in technical appraisals that Andy Stirling (2008) has called "closing down"—that is, they aim to limit debate. The four criteria exclude arguments from the technical phase that are considered to be inappropriate. However, whether subsequent deliberations in a technical phase are done in "opening-up" or "closing-down" mode is left open in the normative SEE approach, which is more concerned with actors and not so much with procedures.

REFERENCES

Brink, Anthony. 2001. *Debating AZT: Mbeki and the AIDS Drug Controversy.* Pietermaritzburg: Open Books. http://www.tig.org.za/pdf-files/debating_azt.pdf.

Brooks, Harvey. 1964. The Scientific Adviser. In *Scientists and National Policy-Making*, ed. Robert Gilpin and Christopher Wright, 72–96. New York: Columbia University Press.

Ceccarelli, Leah. 2011. Manufactured Scientific Controversy: Science, Rhetoric, and Public Debate. *Rhetoric & Public Affairs* 14 (2): 195–228.

Chigwedere, Pride, George R. Seage, Sofia Gruskin, Tun-Hou Lee, and M. Essex. 2008. Estimating the Lost Benefits of Antiretroviral Drug Use in South Africa. *JAIDS Journal of Acquired Immune Deficiency Syndromes* 49 (4): 410–415.

Collingridge, David, and Colin Reeve. 1986. *Science Speaks to Power.* New York: St Martin's Press.

Collins, Harry, ed. 1981. Knowledge and Controversy: Studies of Modern Natural Science. *Social Studies of Science* 11 (Special Issue): 3–158.

———. 2004. *Gravity's Shadow: The Search for Gravitational Waves.* Chicago and London: Chicago University Press.

Collins, Harry, and Robert Evans. 2002. The Third Wave of Science Studies: Studies of Expertise and Experience. *Social Studies of Science* 32 (2): 235–296.

———. 2007. *Rethinking Expertise.* Chicago: University of Chicago Press.

Collins, Harry, and Trevor Pinch. 1979. The Construction of the Paranormal: Nothing Unscientific Is Happening. In *The Sociological Review Monograph No 27: On the Margins of Science: The Social Construction of Rejected Knowledge*, ed. Roy Wallis, 237–270. Keele: Keele University Press.

Collins, Harry, and Martin Weinel. 2011. Transmuted Expertise: How Technical Non-Experts Can Assess Experts and Expertise. *Argumentation* 25 (3): 401–413.

Collins, Harry, Robert Evans, Sergio Pineda, and Martin Weinel. 2016. Modelling Architecture in the World of Expertise. *Room One Thousand* 4: 24–34.

Collins, Harry, Andrew Bartlett, and Luis Reyes Galindo. 2017. Demarcating Fringe Science for Policy. *Perspectives on Science* 25 (4): 411–438.

Connor, Edward M., Rhoda S. Sperling, Richard Gelber, Pavel Kiselev, et al. 1994. Reduction of Maternal-Infant Transmission of Human Immunodeficiency Virus Type 1 with Zidovudine Treatment. *New England Journal of Medicine* 331 (18): 1173–1180.

Coovadia, Hoosen, and Imraan Coovadia. 2008. Science and Society: The HIV Epidemic and South African Political Responses. In *Hot Topics in Infection and Immunity in Children V (Advances in Experimental Medicine and Biology)*, ed. Adam Finn, Nigel Curtis, and Andrew J. Pollard, 16–28. New York: Springer.

Dabis, François, Philippe Msellati, Nicolas Meda, Christiane Welffens-Ekrad, et al. 1999. 6-Month Efficacy, Tolerance, and Acceptability of a Short Regimen of Oral Zidovudine to Reduce Vertical Transmission of HIV in Breastfed Children in Côte d'Ivoire and Burkina Faso: A Double-Blind Placebo-Controlled Multicentre Trial. *The Lancet* 353: 786–792.

Evans, Robert, and Alexandra Plows. 2007. Listening Without Prejudice? Re-discovering the Value of the Disinterested Citizen. *Social Studies of Science* 37 (6): 827–853.

Fleck, Ludwik. 1979. *Genesis and Development of a Scientific Fact*. Chicago, London: University of Chicago Press.

Geffen, Nathan. 2010. *Debunking Delusions: The Inside Story of the Treatment Action Campaign*. Johannesburg: Jacana.

Goldman, Alvin. 2001. Experts: Which Ones Should You Trust? *Philosophy and Phenomenological Research* 63 (1): 85–110.

Hardwig, John. 1985. Epistemic Dependence. *Journal of Philosophy* 82 (7): 335–349.

Jasanoff, Sheila. 1990. *The Fifth Branch: Science Advisers as Policymakers*. Cambridge: Harvard University Press.

———. 1991. Acceptable Evidence in a Pluralistic Society. In *Science and Values in Risk Management*, ed. Deborah Mayo and Rachelle Hollander, 29–47. New York, Oxford: Oxford University Press.

Kuhn, Thomas. 1962. *The Structure of Scientific Revolutions*. Chicago: University of Chicago Press.

Lindblom, Charles E., and Edward J. Woodhouse. 1993. *The Policy-Making Process*. Englewood Cliffs: Prentice Hall.

MacGregor, Karen. 2000. Conspiracy Theories Fuel Row Over AIDS Crisis in South Africa. *The Independent*, p. 12, September 20. http://www.independent.co.uk/news/world/africa/conspiracy-theories-fuel-row-over-aids-crisis-in-south-africa-699302.html.

Martin, Brian, and Gabriele Bammer. 1996. When Experts Disagree. In *Chronic Musculoskeletal Injuries in the Workplace*, ed. Don Ranney, 101–113. Philadelphia: W. B. Saunders.

Mbeki, Thabo. 1999. *Address of President Mbeki, at the National Council of Provinces*. Cape Town: Office of the President. https://www.mbeki.org/2016/06/09/address-to-the-national-council-of-provinces-cape-town-19991028/.

Michaels, David. 2008. *Doubt Is Their Product: How Industry's Assault on Science Threatens Your Health*. Oxford: Oxford University Press.

Myburgh, James. 2007. The Virodene Affair. *Politicsweb*, September 17. http://www.politicsweb.co.za/news-and-analysis/the-virodene-affair-i.

———. 2009. In the Beginning There Was Virodene. In *The Virus, Vitamins & Vegetables: The South African HIV/AIDS Mystery*, ed. Kerry Cullinan and Anso Thom, 1–15. Johannesburg: Jacana.

Nattrass, Nicoli. 2007. *Mortal Combat: AIDS Denialism and the Struggle for Antiretrovirals in South Africa*. Scottsville: University of KwaZulu Press.

———. 2008. AIDS and the Scientific Governance of Medicine in Post-apartheid South Africa. *African Affairs* 107 (427): 157–176.

Nelkin, Dorothy, ed. 1979. *Controversy: Politics of Technical Decisions*. Bloomington, IN: Sage.

Oreskes, Naomi. 2004. The Scientific Consensus on Climate Change. *Science* 306 (December): 1686.

Oreskes, Naomi, and Erik Conway. 2010. *Merchants of Doubt*. New York: Bloomsbury Press.

Papadopulos-Eleopulos, Eleni, Valendar F. Turner, John M. Papadimitriou, David Causer, Helman Alphonso, and Todd Miller. 1999. A Critical Analysis of the Pharmacology of AZT and Its Use in AIDS. *Current Medical Opinion* 15 (Supplement): S1–S45.

Priaulx, Nicky, and Martin Weinel. 2014. Behavior on a Beer Mat: Law, Interdisciplinarity & Expertise. *Journal of Law, Technology & Policy* 2: 361–391.

Rushefsky, Mark. 1982. Technical Disputes: Why Experts Disagree. *Policy Studies Review* 1 (4): 676–685.

Shaffer, Nathan, Rutt Chuachoowong, Philip A. Mock, Chaiporn Bhadrakom, et al. 1999. Short-Course Zidovudine for Perinatal HIV-1 Transmission in Bangkok, Thailand: A Randomised Controlled Trial. *The Lancet* 353: 773–780.

Shwed, Uri, and Peter Bearman. 2010. The Temporal Structure of Scientific Consensus Formation. *American Sociological Review* 75 (6): 817–840.

Stirling, Andy. 2008. 'Opening Up' and 'Closing Down': Power, Participation, and Pluralism in the Social Appraisal of Technology. *Science, Technology & Human Values* 33 (2): 262–294.

Weinel, Martin. 2007. Primary Source Knowledge and Technical Decision-Making: Mbeki and the AZT Debate. *Studies in History and Philosophy of Science* 38 (4): 748–760.

———. 2011. *Technological Decision-Making Under Scientific Uncertainty: Preventing Mother-to-Child Transmission of HIV in South Africa*. Cardiff: Cardiff University.

Whiteside, Alan. 2008. *HIV/AIDS: A Very Short Introduction*. Oxford, New York: Oxford University Press.

Wiktor, Stefan, Ehounou Ekpinia, John Karon, John Nkengasong, et al. 1999. Short-Course Oral Zidovudine for Prevention of Mother-to-Child Transmission of HIV-1 in Abidjan, Côte d'Ivoire: A Randomised Trial. *The Lancet* 353: 781–785.

CHAPTER 5

Judging Social Work Expertise in Care Proceedings

Ann Potter

5.1 INTRODUCTION

This chapter draws on a qualitative, socio-legal study which explored how the judiciary, lawyers and social workers evaluate social work evidence within care proceedings in England, across and between the disciplines of law and social work. First, the contemporary context for social work practice in care proceedings in England is explained, and approaches to studying social work expertise are outlined. The empirical study is then briefly described, followed by a discussion of findings relating to judicial evaluations of social work evidence within legal proceedings. Collins and Evans' (2007) theory of expertises was applied in the study to analyse the presentation of social work evidence, and the evaluation of professional social work expertise by judges in care proceedings, with a focus on interactional and meta-expertises. This new application of the theoretical framework within an empirical, socio-legal study enables a focus on interdisciplinary communication and evaluation within legal proceedings, understanding expertise as more than expertise in "doing" social work or law.

A. Potter (✉)
Manchester Metropolitan University, Manchester, UK
e-mail: A.Potter@mmu.ac.uk

D. S. Caudill et al. (eds.), *The Third Wave in Science and Technology Studies*, https://doi.org/10.1007/978-3-030-14335-0_5

5.2   Context: Care Proceedings, Family Justice Reforms and the Re-positioning of Social Workers as "Experts"

Care proceedings in England are the legal means by which state-employed social workers may apply to the Family Court to remove a child from its family, where parents have caused or may cause significant harm to the child (Children Act 1989 s.31). Care proceedings are civil cases heard by (1) lay magistrates (supported by a legal adviser), or by (2) legally qualified judges (hereafter referred to collectively as "judges"), depending on the complexity of the case. The social worker, via their employing local authority, is the applicant in the proceedings who presents evidence to the Family Court as a professional witness, to support the application. The parents and the child are respondents within this adversarial legal process, and the child is represented by an independent social work professional (the Children's Guardian). The role of the Children's Guardian is to represent the child in court; to make their own enquiries and advise the court on the appropriateness of the local authority's application; to appoint and instruct a lawyer for the child; and to advise if additional evidence is required. All parties are represented by publicly funded lawyers for the duration of the proceedings. During the proceedings, written evidence is provided by all parties and contested evidence may be challenged in oral cross-examination, with factual judgments decided on the balance of probabilities. Prospective judgments at the end of the proceedings, about the most appropriate future plan for the child, are based on the primary principle in the Children Act 1989 that the child's welfare is the court's paramount consideration (Children Act 1989 s.1).

If a decision is made to issue care proceedings, local authority social work evidence is generally comprised of the social worker's written assessments of the children's needs, the capacity of the parents to meet those needs, and consideration of environmental factors that may support or hinder the parenting capacity (Department for Education 2014, 2018). Judges in care proceedings consider evidence from all the parties, including the professional opinion evidence provided by the local authority social worker and the Children's Guardian (on behalf of the child), to decide on the appropriate outcome for the child. Thus all care proceedings have at least two professional witnesses, both of whom are permitted to provide opinion evidence, based on their professional work with the family. Whilst the Children's Guardian plays an important role in care proceedings in representing the child and advising the court, local author-ity social workers' evidence in care proceedings is an under-researched aspect of professional practice and is a focus within family justice system reform, as discussed below. Accordingly, evaluation of the evidence of local authority social workers in care proceedings, and particularly their expertise, was chosen as the focus for this study.

In some care proceeding cases, in addition to the professional witnesses already outlined, the court may appoint one or more independent "expert" witnesses, as defined in court rules (Family Procedure Rules 2010 SI2010/2955, Part 25). For example, a paediatrician, radiographer or neurologist may be required to advise on the potential cause of injuries in a case of suspected physical abuse; a DNA testing company scientist may report on biological relatedness; a psychiatrist may advise on treatment options and prognosis for a parent whose mental disorder is negatively affecting their parenting capacity. Independent expert witnesses are appointed when the court requires specialised areas of knowledge and rec-ognised levels of expertise in relation to particular features of a case. Clearly, the local authority social worker (or the Children's Guardian) is not qualified to provide these types of medical or scientific evidence.

The relative status of professional and expert witnesses in care proceed-ings was addressed in the most recent government-commissioned reform of the family justice system in England. The Family Justice Review (Ministry of Justice 2011b) highlighted a major problem with care pro-ceedings taking too long, causing delayed decision-making for children (and families), with increasing cost to the public purse. In particular, the review identified and confirmed a generalised lack of trust in the quality of local authority social work practice and evidence in care proceedings. This led to an over-reliance on court-appointed, independent expert witnesses, particularly clinical psychologists and independent social workers, which was identified as a significant, contributory factor to unnecessary delay. This view was supported by research which found that additional, inde-pendent expert witnesses were used often in care proceedings to provide a "second opinion" on the prospective, welfare decision-making at the end of proceedings, as a consequence of a lack of confidence in the evidence and professional expertise of local authority social workers (Brophy 2006; Masson et al. 2008). This was in addition, and opposed to, the appropriate need for medical or "scientific" experts in some cases, as explained above. The increasing use of independent social workers and psychologists reflected a perceived hierarchy of professional knowledge and expertise within the Family Court. Evidence from independent social workers and professionals such as clinical psychologists was deemed "more" expert, and therefore preferable to relying solely on evidence from local authority social workers (Ministry of Justice 2011a).

To reduce delay and curb costs, the Family Justice Review (Ministry of Justice 2011b) recommended a mandatory reduction in the use of independent experts in care proceedings. This review recommendation resulted in legislative change, and the Children and Families Act 2014 (s. 13(6)) now formally restricts the use of independent expert witnesses in care proceedings to situations where it is "necessary." In 2013, anticipating this legislative change, the President of the Family Division of the High Court of England and Wales, Sir James Munby, made widely publicised comments about social workers and the lack of trust in them as professional witnesses. With fewer independent expert witnesses, he argued that judges would have to rely more on social work evidence as the main source of professional information, analysis and (hopefully) expertise in relation to outcomes for children. This would require legal professionals to reconsider their approach to evaluating local authority social work evidence within care proceedings. Accordingly, the President of the Family Division outlined his expectation that, as there would be fewer independent experts, the judiciary and lawyers must now perceive and treat social workers in care proceedings as "experts" in their own right (Munby 2013).

These legal and policy changes aimed to influence professional legal practice and attempted to re-position local authority social workers as "experts" within care proceedings, by promoting increased recognition of expertise within this professional group. However, the prevailing social, political and media perceptions of local authority social workers was (and remains) negative, particularly in relation to a well-documented "blame culture" surrounding child protection services, with social workers often seen as failing in their responsibilities to protect children from abuse (Dickens et al. 2017; Care Crisis Review 2018). The potential contradiction between a policy-driven attempt to re-position social workers as experts and a social context of negativity and blame towards social workers provided an appropriate rationale to explore understandings of local authority social work expertise, using legal evaluations of local authority social work evidence within care proceedings as a basis for empirical enquiry.

5.3   Understanding Social Work Expertise

Social work is a relatively new profession and is based on values such as empowerment and social justice—see, for example, the global definition of the social work profession (IFSW 2014). The concept of professional expertise is challenging for some in social work, suggesting associations with and claims to privileged knowledge domains and elite social groups, which may be considered to be potentially "at odds" with the aims of the profession (Parton 2014). However, in the context of a "blame culture" towards child protection services, and a perceived "expertise gap" amongst social workers (Dickens et al. 2017), there is an obvious attraction to the identification and development of features of professional expertise within social work, to improve practice and re-claim professional reputation.

In the literature relating to studies of expertise, theories of the structure, acquisition and performance of expertise have tended to dominate (Dreyfus and Dreyfus 1986; Chi 2006; Ericsson 2006). Studies of social work expertise have usually focussed on the development of expertise, with the mastery and application of a body of knowledge as a key feature, acquired over time and often within professional education and training (Fook et al. 1997, 2000; Drury-Hudson 1999; Taylor and White 2006). In child protection research, studies from across the international social work field have explored social workers' expertise when using different types of knowledge and decision-making tools in practice-based decision-making (Gillingham 2011). Other studies have compared novices and experienced social workers (Davidson-Arad and Benbenishty 2014; Fleming et al. 2014). As in other research relating to professional practice, social work studies often focus on recognisable features of expert performance during practice with children and families, seeking to understand how social workers might become "more expert," through a developmental approach to domain-specific education and training. So far, much less attention has been paid to how social work expertise is understood and evaluated in inter-disciplinary settings, for example, when social workers act as professional witnesses in legal proceedings. Social work expertise in this scenario is about the effective communication of social work knowledge and practice, within a legal (rather than a social work) process. Those making judgments about the social worker's expertise are professionals from a different background (law), seeking to understand a different knowledge base to their own and evaluate evidence (information about practice and professional opinion) from another discipline. As such, questions are raised about how expertise may be communicated, understood and evaluated across disciplinary boundaries. This shifts the focus away from domain-specific considerations of the structure or acquisition of social work expertise in practice with children and families, to the types of expertise involved in inter-disciplinary communication by a social work witness, and evaluation of this by the judge, within a legal process.

Domain-specific, developmental theories of expertise are useful to consider how someone progresses from novice to expert within their own discipline, over time (Dreyfus and Dreyfus 1986; Fook et al. 2000). However such theories do not address the dynamic, social processes involved in communicating knowledge and evaluating expertise across disciplinary boundaries. In contrast, Collins and Evans' (2007) theory identifies a range of different expertises, including contributory expertise (expertise in doing) and interactional expertise (expertise in communicating effectively with non-experts, derived from the expert's reflective and interactional abilities). In social work, expertise "in the field," the practice of social work with families and children—can be categorised as contributory expertise. Following Collins and Evans, this is different to the interactional expertise required to produce excellent written social work evidence for a legal process, or to be evaluated by legal decision-makers as an impressive and authoritative professional witness in a courtroom.

In relation to legal judgments about social work expertise, Collins and Evans also identify types of meta-expertises (expertise in evaluating others) including technical connoisseurship. Technical connoisseurship is described as "the ability to judge an expertise without being able to practice it" (Collins and Evans 2007, 59). It is also related to interactional expertise and is achieved by socialisation not in the practice itself, but in its language and discourses. In other words, judges need to be sufficiently socialised in the language and practices of social work, in order for them to be able to make meaningful evaluations of the expertise (or otherwise) of the social worker as a professional witness. In this study, Collins and Evans' theory was useful in enabling consideration of the different types of expertises involved in inter-disciplinary communication and evaluation of social work expertise in care proceedings.

5.4   THE SOCIO-LEGAL STUDY

This qualitative, socio-legal study explored the views and experiences of local authority social workers, lawyers and the judiciary in relation to the expertise of social workers in care proceedings. This was an in-depth, ethnographic study of how local authority has written and oral evidence was presented and evaluated in a sample of contested care proceedings cases ($n = 4$), within one geographical area in England. Methods included judicial focus groups; observations of court-based professional discussions; observations of the oral evidence of the social work witnesses in the contested hearings; semi-structured interviews with the social work and legal professionals in each case; and analysis of the written social work evidence in each case.

Care proceedings in England are heard in private, with access usually restricted to the parties in the case. The nature of the information presented in evidence by the parties is sensitive. The subsequent legal decisions made may have life-long consequences for the parents and the children involved, and families are often distressed by and within the proceedings. Ethical approval for the research was granted by the University of Bristol Law School Research Ethics Committee. Permissions to conduct the various elements of the study were granted by the Ministry of Justice, the President of the Family Division of the High Court of England and Wales, Her Majesty's Courts and Tribunals Service, Cafcass (the body that employs Children's Guardians) and the local authorities whose cases were included in the study. The focus of the study was professional practice and professionals' experiences of the legal process; however, it was important to be mindful of and acknowledge the importance of the proceedings for each family in the sample cases. No data were collected from or about any family members or children. However, when cases were identified for the study, family members were approached via their lawyer to provide information about the study and to request their agreement to the researcher observations. If any family members objected then the observations did not proceed and the case was not included in the study.

Ethnographic data collection from the sample of cases involved triangulation of a range of qualitative methods, including participant and researcher perspectives (Moran-Ellis et al. 2006). Data were gathered from social work and legal professionals about what they understood social work expertise to be, and their experiences of being a professional witness or evaluating professional witnesses in care proceedings. Analysis of the data (Boyatzis 1998) led to the construction of themes relating to the preparation, content, presentation and evaluation of social work evidence, across and between the professions of social work and law. Part of the analysis involved the application of Collins and Evans' theory of expertises, in particular consideration of the social workers' interactional expertise in presenting their evidence and the judges' meta-expertise (technical connoisseurship) in evaluating the social workers' evidence within the care proceedings, discussed below.

5.5   Discussion

All of the social workers in the study expressed a view that they found being a professional witness in care proceedings intimidating and "nerve-wracking." This was largely due to their desire to perform well, and achieve a favourable evaluation by the judge in relation to their proposed plan to safeguard the children in the cases. The social workers were concerned to ensure that their written evidence addressed the legal requirements of the care proceedings process, in terms of using the correct evidence format, and demonstrating a balancing exercise in their analysis that complied with judicial directions in case law (*Re B-S (Children) [2013] EWCA Civ 1146*). The social workers also considered that, to be evaluated as demonstrating expertise, they should include references to social work theory and research in their written evidence, in addition to an account of their work with the family members and the child. In relation to communicating effectively with the legal decision-maker, the social workers explained that they would need to shape their evidence to the expectations of the court, which required knowledge of the legal process and the practices and etiquette of contested hearings, particularly when giving oral evidence and being cross-examined.

The social workers varied in their level of experience as a professional witness in care proceedings; however, they all described this deliberate approach to the preparation and presentation of their evidence, within which they were mindful of the need to "have the court in mind" when providing their professional opinion. This highlighted a conscious awareness amongst the social workers of the inter-disciplinary nature of the communication of their evidence in legal proceedings. They were aware of potential barriers to understanding across the disciplines of social work and law, and they recognised that the onus was on them, the social workers, to shape the way they communicated their evidence, to meet the requirements of the legal evaluators. Thus, to demonstrate expertise as a professional witness within care proceedings, the social workers needed to be able to operate and communicate expertly with legal professionals, within a legal process. The social workers recognised this and in the study they highlighted the importance of becoming socialised in the language and practices of the legal system and care proceedings processes, in order to maximise their potential to achieve a favourable legal evaluation of their evidence.

These findings in relation to the social workers in the study align with Collins and Evans' theory of expertises, and in particular their identification of Interactional Expertise. Interactional Expertise is explained as the ability of a contributory expert from one domain (discipline) to communicate their expertise effectively to someone from another domain. To achieve Interactional Expertise, the dispositions of reflective ability and interactional ability must be engaged and combined. In this study, reflective ability can be seen in the social workers' deliberate and conscious attempts to reflect on what the decision-maker wants and needs to achieve the legal decision that the social worker is aiming for. Interactional ability is seen in the social workers' purposeful shaping of social work information and professional opinion into a legally acceptable format, including acceding to requirements in case law about setting out the analysis underpinning their social work recommendation in a particular (legally determined) way. According to Collins and Evans it is the combination and application of these reflective and interactional abilities that enables Interactional Expertise to be realised.

I turn now to legal judgments about social work expertise, as explored in the study. In order to be able to evaluate the evidence of a professional witness from a discipline other than law, it follows that a judge must understand enough about the language and practices of the other discipline to enable them to assess the quality of the practice and the professional opinion presented in the evidence. Collins and Evans explain this as "technical connoisseurship." As explained above, all care proceedings involve social workers as professional witnesses and, as such, Family Court judges are likely to acquire technical connoisseurship through hearing cases, in addition to mandatory judicial training that they must undertake, prior to being allocated care proceedings cases.

The judicial focus groups provided some general insights into the experiences and the expectations of the legal decision-makers when evaluating social work evidence in care proceedings. In order to be evaluated favourably, the judges expected the social workers to adhere to the legal requirements for the format of their evidence, and to show that the analysis underpinning their recommendation was compliant with case law. The judges did not place significant emphasis on other potential indicators of expertise such as the length of social workers' practice experience, or the need for social workers always to include theory and research in their evidence (this was in contrast to the expectations of the social workers). Rather, the judges expressed a strong view that social work evidence that demonstrated compassionate, relationship-based practice with children and families (Turney 2012) would be more likely to indicate reliability, credibility and expertise in the social work witness. In summary, the judges identified that, for them, social work expertise would be evidenced by appropriately structured written evidence, with a clearly reasoned recommendation, which demonstrated fair and value-based work with children and families.

The observations of the contested hearings in the sample cases provided an additional opportunity to analyse how the judges evaluated the social workers' evidence and their expertise as professional witnesses during their oral evidence in the sample cases. In adversarial legal systems, the lawyers for the parties in a case usually conduct the questioning of witnesses. However, in contested care proceedings hearings in England, it is also common practice for a judge to ask their own questions directly of a witness, during the oral evidence. In this study, different types of judicial question posed to the social workers in the cases were observed and categorised as clarification questions, elaboration questions and discursive questions. Instances of discursive questions in particular provided examples of observed inter-disciplinary communication and evaluation. This was judicial evaluation "in action," where the social work witness and the legal decision-maker engaged in an exchange of several questions and responses about a particular aspect of the social worker's oral evidence.

Observations of these discursive exchanges between the judge and the social work witness indicated that the judges were applying their own knowledge and experience of social work practice, including social work theory and research evidence, in formulating their questions to the social work witness. In one example, the judge and the social worker "discussed" the social work research evidence for decision-making as to the placement of siblings together or apart. In formulating the discursive questions, the judge demonstrated familiarity with the relevant social work knowledge base for this issue. During the exchange, the judge appeared to respond favourably to the social worker's (knowledgeable) answers to the questions and it became apparent that the judge was eliciting the "expert" opinion of the social work witness on this aspect of the case. This demonstrated technical connoisseurship in the judge. The judge was seeking to evaluate the social worker's expertise about the issue, but in order to do so they needed to know (enough) about social work's language and practices (at least in relation to this particular issue) to initiate and continue the discursive exchange as observed. Interactional expertise was demonstrated by the social work witness, who responded knowledgably and authoritatively to the judge's questions, in effect engaging in a type of professional discussion with the judge. This example highlights a dynamic relationship between the expert (social worker) and the evaluator (judge). The social worker engaged their interactional expertise to communicate their social work knowledge to a legal audience, within a legal process. The judge used technical connoisseurship (about social work), both to initiate the discursive question and answer exchange, and then to evaluate the responses of the social work witness during their evidence.

5.6   Conclusion

This chapter has outlined some examples of the application of Collins and Evans' theory of expertises within an empirical, qualitative socio-legal study of social work expertise in care proceedings. Although developed primarily within the field of Science and Technology Studies, Collins and Evans' theory has potential applications in other inter-disciplinary processes, in particular those involving the communication, presentation and evaluation of professional knowledge across disciplinary boundaries.

The application of the theory within this study enabled a useful differentiation between expertise in child protection social work with children and families, and expertise as a professional social work witness in care proceedings. A social worker may be engaged in excellent, expert social work with children and families "in the field" (contributory expertise within the social work process). However, in order to be judged as an expert professional witness within care proceedings, a social worker must prepare and present their evidence in a form and manner that enables a favourable legal evaluation (interactional expertise within the legal process).

Collins and Evans' theory also enabled identification of a specific judicial meta-expertise, namely technical connoisseurship. This is based on socialisation in the language and practices of another domain or discipline, and was observed in this study in the judicial evaluations of social work witnesses during their oral evidence. Technical connoisseurship underpins expertise in evaluation and the formulation of informed judgments about a familiar domain. It involves "acquaintanceship" with the domain, rather than immersion within it. The example from this study demonstrated how technical connoisseurship was used by a judge to evaluate a specific, knowledge-based aspect of a social work witness' evidence.

The legal and policy context outlined earlier involves the re-positioning of social workers as expert professional witnesses in care proceedings. This requires the judiciary to accept and rely on social work evidence as their main source of expert professional opinion for legal decision-making. Prevailing negative views about social work practice present a challenge to this process. The application of Collins and Evans' theoretical framework offers a deeper understanding of the range of expertises involved in promoting effective inter-disciplinary communication and evaluation in legal proceedings. This understanding has the potential to assist social workers to develop and improve their practice and communication as professional witnesses. It encourages them to focus on socialisation in the language and practices of the court, thus enhancing their interactional expertise. For judges, the importance of technical connoisseurship in effective evaluations of social work witnesses underlines the need for judges to be or become sufficiently acquainted with the knowledge base of the social work witness.

From both perspectives (social worker and judge), it is clear that expertise needs to be understood as more than "doing" social work or law. Rather, and as explained by Collins and Evans, expertise is a social process, involving socialisation within the particular field of knowledge and practice, thereby enabling effective and meaningful communication and evaluation across domains and disciplinary boundaries. This understanding should inform the types of professional development processes that will promote interactional expertise in social work witnesses, and support judges to develop and maintain technical connoisseurship to make informed evaluations of social work evidence within legal proceedings.

Applying Collins and Evans' theory of expertises, it is clear that efforts to improve practice and confidence amongst social work witnesses and judicial evaluators should prioritise effective socialisation across and between the disciplines of social work and law.

REFERENCES

Boyatzis, R.E. 1998. *Transforming Qualitative Information: Thematic Analysis and Code Development*. London: Sage.

Brophy, J. 2006. *Research Review: Child Care Proceedings Under the Children Act 1989*, Department for Constitutional Affairs, DCA Researching Series 5/06. Oxford: Oxford Centre for Family Law and Policy, University of Oxford.

Care Crisis Review: Options for Change. 2018. London: Family Rights Group. https://www.frg.org.uk/images/Care_Crisis/CCR-FINAL.pdf.

Chi, M.T.H. 2006. Two Approaches to the Study of Experts' Characteristics. In *The Cambridge Handbook of Expertise and Expert Performance*, ed. K.A. Ericsson, N. Charness, P.J. Feltovich, and R.R. Hoffman. Cambridge: Cambridge University Press.

Collins, H., and R. Evans. 2007. *Rethinking Expertise*. London: The University of Chicago Press.

Davidson-Arad, B., and R. Benbenbishty. 2014. Child Welfare Attitudes, Risk Assessments and Intervention Recommendations: The Role of Professional Expertise. *British Journal of Social Work* Advanced Access Published October 27: 1–18.

Department for Education. 2014. *Court Orders and Pre-Proceedings for Local Authorities*. https://assets.publishing.service.gov.uk/government/uploads/system/uploads/attachment_data/file/306282/Statutory_guidance_on_court_orders_and_pre-proceedings.pdf.

———. 2018. *Working Together to Safeguard Children: A Guide to Inter-agency Working to Safeguard and Promote the Welfare of Children*. https://assets.publishing.service.gov.uk/government/uploads/system/uploads/attachment_data/file/779401/Working_Together_to_Safeguard-Children.pdf.

Dickens, J., J. Berrick, T. Pösö, and M. Skivenes. 2017. Social Workers and Independent Experts in Child Protection Decision Making: Messages from an Intercountry Comparative Study. *British Journal of Social Work* 47: 1024–1042.

Dreyfus, H.L., and S.E. Dreyfus. 1986. *Mind Over Machine: The Power of Human Intuition and Expertise in the Era of the Computer*. New York: Free Press.

Drury-Hudson, J. 1999. Decision Making in Child Protection: The Use of Theoretical, Empirical and Procedural Knowledge by Novices and Experts and Implications for Fieldwork Placement. *British Journal of Social Work* 29: 147–169.

Ericsson, K.A. 2006. An Introduction to 'Cambridge Handbook of Expertise and Expert Performance': Its Development, Organisation and Content. In *The Cambridge Handbook of Expertise and Expert Performance*, ed. K.A. Ericsson, N. Charness, P.J. Feltovich, and R.R. Hoffman. Cambridge: Cambridge University Press.

Fleming, P., L. Biggart, and C. Beckett. 2014. Effects of Professional Experience on Child Maltreatment Risk Assessments: A Comparison of Students and Qualified Social Workers. *British Journal of Social Work*, Advance Access Published August 27: 1–19.

Fook, J., M. Ryan, and L. Hawkins. 1997. Towards a Theory of Social Work Expertise. *British Journal of Social Work* 27: 399–417.

———. 2000. *Professional Expertise: Practice, Theory and Education for Working in Uncertainty*. London: Whiting and Birch Ltd.

Gillingham, P. 2011. Decision-Making Tools and the Development of Expertise in Child Protection Practitioners: Are We 'Just Breeding Workers Who Are Good at Ticking Boxes'? *Child and Family Social Work* 16: 412–421.

IFSW. 2014. *International Federation of Social Workers – Global Definition of the Social Work Profession*. http://ifsw.org/get-involved/global-definition-of-social-work/.

Masson, J, J. Pearce, and K. Bader, with O. Joyner, J. Marsden, and D. Westlake. 2008. *Care Profiling Study*. Ministry of Justice Research Series, March. www.justice.gov.uk/publications/docs/care-profiling-study.pdf.

Ministry of Justice. 2011a. *Family Justice Review Interim Report*. London: Ministry of Justice/Department for Education.

———. 2011b. *Family Justice Review Final Report*. London: Ministry of Justice/Department for Education.

Moran-Ellis, J., V.D. Alexander, A. Cronin, M. Dickinson, J. Fielding, J. Sleney, and H. Thomas. 2006. Triangulation and Integration: Processes, Claims and Implications. *Qualitative Research* 6 (1): 45–59.

Munby, J. 2013. View from the President's Chambers: The Process of Reform. *Family Law*, May: 548–552.

Parton, N. 2014. *The Politics of Child Protection*. Hampshire: Palgrave Macmillan.

Taylor, C., and S. White. 2006. Knowledge and Reasoning in Social Work: Educating for Humane Judgement. *British Journal of Social Work* 36: 937–954.

Turney, D. 2012. A Relationship-Based Approach to Engaging Involuntary Clients: The Contribution of Recognition Theory. *Child and Family Social Work* 17: 149–159.

LIST OF STATUTES

Children Act 1989 c.41. http://www.legislation.gov.uk/ukpga/1989/41/contents.

Children and Families Act 2014 c.6. http://www.legislation.gov.uk/ukpga/2014/6/contents/enacted.

STATUTORY INSTRUMENTS

Family Procedure Rules 2010 SI2010/2955. https://www.legislation.gov.uk/uksi/2010/2955/contents/made.

LIST OF CASES

Re B-S (Children) [2013] EWCA Civ 1146. https://www.judiciary.uk/wp-content/uploads/JCO/Documents/Judgments/b-s-children.pdf.

CHAPTER 6

Geographical Expertise: From Places to Processes and Back Again

Colin Robertson and Rob Feick

6.1 Introduction

The shift in knowledge production, from experts to the crowd, resulting from information and communication technologies (ICTs) has radically transformed where and how people procure and interpret information. New tensions in knowledge creation and communication are evident, in domains such as health care and climate science, and point to some citizens' diminishing trust in traditional holders of knowledge—a development that many see as one of the principal problems of our time (Hmielowski et al. 2014; Wachinger et al. 2013; Editorial 2017).

This democratization of information, data, and knowledge production has had significant impacts on culture and society in the digital era. For example, citizen science projects allow people without professional

C. Robertson (✉)
Department of Geography and Environmental Studies, Wilfrid Laurier University, Waterloo, ON, Canada
e-mail: crobertson@wlu.ca

R. Feick
School of Planning, University of Waterloo, Waterloo, ON, Canada
e-mail: robert.feick@uwaterloo.ca

© The Author(s) 2019
D. S. Caudill et al. (eds.), *The Third Wave in Science and Technology Studies*, https://doi.org/10.1007/978-3-030-14335-0_6

qualifications to be actively involved in scientific research through data collection and, to varying degrees, analysis, and research design. While citizen science is not new, improved access to internet connectivity, inexpensive data collection instruments, and personal computing now permit collaborative projects to be scaled to much larger participant groups and geographies than was previously possible (Haklay 2013; Buytaert et al. 2014). How community-based and citizen-generated science fits into standard scientific practice and its linkages with governance, planning, and decision-making is still evolving (Cohn 2008).

The relationships between citizens and experts have evolved in response to non-experts' enhanced capacity to engage in information production and sharing through ICT. Such tech-enabled engagements have led to broader changes in societal attitudes towards authority and to the growth of personalized information feeds (e.g., social media) that selectively filter and reinforce self-held perspectives (Pariser 2011). Within academia, traditional understandings of expertise have been critiqued through social constructivism, which highlights how scientists and the knowledge they produce are affected by the social contexts they are embedded within. These critiques describe how the processes of negotiation and compromise engaged in by scientists are rooted in society, economics, politics, and culture. Those processes continually steer and manipulate the evolution of science and technology, and in this light, science can be situated within the same power and political struggles as other facets of society. The knowledge that scientists (i.e., experts) provide may never be totally neutral and detached from these contexts (Kukla 2013).

The 'Third Wave of Science Studies' outlined in Collins and Evans (2002) makes the critical point that while politics may influence science, it is not a *legitimate input* to scientific decision-making. Geography makes an interesting application for Third Wave notions of expertise in that the 'core-set'—those scientists at the heart of the discipline of variant fields of geography (GIScience, economic geography, transportation geography)—navigate subject matter most non-experts feel some mastery of. The naïve geography of the public (Egenhofer and Mark 1995) or even the 'accidental geography' of other scientists enabled with geographic information systems (GIS) and computation (O'Sullivan and Unwin 2014) is detached from the theory and knowledge of academic geographers. And yet perhaps, due to the 'exposure' of geography to the public, the certainty of geographic expertise is more diffuse than other disciplines. Rarely are geographers called upon to give their theories of place attachment or distance-decay effects as evidence in court, for example.

Geographic expertise can therefore provide a case study to link the user-generated prosumers of Web 2.0 (i.e., the crowd) with the more traditional categories of experts identified in the 'Studies of Experience and Expertise' (hereinafter 'SEE') project (Collins and Evans 2002). We will examine the impacts of these coupled social and technological transformations by examining how local geographic knowledge and academic geography have evolved over time. Geographic information is defined here broadly to encompass factual information about features of the earth's surface (e.g., cities and lakes), the patterns that emerge through the arrangements of these phenomena (e.g., habitat fragmentation), as well as more subjective information pertaining to individuals' place-based experiences and values (e.g., local hotspots). In turn, geographic knowledge relates to understanding of events, phenomena and processes that occur (or have occurred) in specific locales as well as the cognitive processes individuals use to detect spatial patterns and to interpret spatial relationships for tasks such as navigation (Downs and Stea 2011; Kitchin and Blades 2002).

SEE may provide a framework for defining the nature of geographic expertise and how it is acquired, recognized, and distributed. In previous work, we have theorized how these two types of geographic knowledge comprise two related but distinct dimensions of geographical expertise (Robertson and Feick 2017). Broadly speaking, we distinguish between knowledge of specific locations versus knowledge of more generic processes that produce particular features or characteristics of specific locations. The dimensions of expertise as articulated in SEE—the traditional acquisition through formal and informal training, the tacit knowledge gained through socialization within the community of experts, and the degree to which expertise is distributed in the population—provide a convenient lens through which to understand local (i.e., experience-based) geographic knowledge (Collins 2011). In this chapter, we consider how geographical expertise has evolved over time and how this framing of expertise can contribute to the integration of local perspectives in environmental policy development, research, and planning.

6.2   Context

In modern history, geographic data and knowledge production have been the domain of professionals with training in cartography, geography, or planning, with important thematic contributions also being made by experts in disciplines where spatial patterns and processes figure prominently (e.g., epidemiology, ecology). Geographical information can be produced through a variety of mechanisms including land surveying methods, personal descriptions of place-based experiences, and marking up of paper maps, as well as satellite imaging and new forms of location sensing technologies (e.g., GPS chips, mobile phone signals). The past decade has witnessed a remarkable expansion in who produces geographic information and how these data are shared (Sui et al. 2013). The proliferation of location-aware devices (e.g., smart phones, vehicles) and widespread internet access have led to new digital participatory and online mapping tools that have greatly expanded peoples' capacity to use and create spatial information about matters of concern to them (e.g., places of personal significance) (Goodchild 2007; Sui et al. 2013). This type of participatory geographic sensing, termed volunteered geographic information (VGI), varies from so-called passive sensing from automated geotagging of online media with GPS coordinates, to active engagement in geographical data collection, analysis, and interpretation—often without expert assistance or mediation. The variety in engagement modes mirrors traditional models of participatory processes (Arnstein 1969; Craig et al. 2002) with many VGI projects seeking to capture important insights that non-experts have concerning local events, history, ecology, and place-based social and/or public health issues. Participatory research practices have been increasing across both social and natural sciences as researchers and planners in the public sector take advantage of new technologies and communication norms to bridge real and perceived gaps with society at large (Kahila-Tani et al. 2016; Brown et al. 2014).

Mechanisms for incorporating local knowledge into planning/policy development and research remain in their infancy (Conklin et al. 2015). In the case of place-based information, the location and boundaries of places referenced by community members and official documents are often different. Hollenstein and Purves (2010) showed how different conceptualizations of the location of 'downtown' in cities across the United States vary as represented in user-generated data (Flickr photos) mapped to a variety of potential boundary configurations. Relatedly, interpretations and descriptions of locally observed species often differ between locally adapted common names and expert taxonomies (Barron et al. 2015). Such distinctions are problematic both from the perspective of building a shared understanding of the issue, but also from viewpoint of knowledge validation and authority, as subsuming local or traditional names under scientific conventions can have the effect of disempowering local perspectives (Barron et al. 2015).

Efforts to incorporate bottom-up or community-held knowledge into environmental planning and management processes have been occurring over the last two decades, often with mixed results (Seltzer and Mahmoudi 2013; Innes and Booher 2004; Agrawal and Gibson 1999). These efforts are hampered by well-known issues: lack of a shared ontology, qualitative versus quantitative approaches and data, systems versus local perspectives, and so on. Moreover, what makes many of the debates about the value of experts' and non-experts' evidence especially challenging is that place and location play key roles in many of these conflicts. Complex challenges such as climate change, for example, are manifested differently from place-to-place and at a range of scales. Effects are often common across specific types of places (e.g., coastal cities); however, these effects are also expressed in locally unique ways. These types of place-based issues can only be addressed adequately with the knowledge that accrues from experiences in a specific locale and/or within an identifiable type of place. To understand how geographic thinking about local expertise has evolved over time, we will review some of the dominant trends in the production of geographic knowledge over the last century.

6.3   Geographic Expertise: From Place to Processes

Our understanding of what constitutes geographic knowledge and expertise, and who holds them, has evolved considerably, albeit not in a linear manner and not without debate since the early twentieth century. At this time, geography as a discipline had a predominant focus on describing places and documenting their differences and similarities in text and map form—a chorographic tradition that can be traced to ancient Greek geographers such as Strabo and Ptolemy (Dilke 1987). A rich tradition generally described as regional geography was built up around Richard Hartshorne among other American geographers who sought to characterize the nature of geographical regions as emergent phenomena in order to understand how areas differ. In this context, geographers' expertise revolved around *synthesizing information about places* (e.g., climate, terrain, cultural practices) to describe how their properties combine to produce differences between places (Hartshorne 1939). This focus on synthesis did not preclude more general knowledge-building within relevant geographic subfields (e.g., geomorphology), but developing holistic characterizations of specific places remained the raison d'être of geography (Cresswell 2013).

Golledge (2002) describes this first half-century of geographic knowledge-building as declarative in nature, as it was aimed at collecting, integrating, and representing facts of the geographical world to improve understanding of localities. Dissatisfaction with this ideographic inventorying and documenting of place-specific character led to a mid-century pivot towards a quantitative or more 'science-based' geography that sought to develop generalizable statements that would be applicable in many locations. This shift to a more scientific geography had several key impacts on how geographic knowledge was constructed in academia. First, broad description was replaced by efforts to explain, often using unambiguous quantitative measurements and mathematical models (Kwan and Schwanen 2009). Second, substantial efforts were made to model processes of change and the dynamics of social, ecological, and physical systems in contrast to the largely static region-based predecessor. Third, new spatially explicit theories were developed to explain spatial patterns (location, dispersion, and configuration) of human and physical phenomena and the spatial processes through which they interact (Golledge 2003).

This quantitative turn splintered the discipline into sub-specialties focused on a range of topics including quantification and model building, social theory and critique, human-environment relations, resource management, and physical and biogeography. As these sub-specialties have evolved, the nature of geographical expertise became detached from physical places, and more focused on generalized form and process. Migration flows between cities, for example, were estimated in gravity models based on Newtonian principles where cities' ability to attract migrants is proportional to their mass (populations) and inversely proportional to the distances separating cities (Kwan and Schwanen 2009). A variety of generic urban models were developed in this period to capture the dynamics of specific sectors and activities (e.g., transportation systems, land use change and population growth) and growth and decline of entire metropolitan areas (Lowry 1964; Forrester 1970; Lee 1973). In SEE terms, geographic knowledge and expertise were highly esoteric as they were held and developed by scholars alone and centred on abstracting from geographic details to develop generalizable models to explain processes of change and spatial variation.

Theoretical models of processes that produce geographic patterns, such as models of rainfall, housing costs, or commuting patterns, tend to work better at larger scales than they do at more localized spatial scales. The typical explanation for this in both natural and social sciences has been lack of data: too little is known about exact local conditions that mediate and control the expression of patterns on the ground, while at larger scales these local features average out to a more predictable outcome. In statistical terms, local predictions are subject to greater variance than larger-scale aggregate predictions and/or understanding. Different disciplinary approaches take on levels of abstraction that align with their view of the world. Economic models typically operate over aggregated quantities, whereas psychological models operate at the individual level. For models of spatial processes, scales might range from the block or street level to the global level. The types and contributors of geographic expertise as inputs to these models vary and have evolved over time.

One of the most well-known quantitative models of geographical patterns is Walter Christaller's central place theory (CPT) which sought to explain the spatial arrangement of urban centres (i.e., central places) of varying size—first across southern Germany and then all of Europe (Berry and Garrison 1958). The model represents cities as functional nodes which service a local area and a surrounding hinterland. As cities grow larger, these service areas also expand, leading to increasing distance between large centres and a hierarchy of recursively smaller centres (e.g., many small villages, fewer regional centres, fewer still large urban centres). CPT is based on economic actors minimizing travel to obtain goods and services, while providing goods and services in direct proportion to demand within a highly idealized homogeneous environment subject to several strenuous simplifying assumptions. As urban geographers began to apply CPT to different regions, additions were made to account for transportation routes, agglomeration effects and spatial changes in cities over time (Beckmann and McPherson 1970; Parr 1973). From a theoretical perspective, this represents a less abstracted view of geographical processes forming spatial networks of cities, and a more bottom-up approach to pattern formation. At a technical level, this means modelling behaviour of individual actors in the system rather than aggregate outcomes of large classes of actors. In current thinking of the spatial organization of economic activities and distribution of settlements, CPT is largely ignored in favour of approaches that encompass both global processes and local context.

6.4   GEOGRAPHIC EXPERTISE: FROM GLOBAL PROCESSES TO PROCESSES IN CONTEXT

A shift in understanding, from identifying theories that explain broad-scale patterns to uncovering how place-based dynamics lead to local anomalies in broad spatial trends, became central to geographic research in the 1990s and 2000s. This new appreciation for understanding local processes in context is evident in both new analytical methods and in research design. For example, in response to criticism that GIS analytical approaches were overly top-down and did not represent community members' concerns, the subfield of public participation GIS (PPGIS) was born. PPGIS projects seek to empower residents by providing them with opportunities to define issues that matter to them, record map data that represent their local knowledge and places of importance, and utilize the same technological tools as government and business experts in land management decision-making. PPGIS projects aim to use GIS as boundary objects that enable the recognition that traditional experts (planners and councillors) do not have the same understanding of local lived conditions or citizens' perspectives as individuals with experience-based expertise (Harvey and Chrisman 1998).

The geographic move to local concerns can also be seen methodologically (Brunsdon et al. 1998; Fotheringham 1997). Developments of local spatial statistics (Getis and Ord 1992; Anselin 1995); spatially explicit forms of regression analysis (Brunsdon et al. 1998) and cluster/hotspot mapping techniques (Nelson and Boots 2008) exploded during this period. Many of these tools were primarily developed to explore local variations from more generic or systemic patterns and relationships. For example, medical geography studies began to focus on identifying and mapping localized areas of high disease risk rather than broad-scale systematic risk factors associated with disease prevalence. Inquiry could then focus on explaining these anomalies through detailed studies of local driving factors.

Local knowledge of various forms was often a component of these studies where areas had been selected a priori based on larger patterns. In the context of health, many studies were initiated by local residents concerned about environmental health issues. Cancer cluster investigations that occurred extensively in the United Kingdom and North America were the result of local residents who worried that an industrial development was leading to a 'cluster' or localized area of high risk in their communities, and who demanded government responses (Jacquez and Greiling 2003).

These concerns led to hundreds of studies by local health authorities investigating these concerns, typically with inconclusive results. New quantitative methods were developed to identify 'real' clusters from those that could be explained by chance (Besag and Newell 1991; Openshaw et al. 1987; Kulldorff and Nagarwalla 1995; Hjalmars et al. 1996). Due to the long latency period with cancers and other chronic health issues with suspected links to environmental exposures, controlling for confounding variables in these studies is extremely difficult.

In one suspected cluster around the Sellafield nuclear facility in Cumbria in northwest England, residents of a nearby village of Seascale raised concerns about childhood leukaemia and other rare cancers to a television producer making a documentary about occupational exposures (Cancer Research UK 2016). The television documentary raised the link between the nuclear site and childhood cancer deaths, leading to a study which confirmed a statistical exceedance in risk over a 10-year period of 1968–1978—six deaths compared to an expected number of 1.4 if local rates were consistent with the national average. Yet defining causal relations between long-term environmental exposures and health outcomes is extremely challenging, and cannot be drawn from statistical evidence of this sort alone. Complexities arise because of several technical factors: local exceedances are expected to occur sometimes even for random distributions, hypotheses are typically determined post-hoc, invalidating statistical inference procedures (i.e., the 'Texas sharpshooter effect'), and depending on how geographic, temporal, and diagnostic categories are specified, statistically significant effects can increase or disappear altogether. These expert-oriented explanations often fail to quell local concerns, which resulted in calls for an end to cluster investigations themselves, as they failed to provide any useful new information and caused significant problems for local health authorities (Rothman 1990). In most cases where high disease risk was found, occupational exposures could be identified as causal. In Sellafield, a case-control study later found that the anomalous risk could be explained by occupational exposures to radiation of fathers employed at the nuclear facility, rather than as a result of outdoor exposures in the environment as was most feared (Gardner et al. 1990). Further studies have found additional links between pre-conception exposure and still-birth risk (Parker et al. 1999).

Such cluster studies present an example of experts recognizing that locals have some understanding of problems that experts don't have. Experience-based expertise of residents identified a heightened risk relative to their experience of the area before there was nuclear facility. For public health authorities, this shows that locals may know something about health problems that deviate from a particular disease's 'average' incidence rate at the regional or state level. This locale-specific expertise is then used to inform a search for more generic understanding (i.e., place-type expertise) through local searches around all similar radiation-producing plants.

Geographic research into health and disease responded to these short-comings by becoming more 'place-based.' Kearns' (1993, 140) seminal paper noted that in medical geography, "little attention has been paid to the understanding of place as that experienced zone of meaning and familiarity," Kearns argues for "a convergence between consideration of the experience of place (a social geographical concern) and socioecological health perspectives and policies (a public health concern)," stressing the need for qualitative/interpretative approaches over statistical/analytical. From the perspective of geographic knowledge, we can see this shift as representing a need to incorporate local perspectives and values into studies of health and environment. In the ensuing 25 years, local inputs into health geographic studies have dramatically changed from subjects being measured to participants being engaged. The types of input in the new health geography are therefore about peoples' individual experiences: access to health services, healthy food, exercise, greenspace, and social opportunities; and an altogether more holistic approach to the concept of health and wellbeing (Kearns and Moon 2002; Kwan 2013). The scope for participation is also wider; including increasing examples of community and professional co-development of health research and policy (Coburn 2005).

The move towards more locally engaged and contextually situated geographies of health is representative of a wider shift to participatory approaches across geographic and environmental studies. In planning, for example, formal models of local engagement in planning processes have expanded greatly over the last two decades. Technological developments such as VGI and online mapping tools have enabled wider participation and easier implementation to harness local perspectives on environmental issues. Public participation in GIS (PPGIS) studies in the 2000s and later geoweb studies (2010s) illustrate how local geographic knowledge can be obtained on place-specific issues and fused with expert knowledge as part of official planning processes (Jankowski et al. 2017; Nyerges and Aguirre 2011).

6.5   LOCAL GEOGRAPHICAL EXPERTISE IN THE GLOBAL CONTEXT

The growing interdependence of societies through international trade, travel, and communications facilitated by ICTs since the 2000s has revealed and exacerbated global problems such as growing income inequality, environmental degradation, and climate change. Yet each of these global issues manifests differently in local communities and local adaptations and responses to global issues is a defining characteristic of much of today's environmental research. By definition, local expertise is bound by local geographies and can therefore be linked horizontally to identify regions of similar and dissimilar experience. The 'processes-in-context' approach to research, simultaneously addressing structures and processes at global scales while engaging with local experiences and perspectives, holds considerable potential in current empirical research in geography (Wilson and Graham 2013).

Climate change, for example, can be understood at a multitude of scales, from global and multi-decadal oscillations in sea surface temperature across the Atlantic Ocean, to timing of ice road closures and impacts on ice-fishing in northern Canada. Local geographic expertise, of regional and localized climate-dependent processes and impacts, is critical to developing policies and research to respond and adapt to a changing climate (Sheppard 2012). Riedlinger and Berkes (2001), for example, report how traditional knowledge can contribute to understanding climate change in the Canadian Arctic, noting that "ecological and environmental expertise found in Inuit communities can highlight parameters rarely measured by scientists and help make sense of scientific findings by placing them in a local context." They also describe how local expertise of Inuit peoples can help to understand regional variability associated with climate change in a historical context, to better discern baselines from which to interpret changes in sea ice, wildlife, permafrost, and weather. This sort of local expertise, termed *locale familiarity* in Robertson and Feick (2017), is distinct from what we call place-type expertise, which might provide predictions of changes expected in locales with specific shared characteristics such as greater permafrost thaw in all Arctic settlements. Place-type expertise is more generic and applicable to a class of place and will lack local detail (e.g., whether a particular stream will be traversable in early June). Local-familiarity expertise will be rich in local detail and lack predictive power (e.g., whether total snowfall will be higher next year).

Locale familiarity as a knowledge base for understanding climate change need not only be based on hundreds of generations of experience. More 'shallow' forms of local knowledge are possible, such as simply asking people about the weather in their local environment at a given time and space. The Snowtweets Project for example, asks people to measure and post-snow measurements (King et al. 2009) from their homes; whereas the RinkWatch Project asks people to report online whether they can skate on outdoor ice rinks (Robertson et al. 2015). With the advent of social media and big data tools, such projects can potentially recruit participants at large scale, enabling the scaling up of locale familiarity to regional, national, and even international scales. These local experiences can then be placed within the global context, supporting richer understanding of how global processes are impacting communities. In the RinkWatch example, we were able to translate IPCC climate scenarios into 'number of skateable days' for specific cities where people had reported observations. Such place-based and two-way flows of knowledge between citizens and experts are increasingly an aspect of all parts of the research process where citizens and communities are involved in local issues, from project design to analysis and interpretation (Haklay 2013; Preece 2016).

6.6   Conclusion

The need to incorporate local expertise into place-based research in the context of complex global issues is evident from the discussion above. New modes of research design are being developed to fuse the technological capabilities of big data and ICT with the collection of local perspectives and knowledge. The language, theory, and conceptual models of SEE provide a set of tools to operationalize the integration of local expertise within applied environmental management. If the problem of extension in Collins and Evans (2002) can be paraphrased as "all voices should be heard on technical debates," in a geographic context that might be phrased as "all problems are local." We envisage that the third phase described here, processes in context, recognizes both the value of local expertise (i.e., locale familiarity) and the importance of a generic understanding (i.e., place-type). To that end, we see direct connections between SEE and incorporating local expertise into environmental research and planning.

The examples provided here show how the consideration of local geographic expertise in academic geography has changed over time. The integration of SEE into applied geography and planning must go beyond translation of concepts across knowledge communities to defining the nature of geographic expertise itself in specific cases. The frameworks and methods for how we measure, evaluate, and handle geographic expertise across dimensions of experience, credentials, tacit/sharedness, and esotericity still need to be defined.

The use of so-called boundary objects between communities as the basis for knowledge sharing has long been proposed as a means for dialogue and socialization between scientists and non-scientists (Star and Griesemer 1989). Boundary objects are "artefacts of practice that are agreed and shared between communities," which in the geographical context may include maps and spatial representations of geographic space. Harvey and Chrisman (1998) consider GIS technology as a case study in boundary objects, noting that:

> Any time in which negotiations lead to the stabilization of GIS technology, this involves boundary objects. As GIS technology carries the values from multiple social groups, there is hardly any part of a local GIS that is not in some sense a boundary object.

The details of these negotiations—the geographic content with which technology objects such as web-based mapping platforms, mobile apps, geosocial media, and so on interact—provide the basis for eliciting and understanding local geographical expertise. While boundary objects may facilitate translation of understandings and values of local geographies (e.g., what constitutes a wetland), by emphasizing shared or agreed-upon elements of knowledge, they tend to discount local or unique understandings, which often are of most interest when it comes to linking process-based or scientific models with place-based or context-specific geographic outcomes.

Participatory research methodologies that aim to foster "co-creation" rather than "translation" of knowledge have been bolstered by recent technological developments. Citizen science in this context can be designed in conjunction with local community interests, engaging citizens as collaborators in project scope, design, implementation, and analysis and synthesis. The 'Extreme Citizen Science' model of Haklay (2013) has been successful in engaging marginalized groups in mapping and monitoring place-based issues such as illegal logging in Africa and sea-ice melt in the Arctic (Stevens et al. 2014). For these projects, the aim is to collaborate with local residents to elicit local geographic knowledge through the use of mobile applications, and empower participants in the control and management of local land and resources. In this way, 'expert' geographic knowledge (e.g., climate forecasts, forest administration boundaries) can be directly integrated with local understandings through place-based mapping.

REFERENCES

Agrawal, A., and C.C. Gibson. 1999. Enchantment and Disenchantment: The Role of Community in Natural Resource Conservation. *World Development* 27 (4): 629–649. https://doi.org/10.1016/S0305-750X(98)00161-2.

Anselin, L. 1995. Local Indicators of Spatial Association—LISA. *Geographical Analysis* 27 (2): 93–115.

Arnstein, S.R. 1969. A Ladder of Citizen Participation. *Journal of the American Institute of Planners* 35 (4): 216–224.

Barron, E.S., C. Sthultz, D. Hurley, and A. Pringle. 2015. Names Matter: Interdisciplinary Research on Taxonomy and Nomenclature for Ecosystem Management. *Progress in Physical Geography: Earth and Environment* 39 (5): 640–660. https://doi.org/10.1177/0309133315589706.

Beckmann, M.J., and J.C. McPherson. 1970. City Size Distribution in a Central Place Hierarchy: An Alternative Approach. *Journal of Regional Science* 10 (1): 25–33.

Berry, B.J.L., and W.L. Garrison. 1958. A Note on Central Place Theory and the Range of a Good. *Economic Geography* 34 (4): 304–311. https://doi.org/10.2307/142348.

Besag, J., and J. Newell. 1991. The Detection of Clusters in Rare Diseases. *Journal of the Royal Statistical Society* 154: 143–155.

Brown, G., M. Kelly, and D. Whitall. 2014. Which 'Public?' Sampling Effects in Public Participation GIS (PPGIS) and Volunteered Geographic Information (VGI) Systems for Public Lands Management. *Journal of Environmental Planning and Management* 57 (2): 190–214.

Brunsdon, C., S. Fotheringham, and M. Charlton. 1998. Geographically Weighted Regression—Modelling Spatial Non-stationarity. *Journal of the Royal Statistical Society: Series D (The Statistician)* 47 (3): 431–443.

Buytaert, W., Z. Zulkafli, S. Grainger, L. Acosta, T.C. Alemie, J. Bastiaensen, and M. Foggin. 2014. Citizen Science in Hydrology and Water Resources: Opportunities for Knowledge Generation, Ecosystem Service Management, and Sustainable Development. *Frontiers in Earth Science* 2: 26.

Cancer Research UK. 2016. Sellafield, Radiation and Childhood Cancer – Shedding Light on Cancer Clusters Near Nuclear Sites. Accessed June 14, 2018 http://scienceblog.cancerresearchuk.org/2016/10/31/sellafield-radiation-and-childhood-cancer-shedding-light-on-cancer-clusters-near-nuclear-sites/.

Coburn, J. 2005. *Street Science: Community Knowledge and Environmental Health Justice*. Cambridge, MA: The MIT Press.

Cohn, J.P. 2008. Citizen Science: Can Volunteers Do Real Research? *BioScience* 58 (3): 192–197. https://doi.org/10.1641/B580303.

Collins, H. 2011. Three Dimensions of Expertise. *Phenomenology and the Cognitive Sciences* 12 (2): 253–273. https://doi.org/10.1007/s11097-011-9203-5.

Collins, H.M., and R. Evans. 2002. The Third Wave of Science Studies: Studies of Expertise and Experience. *Social Studies of Science* 32 (2): 235–296.

Conklin, A., Z. Morris, and E. Nolte. 2015. What Is the Evidence Base for Public Involvement in Health-Care Policy?: Results of a Systematic Scoping Review. *Health Expectations* 18 (2): 153–165.

Craig, W.J., T.M. Harris, and D. Weiner. 2002. *Community Participation and Geographic Information Systems*. Boca Raton, FL: CRC Press.

Cresswell, T. 2013. Geographic Thought: A Critical Introduction. Chichester, West Sussex, UK: Wiley-Blackwell. Editorial: Trust We Must. *Nature Geoscience* 10 (6): 395.

Dilke, O.A. 1987. The Culmination of Greek Cartography in Ptolemy. *The History of Cartography* 1: 177–200.

Downs, R.M., and D. Stea. 2011. Cognitive Maps and Spatial Behaviour: Process and Products. In *The Map Reader: Theories of Mapping Practice and Cartographic Representation*, ed. M. Dodge, R. Kitchin, and C. Perkins, 312–317. Hoboken: John Wiley & Sons.

Editorial. 2017. Trust We Must. *Nature Geoscience* 10 (6): 395.

Egenhofer, M.J., and D.M. Mark. 1995. *Naive Geography. Spatial Information Theory: A Theoretical Basis for GIS*. Conference Proceedings, Published in the Lecture Notes in Computer Science Series, 1–15. Berlin: Springer. https://doi.org/10.1007/3-540-60392-1_1.

Forrester, J.W. 1970. Urban Dynamics. *IMR; Industrial Management Review (Pre-1986)* 11 (3): 67.

Fotheringham, A. 1997. Trends in Quantitative Methods I: Stressing the Local. *Progress in Human Geography* 21 (1): 88–96.

Gardner, M.J., M.P. Snee, A.J. Hall, C.A. Powell, S. Downes, and J.D. Terrell. 1990. Results of Case-Control Study of Leukaemia and Lymphoma Among Young People Near Sellafield Nuclear Plant in West Cumbria. *BMJ* 300 (6722): 423–429. https://doi.org/10.1136/bmj.300.6722.423.

Getis, A., and J.K. Ord. 1992. The Analysis of Spatial Association by Use of Distance Statistics. *Geographical Analysis* 24 (3): 189–206.

Golledge, R.G. 2002. The Nature of Geographic Knowledge. *Annals of the Association of American Geographers* 92 (1): 1–14.

———. 2003. Human Wayfinding and Cognitive Maps. In *The Colonization of Unfamiliar Landscapes*, 49–54. London: Routledge.

Goodchild, M.F. 2007. Citizens as Sensors: The World of Volunteered Geography. *GeoJournal* 69 (4): 211–221.

Haklay, M. 2013. Citizen Science and Volunteered Geographic Information: Overview and Typology of Participation. In *Crowdsourcing Geographic Knowledge*, ed. M. Sui, S. Elwood, and M. Goodchild, 105–122. Dordrecht: Springer.

Hartshorne, R. 1939. The Nature of Geography: A Critical Survey of Current Thought in the Light of the Past. *Annals of the Association of American Geographers* 29 (3): 173–412.

Harvey, F., and N. Chrisman. 1998. Boundary Objects and the Social Construction of GIS Technology. *Environment and Planning A: Economy and Space* 30 (9): 1683–1694. https://doi.org/10.1068/a301683.

Hjalmars, U., M. Killdorff, G. Gustafsson, and N. Nagarwalla. 1996. Childhood Leukaemia in Sweden: Using GIS and a Spatial Scan Statistic for Cluster Detection. *Statistics in Medicine* 15: 707–715.

Hmielowski, J.D., L. Feldman, T.A. Myers, A. Leiserowitz, and E. Maibach. 2014. An Attack on Science? Media Use, Trust in Scientists, and Perceptions of Global Warming. *Public Understanding of Science* 23 (7): 866–883.

Hollenstein, Livia, and Ross Purves. 2010. Exploring Place Through User-Generated Content: Using Flickr Tags to Describe City Cores. *Journal of Spatial Information Science* 1: 21–48.

Innes, J.E., and D. Booher. 2004. Reframing Public Participation: Strategies for the 21st Century. *Planning Theory & Practice* 5 (4): 419–436.

Jacquez, G.M., and D.A. Greiling. 2003. Geographic Boundaries in Breast, Lung and Colorectal Cancers in Relation to Exposure to Air Toxics in Long Island, New York. *International Journal of Health Geographics* 2 (1): 4.

Jankowski, P., M. Czepkiewicz, M. Młodkowski, Z. Zwoliński, and M. Wójcicki. 2017. Evaluating the Scalability of Public Participation in Urban Land Use Planning: A Comparison of Geoweb Methods with Face-to-Face Meetings. *Environment and Planning B: Urban Analytics and City Science*. https://doi.org/10.1177/2399808317719709.

Kahila-Tani, M., A. Broberg, M. Kyttä, and T. Tyger. 2016. Let the Citizens Map—Public Participation GIS as a Planning Support System in the Helsinki Master Plan Process. *Planning Practice & Research* 31 (2): 195–214.

Kearns, R.A. 1993. Place and Health: Towards a Reformed Medical Geography. *The Professional Geographer* 45 (2): 139–147. https://doi.org/10.1111/j.0033-0124.1993.00139.x.

Kearns, R., and G. Moon. 2002. From Medical to Health Geography: Novelty, Place and Theory After a Decade of Change. *Progress in Human Geography* 26 (5): 605–625. https://doi.org/10.1191/0309132502ph389oa.

King, J.M., A.R. Cabrera, and R.E. Kelly. 2009. The Snowtweets Project: Communicating Snow Depth Measurements from Specialists and Non-Specialists via Mobile Communication Technologies and Social Networks. *AGU Fall Meeting Abstracts* 11, ED11A-0562.

Kitchin, R., and M. Blades. 2002. *The Cognition of Geographic Space*. Vol. 4. London: I.B. Tauris.

Kukla, A. 2013. *Social Constructivism and the Philosophy of Science*. New York: Routledge.

Kulldorff, M., and N. Nagarwalla. 1995. Spatial Disease Clusters: Detection and Inference. *Statistics in Medicine* 14: 799–810.

Kwan, M.-P. 2013. Beyond Space (As We Knew It): Toward Temporally Integrated Geographies of Segregation, Health, and Accessibility. *Annals of the Association of American Geographers* 103 (5): 1078–1086. https://doi.org/10.1080/000 45608.2013.792177.

Kwan, M.-P., and T. Schwanen. 2009. Quantitative Revolution 2: The Critical (Re)Turn. *The Professional Geographer* 61 (3): 283–291.

Lee, D.B., Jr. 1973. Requiem for Large-Scale Models. *Journal of the American Institute of Planners* 39 (3): 163–178.

Lowry, I.S. 1964. *A Model of Metropolis* (No. RM-40535-RC). RAND Corporation, Santa Barbara, CA.

Nelson, T.A., and B. Boots. 2008. Detecting Spatial Hot Spots in Landscape Ecology. *Ecography* 31 (5): 556–566. https://doi.org/10.1111/j.906-7590.2008.05548.x.

Nyerges, T., and R. Aguirre. 2011. Public Participation in Analytic-Deliberative Decision Making: Evaluating a Large-Group Online Field Experiment. *Annals of the Association of American Geographers* 101 (3): 561–586.

O'Sullivan, D., and D. Unwin. 2014. *Geographic Information Analysis*. Hoboken, NJ: John Wiley & Sons.

Openshaw, S., M. Charlton, C. Wymer, and A. Craft. 1987. A Mark 1 Geographical Analysis Machine for the Automated Analysis of Point Data Sets. *International Journal of Geographical Information Systems* 1 (4): 335–358.

Pariser, E. 2011. *The Filter Bubble: What the Internet Is Hiding from You*. London: Penguin.

Parker, L., M.S. Pearce, H.O. Dickinson, M. Aitkin, and A.W. Craft. 1999. Stillbirths Among Offspring of Male Radiation Workers at Sellafield Nuclear Reprocessing Plant. *The Lancet* 354: 1407–1414. https://doi.org/10.1016/S0140-6736(99)04138-0.

Parr, J.B. 1973. Growth Poles, Regional Development, and Central Place Theory. *Papers of the Regional Science Association* 31 (1): 173–212. Berlin: Springer-Verlag.

Preece, J. 2016. Citizen Science: New Research Challenges for Human–Computer Interaction. *International Journal of Human-Computer Interaction* 32 (8): 585–612.

Riedlinger, E.D., and F. Berkes. 2001. Contributions of Traditional Knowledge to Understanding Climate Change in the Canadian Arctic. *Polar Record* 37 (203): 315–328. https://doi.org/10.1017/S0032247400017058.

Robertson, C., and R. Feick. 2017. Defining Local Experts: Geographical Expertise as a Basis for Geographic Information Quality. *Proceedings of the 13th International Conference on Spatial Information Theory* (COSIT 2017) 22: 1–14.

Robertson, C., R. McLeman, and H. Lawrence. 2015. Winters Too Warm to Skate? Citizen-Science Reported Variability in Availability of Outdoor Skating in Canada. *The Canadian Geographer/Le Géographe Canadien* 59 (4): 383–390. https://doi.org/10.1111/cag.12225.

Rothman, K. 1990. A Sobering Start for the Cluster Busters' Conference. *American Journal of Epidemiology* 132 (supp 1): 6.

Seltzer, E., and D. Mahmoudi. 2013. Citizen Participation, Open Innovation, and Crowdsourcing: Challenges and Opportunities for Planning. *Journal of Planning Literature* 28 (1): 3–18.

Sheppard, S.R. 2012. *Visualizing Climate Change: A Guide to Visual Communication of Climate Change and Developing Local Solutions.* New York: Routledge.

Star, S.L., and J.R. Griesemer. 1989. Institutional Ecology, 'Translations' and Boundary Objects: Amateurs and Professionals in Berkeley's Museum of Vertebrate Zoology, 1907–39. *Social Studies of Science* 19 (3): 387–420. https://doi.org/10.1177/030631289019003001.

Stevens, M., M. Vitos, J. Altenbuchner, G. Conquest, J. Lewis, and M. Haklay. 2014. Taking Participatory Citizen Science to Extremes. *IEEE Pervasive Computing* 13 (2): 20–29. https://doi.org/10.1109/MPRV.2014.37.

Sui, D., S. Elwood, and M. Goodchild, eds. 2013. *Crowdsourcing Geographic Knowledge: Volunteered Geographic Information (VGI) in Theory and Practice.* New York: Springer Science & Business Media.

Wachinger, G., O. Renn, C. Begg, and C. Kuhlicke. 2013. The Risk Perception Paradox-Implications for Governance and Communication of Natural Hazards. *Risk Analysis* 33 (6): 1049–1065. https://doi.org/10.1111/j.1539-6924.2012.01942.x.

Wilson, M., and M. Graham. 2013. Neogeography and Volunteered Geographic Information: A Conversation with Michael Goodchild and Andrew Turner. *Environment and Planning A* 45 (1): 10–18.

Imitation Games

Martin Weinel

1.1 INTRODUCTION TO PART II

This part contains four chapters that all draw upon the Imitation Game method. The chapters taken together showcase the flexibility of the Imitation Game as a social scientific mixed method (Collins et al. 2017; see Chap. 7 of this volume). In two of the four chapters, the authors used (relatively) easy-to-run, small-scale Imitation Games, relying on small numbers of participants to generate some qualitative data. In one of those two chapters (Chap. 8), that qualitative data was then used to explore anew an established topic, namely whether broadcasters understand and should understand their audiences. Philippe Ross approaches this question by playing Imitation Games with the producers of a particular radio program broadcasted in Quebec, Canada, and members of the audience. The Imitation Games in the context of that chapter is exploratory, as one Ross's aims is to establish whether Imitation Games are a useful method to shed new light on the issue of audience research.

Small-scale Imitation Games can also be used to make initial forays into un- or under-explored research topics such as the identities of marginalized groups (see Chap. 10 of this volume, written by participants of a research seminar at the Humboldt University in Berlin). Guided by their course conveners, students were organized in small teams and asked to explore identities in Germany. The students chose their own topics and produced exploratory *and* interesting research reports on marginalized and under-researched groups. The chapter highlights three particular research projects, focused on black Germans, German Muslims, and

Berliners (people born or socialized in Berlin). The interesting twist in this particular application of the Imitation Game method is that the student-led research teams also included their own ethnographers, who were able to reflect critically on the overall research process. One section in Chap. 10 offers a critique of the Imitation Game method, informed by such reflexive ethnography. The chapter demonstrates that Imitation Games can be fruitfully combined with other research methods (Wehrens 2016; Collins et al. 2017).

In contrast, Chaps.7 (Collins et al.) and 9 (Kubiak) make use of the complex, large-scale version of the method, which requires both the use of elaborate and bespoke Imitation Game software and large samples. While more challenging to organize and run, this type of Imitation Game generates both meaningful qualitative and quantitative data. Both chapters study contrasting regional identities—Scottish-ness and English-ness in the case of Chap. 7, and East- and West-German-ness in the case of Chap. 9. While both chapters come to similar conclusions—dominant identities are treated as normal to the degree that they are not even recognized as identities—the role that Imitation Games play in the respective chapters is different. Chapter 7 is, in a sense, a proper methods chapter, as it not only uses the Imitation Game method to generate qualitative and quantitative data on Scottish and English identities, as constructed by Scottish and English students in Edinburgh and Southampton, but it also reflects on innovative features of the Imitation Game as used during this particular research project. It thus advances not only our understanding of English and Scottish identities, but also our knowledge of the Imitation Game method.

Chapter 9 by Daniel Kubiak, in contrast, uses the Imitation Game simply as a means to an end—to generate data that help to understand contemporary German debates about East Germans and East Germany. His research not only shows that West-German-ness is widely regarded as the norm, and therefore is essentially equated with German-ness, but also that East-German-ness continues to be linked to the former German Democratic Republic, even though many of those who are constructed as being East German have never lived in that particular state, as they were born after its demise in 1990.

One can also change perspective and look at the following four chapters in a different way, to explain why some authors chose to utilize the complex version of the Imitation Game and why others relied on the small-scale version. While the topics chosen for research have something to with the choice of Imitation Game version—it is hard to play large-scale Imitation Games on sensitive topics or topics that deal with very small populations—the explanation offered here turns on the respective authors' degrees of immersion into the Imitation Game research community. As pointed out in Chap. 1, the Imitation Game is a method that affords the systematic exploration of expertise, but the ability to successfully play Imitation Games as part of research projects is, of course, in itself an expertise. We can therefore reflexively apply one of the central ideas of the Studies of Expertise and Experience (SEE) research program—the idea that expertise, whether it is interactional or contributory, requires social-ization into a wider community that holds and maintains relevant bodies of tacit knowledge. Looked at it in this way, it becomes obvious why the two chapters use the complex version of the method, while the other two utilize the simpler small-scale version.

Chapter 7 by Collins et al. can thus be regarded as the contribution from the core set of Imitation Game researchers. The collective of authors shares several decades of experience in thinking about and playing Imitation Games. Closest to the core set is Daniel Kubiak, who acted as a "local organizer" in Berlin during the five-year period when Imitation Game research was funded by the European Research Council. In this role, Kubiak was not only responsible for the preparation and organization of Imitation Games that were played in Germany, but he also attended Imitation Game workshops and received face-to-face training in how to use the Imitation Game software and how to organize the games. It is therefore unsurprising that the chapters authored by the Cardiff collective and by Kubiak succeed in using the more complex version of the method.

In contrast, the authors of the other two chapters (Chaps. 8 and 10), which utilize a simple version of the Imitation Game, are more removed from the community of Imitation Game experts. Philippe Ross's interest in Imitation Games was developed while attending several of the annually held "Studies in Expertise and Experience" workshops (SEESHOPs). While he received face-to-face training in how to use the software and how to organize and conduct Imitation Games from one of the Cardiff-based Imitation Game researchers in Ottawa in May 2017, he was on his own when he conducted his research just a few weeks later. The students who authored Chap. 10 were even further removed from the core set. Until their projects were completed, none of them had any personal interactions with members of the core set. Instead, they received their training and instructions from Kubiak, who had been trained by core set members.

REFERENCES

Collins, Harry M., Robert Evans, Martin Weinel, Jennifer Lyttleton-Smith, Andrew Bartlett, and Martin Hall. 2017. The Imitation Game and the Nature of Mixed Methods. *Journal of Mixed Methods Research* 11 (4): 510–527.

Turing, Alan. 1950. Computing Machinery and Intelligence. *Mind* 59 (236): 433–460. https://doi.org/10.1093/mind/LIX.236.433.

Wehrens, Rik. 2016. De Imitation Game als blikopener: Praktijkervaringen met patiënten met eetstoornissen en hun behandelaren. *KWALON: Tijdschrift voor Kwalitatief Onderzoek in Nederland* 21 (2): 31–37.

CHAPTER 7

Bonfire Night and Burns Night: Using the Imitation Game to Research English and Scottish Identities

Harry Collins, Robert Evans, Martin Hall,
Hannah O'Mahoney, and Martin Weinel

Authors are listed alphabetically. The authors would like to thank Helia Marreiros and Michael Kattirtzi for their invaluable assistance in fieldwork and data collection. The contributions to research described in this chapter are as follows:
- Research design: Collins, Evans, Weinel
- Software: Hall
- Fieldwork and Data Collections: Weinel and Kattirtzi (Edinburgh), Evans and Marreiros (Southampton)
- Data Analysis: Evans, Weinel, O'Mahoney
- Writing up: Evans

The research was funded by a European Research Council Advanced Research Grant (269463 IMGAME) awarded to Collins.

H. Collins • R. Evans (✉) • H. O'Mahoney • M. Weinel
Cardiff University, Cardiff, UK
e-mail: CollinsHM@Cardiff.ac.uk; EvansRJ1@Cardiff.ac.uk;
OMahoneyH@Cardiff.ac.uk; WeinelM@Cardiff.ac.uk

M. Hall
University of Winchester, Winchester, UK
e-mail: martin.hall@winchester.ac.uk

© The Author(s) 2019
D. S. Caudill et al. (eds.), *The Third Wave in Science and Technology Studies*, https://doi.org/10.1007/978-3-030-14335-0_7

7.1   INTRODUCTION

This chapter is primarily about the Imitation Game as a research method, the kinds of data it is able to generate, and the ways in which these data can be analyzed. In describing the use of the method we do, of course, say something about the nature of being English or Scottish but the chapter should be read as an attempt to open up a domain of research by demonstrating its possibilities and not as a definitive account of national identities in the two nations. Our baseline finding is that English people are markedly less successful at pretending to be Scottish than vice versa. We argue that this indicates a stronger, more reflexive, sense of national identity on the part of Scottish people and suggest two possible reasons for this. First, Scottish people are more aware of their distinct identity within the UK than English people, who may find regional identities more salient and/or struggle to identify characteristics that unite the English while also differentiating them from (say) the British. Second, and closely linked to this, Englishness functions as a hegemonic or dominant identity within the UK as a whole, not just England, and this makes it much more visible to Scottish people than Scottishness is to the English.

The inspiration for the research was Kubiak and Weinel's use of the Imitation Game to explore the changing nature of East German identities after the fall of the Berlin Wall in 1989 (Kubiak and Weinel 2016), a phenomenon discussed in Chap. 9 of this volume. In the case of Scotland and England, the referendum that was held in September 2014 created the possibility of a similarly momentous change, though in this case the outcome would be the division of a nation rather than its reunification. Our idea was that, should the referendum lead to independence for Scotland, capturing the ideas of Englishness and Scottishness that were in circulation at the time would provide a useful benchmark against which later data could be compared. For example, would the identities diverge following independence and, if so, in what ways? In the end, the referendum was won by the pro-unionist campaign and Scotland remains part of the United Kingdom. Nevertheless, in conducting the research we were able to develop and test some important methodological innovations that will improve future Imitation Game research and also demonstrate the potential of the method to gather revealing and meaningful data that can support comparative and longitudinal research.

In what follows, we briefly summarize the political and cultural context leading up to the referendum on Scottish independence before turning to the details of the research we carried out. Here, we begin with a generic overview of the Imitation Game method, followed by a more detailed account of how we collected the data used in this chapter. Next, we report a variety of results, drawing on both qualitative and quantitative data. We conclude by identifying some of the limitations of our study and outline how the research could be developed in the future.

7.2   England and Scotland: A Very Brief History

The United Kingdom of Great Britain and Northern Ireland is four countries—England, Scotland, Wales, and Northern Ireland—and a single country that is known, variously, as the United Kingdom, the UK, or Great Britain. Of the four countries that make up the UK, England is by far the biggest in terms of population and is home to 84 percent (or approximately 55.6 million) of the total UK population of just over 66 million. By comparison, the populations of the remaining countries are 5.4 million for Scotland, 3.1 million for Wales, and 1.9 million for Northern Ireland, which means that the combined populations of Wales and Scotland are roughly the same size as the population of London (ONS 2018).

The links between the constituent parts of the UK are enshrined in a number of treaties through which formerly independent nations were joined with England. Wales became part of the Kingdom of England as a result of Acts of Union passed under the reign of King Henry VIII in 1536 and 1543. Scotland formally joined the Kingdom of England (and Wales) in 1707, with Treaties of Union passed in both the English and Scottish parliaments creating the new country of Great Britain. Ireland was incorporated into the new United Kingdom of Great Britain and Ireland in 1801 but, following sustained campaigns for independence, the Anglo-Irish agreement of 1921 partitioned the island of Ireland into an independent Republic of Ireland and the six counties of Northern Ireland. The latter chose to remain within what then became—and remains—the United Kingdom of Great Britain and Northern Ireland.

In terms of its political institutions, the UK is a constitutional monarchy, with Queen Elizabeth II the current head of state, and the national Parliament based in Westminster. Below this level, however, each nation has a different degree of devolved government. England has no national parliament of its own, and proposals for a regional assembly for the North East of England were rejected in a referendum held in 2004. In contrast, the other three nations all have some degree of devolved administration, though the powers available to each vary. In Scotland, the Scottish Parliament was established in 1999, following a referendum it held in 1997. Of the three devolved administrations, the Scottish Parliament has the most extensive powers and is, for example, the only one that has the power to vary tax rates.

It should also be noted that voting patterns in Scotland are often different from those of England. For example, in the UK general elections of 1997, 2001, 2005, 2010, and 2015, there was never more than one Conservative Member of Parliament (MP) elected in Scotland and, prior to this (1979, 1983, 1987, 1992), the Labour Party was dominant in Scotland even though the UK government was led by the Conservative Party. More recently, the rise of the Scottish National Party has radically reduced the number of Labour MPs elected in Scotland to just one in 2015 but, until 2017 when thirteen Conservative MPs were elected, there was no increase in the number of Conservative MPs. As a result of these differences there is a sense among some Scots that the UK parliament, which is dominated by MPs representing English constituencies, does not always give due care and attention to the particular needs and problems of the Scottish people.

Culturally, Scotland has a number of traditions—music, literature, sports, food, clothing—that are not found elsewhere in the UK. It is also worth noting that it has always retained distinct and different legal and education systems as well as its own bank notes. In sport, Scotland competes as an independent nation (as do Wales, England, and Northern Ireland) in a number of international competitions (e.g., football, rugby union, and cricket, though not the Olympic Games), with matches against England often being the highlight of these competitions for many spectators.

Given this, it is perhaps no surprise that the creation of the Scottish Parliament in 1999 was not enough for some Scots and that, having been granted some autonomy, a significant proportion continued to feel that something more radical was needed. It was the success of these calls for Scottish independence and the referendum—held on September 18, 2014—that prompted the research described in this chapter.

7.3   The Imitation Game

The Imitation Game is a formal version of the parlor game that inspired the Turing Test (Turing 1950) for artificial intelligence. When used for social research, it reveals the content and distribution of interactional expertise about the experiences of particular social groups and, by implication, the nature and depth of the interactions between communities (Collins et al. 2006; Collins and Evans 2014). In the research described here, we started with the assumption that the Scottish and English form two distinct social groups, with two distinct sets of experiences, and used the Imitation Game to (a) investigate the extent to which members of these groups can recognize each other as group members and (b) the ways in which they make these judgments.

There are a number of different ways to play Imitation Games[1] (Collins et al. 2017), but all build on the three-player game described by Turing. In this basic version of the Game, two players are drawn from the same social group—the target group—with one playing the role of Interrogator/Judge and the other playing the role of Non-Pretender.[2] The third player— the Pretender—is the person whose expertise is being tested and they are drawn from another social group. The challenge is for the Interrogator/Judge to ask questions of the other players and, based solely on the answers provided, work out which set of answers comes from the Non-Pretender, who has been instructed to answer "naturally," and which from the Pretender, who has been told to answer as if they were a member of the target group.

The set up for a basic three-player Imitation Game, which we now refer to as the "Classic" format to distinguish it from the more complex variant described later, is illustrated in Fig. 7.1. Each Imitation Game generates the following kinds of data:

Fig. 7.1   Schematic representation of the Imitation Game

- **Questions** that reveal which of their experiences the Interrogator/ Judge thinks are shared with the Non-Pretender but are unknown to the Pretender
- **Non-Pretender answers** that reveal the extent to which Interrogator/ Judge's expectations are met and, in so doing, give an indication of the range of experiences that characterize the target group
- **Pretender answers** that reveal what the Pretender knows about the target community
- **Decisions** by the Interrogator/Judge, including **reasons** and **confidence levels**, that record how successful they were in distinguishing between the two players.

The hypothesis is that, where the Pretender has extensive interaction with the target group, the Pretender will have developed sufficient interactional expertise (Collins and Evans 2002, 2007, 2016; Collins et al. 2006) to provide answers that are as authentic and plausible as those given by Non-Pretender. In these cases, the Interrogator/Judge will find it hard to work out which answers come from which player. In contrast, where there is little interaction between the groups, the Pretender will lack the knowledge needed to provide good answers and the Interrogator/Judge will find it easy to work out who is who.

In the case of the Scots and the English, the hypotheses can be stated more formally as follows:

- If Englishness is the dominant identity within the UK, then Scottish people should be good at pretending to be English. The reason is that Scottish people will have access to a lot of the interactional expertise associated with being English because, at least within the UK, this expertise will be almost ubiquitous. The parallel is with notions of double consciousness (du Bois 1903), hegemonic masculinity (Connell and Messerschmidt 2005), and heteronormativity (Butler 2006) all of which suggest that dominant cultures and values are accessible to, and understood by, all social groups, including those who do not necessarily identify with or live by those norms.
- In contrast, if Scottishness is not a widely available or discussed identity outside of Scotland, then the interactional expertise associated with being Scottish will not flow south across the border into England. As a result, English people should struggle to pretend successfully as there will be a range of specifically "Scottish" experiences about which they have little or no knowledge.

In making these assumptions we are extending the ideas of contributory and interactional expertises beyond the narrowly specialist domains of esoteric expertise in which they were first discussed (Collins and Evans 2002, 2007) to suggest that contributory, and hence interactional expertises, can be used to characterize large and otherwise diverse social groups (Collins 2011; Collins and Evans 2017). The research is, therefore, also a test of this extension of the theory.

7.4   FIELDWORK

For this project, we used a more complex version of the Imitation Game in which the key parts of the Classic three-player Game are separated into a four-step process that proceeds as follows (Collins et al. 2017):

- **Step 1**: A number of real-time, three-player Imitation Games are played simultaneously, with the questions and Non-Pretender answers being used in the subsequent steps.
- **Step 2**: Questions generated at Step 1 are turned into an online survey through which large numbers of Pretenders provide free-text responses.
- **Step 3**: This is a database operation in which new and unique transcripts are created by combining each set of Pretender answers collected at Step 2 with the corresponding set of questions and Non-Pretender answers from Step 1.
- **Step 4**: A new set of Judges (i.e., players who have not been involved at Step 1) read the transcripts created at Step 3 and attempt to identify the Pretender. Each Judge typically receives six to eight transcripts and, if enough Judges are recruited, it is possible to ensure that each transcript is judged twice. Judging at Step 4 is conducted as an online activity with participants being emailed a unique URL that gives them access to their set of transcripts.

Step 1 Games were played in Edinburgh and Southampton on November 19, 2014; ten in the morning and ten in the afternoon. Participants were students at each university, with each participant satisfying the criteria that he or she was born in England (Southampton) or Scotland (Edinburgh) and had not lived abroad for a significant period of time. The same criteria were also used in Steps 2 and 4. In total, 53 Step 1 participants were recruited in Southampton (27 for the morning session, 26 for the afternoon session) and 29 in Edinburgh (19 in the morning, 10 in the afternoon). As a result, all Southampton Step 1 Games were played as "group Games" (Collins et al. 2017; Evans et al. 2018), by which we mean that each role was taken by a small group of two or three students rather than a single person. In Edinburgh, nine out of the ten Step 1 Games played in the morning session were played with pairs of students, with the tenth Game and all afternoon Games being played by individual students. The total numbers of participants in all Steps of the research are summarized in Table 7.1.

Step 2 was carried out in both Edinburgh and Southampton in the week following Step 1. The target was to recruit 200 students in each location so that each set of questions from Step 1 would be answered by ten new Pretenders. In practice, we were not able to recruit all the necessary participants before the end of the first semester, and so Step 2 was completed in February 2015. In total, we recruited the following:

- 194 English students in Southampton who pretended to be Scottish by answering the questions set by Step 1 Interrogators/Judges in Edinburgh
- 205 Scottish students in Edinburgh who pretended to be English by answering the questions set by Step 1 Interrogators/Judges in Southampton

Each Pretender response was reviewed by a member of the research team in order to weed out responses where, for example, it was clear that the Pretender had either failed to understand the instructions or simply not tried (e.g., provided one-word answers to all questions). At Step 3, the accepted Pretender answers were combined with the original questions and Non-Pretender answers from Step 1, producing 150 transcripts in which English Step 2 participants pretended to be Scottish and 185 transcripts in which Scottish Step 2 participants pretended to be English.

In Step 4, which took place during April 2015, a further 40 participants were recruited at each location and asked to judge the transcripts pro-

Table 7.1 Summary of participants recruited

	Fieldwork date	English participants	Scottish participants
Step 1	Nov. 2014	53	29
Step 2	Nov. 2014, Feb. 2015	194 (total)150 (usable)	205 (total)185 (usable)
Step 4	April 2015	40	40

duced at Step 3. At Step 4 each Judge received between six and eight transcripts to consider and was able to read the entire transcript before being asked to make their decision about who was who. As with Step 1, Judges' decisions about which participant was the Non-Pretender (and hence which was the Pretender) were accompanied by a self-assessed confidence rating in the judgment, ranging from 1 (I have little or no idea) to 4 (I am pretty sure I know who is who) and free-text box in which the Judge was asked to explain the reason for their decision.

The Step 1 Imitation Games played for this project also saw the first use on a large scale of a new software feature: the randomized display of answers for each question. By this we mean that, when the Pretender and Non-Pretender answers are displayed to the Judge, the Pretender answer will sometimes appear on the right-hand side of the screen and sometimes on the left-hand side. An example of the screen seen by Judges, with placeholder data rather than real data, is shown in Fig. 7.2.

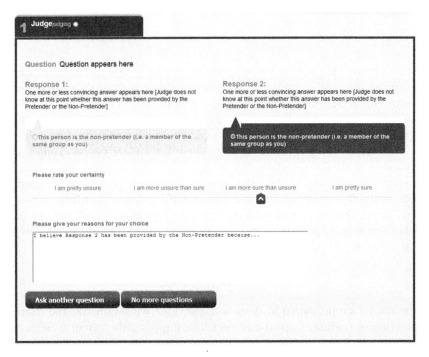

Fig. 7.2 Judge Screen, as seen after each question

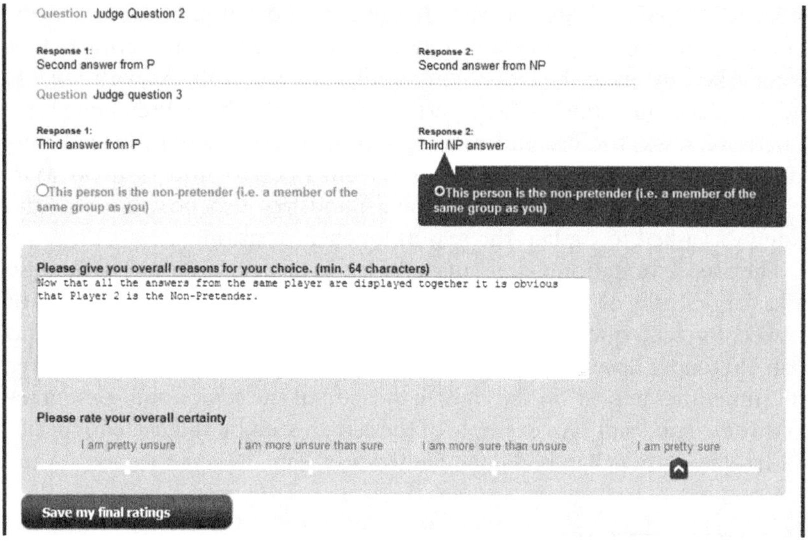

Fig. 7.3 Judge Screen, as seen after all questions have been asked/answered

This means that Judges have to consider each question and answer turn independently and cannot use judgments about a previous answer to inform their decision about the current question. We introduced this innovation because analysis of data from previous Imitation Games suggested that Judges rarely, if ever, changed their mind after the first question. Once the Step 1 Game is completed, each Interrogator/Judge is presented with the complete set of questions and answers from their Game, now arranged so that the answers from each player are grouped together, as shown in Fig. 7.3, and a final Step 1 judgment is made. In this way, we are able to analyze both turn-by-turn data from Step 1 and, using data from Step 4, holistic judgments based on the entire set of questions and answers.

7.5   PASS RATES

The results are presented in three sections. First we summarize the main quantitative findings from the project by comparing the extent to which English and Scottish players were successful in their different roles. Next we analyze the questions and answers in more detail and, finally, we explore some of the methodological insights gained from the project.

For Imitation Games, the basic summary statistic is the "pass rate." Presented as a percentage, this is based on Step 4 Judges' guesses about who is who and calculated using the formula:

$$\text{Pass Rate} = 1 - \left(\frac{\text{Right Guesses} - \text{Wrong Guesses}}{\text{Total Guesses including "Don't Know" responses}} \right)$$

In determining the number of right, wrong, and don't know responses, all answers with a confidence level of 1 or 2 are treated as "don't know" responses regardless of whether they are right or wrong. The rationale for this is that the label for confidence level 2 on the rating scale is "I am more unsure than sure." All answers with a confidence level of 3 or 4 are treated as definite identification attempts and are then counted as either right or wrong. If the Judges' guesses turn out to be split evenly between right and wrong, then the pass rate will be 100 percent. This seems intuitively plausible as such a "chance" outcome implies that the Judges are effectively guessing in the absence of any clear information. A further advantage of the pass rate formula given above is that it is not affected by the relative proportion of "don't know" responses. Even if some Judges are more risk averse than others, and so tend to favor a low confidence rating, thus creating a higher proportion of don't know responses, this will make no difference to the overall pass rate so long as equal numbers of potentially right and wrong guesses are diverted to the "don't know" category.

Finally, and as noted above, Step 4 can be used to ensure that two different Judges evaluate each transcript. The allocation system used gives each Judge between six and eight transcripts while also ensuring that each Judge gets a unique permutation of transcripts. In other words, although each transcript gets judged twice, no two Judges should ever have more than one transcript in common. For simplicity, and to distinguish between the two sets of judgments, we call one set of transcripts "Blue" and the other set "Orange."[3] Table 7.2 shows the aggregate totals for each set of judgments and the average of Blue and Orange sets for English Judges attempting to identify Scottish Pretenders and for Scottish Judges attempting to identify English Pretenders.

The pass rates for English and Scottish Pretenders, calculated using the formula given above and using the frequencies contained in the average column for each group, are as follows:

Table 7.2 Judges' verdicts

	English Judges, Scottish Pretenders			Scottish Judges, English Pretenders		
	Blue	*Orange*	*Average*	*Blue*	*Orange*	*Average*
Wrong	17	17	17	8	9	9
Don't know	64	68	66	16	17	17
Right	104	100	102	126	122	124
Total	185	185	185	150	148	149

- For Scottish Pretenders being judged by English Judges: 54.1 percent
- For English Pretenders being judged by Scottish Judges: 22.5 percent

The difference between the two pass rates is 22 percent and is consistent with our initial hypothesis that Scottish Pretenders would be more successful than English Pretenders. This lends support to the idea that Scottish players are more aware of both English and Scottish identities and that Englishness is a dominant or hegemonic identity within the UK. Although not strictly necessary given the size of the difference between the groups, the statistical significance of the difference in pass rates can be calculated using a bootstrap simulation method in which the frequencies in the table provide the initial weights. Alternatively, if the three possible outcomes are coded as -1, 0, and $+1$ respectively, then a t-test can be used to compare the mean score for each group. Using the simulation method, the probability of this difference coming about by chance is less than 0.0001; using the t-test the outcome is very similar ($t(333) = -4.568$, $p < 000$).

As an aside, the difference is likely to be robust for a second reason. In other Games, we have found that playing Step 1 with groups has the effect of reducing the pass rate (Collins et al. 2017; Evans et al. 2018). We think this is because playing as group improves the quality of questions asked and helps to eliminate idiosyncratic Non-Pretender answers. Applying this insight to the English and Scottish Imitation Games suggests that, to the extent that the variation in Step 1 procedures, where some Games were played by individuals and some by groups, had an impact on the results, this should have worked against the Scottish Pretenders. Specifically, as all Scottish Pretenders contributed to Games in which all questions and comparator answers were created by groups the pass rate they were able to achieve should have been minimized. In contrast, at least some English

Pretenders were responding to, and being compared against, data generated in individual Step 1 Games. We suspect this makes their task somewhat easier and any impact would therefore tend to increase the pass rate for English Pretenders. In other words, if Step 1 recruitment had been more successful and the same protocols followed in both Edinburgh and Southampton, the most likely outcome would be that the difference in pass rates would increase as English Pretenders would be (even) more likely to be identified.

7.6   ANALYZING QUESTIONS AND ANSWERS

This research saw the introduction of a new software feature that randomized the way in which the responses to questions displayed in Step 1. As with earlier versions of the Game, both Pretender and Non-Pretender answers were presented simultaneously. The additional feature was that the allocation of Pretender or Non-Pretender answers to "Response 1" or "Response 2" on the screen seen by the Interrogator/Judge (Fig. 7.2) was randomized for each turn. The advantage of this is twofold:

1. It forces Interrogators/Judges at Step 1 to analyze each pair of answers in relation to the question asked and nothing else. In earlier research (Collins et al. 2006), we had thought that players would use previous answers to inform their next question and that seeing the whole transcript at each turn would be important. In practice, questions rarely, if ever, developed in this way, and the more obvious effect was that the decision made by Judges in response to the first question often became a schema into which all subsequent answers were made to fit. The holistic judgment based on all questions and answers is recorded but it is now collected at the end of the Game and only after the Interrogator/Judge has indicated that they do not wish to ask any further questions.
2. Because each decision and reason are linked to a specific question and the associated pair of answers, it is possible to analyze the turn-by-turn data in more detail. We had previously coded questions for "type" and "thematic content" (Collins et al. 2017) but had no way of knowing how individual questions and answers had been interpreted and which, if any, had proved particularly significant in reaching the final judgment.

Turning first to the types of questions asked, it is possible to code questions as falling into one of the four categories listed below[4]:

- **Biographical** questions such as "Where did you holiday as a child?"
- **Knowledge** questions such as "In cockney rhyming slang, what would i [sic] mean by saying 'apples and pears'?"
- **Opinion** questions such as "Should Scottish nationals pay the same fees for university as English people?"
- **Preferences** such as "What is your preferred hierarchical order of scone toppings?"

Based on this, we can then examine the distribution of question types across Step 1—that is, what types of question were most common—and the pass rate for each type of question—that is, which types of question were most successful. The summary statistics are listed in Table 7.3 and reveal a number of insights into the approaches of Interrogators/Judges and the differing abilities of English and Scottish Pretenders.

Two things in particular stand out as worthy of further note. First is the relative overreliance of English Interrogators/Judges on knowledge questions (60 percent of questions) at the expense of biographical, opinion, and preference questions. One possible interpretation of this is English Judges struggled to articulate personal and cultural experiences that they felt were both quintessentially "English" and likely to be unknown to Scottish Pretenders. As a result, questions about knowledge appeared to provide a more likely route to success. In contrast, Scottish Interrogators/Judges had a more balanced portfolio of questions in which knowledge questions were the largest category (36 percent) but by a much smaller margin, suggesting that Scottish Interrogators/Judges were able to iden-

Table 7.3 Question types and associated pass rates by nationality

	English Judges, Scottish Pretenders		Scottish Judges, English Pretenders	
	Proportion (%)	Pass rate (%)	Proportion (%)	Pass rate (%)
Biographical	11	59	18	48
Knowledge	60	59	36	31
Opinion	16	104	26	36
Preferences	13	95	21	48

tify biographical and cultural experiences that were both Scottish and likely to discriminate.

The second feature of note is the variations in pass rates, both within each group of Pretenders and between them. As might be expected given the difference in holistic judgments made by Judges at Step 4, the question-by-question pass rates for English Pretenders being evaluated by Scottish Interrogators/Judges at Step 1 are all much lower than the equivalent pass rates for Scottish Pretenders responding to English Interrogators/Judges. Thus, the pass rate for all question types is below 50 percent for English Pretenders and below 40 percent for two of the four types (knowledge and opinion), suggesting that they often struggled to provide plausible answers. In contrast, for opinion and preference questions, Scottish Pretenders achieved a pass rate of around 100 percent, suggesting that their responses were indistinguishable from those of the English Non-Pretenders. This provides another possible explanation for the reliance of English Interrogators/Judges on knowledge questions: quite simply, other questions did not work![5]

In addition to coding for question type, we also coded questions for their thematic content. As with question type, we can identify both the most common question themes and, by considering the pass rates associated with each, the most discriminating question themes. This, in turn, gives some insights into the ways different domains knowledge and experience are shared between groups. The data are summarized in Table 7.4 for most common questions and Table 7.5 for most effective questions.

As with the analysis of question types, it is noticeable that English Interrogators/Judges have a different pattern of questions to Scottish Interrogators/Judges. While both groups use a high proportion of geographical questions such as "How would you describe the difference between West and East London?" or "Where would you define as the Highlands, both culturally and geographically?," the most common categories for Scottish Interrogators/Judges are the more obviously cultural categories of "Traditions" and "Special Occasions." This suggests, once again, that Scottish Interrogators/Judges have access to what they expect to be a distinctive set of cultural resources. In contrast, geography questions tend to be more knowledge based (e.g., what is X, where is Y, give three examples of Z) and less likely to tap into wider aspects of cultural experience.

If the distribution of question themes reveals something of the ways in which Interrogators/Judges expect the two groups to be differentiated, then calculating the pass rate for each thematic group tells us about the

Table 7.4 Most common question themes

English Judges, Scottish Pretenders	% of questions	PR (%)	Scottish Judges, English Pretenders	% of questions	PR (%)
Geography	23	58	Traditions	13	29
Food and drink	13	81	Special occasions	11	33
Traditions	9	80	Geography	10	27
Education	9	64	Language	10	27
Sport	7	100	Food and drink	9	30

Table 7.5 Most effective question themes

English Judges, Scottish Pretenders	% of questions	PR (%)	Scottish Judges, English Pretenders	% of questions	PR (%)
Special occasions	3	20	Education	6	0
Transport	6	40	Money	3	0
Geography	23	58	Music and dance	6	0
Money	5	63	Transport	1	0
Education	9	64	Politics	7	25

extent to which these expectations were met. Looking at Table 7.4, it is clear that the most popular question themes were not necessarily the most discriminating for either English or Scottish Interrogators/Judges. Thus, for example, questions about "Sport," "Traditions," and "Food and Drink" were generally ineffective for English Interrogators/Judges in Step 1 with Scottish Pretenders achieving pass rates of over 80 percent for these items. Questions coded as "Geography" and "Education," which were typically more knowledge based had lower pass rates but were still generally answered well by a significant proportion of Scottish Pretenders.

The mismatch between the expectations of Interrogators/Judges about what will discriminate and what actually does the job can be seen by comparing Tables 7.4 and 7.5. For English Interrogators/Judges two of the most popular question themes—Geography and Education—do appear in the list of themes with the lowest pass rates, although given the relative success of Scottish Pretenders, the pass rates remain quite high. In the case of Scottish Interrogators/Judges, however, none of the five most popular question themes appear in the top five when the list is ranked by pass rate. Instead, questions relating to the Scottish education system, money, or cultural events like *ceilidhs* (a traditional form of Scottish dancing) tended to be more effective in revealing the gaps in the knowledge of English Pretenders. That said, it must be noted that, as the analysis becomes more disaggregated, the number of cases used to calculate the pass rates is very small and the figures do need to be treated with caution.

We therefore conclude this analysis of the data by offering a more holistic summing up of the difference between the two sets of Players. To create this we have taken the key words and phrases from each of the questions produced by participants at Step 1 and created "Word clouds" in which the size of each word is determined by its frequency in the corpus of text. Word clouds for both English and Scottish Interrogators/Judges are reproduced as Figs. 7.4 and 7.5, respectively.[6]

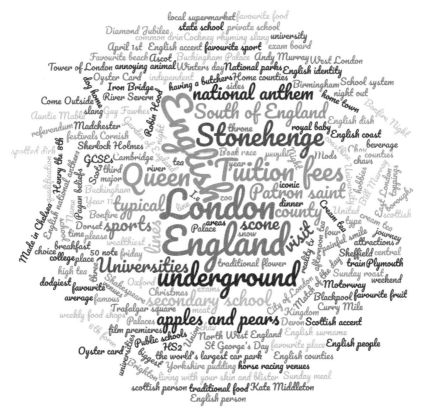

Fig. 7.4 Word cloud for questions set by English Interrogators/Judges

Fig. 7.5 Word cloud for questions set by Scottish Interrogators/Judges

What is apparent from the questions set by English Interrogators/ Judges is their emphasis on "living in England" as opposed to "being English." This is manifested in the emphasis on knowledge questions noted above and in the absence of questions about cultural aspects of their lives. Indeed, while supervising and observing the players during Step 1, it was clear that many of them struggled to come up with questions about what it meant to be English. In some cases, they took inspiration from the questions they received from Scottish Interrogators/Judges when they were playing a different role (e.g., questions about the meaning of words in a local dialect). In others, they resorted to questions about their immediate environment in the south of England, hence the relative importance of questions about the London underground, visitor attractions like Stonehenge, and their experiences of education. In contrast, the word cloud for Scottish Interrogators/Judges highlights the importance of many more distinctively cultural activities and experiences—ceilidhs, haggis, Hogmanay, Burns Night—for this group.

The word clouds also reveal the existence of distinctively Scottish practices that are not accessible to those living in England. In some cases, these are television programs created by BBC Scotland and either not shown in England or not watched by the English Pretenders we recruited. Questions about "Still Game" and Jackie Bird thus left English Pretenders dumbfounded as neither the program nor the presenter were known to them. In contrast, almost all television programs shown in England are also shown in Scotland, unless they are explicitly identified as "regional" in which case they will not be available to all English viewers either. This could be one of the ways in which the hegemonic nature of English identity is constructed: it is not necessarily a deliberate act by its citizens but a consequence of the absence of a meaningful distinction between England and the UK in the country's institutions.

7.7 Caveats and Challenges for Future Research

The aim of this chapter has been to illustrate the potential of the Imitation Game to research questions of national identity. The results are broadly consistent with our initial hypotheses, with the comparison of pass rates and the initial analysis of the textual data being consistent with the idea of an asymmetric relationship between Englishness and Scottishness. That said, there is clearly more work to do. We can classify this into two main areas, one of which is relatively straightforward to describe, the second of which requires further innovations.

The first, and most obvious, lacuna that needs to be filled is the detailed analysis of the qualitative data and, in particular, the integration of this with theories about the nature of social groups and national identity (Brubaker 2004; Jenkins 1996). We have not had the space to examine the data in the detail needed in this chapter but this is a task to which we could turn our attention in the future. The chapters that follow in this volume by Ross (Chap. 8), Kubiak (Chap. 9), and Bauch et al. (Chap. 10) all provide examples of how this might be done.

The second, more challenging, problem is how to explain the absence of a clear "English" identity. In the case of the Scottish participants, there was a distinctive and relatively uniform Scottish identity that emerged and which almost all players were all able to recognize and call upon. In contrast, no such shared identity was articulated by the English students, who ended up asking questions about the experience of living in (the South of) England rather than their experiences of being English. This may be because no such identity exists, which would be a clear difference between the two nations. Alternatively, it may be that, because all the English participants were recruited in a single location, this encouraged them to focus on relatively local aspects of their life and this masked a weaker, but wider, identification with Englishness. Again, this would be a difference with Scotland, where a clear national identity was articulated despite a similar recruitment process, but it would be a difference of degree rather than of kind.

To test which of these explanations is most plausible would require collection of data over a wider range of locations within England and Scotland. The effect of this would be to require Interrogators/Judges to come up with questions that unite the experiences of players from across the whole nation. Thus, English Interrogators/Judges would have to devise questions that were equally accessible to Non-Pretenders from Southampton (on the south coast) to Birmingham (in the middle of the country), and Leeds or Manchester (in the north). Quite what the outcome of this would be is hard to say. It might facilitate the articulation of a trans-regional English identity or it might show that there is no shared English identity at all, just a series of regional identities that happen to be located within a single administrative unit. Either way, the result would be an interesting finding.

7.8   Conclusions

We have reported on an opportunistic research project that responded to a decision by the UK government to allow the Scottish people to vote on their relationship with the UK. By using the Imitation Game, we hoped to document how citizens in Scotland and England constructed the distinctive features of their own national identities and the understanding they had of each other's experiences. Our hypothesis was that the dominant position of England in the UK would mean that English identity would have a more hegemonic character, making it more accessible to Scots, but harder for the English players to articulate as it is taken for granted and unremarked in everyday life. In contrast, Scottish identity would be more explicit for Scots but more restricted geographically, thus rendering it less accessible to English participants in the research.

The data collected broadly confirmed these hypotheses. The pass rate for Scottish Pretenders was significantly higher than that for English Pretenders, with a more detailed analysis of the dialogues revealing a number of differences in the content and nature of the questions asked by each group. More work remains to be done but we believe the data presented so far demonstrates the potential of the Imitation Game to support longitudinal and comparative social research that can complement existing investments such as the Eurobarometer and Mass Observation Archive.

Notes

1. For clarity, we capitalize the Imitation Game when referring to its use as a social science research method.
2. The Interrogator/Judge is a role played by a single person in the three-player Game but actually contains two distinct tasks—asking questions and evaluating answers—that can be performed by different people. This difference becomes important later, hence the use of the more complex terminology at this stage.
3. We differentiate by color to avoid the implication of chronology or ranking that is created by numerical labels such as "first judging" and "second judging."
4. This is a simplified version of the list set out in Collins et al. (2017). Some questions will be coded as belonging to more than one category as they might, for example, as if the Players know about something and, if so, what their opinion is—for example, "What is X and do you like it?"
5. Note that, in this context, "work" refers to the extent to which the answers produced enabled Judges to distinguish between Pretenders and Non-Pretenders. This emphasis on identifying differences between groups is a particular feature of the Imitation Game. One corollary of this is that knowledge that is shared between the two groups is not explored directly, though questions that "fail" to discriminate may unwittingly reveal some of the cultural knowledge that is common to both groups.
6. Wordles were created using https://www.wordclouds.com/ (accessed Feb. 25, 2019).

REFERENCES

du Bois, W.E.B. 1903. *The Souls of Black Folk.* Chicago, IL: A.C. McClurg and Co. http://www.gutenberg.org/ebooks/408.

Brubaker, Rogers. 2004. *Ethnicity Without Groups.* Cambridge, MA: Harvard University Press.

Butler, Judith. 2006. *Gender Trouble: Feminism and the Subversion of Identity*, Routledge Classics. New York: Routledge.

Collins, Harry M. 2011. Language and Practice. *Social Studies of Science* 41 (2): 271–300. https://doi.org/10.1177/0306312711399665.

Collins, Harry M., and Robert Evans. 2002. The Third Wave of Science Studies: Studies of Expertise and Experience. *Social Studies of Science* 32 (2): 235–296. https://doi.org/10.1177/0306312702032002003.

———. 2007. *Rethinking Expertise.* Chicago: University of Chicago Press.

———. 2014. Quantifying the Tacit: The Imitation Game and Social Fluency. *Sociology* 48 (1): 3–19. https://doi.org/10.1177/0038038512455735.

———. 2016. Expertise Revisited, Part I – Interactional Expertise. *Studies in History and Philosophy of Science Part A* 54: 113–123. https://doi.org/10.1016/j.shpsa.2015.07.004.

———. 2017. Probes, Surveys, and the Ontology of the Social. *Journal of Mixed Methods Research* 11 (3): 328–341. https://doi.org/10.1177/1558689815619825.

Collins, Harry M., Robert Evans, Rodrigo Ribeiro, and Martin Hall. 2006. Experiments with Interactional Expertise. *Studies in History and Philosophy of Science Part A* 37 (4): 656–674. https://doi.org/10.1016/j.shpsa.2006.09.005.

Collins, Harry M., Robert Evans, Martin Weinel, Jennifer Lyttleton-Smith, Andrew Bartlett, and Martin Hall. 2017. The Imitation Game and the Nature of Mixed Methods. *Journal of Mixed Methods Research* 11 (4): 510–527. https://doi.org/10.1177/1558689815619824.

Connell, R.W., and James W. Messerschmidt. 2005. Hegemonic Masculinity: Rethinking the Concept. *Gender & Society* 19 (6): 829–859. https://doi.org/10.1177/0891243205278639.

Evans, Robert, Harry M. Collins, Martin Weinel, Jennifer Lyttleton-Smith, Hannah O'Mahoney, and Willow Leonard-Clarke. 2018. Groups and Individuals: Conformity and Diversity in the Performance of Gendered Identities. *British Journal of Sociology.* https://doi.org/10.1111/1468-4446.12507.

Jenkins, Richard. 1996. *Social Identity. Key Ideas.* London; New York: Routledge.

Kubiak, Daniel, and Martin Weinel. 2016. DDR-Generationen revisited – Gibt es einen Generationszusammenhang der "Wendekinder"? In *Die Generation der Wendekinder*, ed. Adriana Lettrari, Christian Nestler, and Nadja Troi-Boeck, 107–129. Wiesbaden: Springer Fachmedien Wiesbaden. https://doi.org/10.1007/978-3-658-11480-0_8.

ONS. 2018. Population Estimates for the U.K., England and Wales, Scotland and Northern Ireland – Office for National Statistics. *Statistical Bulletin*. Office for National Statistics, June 28, 2018. https://www.ons.gov.uk/peoplepopulationandcommunity/populationandmigration/populationestimates/bulletins/annualmidyearpopulationestimates/mid2017.

Turing, Alan. 1950. Computing Machinery and Intelligence. *Mind* 59 (236): 433–460. https://doi.org/10.1093/mind/LIX.236.433.

CHAPTER 8

How (Well) Do Media Professionals Know Their Audiences? SEE Meets Media Studies

Philippe Ross

8.1 Introduction

It is increasingly obvious that digital and social media pose a threat to the power of established, institutional producers of information and culture to define social reality. What is less clear is whether the exercise of this "symbolic power" (Thompson 1995; Silverstone 2005) or "media power" (Couldry and Curran 2003) requires anything specific in the way of competence or knowledge. The matter is particularly vexing now that it is apparently shared with a social group that is anything but exclusive: the general public. While notions like that of "creative audience" (Castells 2009), "producer" (Bruns 2008), and "cocreator" (Burns 2009) seem apt to describe both increased audience agency and diminished producer power, the broader academic and popular discourse surrounding this change tends to perpetuate a false dichotomy between the general public or audience, on the one hand, and (traditional, professional) media producers, on the other. One typical argument contends that social media offer the potential for "ordinary people to define a reality from their own

P. Ross (✉)
University of Ottawa, Ottawa, ON, Canada
e-mail: pross@uottawa.ca

© The Author(s) 2019
D. S. Caudill et al. (eds.), *The Third Wave in Science and Technology Studies*, https://doi.org/10.1007/978-3-030-14335-0_8

perspectives" (Tang and Yang 2011, 677) via the production and transmission of symbolic goods rather than rely on traditional mass media. The opposition it draws between traditional media and so-called ordinary people is shaky in that it implies (A) that the newly empowered individuals possess no special ability and/or (B) that, insofar as the media are populated by individuals (something you would not know from reading much scholarship on media production), these are not ordinary individuals. Yet access to the production of symbolic goods does not depend on definite training and credentials (Bourdieu 1979). Perhaps more importantly, the producers' subservience to audience tastes and behaviors precludes neat distinctions between both groups on the basis of their knowledge and competence—because ordinary audience members have knowledge that established producers desperately want.

This "circular relationship" between producers and audiences (Gans 1957; Gitlin 1983; McQuail 1987; Ross 2014) poses a challenge to our understanding of what producers know and the extent to which their knowledge is specialist or exclusive. This chapter takes up the challenge, first, by problematizing the expertise of media production through a dialogue between *production studies* and the Studies of Expertise and Experience (SEE), and, second, by reporting on exploratory imitation games that were carried out as part of a research project on the relationship between the production staff of a Canadian Broadcasting Corporation (CBC)/Radio-Canada regional branch and its audiences.

8.2   ETHNOGRAPHIES OF MEDIA PRODUCTION

Some of the intricacies and implications of the "circular relationship" between producers and their audiences can be appreciated by considering studies of media production which explore the routinized aspects of creative labor and media work, and which give the audience a central role in the lived experience of media producers, from high-profile executives to technicians and laborers. For instance, McQuail defined the "key media skill" as the ability to "assess public taste" (McQuail 1987, 149). Gitlin described the work of television executives as being geared to determining "what the audience wants" (Gitlin 1983, 19–46). Dornfeld characterized television producers as "popular anthropologists" (Dornfeld 1998, 141–143) concerned with understanding the culture and behavior of their audience. Some have noted the "social distance" (Thompson 1995) between producers and audiences, which is expressed in terms of geography and class (Zafirau 2009, 194), a status or special talent beyond the reach of ordinary individuals (Meyer 2011, 7), or a lack of direct interaction between producers and their audiences that is deemed typical of the cultural industries (Hesmondhalgh and Baker 2011; Caldwell 2008; Deuze 2007).

Production studies also reveal how the inherent limitations of mediated mass communication are overcome by "ordinary" social knowledge or cultural competence. Despite the extensive use of market research techniques, production in institutional settings is pervaded by the use of common sense (Caldwell 2008; Dornfeld 1998; Gitlin 1983), intuition and tacit understandings (Zafirau 2009), as well as beliefs (Ross 2011a) about the audience. This kind of "audience theorizing" (Caldwell 2008) often stems from ordinary, everyday experience with or of social groups such as family members and friends that serve as proxy audience members at various stages of the production process. These informal knowledge claims have been shown to be key in the decision-making process (Zafirau 2009) and even to trump all other arguments (Caldwell 2008, 336). They are invoked to support or to refute empirical evidence (Gitlin 1983, 44), by individuals in a position of authority (Caldwell 2008, 221) or otherwise (Ross 2011b, 11). Much of this recalls user-centered approaches to technology design in Science and Technology Studies (STS). For instance, the tension between "explicit techniques" for engaging users, like market research, and the more powerful effects of so-called implicit techniques, whereby designers rely on their own personal experience to represent their target user (Akrich 1995). Others have termed this reflexive mechanism the "I-methodology" (Oudshoorn et al. 2004).

The recourse to ordinary, implicit social knowledge pertaining to the audience is a feature of production, the nature and extent of which call for sustained empirical investigation. Beyond suggesting that ordinary members of the public may be competent contributors to production endeavors meant for a mass audience—equally or perhaps more so than established producers—it implies a social proximity between the spaces of production and reception more than it does any kind of "social distance." The means for testing this proposition can be found in the methodology associated with Studies of Expertise and Experience.

8.3   Studies of Expertise and Experience (SEE) and the Imitation Game

In their program known as SEE, Collins and Evans (2002, 2007) explored the extent to which technical decision-making is amenable to public involvement. Their sociological theory of expertise aims to enable distinctions between those who "know what they are talking about" (Collins and Evans 2007, 2) in a given field and those who do not. Following Wynne (1989) and his recognition of the contributions of "experience-based experts," Collins and Evans' conception of expertise did not rest on the exclusivity of credentials, knowledge, or practices. Instead, it valued experience over formal certifications; it afforded tacit knowledge a more central role than explicit (or propositional) knowledge; and it resisted equating the ubiquity of a given practice in a particular social setting with an absence of expertise (Collins and Evans 2007, 3). This aligns usefully with the conception of production described in the foregoing section.

Collins and Evans distinguished between "ubiquitous tacit knowledge" and "specialist tacit knowledge": the former is acquired through the ordinary experience of everyday life, while the latter indicates a higher level of competence not possessed by most people because it requires immersion in a specialist domain. Expertise hinges on the latter and its acquisition is thus "a social process—a matter of socialization into the practices of an expert group" (Collins and Evans 2007, 2–3). As my reading of production ethnographies in both media studies and STS suggests, the fact that first-hand experience can trump specialist knowledge makes it difficult to determine in absolute terms which social group—of professional producers or the audience—embodies the expertise of production and thus provides the requisite socialization to would-be producers. These studies nevertheless substantiate the producers' overriding need to understand their audiences, and they suggest that this understanding stems from (naturally occurring) interactions between both groups. This key insight justifies using the major innovation of Collins and Evans' theory: the concept of "interactional expertise" (Collins and Evans 2002, 2007, 2011, 2013).

Defined as "the ability to acquire a thorough understanding of a technical (or cultural) domain through deep immersion in the spoken discourse alone" (Collins and Evans 2011, 10), it applies to the experience of a domain gained through interaction with its practicing members rather than an effective belonging to it as attested by practice. It posits that immersion in the language of a practice (or "sociolect") allows individuals to acquire the tacit knowledge required to make good judgments in a given domain, if not outright technical proficiency. Interactional expertise thus seems amenable to producers-as-popular-anthropologists: individuals whose works as producers requires a thorough understanding of their audiences, but whose understanding is gained through everyday life, that is, interactions with (putative) audience members which may have nothing to do with production as such (cf. Ross 2014).

Accordingly, I set out to explore the social proximity between production and reception as evidenced by the producers' tacit knowledge of their audience—their interactional expertise—by asking the question: How well do producers know their audiences? And in order to do so I deployed the imitation game methodology.

The Imitation Game (IMGame) is the precursor of the Turing Test, developed by Alan Turing in the 1950s to assess the ability of computers to mimic human intelligence (Collins 1990). In IMGames, all three participants are human and they communicate in real time via a bespoke Web-based application. Here, a member of a given cultural group (or "target culture/expertise") plays against a non-member, who is pretending to be a member of that culture. The judge, who is always a member of the target culture, asks the questions and tries to identify the pretender. The extent to which non-members of the target culture can pretend to be members indicates the extent to which that group understands the other. The method measures the possession of interactional expertise—that is, the fluency of individuals in the "sociolect" of groups to which they do not effectively belong—because it urges the judge, who is an effective member of the target culture, to think of questions that only a fellow, experienced, practicing member of the group would know how to answer. Thus it urges a focus on the tacit knowledge, and not the explicit/propositional knowledge, that is deemed to be at the core of a given culture, social practice, or profession. According to the theory of interactional expertise, this can be displayed by individuals who are not effective members of the target culture but who, through "social mixing [with effective members] or a special need to become fluent" (Collins and Evans 2011, 1), acquire the requisite language. Their fluency is measured by the success (or otherwise) of the judge in identifying who is who over a series of questions and answers: the longer the pretender confounds the judge, the more fluent in the target culture/expertise he or she is deemed to be. The promise of this method has been discussed in *Nature* (Giles 2006) and other influential publications (Reisz 2011; Selinger 2012). Collins and his team pioneered its use for the study of cultural integration across four European regions. With respect to the research question stated above, the method is remarkably suited to the task.

8.4   CASE STUDY: RADIO-CANADA OTTAWA-GATINEAU

Imitation games were set up as part of a larger project on the relationship between Radio-Canada Ottawa-Gatineau—the Canadian Broadcasting Corporation's French-language regional branch located in Canada's capital—and its audiences. For the purposes of that project, I approached members of the full-time production staff involved in the creation of original content across the branch's various platforms: radio and television as well as its website and social media accounts. They number 27 individuals in total, 9 of whom agreed to take part, including producers and assistant producers; the host of a popular radio program; reporters/writers; cultural commentators; the head of programming; and the traffic reporter for the morning and afternoon radio broadcasts.

The larger project involved carrying out qualitative interviews with all nine participants in order to obtain biographical data (background, training, credentials, etc.) and to gain a sense of what these media professionals know, or think they know, about their audiences. The interview data played no part in the experimental study that is the subject of this chapter beyond helping to set up the imitation games, which would involve the producers as well as members of their audience.

A crude preliminary analysis of the interview data revealed no real consensus as to the identity of the branch's audience. Instead it revealed a general distrust of market research and notions of the audience fostered by the (regional) managers and CBC corporate headquarters; and the prevalence of ordinary and intuitive conceptions of the audience. A number of recurrent audience features did emerge from the interviews, most notably its (presumed) high level of education; its (presumed) average age of 40 and over; and its (presumed) "love of culture." As at least two interviewees put it: "Our listeners are the kind of people who attend the book fair" (translated from French by author). Based on this, and encouraged by the fact that Radio-Canada Ottawa-Gatineau was to broadcast its Saturday morning radio program to a live audience on site, the recruitment of audience members was carried out at the *Salon du livre de l'Outaouais* (the Ottawa-Gatineau region's annual, French-language book fair) in February 2017. There I collected 20 or so names of individuals who identified as regular listeners of Radio-Canada's radio broadcasts, including that Saturday morning program, *Les Malins* (which translates roughly as the "clever clogs"). Of those, six agreed to take part in the imitation games when they were contacted a few weeks later. One dropped out after reading the instructions, which were sent to participants a few days in advance.

This left five audience members for the games, which took place one evening in May 2017.

The target culture/expertise to be explored through these games was: the Radio-Canada Ottawa-Gatineau/*Les Malins* audience. The games would feature a professional producer and an audience member as Pretender and Non-Pretender, respectively. The Judge would be an audience member. Thus, the games were framed as a test of how well the producers know their audience—or their ability to pass as regular listeners of Radio-Canada Ottawa-Gatineau/*Les Malins*.

Two separate rounds were conducted using the software developed and hosted by the Centre for the Study of Knowledge Expertise Science (KES) at Cardiff University. The full sequence of questions/answers was recorded by the software. After each pair of answers to a same question, the Judge registers a guess as to the respondents' identity, his/her confidence in this guess, as well as an explanation—all of which was also recorded. The guess and confidence level after each question enable a quantitative expression of the participants' interactional expertise but the qualitative content is, at this exploratory stage, of primary interest. The recorded exchanges between participants, as well as the Judges' evolving reasoning, were analyzed using a thematic content analysis in order to shed light on the research question.

After much reflection on the setup, it was decided that audience members would play the roles of Judge and Non-Pretender in groups rather than individually. This owed mainly to the trial nature of the games and the relative "looseness" of the target culture/expertise, and time constraints. Roles were distributed as follows (Table 8.1).

It should be noted that audience members Martin and Michelle, as well as Suzie and Pierre, are partners. This was not planned initially but faced with recruitment issues, enabling participants to play as partners seemed an incentive for participation. It was also anticipated that this would help participants reflect on their experience as regular listeners in everyday life

Table 8.1 Participant roles by round

	Round 1	Round 2
Judge (audience member)	Suzie	Martin
	Pierre	Michelle
	Marie	Marie
Pretender (producer)	Jean	Jean
Non-Pretender (audience member)	Martin	Suzie
	Michelle	Pierre

in contexts such as the home, the car, and so on, and thus prompt useful questions. The partners played the role of Non-Pretender together. When they played as Judge, an extra player—Marie—was added to the mix. On the whole I felt this would offer a good balance between idiosyncratic and more broadly shared experiences, and between familiarity and the need to spell out one's thoughts.

I was in the room with the Judge, and a research assistant was with the Non-Pretender. The Pretender played remotely from home. We managed to play two games (or rounds) on the night—each lasting roughly 90 minutes. We recorded the audio and took notes. The data presented in what follows was translated from French by the author.

8.5   Some Results and What They Mean

Round 1 yielded five sets of question, responses, and judgments. Round 2 yielded six sets. What follows is, first, a summary of the questions and results for each round, which were very different; and, second, a discussion of the judgments and their justification, which were fairly consistent across both rounds. Outstanding issues and next steps are addressed in the conclusions.

In Round 1, the Judges asked the following questions:

Q1.1. Is there a difference for you between the Saturday morning program and the Sunday morning program?

Q1.2. What interests you most about the Saturday morning program?

Q1.3. Do you feel there is enough cultural content in the Saturday morning program?

Q1.4. Do you like participating in competitions to win tickets to shows and so on?

Q1.5. What do you enjoying listening to besides the Saturday morning program?

These questions seemed to me a bit too general but they focused on perceptions, tastes, and personal experience, and they produced more revealing responses on the whole. The Judges correctly identified the Pretender on all five questions and with a confidence level that started at 3 ("I am more certain than uncertain") for Question 1 and rose to 4 ("I am certain") for all subsequent questions.

The following example from the dialogue hints at the reasons for this:

Q1.2. What interests you most about the Saturday morning program?

R1.2.1. The show has a contagious energy. I feel like I'm sitting at the table with the team, in my kitchen. I can be informed and entertained while learning interesting things.
R1.2.2. [Host] Jade Montpetit's voice. She has a soft and warm voice. I find her lovely, a good listener, she has empathy and an easy laugh. I also very much like the show portion with [regular guest] Olivier Scott and his dad. The show is a good way to start the day, on a relaxed and positive note. (Translated from French by author)

In this instance the Judges registered a correct judgment (R1.2.2 is the Pretender's) with a confidence level of 4. Their reasons stressed the fact that R1.2.1 evokes a mood or feeling, it refers to the context or setting of reception, and it describes a motivation that was fairly general but rang true for the Judges; while R1.2.2 was deemed too specific with respect to content and contributors to the show (naming them explicitly), and it was deemed to use a technical term—"show portion"—that listeners typically would not use. Responses and judgments are discussed in more detail below.

In contrast to Round 1, Round 2 featured questions that focused on more specific aspects, contents, and experiences but it yielded less revealing dialogue, ostensibly because the Pretender's responses were less elaborate than in Round 1.

The Judges in Round 2 asked the following questions:

Q2.1. During the week, do you listen in the morning or in the afternoon, and why?
Q2.2. Are the morning traffic reports useful with respect to your everyday habits?
Q2.3. Describe the regional flavor of the weekday morning program.
Q2.4. How would you describe the quality of language in the programs you listen to, specifically Les Malins? Please give examples.
Q2.5. Do you use electronic platforms (Facebook, Twitter, etc.) to express your opinion? Do you phone in when listeners are asked for their thoughts and opinions on a topic?
Q2.6. What is your relationship with the broadcasters? Do you feel an attachment to personalities and contents?

Here the Judges correctly identified the Pretender only half the time and when they did, it was with a confidence level of only 1 ("I am uncertain") or 2 ("I am more uncertain than certain"). Their overall judgment was correct but with a confidence level of only 2.

As an example, consider the responses to Q4:

Q2.4. How do you find the quality of the language used in the shows you listen to, specifically Les Malins? Please justify your answer with examples.

R2.4.1. I find the quality of language acceptable considering it is live. But sometimes there are anglicisms and expressions that are too colloquial. I don't have concrete examples in mind right now, but I recall noticing the occasional colloquial language and the use of English words. But in general, the broadcasters correct themselves or they make fun of their mistakes. Which is reassuring because it means they are mindful of language quality.

R2.4.2. The host uses a rather polished French and she doesn't make glaring mistakes. For instance, English words are sometimes used in the program.

Here the Judges were unable to tell who is who (incorrect judgment, confidence level 1) as both responses were deemed plausible. The Judges felt R2.4.1 might be from the Pretender because it was "too articulate" (Suzie and Pierre both have graduate degrees and they work in education), while the concision and perceived "neutrality" of R2.4.2 suggested the Pretender.

On the whole, and taking both rounds into account, responses that were (generally correctly) attributed to the Pretender were those which:

• Were deemed too well-written
• Used terms deemed technical
• Tried too hard to justify program quality and efforts to please, or connect with, the audience
• Expressed a clichéd view of Ottawa (as serious or boring)
• Gave too much importance, and were too detailed with respect, to contents and features
• Contained "inconsistencies" in reference to the listening context.

In making sense of these results one notes, first, that the Judges knew the Pretender was being played by a Radio-Canada Ottawa-Gatineau producer. Indeed, the first five points listed above were attributed not to a generic Pretender—that is, someone who is not a regular listener of Radio-

Canada Ottawa-Gatineau or of *Les Malins*—but rather to a Pretender who is specifically a producer.

The first two—quality of writing and use of a so-called technical term—were attributed to "a communications or media professional," while the next three were attributed, more specifically, to a producer at Radio-Canada Ottawa-Gatineau. The third, the statement that Radio-Canada Ottawa-Gatineau does a good job of "reaching out to their audience" (R1.3.2), was deemed a generalization, a justification that only such a producer would make. Regarding the fourth, the same Judges felt the view of Ottawa as a serious or boring city (R1.5.2) was clichéd and could only be harbored by someone influenced by the Montréal-centric world-view, which Radio-Canada is traditionally accused of fostering. As for the fifth point, the Judges felt a typical listener would not attach so much importance to content features or the names of program hosts or other contributors, or to the quality of their voice. They felt only a producer of the program would do.

How might these elements have been interpreted, had the Judges not known a Producer was involved? For instance, if we consider the responses to Q2 again, it is arguable whether the terms "show portion" (R1.2.2) or "guest and experts" (R1.3.3) would be deemed too technical, as they were in this instance. And would response 1.2.2 as a whole be attributed to anything other than a very loyal listener?

As for the sixth and last point on the list, the Judges in both rounds pointed to "inconsistencies" in the Pretender's responses that referred to the context in which they listen to the radio. The Judges in Round 1 felt it was odd that someone would claim to listen to the Saturday morning show but not the Sunday morning show. Similarly, Round 2 Judges were suspicious of the fact that someone would claim to tune in on their drive to work in the morning but not on their evening drive back home. Such experiences would likely ring true to some regular listeners (the author of this chapter included) and thus entail different results, thereby suggesting the need to better define the target expertise/culture and who counts as an effective practitioner/member—an issue which is taken up in the conclusions. But the dialogue is encouraging nonetheless in that it illustrates the players' willingness and capacity to reflect on their experience in a way that is consistent with the Imitation Game methodology's aims. Without wanting to overstate this, it was clear from the exchanges around these responses that the Judges were not so much trying to catch out the Pretender from a logical standpoint—there was no sense of a "gotcha!"

moment. Rather, the exchanges suggest they were trying but failing to recognize the circumstances in which someone who claims to be a regular listener would tune in on Saturday but not Sunday, or in the morning but not the evening. They could not square the described practices with their own experience as regular listeners.

Most notably, this willingness and capacity to draw upon their experience is reflected in the responses the Judges (generally correctly) attributed to the Non-Pretender. These responses:

- Tended, in the Judges' words, to "contextualize" (JX-X) their listening
- Echoed their own general motivation
- Were deemed more "spontaneous" and about "feeling" than about specific contents or personalities.

The first point follows from what was described previously. The Judges in Round 1 felt a real listener would evoke the context of reception—but not too specifically. So, for instance, saying that "you like to listen to the Saturday morning show in the kitchen" was accepted as typical by Round 1 Judges, while a response about "listening to the show live from the book fair back in February" was deemed suspiciously detailed. The three Judges in this instance were recruited at that very live broadcast, so the Pretender's response reflected their own experience. But none recalled it was specifically in February, and they said they had no reason to.

One way of reading this suggests, perhaps counterintuitively, that the detailed account of a practice may in fact be inconsistent with its repetition or habitual status (or vague/generic account may be consistent with it). Indeed, the detailed account was treated with suspicion because it is punctual or exceptional—it stands out—while the more generic account suggests habit, something which a real loyal listener could not, or would feel it is unnecessary to, describe in detail because it is taken for granted. Although perplexing with respect to the methodology's applicability in this context, this fits with something that was observed on the day of the morning show's live broadcast. Many people sitting in the audience—which was set up like a café, with the broadcasters sitting around a table on a stage at the front of the room—seemed not to pay much attention to what was happening on stage. Many were enjoying their coffee, chatting, and reading the newspaper while (presumably) listening to the program, like they might do at home, rather than watching the interactions onstage as they might a play. Similarly, the second and third points above indicate that the Judges identified with motivations that were expressed in fairly general terms, such as "listening to learn interesting things" (R1.2.1) or "to find out what's going on in the region" (R2.3.1), and with expressions of mood and feeling—like the show's "contagious energy" (R1.2.1)—rather than specific contents and features.

Two sets of notions in media studies may shed light on these results. The first is the rather intuitive idea of radio as the medium users have on "in the background," for company or while they are busy doing other things, which perhaps supposes a kind of unfocused engagement unlikely to yield detailed accounts. The results are too preliminary to support this in any significant way, but they are consistent with Marshall McLuhan's (1964) characterization of radio as a "hot" medium, that is, a medium that engages only one of the individual's senses through content that is complete and not subject to onerous decoding, such that it entails little or no participation on the part of the listener. The second relates to production studies and the circular relationship between producers and audiences discussed earlier. Best expressed by Gitlin (1983), it is the idea that the audience does not explicitly articulate its wants or likes or needs in the abstract; that these things only become known once a product exists that enables them to materialize around it—or not. In other words, the audience does not get what it wants; it wants what it gets. This may explain why listeners evoke moods and feelings, why they express motivations in fairly general terms, and why they recognize these as typical of the group. More games are needed in order to refine the methodology and to validate such tentative findings. The concluding remarks point to ways forward in this respect.

8.6   Concluding Remarks

One source of concern, and a time-consuming task, in preparation of the imitation games described in this chapter was the written instructions provided to the players, especially the Judges. It was difficult to convey what the experiment was about and what useful questions might be without giving examples, which might have been too leading and constraining for participants. In particular, there was a concern that the Judge's questions would focus on the contents broadcasted by Radio-Canada Ottawa-Gatineau/*Les Malins* rather than *how listeners experience these contents*, or the experience of being a listener more broadly, which was the target culture/expertise the study aimed for. I feared that a focus on the contents would make it too difficult for the Judges to tell who was who because a producer would be expected to know at least as much as even the most loyal listener about contents. As it turns out, this apprehension was founded—but only partly.

On the one hand, this turned out to be the case but arguably it was because the Judges knew the Pretender was a Producer and not a non-listener. Thus, the perceived excess of detail regarding program contents and contributors led to the Judges' catching him out. Clearly this knowledge introduced some measure of noise or reverse psychology in the Judge's reasoning which begs further reflection on the games' setup. However, this seems unavoidable in the context of a study designed specifically to address the producers' knowledge of their audience by measuring their ability—and not that of generic non-experts—to pass as members of their audience. Even deceiving the Judges as to the Pretender's function, or simply not disclosing it to them, hardly seems preferable: as the analysis suggests, this might skew the results significantly yet not give them any more consistency. Indeed, some of the criteria (e.g. the use of technical terms, inconsistent accounts) evoked by the Judges in the present study to identify the producer-as-pretender might well produce similar judgments in games with a nominal generic Pretender, while others (e.g. justification of programs, detailed accounts of contents and features) might serve to fool the Judges into thinking they are dealing with nothing other than a very loyal listener. Others still (e.g. quality of writing, clichéd view of Ottawa) might not apply either way.

In addition to considering how best to frame the Pretender's participation, further studies of producers using this methodology will require reflection on the category of "audience." The audience is in many ways a product of theory—media theory but also the producer's theorizing—not a social group in the way a cultural minority or a community might be. This raises issues of recruitment. In its current setup, the approach used here relies on regular listeners self-identifying as such and this makes for a broad, rather loose definition of the group. Thus one might consider recruiting members of the audience that are part of something closer to a community—active members of online forums related to Radio-Canada Ottawa-Gatineau and its contents, for instance. However, their legitimacy might still be questioned as, according to the producers that were interviewed, these groups are not deemed representative of the total audience and the producers do not engage them or hope to respond to them in any sustained way.

On the other hand, the games carried out as part of this study provided substantial encouragement with respect to audience members attempting to verbalize their experience and to pinpoint the group's specificity—hence the apprehension that the Judges would fail to ask useful questions being only party founded. On the whole, the Judges really "got" the purpose of the imitation games. They asked a number of useful questions drawing on their experience, and their reasoning and judgments were promising in this respect too. In particular, the questions in Round 2 seemed very specific to the target culture/expertise, resonating with widely held conceptions of the Radio-Canada audience (e.g. its notorious attention to the quality of French used in broadcasts), and focusing on regional specificity and the relationship between audiences and producers. In this instance it was the Pretender's concision, perhaps caused by fatigue, which arguably prevented the dialogue from yielding more telling results. In order to verify this, the questions produced by participants in the present study went into a bank for use in a follow-up study that is currently underway: asynchronous, email-based imitation games involving the eight remaining professional producers recruited for the project on Radio-Canada Ottawa-Gatineau and its audiences, and additional members of their audience recruited at the regional book fair.

In sum, while more work is needed to fully exploit the potential of Imitation games in the context of media production, it appears more of a logistical challenge than an epistemological dead end. Indeed, the premise for such an approach remains sound: the audience is a group that producers have a special reason for knowing, and indeed one which they claim to know and to interact with. These claims warrant sustained empirical investigation and, as this chapter has argued, SEE and the Imitation Game methodology seem fit for the purpose.

References

Akrich, Madeleine. 1995. User Representations: Practices, Methods and Sociology. In *Managing Technology in Society: The Approach of Constructive Technology Assessment*, ed. Arie Rip, Thomas Misa, and Johan Schot, 167–184. New York: St. Martin's Press.

Bourdieu, Pierre. 1979. *La distinction. Critique sociale du jugement*. Paris: Éditions de Minuit.

Bruns, Axel. 2008. *Blogs, Wikipedia, Second Life and Beyond: From Production to Produsage*. New York: Peter Lang.

Burns, Andrew. 2009. *Making New Media: Creative Production and Digital Literacies.* New York: Peter Lang.

Caldwell, John T. 2008. *Production Culture: Industrial Reflexivity and Critical Practice in Film and Television.* Durham: Duke University Press.

Castells, Manuel. 2009. *Communication Power.* Oxford: Oxford University Press.

Collins, Harry M. 1990. *Artificial Experts: Social Knowledge and Intelligent Machines.* Cambridge: MIT Press.

Collins, Harry M., and Robert Evans. 2002. The Third Wave of Science Studies: Studies of Expertise and Experience. *Social Studies of Science* 32 (2): 235–296.

———. 2007. *Rethinking Expertise.* Chicago: The University of Chicago Press.

———. 2011. *A New Method for Cross-Cultural and Cross-Temporal Comparison of Societies.* Grant Proposal Submitted to European Research Council Advanced Grant Program. http://www.cf.ac.uk/socsi/contactsandpeople/harrycollins/expertise-project/imitationgamehome.html.

———. 2013. Quantifying the Tacit: The Imitation Game and Social Fluency. *Sociology* 48 (1): 3–19.

Couldry, Nick, and James Curran, eds. 2003. *Contesting Media Power: Alternative Media in a Networked World.* Oxford: Rowman and Littlefield.

Deuze, Mark. 2007. *Media Work.* Cambridge, UK: Polity.

Dornfeld, Barry. 1998. *Producing Public Television, Producing Public Culture.* Princeton, NJ: Princeton University Press.

Gans, Herbert J. 1957. The Creator-Audience Relationship in the Mass-Media: An Analysis of Movie Making. In *Mass Culture: The Popular Arts in America*, ed. Bernard Rosenberg and David Manning White, 315–324. Glencoe, IL: The Free Press.

Giles, Jim. 2006. Sociologist Fools Physics Judges. *Nature* 442: 8. https://doi.org/10.1038/442008a.

Gitlin, Todd. 1983. *Inside Prime Time.* New York: Pantheon Books.

Hesmondhalgh, David, and Sarah Baker. 2011. *Creative Labour. Media Work in Three Cultural Industries.* London: Routledge.

McLuhan, Marshall. 1964. *Understanding Media.* New York: McGraw-Hill.

McQuail, Dennis. 1987. *Mass Communication Theory: An Introduction.* 2nd ed. London: Sage.

Meyer, Vicki. 2011. *Below the Line: Producers and Production Studies in the New Television Economy.* Durham: Duke University Press.

Oudshoorn, Nelly, Els Rommes, and Marcelle Stienstra. 2004. Configuring the User as Everybody: Gender and Design Cultures in Information and Communication Technologies. *Science, Technology & Human Values* 29 (1): 30–63.

Reisz, Matthew. 2011. Imitation of Life: Plaything Promises to Offer Insight into Stereotyping. *Times Higher Education*, March 10.

Ross, Philippe. 2011a. Problematizing the User in User-Centred Production: A New Media Lab Meets Its Audiences. *Social Studies of Science* 41 (2): 251–270.

———. 2011b. Is There an Expertise of Production? The Case of New Media Producers. *New Media & Society* 13 (6): 912–928.

———. 2014. Were Producers and Audiences Ever Separate? Conceptualizing Production as Social Situation. *Television and New Media* 15 (2): 157–174.

Selinger, Evan. 2012. What Happens When We Turn the World's Most Famous Robot Test on Ourselves? *The Atlantic*, June 20.

Silverstone, Roger. 2005. The Sociology of Mediation and Communication. In *The Sage Handbook of Sociology*, ed. Craig Calhoun, Chris Rojek, and Bryan Turner, 188–207. London: Sage.

Tang, Lijun, and Peidong Yang. 2011. Symbolic Power and the Internet: The Power of a 'Horse'. *Media, Culture & Society* 33 (5): 675–691.

Thompson, John B. 1995. *The Media and Modernity: A Social Theory of the Media.* Cambridge, UK: Polity.

Wynne, Brian. 1989. Sheep Farming After Chernobyl: A Case Study in Communicating Scientific Information. *Environment* 31 (2): 10–39.

Zafirau, Stephen. 2009. Audience Knowledge and the Everyday Lives of Cultural Producers in Hollywood. In *Production Studies: Cultural Studies of Media Industries*, ed. Vicki Mayer, Miranda J. Banks, and John T. Caldwell, 190–202. London: Routledge.

CHAPTER 9

East German Identity: A Never-Ending Story?

Daniel Kubiak

9.1 INTRODUCTION

While there is a question mark in the title of this chapter regarding East German identity, upon further thinking and writing on this topic, it seems the answer is already clear, and perhaps the question mark is not needed. After all, the German public regularly experience discussions about *East Germans* and *East German-ness*[1] concerning whether this social group

This chapter would not be possible without the support of an academic and personal network of people, who inspire and also criticize me and my thoughts. I have to thank Sandra Matthäus for discussing East Germany with me for more than six years in self-organized workshops, books and private meetings. Also, I have to thank Johannes Staemmler and Martin Weinel for having the idea for East-West Imitation Games. Last but not least I need to thank the whole Cardiff Team and all the local organizers, who set up the Imitation Game community, especially Martin Hall for giving me the technical support to run the Imitation Games.

D. Kubiak (✉)
Humboldt-Universität zu Berlin, Berlin, Germany
e-mail: daniel.kubiak@hu-berlin.de

© The Author(s) 2019
D. S. Caudill et al. (eds.), *The Third Wave in Science and Technology Studies*, https://doi.org/10.1007/978-3-030-14335-0_9

151

reacts differently to cultural developments, and providing explanations as to why East Germans are still less democratic and less integrated into normal German society. "Normal German," in this kind of discourse, seems to mean white, male, heterosexual and West German.

A recent example of such a discourse is the way public commentators reacted to the outcome of the German parliament elections in the early autumn of 2017. These elections were a big success for the right-wing-radical political party "Alternative für Deutschland" ("Alternative for Germany," hereinafter "AfD"), as it gained nearly 13 percent of the votes. This meant that for the first time in decades, a right-wing-radical party managed to win seats—92 out of 709—in the German parliament. In its attempts to explain this new and historically unusual situation, German political commentators focused on East Germany and in particular on East German male[2] voters (Bennhold 2018; Machowecz 2017). Interestingly, the majority (66 percent, or 3.9 of the 5.9 million voters) of the AfD voters live in the West German federal states.[3] However, because of the smaller East German population, this still means that in all East German federal states, the percentage of AfD voters was much higher than in the West German federal states (Burn-Murdoch et al. 2017). This fact was explained afterwards by dozens of newspaper commentaries, describing the East Germans as different from the normal voters. Some suggested that the "abnormality" or "otherness" of East Germans is linked to their experiences in an autocratic system. Others explained it with a lack of civic education in democratic societies. Some even suggested that the voting behavior of East Germans reflects a lack of gratefulness.

What all these articles demonstrate is that *East German* as an identity still exists, certainly in the heads of the journalists. Social scientists ought to recognize the constructed character of this identity, and they might point to structural social and economic disadvantages in the East to explain partially the observed voter behavior. Such reflexivity about East German identity is, however, largely missing in German public discourse that involves East Germany. Most political commentators "naturalize" the postulated East German identity and use it as an explanation for all perceived social and political ills supposedly afflicting the East. The asymmetry of this kind of political analysis becomes obvious when it is recognized that no one would invoke West German-ness to explain why 10–15 percent of West Germans in the federal states of Bavaria and Baden-Württemberg voted for the AfD in the regional elections.

In this debate, and in many other similar debates, we can see how East Germans are constructed as different kinds of Germans—Germans who are not normal like all other (West) Germans. And, as I will argue in this chapter, it is this *othering* of East Germans that shapes the self-image of East Germans. This is particularly interesting because one might think that nearly 30 years after the fall of the Berlin Wall, the notion of a distinct and somehow abnormal East German identity would disappear. This chapter illustrates that this is not happening. Instead of disappearing, we can see that the construction of East German identity is shifting. I will present my findings based on German-German Imitation Games with different East- and West German cohorts, beginning with cohorts born before 1970 until cohorts born after 1990.

9.2   Theories on (East German) Identity

The term "identity" has been used, and the concept researched, in a variety of academic disciplines, including psychology, political science, history, archaeology and sociology. It is therefore important to define identity as used in this chapter. The first theories in social science about identity were proposed at the beginning of the twentieth century by Charles C. Cooley (1902) and George Herbert Mead (2015 [1934]), in the context of the rise of modern society. The establishment of sociology as a science was connected to the idea of class and stratification, and also to the idea of individuality (Simmel 1983). In this context, identity is influenced or shaped by social interaction with the environment. Mead (2015 [1934]) introduced the distinction between *I* and *Me*, which makes the difference between two aspects of identity salient—the incorporated *I*, and a *Me* that is formed by the interaction with the external world. One could say that the *I*, as self-image, needs to be mirrored by the society, so the individual creates a representative *Me*. Until now, this distinction has been relevant for research on identity in general and is particularly relevant for this chapter because identity can only exist through the interaction with the other. According to Mead, Simmel and Cooley, the rise of individual identities (not group identities) has only occurred in the context of modernity. For those early social psychologists, identity was a fixed construct that develops in linear fashion over the course of a lifetime.

The onset of reflexive modernity (Beck and Bonß 2001) marks a new crisis[4] of identity, described by numerous scholars (Goffman 2012 [1975]; Giddens 1991; Taylor 2012; Jenkins 2008 [1996]; Abels 2010). At the end of the twentieth century, identity became a troubled concept, as some authors started to question its usefulness and some even refused to use it for social scientific purposes. They promoted research which apparently goes "beyond identity" and presented alternative terms like identification, categorization, self-understanding, social location, commonality, connectedness and groupness (Brubaker and Cooper 2000), or they introduced concepts like "belonging" (Savage et al. 2015) or "symbolic boundaries" (Lamont and Molnár 2002).

But there are also authors who have tried to fill the sociological concept of "identity" with new content. The concept of "Bastelidentität" (puzzle identity) (Eickelpasch and Rademacher 2013 [2004]) is one example. According to this view, people have the opportunity to puzzle their own identity together day by day. Keupp et al. (2002 [1999]) introduced another concept which they refer to as the "patchwork of identities." For these scholars, the process of identity construction seems to be a meaningful starting point to analyze identity in postmodern society. The construction of identity out of social categories is a daily process, and the building of one's identity never stops. For my research about German-German identities, I found this concept very helpful, since German-German identities are not only separated into East German and West German identities, but also into an array of regional and local identities. My assumption is that depending on the social context and situation, East German-ness as an identity is sometimes foregrounded and emphasized, and sometimes hidden from others. People can decide which part of their identity they want to use in which situation. It is possible to identify as East German, as German, and as a person from East Berlin at the same time. Some East Germans report that they have experienced their East German-ness for the first time when they left the geographical region of East Germany. To be East German is not considered to be important when they actually are in East Germany (Hacker et al. 2012). Therefore, Mead's concept is still useful, because young East Germans create their "Me" in social interactions in the West German environment.

Research on East German identity and the social construction of East German-ness has been a very important part of what is often referred to as "East Germany studies." This field has developed massively since 1990, and a large variety of descriptions of East German identities has been proposed. These range from the public perception of East Germans as "Untertanen" (subordinates/subjects) (Maaz 2010 [1990]), as members of under- and working class (Geißler 2014), as aggressive right wingers (Bittermann 1999), as the avant-garde of the precariat (Engler 2002) or as pioneers of the precariat (Buck and Hönke 2013), as minority in their own land (den Hertog 2004)—where the young "generation"[5] are called the "voiceless generation" (Staemmler 2011)—to depictions of East Germans, who are not integrated into the German elite (Mau 2012; Best and Vogel 2011; Deutsche Gesellschaft e.V. 2017), as "symbolic foreigners" (Pates and Schochow 2013), or of the East as a discursive intersection (Matthäus and Kubiak 2016). The last depiction is from a recent essay collection on "Der Osten" (The East), where some articles use the concept of "Orientalism" (Said 2012 [1978])—which basically includes the construction of "We" and "They" in a postcolonial context, but appears to be useful to inform research about East Germans (Wilke 2016; Straughn 2016; Ringel 2016).[6]

Most of the foregoing depictions assume or imply that East Germans are different from real or normal Germans. Even though some of these sources mention the concept of *othering* explicitly, the othering of East Germans remains mostly implicit in this literature. If West German is constructed as normal (Roth 2008; Quent 2015), what is it that makes it normal? Is there also a separate West German identity, or is being West German the same as being German?

Thomas Ahbe (2004) argues that West Germans have only been constructed recently in response to the German East—a space to which West Germans do not want to belong. This corresponds with the identity depictions mentioned above. Another interesting question is as to whether East Germans really are "symbolic foreigners," as Pates and Schochow (2013) argue. If true, it would mean that East Germans are essentially the same as non-German citizens, or "Menschen mit Migrationshintergrund" ("people with migration background").[7] Here it is worth asking why Germans with "Migrationshintergrund" are also still being othered by hegemonic discourses (Foroutan 2010; Terkessidis 2010; also Geißler 2014).

The central question asked and answered in this chapter is whether symbolic othering has influenced the self-identification of East Germans. To answer this question, I draw on data generated by playing a series of Imitation Games involving East- and West German participants. The Imitation Game research and its findings are discussed in the next section.

9.3   German-German Imitation Games

As other contributions in this volume explain the Imitation Game research method in great detail (see, e.g., Chap. 7), it is sufficient to keep the following exposition of the Imitation Game method brief. Each of the almost

200 Imitation Games played as part of this research project involved three participants. The three players were connected via the Internet using bespoke Imitation Game software, and each player was playing one of three available roles: Interrogator/Judge (hereafter "Judge"), Non-Pretender or Pretender. In any single Game, the Judge and the Non-Pretender always belonged to the same social category, while the Pretender belonged to another social category. With regard to the Imitation Games that were played as part of this research project, the two available social categories into which participants were divided in East German and West German.

While each individual Imitation Game involved three players, each individual participant was simultaneously involved in three Imitation Games, in which they played each role respectively. In other words, each participant played each of the three available roles respectively in the three Imitation Games in which they were involved.

The task of Judges was to ask questions related to the topic of the Imitation Game—in this case about "being East German" or "being West German" in the widest sense—and to decide which of the two anonymized answers they received in response to each question from the other two participants, whose exclusive task it was to provide answers, was written by the Pretender and which was written by the Non-Pretender. Non-Pretenders were instructed to "be themselves" and answer "naturally," while Pretenders had to produce an answer that imitated the answer that they believed a member of the other social category (the social category to which both Judge and Non-Pretender belonged) would give.

For example, an East German Judge could ask how the participants have personally experienced November 9, 1989, the day the Wall fell. While the East German Non-Pretender should be able to draw on personal experiences, the West German Pretender would be unable to draw on personal experiences and would have to rely on what they have heard from East Germans (if they know any), or they might have to imagine how an East German might have experienced the fall of the Wall. Because Judges in an Imitation Game only know that they are playing with someone from their own social category, and with someone from another social category, without having any more specific information, the questions that Judges ask usually focus on their collective experiences and knowledge, which also means the Imitation Game dialogues that are created in each Game reproduce popular discourses about the social categories or groups.

This feature of the Imitation Game method makes it potentially useful to generate interesting data about East and West Germans.

Data generation, that is, playing Imitation Games with East and West Germans, occurred in two stages. During the first stage, we ran 122 Imitation Games in 2014 in Berlin with 122 participants at the Humboldt University.[8] At this stage, we recruited participants according to their age so that we could assign each of them into one of six available cohorts: (1) those born before 1970 (n = 18), (2) those born between 1971 and 1980 (n = 18), (3) those born between 1981 and 1985 (n = 24), (4) those born between 1985 and 1988 (n = 22), (5) those born between 1989 and 1991 (n = 18), and (6) those born between 1991 and 1995 (n = 22). The participants were mostly, but not exclusively, students at Humboldt University.[9] In 2015, during the second stage of data generation, we ran another 72 Imitation Games, but this time we focused exclusively on those born between 1990 and 1995. Also, instead of running these Games in Berlin, we conducted them simultaneously in two cities—in Bremen, located in Northwest Germany, where the West German participants were recruited, and in Rostock, in Northeast Germany, where the East German participants were recruited.

In both stages, the participants were categorized as East or West German, according to the geographic place they were born. In most cases, this categorization worked very well, although we encountered some participants who had lived for significant periods of their lives in both geographic parts of Germany, or who had parents from both parts of Germany.

9.4   Results

I bring together two concepts. One concept is the identification of different *generations* within the German Democratic Republic (GDR), which was a separate state from 1949 until 1990, and was a part of the Eastern Bloc during the Cold War, from 1949 to 1990. The second concept is the so-called *Post-Wende-Generation* (Post-Unification-Generation). This is a reference to those who were born in the geographic area of the former GDR, that is, East Germany, without ever having lived in that socialist state. An interesting question to ask in this context is whether persons born after 1990 still develop a distinct East German identity?

9.4.1   Differences Between the Age Groups: Are There East German Generations and Why Is the "Post-Unification Generation" Interesting?

An analysis of the Imitation Games involving cohorts of East and West Germans was published in a German-language article in the edited volume about the so-called *Dritte Generation Ost*,[10] also sometimes referred to as *Wendekinder* (Children of Change). That paper focused on the East German participants and asked whether those born between 1973 and 1984 in the GDR really constituted a generation in the sociological sense (Kubiak and Weinel 2016).

The present research project responded to other sociological work on generations in East Germany. Thomas Ahbe and Rainer Gries (2006), for example, distinguish between six different GDR generations, spanning people born between 1892 (those born that year were in their 50s when the GDR was founded in 1949) and 1985.[11] The last of their postulated GDR generations, which was of particular interest to us, and referred to as *Wendekinder* ("Children of Change"), was described as very performance oriented and pragmatic, on the one hand, and as very disoriented about their roots, on the other. Their parents could not help them with orientation in their youth, because they were similarly confused and disoriented as well. Interestingly, the academic discourse about East German generations in general, and about *Wendekinder* in particular, appeared to be complemented and supported by real-life developments in Germany. In 2009, a network called *Dritte Generation Ost* (Third Generation East) was founded in Germany in an explicit effort to create a vehicle to represent the supposedly generation-specific interests of those born between 1975 and 1985, and to bring the idea of a generation of "Wendekinder" to life. This network has generated publicity and a widespread discourse about the heritage of GDR and the experiences of those born in the last years of the GDR's existence, who grew up in times of great societal change.

The first stage of our Imitation Game research was explicitly designed to focus on this last generation of GDR citizens and to ask if the label *generation* is appropriate. Put differently, the aim was to find out whether those born between 1973 and 1985 are really bound together through similar experiences and identities.

We used the method of qualitative content analyses (Mayring 2000) to analyze the questions the participants asked their counterparts. We concluded that there is no "Third Generation East" in terms, for example, of

Karl Mannheim's concept of generations (Mannheim 1964). Our main explanation is that there is simply too much divergence in the experiences of those born between 1973 and 1985. The members of this supposed generation were, in general terms, differently socialized in the GDR. In particular, their levels of integration into GDR institutions were very different. For example, a person born in the mid-1970s was integrated for at least 8 years into the GDR school system and likely had experiences in the Freie Deutsche Jugend (Free German Youth, the state-controlled youth organization). Also, the experience of the fall of the Berlin Wall was more important for the older members of that age group than for persons born after 1981, who tend to have very few personal memories of the fall of the Wall. We found similarities between those born in the late 1970s and in the early 1980s, respectively, but in the relevant categories (culture, language and institutions), we found significant differences. Thus the term "generation" is not sociologically useful to describe the age cohort born between 1973 and 1985, even though it seems to have some political use in mobilizing people, as well as shaping and influencing some of the inner-German discourses. In this age group, we also saw a change in the priority of questions. While the older age groups were predominantly asking questions trying to elicit knowledge about the GDR,[12] the younger age groups were asking more biographical questions.[13] Up to 89 percent of the questions in the older group were knowledge questions.[14] In the group of participants born between 1986 and 1988, only 48 percent of the questions were knowledge questions. This appears to confirm that the older age groups were much more integrated in the GDR society, as they were able to ask questions that required deep knowledge of life in the GDR—in order to ask the questions in the first place, and also to be able to answer such questions (Fig. 9.1).

Interestingly, the percentage of knowledge questions in the group of participants born after 1990 is high similar to the questions of the oldest cohort. The qualitative analysis reveals, however, that the content of the questions is very different, mainly because these questions were not about the time before 1990—knowledge about the GDR—but about the time after 1990—knowledge about post-reunified East Germany. Most interesting were the great number of questions where the participants did not really recognize that difference. There were questions about the time after 1990, but questions asked by those who grew up in the GDR were different from those asked by people born after 1990. These interesting findings generated a new research question: How do those born in the

160 D. KUBIAK

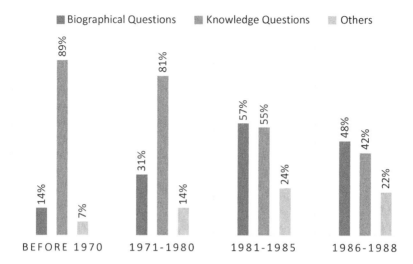

Fig. 9.1 Percentage of questions of number of all questions. Source: Kubiak and Weinel (2016)

geographical territory of the former GDR construct their identities, and how do they differ from those born in the GDR? Therefore, in the next section, I take a closer look at this age group born after 1990 and their construction of East German identity.

9.4.2   The Constitution of Identity of Young East Germans

Those born between 1990 and 1995 were selected because they were born in the new federal states in the territory of the former GDR, but not in the GDR. The question is whether this group is somehow linked to an East German identity. If the answer is yes, it shows that identification shifts from belonging to the GDR (e.g., because it's one's place of birth or the place where one grew up) to East Germany as a constructed region. While it was easy to say what and where the GDR was, it is not that easy to say what and where East Germany is now. Some regions in the federal state of Mecklenburg-West Pomerania can be seen as being more North than East, and some regions in Saxony-Anhalt and Thuringia can be seen as more central than east, geographically speaking. But the term "East German" describes more than a geographical heritage—it describes a constructed identity of Germans, mostly living in the new federal states founded in 1990, which before 1990 constituted the GDR. So normally when we say East Germany, we mean the former territory of the GDR; but the interesting question is whether the inhabitants there still see themselves as East Germans, in a cultural and not in a purely geographical sense.

Based on the approach introduced at the beginning of this chapter, I identified three narratives that refer to or construct an East German identity. Research on narratives, prominent in historical research, has grown in the social sciences in the last two decades. I interpret the narratives here using Margaret Somers's approach (Somers 1994). She presents four dimensions of narratives: ontological, public, conceptual and meta. For this chapter, public narratives, defined as "narratives attached to cultural and institutional formations larger than the single individual," are especially important (Somers 1994, 619). For the process of identity construction, one can identify specific reasons for an East German identity.

First, I propose that young people born and raised in the new federal states identify as East Germans through their knowledge about, and discussions with, their parents. This first narrative is based on the idea that identity is constructed by life experience and socialization (Mead 2015 [1934]; Cooley 1902; Keupp et al. 2002 [1999]). In the case of East Germany, the participants do not have any personal memories of the GDR, so the experiences of their parents are very important for them to establish differences between East and West. The second narrative is connected to the negative connotation of East German ancestry, as participants from the new federal states experience discrimination due to their East German-ness. In everyday life, it is possible to hide your ancestry if necessary, but in the Imitation Game this shared experience could be used to distinguish the East Germans from the other group. The participants got this self-image because of the existing public image of East Germans, and then it got reproduced within their social environment (Jenkins 2008 [1996]). As a third narrative, I analyze the West German view of East German identities, primarily created by *othering* East Germans as not part of the normal Germany. By challenging what it means to be East German, they are playing with their own identity and existing stereotypes. In this sense, East Germans are the *others* who ought to answer questions differently compared to "normal" Germans. In the next three sections, each of the three narratives will be discussed by drawing on one exemplary dialogue respectively from the Imitation Games.

9.4.3   The Influence of Parents on East German
Identification Processes

For those East German participants who were born after the demise of the GDR, their knowledge from and experiences with their parents created an identification process through socialization. The biographies of their parents were shared in their families, and the participants were influenced by their parents' reactions to certain situations. The social status of their parents was very important for resources and opportunities for the participants. I demonstrate this using a typical dialogue. An East German Judge asks: "Welche Sprachen haben deine Eltern in der Schule gelernt? [Which languages did your parents learn in school?]." As Judges need to record the reasons for asking each question, the Judge in this dialogue explained her choice as follows: "Die meisten hatten wahrscheinlich kein Russisch in westdeutschen Schulen [Most people probably did not learn Russian in West German schools]." The answers are different in length but also in content. The Pretender gives a long answer and appears to speak to the intentions of the judge:

Also da mein Vater jedes Mal im Restaurant eine 'Schpreit' statt 'Sprite' bestellt, kann ich definitiv bezeugen, dass er niemals in seinem Leben auch nur eine Stunde Englischunterricht besucht hat. Bei meiner Mutter sieht das schon besser aus. Wenn es um Fremdsprachen geht, werden allerdings nur bei Familienfeiern mal die paar Brocken Russisch zum Besten gegeben. Der ewig gleiche Satz minjasavut […] (keine Ahnung, wie man das schreibt).

[Since my father always orders a 'Shprite'[15] instead of 'Sprite' in restaurants, I can definitely say that he never attended a single English lesson in his life. Regarding my mother, things look a little bit better. But when it comes to foreign languages, they might just drop in some Russian words or phrases into the conversation at family parties. Always the same sentence: minjasavut […] (no idea how to write it).]

In contrast, the answer of the East German Non-Pretender is much shorter and speaks more directly to the intentions of the Judge:

Einmal natürlich Deutsch. Mein Vater hat zusätzlich Russisch gelernt, meine Mutter noch Französisch und Englisch, sie kommt aber auch aus West-Berlin.

[First of all, German. Additionally, my father learned Russian, my mother also French and English, but of course she is from West Berlin.]

In this case, the Judge appears to have little trouble in identifying the Pretender. This is mainly because she does not believe the "Schpreit" example. The Judge argues that the short answer seems to be more authentic:

> Das klingt nach der typischen Anekdote, die jedes ostdeutsche Kind von seinen Eltern kennt. Das klingt irgendwie unecht oder nacherzählt. Die zweite Antwort ist knapp und klingt 'echter'. Auch wenn unsere Eltern-Generation Englisch hatte, dann können die meisten, sofern sie das nicht im Job brauchen, auch kein Englisch mehr bzw. die Aussprache ist recht lustig. Selbst in Ostdeutschland gab es Englischunterricht, zumindest hatten es meine Eltern.
>
> *[That sounds like a typical anecdote every East German knows about their parents. It sounds somehow false or regurgitated. The second answer is brief and sounds more 'authentic.' But even if our parents' generation had English lessons in school, they usually cannot speak English, unless they need it professionally, and the pronunciation is kind of funny. Even in East Germany they had English lessons, at least my parents did.]*

Socialization is a very important part of the process of identity formation. In this and numerous other examples, it is obvious that participants identify themselves as East Germans by identifying with their parents. The intergenerational memory shared with the parents is stronger than their personal knowledge. The participants do not know much about GDR, but they know a lot about their parents, whom they identify as East Germans. Thus, we can see that this process of socialization still influences the identity of East Germans.

9.4.4   East German Identity Politics in Relation to Downgrading Experiences

In the Imitation Games, the participants who were categorized as East German were more successful in pretending to be West German than the other way around. They were also better at identifying the Pretenders. There is a public image of the meaning of being East German, and in the discourse East Germans react to that. East Germans are very often shown as people who vote for extremist parties (mostly of the right-wing variety) (Quent 2015), kill their babies (Heft 2013), have terrible dialects, and are relatively unfamiliar with the democratic and capitalist system (Edinger and Hallermann 2004). These and other mainly demeaning and negative stereotypes often come to the fore in jokes about East Germans, but they also become visible when we analyze how East Germans are portrayed in the national media (Meyen 2013; Ahbe et al. 2009). They still engage in identity politics, because in some way they need to belong to the East German social group, which in the context of studies focusing on German Muslims is called neo-identification (Amirpur 2011). They command a special kind of knowledge about East Germany that West Germans cannot match.

They are therefore more successful in the Imitation Game, as they create the narrative I will introduce with another typical dialogue. One East German Judge asked the following question during an Imitation Game: "Würdest du lieber in einem anderen Teil Deutschlands leben? Und wenn ja, in welchem? [Would you prefer to live in another part of Germany, and if so, in which one?]." The Judge asked this question because he believed that West Germans usually have a negative image of the East. This self-identity on the part of East Germans is constructed by the idea of how one feels perceived by the West as the other group. Thus, the judge outlines the intention as follows: "Ich denke, dass häufig die Annahme im Westen besteht, dass es im Osten nicht so schön ist, beziehungsweise, wenn man kann, man doch eher in den Westen geht. [I think that in the West, the assumption that it is not very nice in the East, or that if one could leave the East for the West, one is likely to do so, is quite prevalent]." The Pretender plays right into the hand of the Judge:

> Ja, später würde ich lieber in Süddeutschland leben, weil es dort bessere Jobs und weniger politisch sehr links oder sehr rechts eingestellte Menschen gibt. Allerdings sprechen die Leute im Süden auch kein verständlicheres Deutsch als hier und sind alle so katholisch, von daher müsste ich das noch mal überdenken.
>
> *[Yes, later on I want to live in Southern Germany as there are better jobs there and people are not as politically extreme to the left or the right. However, the people in the South do not speak a more intelligible German than they do here and they are all very Catholic. I might have to think it over.]*

It is interesting that in this attempt to be East German, the Pretender uses several stereotypes, such as extreme political attitudes, poor job opportunities and strong dialects. While she does not explicitly mention West Germany as a preferred destination, it is very clear from the content of the answer that the "Southern Germany" she refers to is located in the territory of the old West Germany. It is also interesting that the Imitation Game that generated this dialogue took place in two northern German port cities which are both facing economic difficulties. Bremen, the West German location, is struggling in many ways, yet this does not seem to prevent the Pretender from making use of the stereotype of the economically underdeveloped East.

Interestingly, the East German Non-Pretender also wants to leave her current place of residence, but the justification for this is entirely void of any pejorative stereotyping of the East: "Definitiv! Ich würde gerne wieder in Hamburg leben, da ich dort schon mal paar Jahre gewohnt habe [Definitely. I'd like to live in Hamburg again because I've already lived there for a few years]." In this particular exchange, the Judge appears to have no problem in identifying the Pretender due to their unreflective use of stereotypes:

> Ich denke, dass Antwort 1 der Imitator ist, da in dieser Antwort auch mit Vorurteilen gespielt wird. Es hört sich so an, als wenn ein 'Ostdeutscher' gern im reichen Westen leben würde und nur die religiöse Haltung stört, da es im Osten ja weniger gläubige Menschen gibt.
>
> *[I think Response 1 comes from the Pretender because this answer also plays with stereotypes. It sounds like an 'East German' wants to live in the rich West; only the religiosity there is disturbing, as there are fewer religious people in the East.]*

This narrative, while surfacing in the Imitation Games, is mostly derived from a discourse that is particularly entrenched in the media. The East is usually depicted as worse than the West in the eyes of the German public, but East Germans also employ this denigration of the new federal states to create their self-perception. In the next section, I will try to explain this by focusing on the narrative of *othering* the East.

9.4.5   West German as the Norm: The Others Are the East Germans

In the Imitation Games, it was striking that West German Judges attempted to construct the stereotype of an East German identity instead of asking questions about their own group. Identifying East Germans due to their "otherness" was apparently considered to be easier than trying to identify "genuine" West German responses. This implies that there is an image of how the others would answer certain questions. One example in the Imitation Games is the attitude toward extreme right-wing opinions or movements. The assumption is that East Germany is homogeneously different from the norm in this regard. For example, in the following dialogue, the West German judge asks[16]:

> In letzter Zeit wurden in Freital und Tröglitz Asylbewerberheime angegriffen, die NSU Terrorzelle hat aus Zwickau heraus agiert und in Dresden spaziert Pegida jeden Montag, ihre rassistische Hetze kundgebend. Ist diese zunehmende Fremdenfeindlichkeit über eine Benachteiligung der neuen Bundesländer nach der Wende, oder über eine fehlende Aufarbeitung des 3. Reichs in der ehemaligen DDR zu erklären?
>
> *[Recently, the accommodations of asylum seekers in Freital and Tröglitz (a town and a village respectively located in Southern Saxony) were attacked. The (far-right) terrorist group NSU operated out of Zwickau (a city in Saxony), and in Dresden (the capital of Saxony) PEGIDA (a right-wing social movement) parades through the city every Monday, showcasing their racist propaganda. Can this increasing xenophobia in the East be explained by the disadvantages of the new federal states after reunification, or does it originate from the GDR's failure to learn the lessons of the Third Reich?]*

The intention behind asking this question is explained by the Judge as follows:

> Da sich Menschen häufig mit der ihr eigenen Bezugsgruppe solidarisieren, würde ich vermuten, dass sie die Schuld auf der jeweils anderen Seite suchen. Hier gibt es nur zwei klare Antwortmöglichkeiten (was sicher zu undifferenziert ist, um die Frage wirklich zu beantworten).
>
> *[As people mostly express solidarity with their own peer group, I would suspect that they lay blame on the other side. There are just two possible clear answers (which is surely too undifferentiated to answer the question properly).]*

For the Judge, it is patently obvious that the East has bigger problems with right-wing extremism than the West. The judge is only interested in the reasons for this fact. In an intersectional analysis, one might ask if right-wing extremism is really only a problem of the East. However, the Pretender (in this case, an East German) does not question this assumption and answers as follows:

Wahrscheinlich haben beide Aspekte mit dem Thema zu tun, aber über die Aufarbeitung des Dritten Reiches in der DDR weiß ich nicht besonders viel. Ich kann nur so viel vermuten: dadurch, dass die DDR-Bürger in ihrem Staat eingesperrt waren, hatten sie natürlich auch nicht viel Kontakt mit unterschiedlichen Kulturen. Und so entsteht Angst vor Fremden. Außerdem sind viele DDR-Bürger nach der Wende unzufrieden gewesen. Viele haben ihren Job verloren oder waren unzufrieden, dass einfach ein neues System über sie 'gestülpt' wurde. So entsteht auch Hass gegenüber anderen.

[Perhaps both aspects are related to this topic. But I do not know much about how the Third Reich was dealt with in the GDR. I can only suggest that GDR citizens were imprisoned in their country and that's why they did not have much contact with other cultures. This creates fear of foreigners. Additionally, many GDR citizens were frustrated after the transition. Many lost their jobs and were dissatisfied that a new system was simply imposed on them and they had to accept it. That's also how hate of others is generated.]

The West German, who was not supposed to pretend, answers in a similar vein:

Ich könnte mir eher vorstellen, dass das über die Benachteiligung der neuen Bundesländer zu erklären ist. Viele verstehen es glaube ich nicht, wieso die Flüchtlinge auf unsere Hilfe angewiesen sind bzw. wieso die Gelder für sie vorgesehen sind bzw. ausgegeben werden und nicht für die Menschen, die in den neuen Bundesländern leben. Viele sind in ihrem Denken so eingeschränkt, und einen Sündenbock findet sich ja immer.

[I can only imagine that it can be explained with the discrimination of the former East German federal states. I believe that many do not understand why the refugees need our help. Also, they do not understand why money is allocated to these people instead of being given to the new federal states. Many are very limited in their thinking, and a scapegoat can always be found.]

In this dialogue, the Judge is able to identify the Pretender and explains the decision as follows:

Unwissen über die Geschichte der DDR + vage Vermutungen der ersten Person. Die zweite Person dagegen scheint sich mit der Situation auseinandergesetzt zu haben und ist in ihrer Antwort deutlich präziser.

[No knowledge about the history of the GDR + vague assumptions by the first person (pretender). The second person (non-pretender) seems to have thought through the situation and is much more precise in their answer.]

Without any reference to West Germany, this dialogue tries—and succeeds—in identifying the West German by talking about the East. Strikingly, the West German here is assumed to be the one who has better and more reflective knowledge about the East, and especially about the GDR. The West is viewed as normal, enlightened and well educated, and the participants do not appear to see the risk that right-wing positions could also gain strength in the West.[17] The West German constructs a self-definition by treating the East as the *other*. It seems that without the East there is no West, and therefore no norm. It is significant that the West German judges primarily asked questions about East German topics—on which subject one could argue they were not experts. Questions about the uniqueness of West Germany were not nearly as common.

9.5   Conclusion

The analysis of the different datasets of the Imitation Games (played in Berlin, Bremen and Rostock) supports the notion of a shift in what it means to identify as East German. While the questions of the age groups born in the GDR heavily reflect lived experience in the GDR, the content of the questions for the younger age groups shifts toward experiences of being *othered* and disparaged as East Germans. Among the older age groups, knowledge questions dominate, while the younger age groups predominantly ask biographical questions. Among those born between 1990 and 1995, we find three narratives that offer clues as to how an East German identity is constructed and constituted. Their identity is linked to GDR due to the biographies of the parents and their parents' special knowledge about being in the GDR. The three narratives hint at the formation of East German identities through the socialization of the parents, the disparagement of "East German" biographies, and the othering of East Germans. The most interesting finding is that the age group born between 1990 and 1995 experiences a *double othering*: when they are addressed as East Germans, this identity is intrinsically linked to the existence of the GDR, even though they have never lived in that country. They have to identify with their parents to get in touch with their East German-ness without having ever been former citizens of the GDR. This means that while they are not real East Germans like their parents, they are also not seen as normal Germans. Put differently, they are constructed as both not real Germans and not real East Germans. This is, by the way, a very interesting parallel to the children and grandchildren of migrants in Germany (see Kubiak 2017; Foroutan and Kubiak 2018). Like second- and third-generation immigrants, young East Germans are caught in a dilemma: on the one hand, they might want to move away from attributions of "being East Germans," but, on the other hand, their specific knowledge and expertise of East Germany, and about being East German, offer an easily accessible repository on which they can rely.

Notes

1. Terms like "East Germans," "West Germans" or indeed "East German-ness" are problematic constructs that can easily be criticized for constructing a version of reality that is contestable and is in fact contested. They can also have very different meanings in different contexts: East German, for example, can refer to a person in or from the "politico-geographic" region of Germany that is called East Germany, which is congruous with the territory of the former German Democratic Republic but the term can also be used to convey certain cultural assumptions and stereotypes. While these terms will only be occasionally highlighted through the use of italics, this does not mean that they are used in a "realist" sense.
2. This is because the majority of AfD voters are male.
3. Germany has 16 federal states. Only five of them are in the territory of the former German Democratic Republic. One of them is Berlin, of which a large part belonged to West Germany before the fall of the Berlin Wall.
4. The first crisis arose with the beginning of the industrial revolution and enlightened societies.
5. Concerning the problem of separating East Germans by generations, I wrote an article with Martin Weinel arguing that there is no "Third Generation East," as it is defined by the founders of the network. We would divide this cohort in two generations (Kubiak and Weinel 2016).
6. A much more detailed overview of research about East Germans, combined with the idea of calling East Germans the "subaltern," can be found in a very informative article by Raj Kollmorgen (2011).
7. "Menschen mit Migrationshintergrund" ("people with migration background") is the official term, in the national statistics, for people who have no German citizenship or familial relations to at least one parent with no German citizenship.
8. Because each individual participant was involved in three Imitation Games simultaneously, and each Imitation Game involves three participants, the number of Imitation Games equals the number of participants. The *we*, which appears in the sentence, will be used in this chapter on occasions to emphasize the collaborative nature of data generation. Both stages were planned and conducted by myself and Martin Weinel.

9. The age cohorts were "conveniently" constructed by the researchers in accordance to the available number of participants with different ages. Given that most participants were students, it was easier to find participants born between 1985 and 1995 than older participants.

10. The "Third Generation East" is a network of young East and West Germans founded in 2010. The idea of the founders is to bring East Germans into the public discourse to influence German discourse on East and West Germany. See, for example: https://www.huffingtonpost.com/john-feffer/germanys-third-generation_b_4026560.html.

11. The first five generations are called *mißtrauische Patriarchen* (distrustful patriarchs) (1892–1916), *Aufbaugeneration* (construction/rebuilding generation) (1925–1935), the *funktionierende Generation* (functioning generation) (1935–1948), the *integrierte Generation* (integrated generation) (1950–1959), and the *entgrenzte Generation* (delimitated generation) (1960–1972).

12. "How much was a bun in the GDR?" (Question in the age group 1981–1985), or "What was the name of a character in a children's magazine, and describe what kind of character it was?" (Question in the age group 1981–1985).

13. "How long was your mother at home after your birth, before she went back to work?" (Question in the age group 1981–1985).

14. The same question could be coded in different ways, so a question can be *biographical* and *knowledge* at the same time.

15. 'Shp' represents a typical pronunciation of 'sp' by someone speaking with a Saxon dialect, that is, a version of German that is spoken across the two East German federal states of Saxony and Saxony-Anhalt.

16. This Imitation Game took place on July 1, 2015, two months before a large number of refugees came to Germany (called the "summer of migration").

17. The election results of the right-wing-radical party AfD in March 2016 in the West German federal states of Baden-Württemberg and Rhineland-Palatinate provide evidence to challenge this assumption.

REFERENCES

Abels, H. 2010. *Identität*. Wiesbaden: Verlag für Sozialwissenschaften.

Ahbe, T. 2004. Die Konstruktion der Ostdeutschen. Diskursive Spannungen, Stereotype und Identitäten seit 1989. *Aus Politik und Zeitgeschichte* 41–42: 12–22.

Ahbe, T., and R. Gries. 2006. Die Generationen der DDR und Ostdeutschlands. Ein Überblick. *Berliner Debatte Initial* 17 (4): 90–109.

Ahbe, T., R. Gries, and W. Schmale. 2009. *Die Ostdeutschen in den Medien. Das Bild von den Anderen nach 1990*. Leipzig: Leipziger Univ.-Verl.

Amirpur, K. 2011. Die Muslimisierung der Muslime. In *Manifest der Vielen. Deutschland erfindet sich neu*, ed. H. Sezgin, 197–204. Berlin: Blumenbar-Verl.

Beck, U., and W. Bonß. 2001. *Die Modernisierung der Moderne*. Frankfurt am Main: Suhrkamp.

Bennhold, K. 2018. One Legacy of Merkel? Angry East German Men Fueling the Far Right. *New York Times*, November 11. Accessed November 7, 2018. https://www.nytimes.com/2018/11/05/world/europe/merkel-east-germany-nationalists-populism.html.

Best, H., and L. Vogel. 2011. Politische Eliten im vereinten Deutschland. Stukturen, Einstellungen und Handlungsbedingungen. In *Ostdeutschland und die Sozialwissenschaften. Bilanz und Perspektiven 20 Jahre nach der (Wieder-) vereinigung*, ed. A. Lorenz, 120–152. Wiesbaden: Barbara Budrich.

Bittermann, K. 1999. *Der rasende Mob. Die Ossis zwischen Selbstmitleid und Raserei*. Berlin: Edition Tiamat.

Brubaker, R., and F. Cooper. 2000. Beyond "Identity". *Theory and Society* 29: 1–47.

Buck, E., and J. Hönke. 2013. Pioniere der Prekarität. Ostdeutsche als Avantgarde des neuen Arbeitsmarktregimes. In *Der "Ossi". Mikropolitische Studien über einen symbolischen Ausländer*, ed. R. Pates and M. Schochow, 23–53. Wiesbaden: Springer VS.

Burn-Murdoch, J., B. Ehrenberg-Shannon, S. Bernard, H. Maier-Borst, and M. Stabe. 2017. Germany's Election Results in Charts and Maps. *Financial Times*. https://www.ft.com/content/e7c7d918-a17e-11e7-b797-b61809486fe2.

Cooley, C.H. 1902. *Human Nature and Social Order*. New York: Scribner's.

den Hertog, F. 2004. *Minderheit im eigenen Land? Zur gesellschaftlichen Position der Ostdeutschen in der gesamtdeutschen Realität*. Frankfurt am Main: Campus Verlag.

Deutsche Gesellschaft e.V. 2017. *Ostdeutsche Eliten. Träume, Wirklichkeiten und Perspektiven*. Accessed November 13, 2017. http://www.deutsche-gesellschaft-ev.de/images/Deutsche_Gesellschaft_eV_Broschuere_Ostdeutsche_Eliten.pdf.

Edinger, M., and A. Hallermann. 2004. *Politische Kultur in Ostdeutschland. Die Unterstützung des politischen Systems am Beispiel Thüringens*. Frankfurt am Main: Lang.

Eickelpasch, R., and C. Rademacher. 2013 [2004]. *Identität*. Bielefeld: Transcript.

Engler, W. 2002. *Die Ostdeutschen als Avantgarde*. Berlin: Aufbau Verlag.

Foroutan, N. 2010. Neue Deutsche, Postmigranten und Bindungs-Identitäten. Wer gehört zum neuen Deutschland. *Aus Politik und Zeitgeschichte* 46–47: 9–15.

Foroutan, N., and D. Kubiak. 2018. Ausschluss und Abwertung. Was Muslime und Ostdeutsche verbindet. *Blätter für deutsche und internationale Politik* 63: 93–102.

Geißler, R. 2014. *Die Sozialstruktur Deutschlands*. Wiesbaden: Springer VS.

Giddens, A. 1991. *Modernity and Self-Identity. Self and Society in the Late Modern Age*. Stanford: University Press.

Goffman, E. 2012 [1975]. *Stigma. Über die Techniken der Bewältigung beschädigter Identität*. Frankfurt am Main: Suhrkamp.

Hacker, M., S. Maiwald, and J. Staemmler. 2012. Dritte Generation Ost. Wer wir sind, was wir wollen. In *Dritte Generation Ost. Wer wir sind, was wir wollen*, ed. M. Hacker, S. Maiwald, J. Staemmler, J. Enders, A. Lettrari, H. Petzcker, et al., 9–16. Berlin: Christoph Links.

Heft, K. 2013. Kindsmord als Phänomen Ostdeutschlands? – Eine Analyse medialer Diskursverschiebungen. In *Mörderinnen. Künstlerische und mediale Inszenierungen weiblicher Verbrechen*, ed. H. Lee and I. Maurer Queipo, 305–327. Bielefeld: Transcript.

Jenkins, R. 2008 [1996]. *Social Identity*. London and New York: Routledge.

Keupp, H., T. Ahbe, W. Gmür, R. Höfer, B. Mitzscherlich, W. Kraus, and F. Straus. 2002 [1999]. *Identitätskonstruktionen. Das Patchwork der Identitäten in der Spätmoderne*. Reinbek: Rowohlt Taschenbuch Verlag.

Kollmorgen, R. 2011. Subalternisierung. Formen und Mechanismen der Missachtung Ostdeutscher nach der Vereinigung. In *Diskurse der deutschen Einheit. Kritik und Alternativen*, ed. R. Kollmorgen, F.T. Koch, and H.-L. Dienel, 301–359. Wiesbaden: VS Verlag für Sozialwissenschaften.

Kubiak, D. 2017. Der Fall "Ostdeutschland". "Einheitsfiktion" als Herausforderung für die Integration am Fallbeispiel der Ost-West-Differenz. *Zeitschrift für Vergleichende Politikwissenschaft*. https://doi.org/10.1007/s12286-017-0372-7.

Kubiak, D., and M. Weinel. 2016. DDR-Generationen revisited. Gibt es einen Generationszusammenhang der "Wendekinder"? In *Die Generation der Wendekinder. Elaboration eines Forschungsfeldes*, ed. A. Lettrari, C. Nestler, and N. Troi-Boeck, 107–129. Wiesbaden: Springer VS.

Lamont, M., and V. Molnár. 2002. The Study of Boundaries in the Social Sciences. *Annual Review of Sociology* 28: 167–195.

Maaz, H.-J. 2010 [1990]. *Der Gefühlsstau. Psychogramm einer Gesellschaft*. München: C.H. Beck.

Machowecz, M. 2017. "Oh, Ostmann!". *ZEIT*. Accessed November 7, 2018. https://www.zeit.de/politik/deutschland/2017-09/ostdeutschland-maenner-wut-frauen-ddr.

Mannheim, K. 1964. Das Problem der Generationen. In *Wissenssoziologie. Auswahl aus dem Werk*, Soziologische Texte, Bd. 28, ed. K. Mannheim and K.H. Wolff, 509–565. Berlin [u.a.]: Luchterhand.

Matthäus, S., and D. Kubiak, eds. 2016. *Der Osten. Neue sozialwissenschaftliche Perspektiven auf einen Gegenstand jenseits von Verurteilung und Verklärung*. Wiesbaden: Springer VS.

Mau, S. 2012. Ossifreie Zone. *ZEIT*, 16/2012. Accessed November 13, 2014. http://www.zeit.de/2012/16/P-Ostdeutsche-Elite.

Mayring, P. 2000. Qualitative Content Analyses. *FOS Forum Qualitative Social Research, 1* (2). Accessed November 15, 2017. http://nbn-resolving.de/urn:nbn:de:0114-fqs0002204.

Mead, G.H. 2015 [1934]. *Mind, Self, and Society.* Chicago: University of Chicago Press.

Meyen, M. 2013. *Wir haben freier gelebt. Die DDR im kollektiven Gedächtnis der Deutschen.* Berlin; Bielefeld: De Gruyter; Transcript.

Pates, R., and M. Schochow, eds. 2013. *Der "Ossi". Mikropolitische Studien über einen symbolischen Ausländer.* Wiesbaden: Springer VS.

Quent, M. 2015. Sonderfall Ost–Normalfall West? In *Rechtsextremismus und "Nationalsozialistischer Untergrund": Interdisziplinäre Debatten, Befunde und Bilanzen*, ed. W. Frindte, D. Geschke, N. Haußecker, and F. Schmidtke, 99–117. Wiesbaden: Springer VS.

Ringel, F. 2016. Neue Gegenwärtigkeiten in Hoyerswerda: Zur Anthropologie und Zukunft Ostdeutschlands. In *Der Osten. Neue sozialwissenschaftliche Perspektiven auf einen Gegenstand jenseits von Verurteilung und Verklärung*, ed. S. Matthäus and D. Kubiak, 141–167. Wiesbaden: Springer VS.

Roth, K.S. 2008. Der Westen als 'Normal-Null'. Zur Diskurssemantik von 'ostdeutsch' und 'westdeutsch'. In *Diskursmauern. Aktuelle Aspekte der sprachlichen Verhältnisse zwischen Ost und West*, ed. K.S. Roth and M. Wienen, 69–89. Bremen: Hempen-Verlag.

Said, E. 2012 [1978]. *Orientalism. Western Conceptions of the Orient.* London: Penguin Books.

Savage, M., G. Bagnall, and B. Longhurst. 2015. *Globalization and Belonging.* London: SAGE.

Simmel, G. 1983. *Schriften zur Soziologie. Eine Auswahl.* Frankfurt am Main: Suhrkamp.

Somers, M.R. 1994. The Narrative Constitution of Identity: A Relational and Network Approach. *Theory and Society* 23: 605–649.

Staemmler, J. 2011, August 18. Wir, die stumme Generation. ZEIT, 34/2011. Accessed November 7, 2018. http://www.zeit.de/2011/34/S-Generation-Ost.

Straughn, J. 2016. Wo "der Osten" liegt. Umrisse und Ambivalenzen eines verschwundenen und verschwindenden Landes. In *Der Osten. Neue sozialwissenschaftliche Perspektiven auf einen Gegenstand jenseits von Verurteilung und Verklärung*, ed. S. Matthäus and D. Kubiak, 195–223. Wiesbaden: Springer VS.

Taylor, C. 2012. *Quellen des Selbst. Die Entstehung der neuzeitlichen Identität.* 8th Aufl. Frankfurt am Main: Suhrkamp.

Terkessidis, M. 2010. *Interkultur.* Berlin: Suhrkamp.

Wilke, C. 2016. Östlich des Rechtsstaats: Vergangenheitspolitik, Recht und Identitätsbildung. In *Der Osten. Neue sozialwissenschaftliche Perspektiven auf einen Gegenstand jenseits von Verurteilung und Verklärung*, ed. S. Matthäus and D. Kubiak, 169–193. Wiesbaden: Springer VS.

CHAPTER 10

The Game with Identities: Identifications and Categorization as Social Practice

Justus Bauch, Celia Bouali, Teresa Hoffmann, Ida Lübben,
Lara Danyel, Nuriani Hamdan, Daria Kappel,
Yannik Markhof, Bastian Neuhauser, Bafta Sarbo,
Laura Schlagheck, Philip Seitz, Leon Spiegelberg,
Aylin Yavaş, Rosa Zylka, Daniel Kubiak,
and Henrik Schultze

10.1   INTRODUCTION

This chapter presents some results of a students' research class at Humboldt-Universität zu Berlin's Department of Social Sciences. More than 40 students attended the class. The idea was to give students the

J. Bauch (✉) • C. Bouali • T. Hoffmann • I. Lübben • N. Hamdan
D. Kappel • Y. Markhof • B. Sarbo • L. Schlagheck • P. Seitz • L. Spiegelberg
A. Yavaş • R. Zylka • D. Kubiak • H. Schultze
Humboldt-Universität zu Berlin, Berlin, Germany
e-mail: celia.bouali@cms.hu-berlin.de; nuriani.hamdan@hu-berlin.de;
daria@kappel-web.com; yannik.markhof@hu-berlin.de; bafta.sarbo@hu-berlin.de;
aylin.yavas@ufuq.de; daniel.kubiak@hu-berlin.de; henrik.schultze@hu-berlin.de

L. Danyel
Berlin, Germany

© The Author(s) 2019   175
D. S. Caudill et al. (eds.), *The Third Wave in Science and Technology Studies*, https://doi.org/10.1007/978-3-030-14335-0_10

opportunity to create their own research questions and answer them by using self-collected data. In advance, we had already decided that the data would be collected with the help of Imitation Games. The overarching goal of this seminar was to consider different aspects of the rather broad term "identity." Therefore, we invited the students to think about possible theories of identity and asked them to develop questions that could be connected with "identity" in a fruitful way. We ended up with six research questions for six Imitation Games in December 2015 in Berlin. In this chapter, three of the students' approaches will be presented very briefly. The research papers were up to 120 pages long and the students presented a very detailed report on their research project. The results have necessarily been abbreviated for this chapter.

To begin with, we would like to present some motivations for choosing the seminar topic and the following research. Since 2015, German society has been challenged by various questions about identity. In the "summer of migration" of 2015, nearly one million asylum seekers came to Germany. Chancellor Angela Merkel welcomed the mostly Muslim group, who had often been treated badly on their journey through the so-called West Balkan route (which ended at the main train station of Budapest, as Hungary was the first EU country on route). This large number of refugees challenged German ideas about what society should be and what constitutes German identity. Germany had not seen similar solidarity for incoming people since perhaps 1989–1990, when thousands of East Germans came to West Germany to seek a better life there. At the same time, right-wing movements like PEGIDA[1] and HOGESA,[2] and the Alternative for Germany (AfD), a right-wing party, became more and more popular. The AfD started to win one election after another and was elected to the German national parliament in September 2017.

Thinking and speaking about identity nowadays is common among Germans. One task of sociologists, then, is to analyze what the concept of identity means both theoretically and empirically. As a foundation for the students' research, we developed a conceptual framework of identity (together with the students), which is very much informed by the work of Richard Jenkins (2008), Michèle Lamont and Virág Molnár (2002), and Rogers Brubaker (2004). The idea was to discuss the concept of identity not as an entity but as the simultaneous interplay of internal identification

B. Neuhauser
Sciences Po, Paris, France
e-mail: bastian@neuhauser-online.de

and external categorization (Jenkins 2008, 44). People interact with each other at the boundary of difference and similarity, which is in turn strongly related to practices (Jenkins 2008, 38). Lamont and Molnár were concerned with the relationship between social and symbolic boundaries, which also helps us understand how differences of social categories are constructed (Lamont 1992; Lamont and Molnár 2002). This brings us to Rogers Brubaker's concept of "ethnicity without groups" (2004), which is a plea for a cognitive perspective on ethnicity:

> [C]ognitive perspectives address the social and mental processes that sustain the vision and division of the social world in racial, ethnic, or national terms. Rather than take "groups" as basic units of analysis, cognitive perspectives shift analytical attention to "group-making" and "grouping" activities such as classification, categorization, and identification. (Brubaker 2004, 79)

Interestingly, the imitation game as a method occupies a rather ambiguous position in this regard, as researchers look for those very practices like "group-making" and "grouping" at the same time as they actively group their participants.

Nevertheless, the three concepts mentioned above have greatly helped to connect the notion of identity with empirical research using Imitation Games. While not unproblematic, we sorted a group of people into two categories (such as born and bred Berliners vs. newcomers) and had them interact in a computer game. When analyzing the data, it was therefore crucial to reflect on the ways we were, to a certain degree, producing social groups and risking that these groups would not correspond to the social reality of the participants. However, in order to investigate what happens when people build "us-and-them" groups, we had to generate the kind of artificial social situation that the Imitation Game requires. Regarding our aim to learn more about how individuals are *doing* identity, this approach worked quite well.

The student groups then thought about the following research questions: Is there an academic identity by students with or without academic parents? Can the subcultures of punks and hip hoppers find more collective distinctions from mainstream society or do the differences between these two subcultural groups predominate? Another question focused on different Latin American identities and compared South American people living in South America with those who live in Germany.

For this chapter, we focus on the following three student groups: (1) those researching the identity of students born in Berlin or not, (2) those investigating Muslim identities and anti-Muslim racism, and (3) those

concerned with the construction of whiteness via symbolically placing
Black Germans outside the national collective. We also had some students
working as research observers, which means that they did not have their
own research project, but they observed and reviewed the research process
of a student group. The goal of these research observers was to evaluate
and critique the method of the Imitation Game. One of the observers will
also present her critique in this chapter.

10.2   STUDENT PROJECTS: BERLIN, MUSLIM IDENTITY, WHITENESS

10.2.1   The Construction of a Berlin Identity Among Students

In September 2017, a group of approximately 100 activists and artists
occupied the well-known Berlin theatre Volksbühne am Rosa-Luxemburg-
Platz. What had been rumored among left-wing groups and the artistic
scene in Berlin, following the widely discussed appointment of Chris
Dercon as Theatre Manager, was put into action:

> Using our transmedia theatre production we want to send a message against
> the current politics within the field of culture and urban development.
> Additionally, to the unapologetic and extreme expulsion of the resident
> population there is an equally strong banishment of cultural institutions
> such as theatres, night clubs and studio communities in favor of a mass tour-
> ism and profit orientated cultural scene. (Press statement of the so-called
> initiative "vb61-12"[3])

The Volksbühne controversy is not alone; discussions on spaces for participation—and particularly, on the legitimacy of political decisions pertaining to cultural productions, cultural sights, and the development of
inner-city spaces—are becoming more frequent. Symbolic fights over
authenticity and the initial identity of Berlin seem omnipresent in public
discourse (as shown in the documentary "Wem gehört Berlin?"), political
initiatives, and city marketing strategies ("be Berlin"[4] or "das B"[5]). Despite
their broad reach, these marketing campaigns can be interpreted as a
"proxy war" and are interwoven with the more fundamental and emotional questions: "Who belongs to the city? or Who owns the city?" Such
strategies emphasize Berlin's image as an open-minded city where everyone has the freedom of (identity) choice due to the cultural and social
diversity for which Berlin is famous. The social and economic realities,

however, suggest otherwise—through the process of gentrification, discrepancies exist, and grow, between the lived reality of Berlin citizens and the images transmitted by the media.

We understand universities as spaces where these emotional questions are being discussed on a daily basis, where debates on Berlin's authenticity and identity, and the right to the city, may freely be explored. Therefore, our analysis focused on individuals studying in Berlin. The project uses Imitation Games to answer the research question of whether students socialized in Berlin use the city in a different way to construct and communicate their identities, compared to students who moved to the city due to their studies or due to secondary reasons. What knowledge about Berlin identifies "Berliners" and "New Berliners?" As the ascribed pioneers of gentrification, students play a central role in this complex. They are identified as a main cause of gentrification thanks to high mobility and cohabitation constellations, yet this group is also being affected by rising rents and a competitive housing market.

We now describe the main concepts that were used to develop the categories, as well as to highlight them. Identities are products of social processes. Jenkins (2008) differentiates between individual and collective social identities. Even though individual identity and social identity are entangled, it does not mean that they are congruent. While individual identity stands for the singularity and particularity of a personality, social identity describes commonalities and the belonging to a group (Jenkins 2008, 24ff.). Actions, expressed mentalities, and symbols as "performed" individual identity need to be validated by the social environment to become part of a larger understanding of the self. Social identity requires approved coherence and authenticity.

To understand identification in relation to a place, the concept of *elective belonging* by Savage et al. (2005) was integrated into the individualized concept of identity and identification. This concept of Savage et al. articulates spatial attachment, social position, and forms of connectivity to other places. By analyzing the distinction between the "born and bred" locals and incoming migrants in different cities, Savage et al. (2005, 29) come to the conclusion that both groups attach to the city very differently. While the migrant incomers are forced to become acquainted with the city and to build up their new social network, the locals are less likely to have a sense of belonging (Savage et al. 2005, 37ff.). Because incomers *choose* their place of residence, they have a strong feeling of attachment. The possibility to participate and to shape a place are meant by *elective belonging*.

What happens if the feeling of belonging is missing? Savage et al. ascertained that the locals dissociate from their place, especially with respect to the changes and innovations with which they cannot identify (Savage et al. 2005, 49).

On the basis of the concepts of *identity* and *elective belonging* by Jenkins and Savage et al., the research question could be analyzed with respect to current conflicts surrounding gentrification, displacement, and the feeling of *who owns the city.*

The Imitation Games were conducted at the Institute of Social Sciences at the Humboldt-Universität zu Berlin. To recruit as many participants as possible, we decided to limit the options to students from universities in Berlin. The group attending was categorized into "Berliners" and "New Berliners," both defined by their place of birth and graduation. Thirty participants were recruited. In the context of the first Imitation Game, 16 people played with each other, and in the second, 14 people attended. Both games lasted approximately two hours. Afterwards, all participants had the opportunity to attend a group discussion in which they could talk about their experiences, impressions, and their opinions on the topic in general.

The categories *mobility, identification, groups, categorization,* and *drawing the line* were easy to imitate. Because the participants accessed factual knowledge as well as knowledge obtained through experiences and memories, the dimensions of implicit and explicit knowledge were the crucial factors to answer the question of research. Judges who tried to identify the Pretenders by testing their *explicit knowledge* (factual knowledge) mostly failed, because for New Berliners, it is easy to adopt that knowledge.

The category *knowledge through experience and memory* turned out to be essential for answering the research question. This category, which was first created intuitively, is consistent with the concept of *tacit knowledge* by Collins and Evans (2010). Tacit knowledge is understood to be knowledge which has not or cannot be made explicit (Collins and Evans 2010, 85). Who has access to that kind of knowledge? "*Knowledge is a collective phenomenon that depends on tacit knowledge that can only be acquired* via *socialization into the relevant community*" (Collins et al. 2015, 4). Accordingly, Berliners have different tacit knowledge from that of "New Berliners." The majority of participants (high number of cases: 219) were trying to reveal identity through this vague concept of *more than factual knowledge.* Explicit and tacit knowledge are almost identical but the difference of the *more* was difficult to reveal, and most of the time, the participants tried to catch it through childhood memories or other memories from the past. Therefore, "New Berliners" may be able to *know theoretically* but only Berliners have the ability to *practically know/can*. The material shows that, even if it is simply not possible for "New Berliners" to know things Berliners learned through socialization, the imitation of that knowledge was often successful. The assumption that *explicit knowledge* about the city could easily be adopted was in fact affirmed during group discussions.

This vague concept of *more than factual knowledge* can be compared with something the participants noted during the group discussion: that the Berlin identity is "fluid"—that is, the personality of Berlin is characterized by transition. Consequently, is it possible for anyone—Berliners and "New Berliners"—to develop an identity in Berlin which is defined by hybridity? Bhabha defines cultural hybridity in the following way:

> For a willingness to descend into that alien territory—where I have led you—may reveal that the theoretical recognition of the split-space of enunciation may open the way to conceptualizing an international culture, based not on the exoticism of multiculturalism or the diversity of cultures, but on the inscription and articulation of culture's hybridity. To that end we should remember that it is the "inter"—the cutting edge of translation and negotiation, the in-between space—that carries the burden of the meaning of culture. (1994, 38)

Bhabha's "in-between space" could be seen as congruent to the description "fluid" the participants came up with in the context of the group discussion. Looking at the (sub-)cultural, political, and religious diversity of identities, the question, if anyone can develop an identity in Berlin which is defined by hybridity, can be affirmed. But urban renewal and displacement processes threaten the hybrid character of the Berlin that Berliners know.

Although participants agreed that among themselves and among their friends, it is not relevant whether one is a Berliner or a "New Berliner," they were still aware of the problems the migrant incomers bring with them. These migrants often have more financial resources available than locals, and thus consume more housing space, culture, and goods; naturally, political consequences arise: Berliners alienate from their neighborhoods, as Savage et al. (2005) describe. This means that gentrification does influence identification with Berlin, and that actions like the occupa-tion of the theatre Volksbühne am Rosa-Luxemburg-Platz might be a reaction, a cry of protest, of the citizens.

10.2.2   Muslim Identities and Anti-Muslim Racism in Germany

Much like other parts of Europe, Germany is witnessing a rise of right-wing, anti-Muslim forces with the electoral success of the right-wing pop-ulist party AfD, which represents merely one expression of widespread anti-Muslim racism (Zick et al. 2011; Bayraklı and Hafez 2015; Zick et al. 2016, 44, 50). The research discussed in this section addresses how Muslim identities are constructed in the face of anti-Muslim racism in Germany. On the one hand, we are interested in the effects of "external perception," as well as experiences of racism on Muslim identity forma-tion. On the other hand, we also look at the issues concerning identity and difference among Muslims. We analyze where non-Muslim narratives draw boundaries between themselves and Muslims, and we explore how Muslims assert their identity inside and outside of those narratives. In this short summary of our research, we focus on some of our findings on Muslim identity construction and address non-Muslim perspectives only as they interact with the former.

We based our research on two conceptual pillars: anti-Muslim racism and Muslim identities. The first, anti-Muslim racism, draws on Said's (2003) theory of *Orientalism*, as well as on the concept of *cultural racism* as theorized, for example, by Balibar (1991). Our definition of anti-Muslim racism[6] is mainly based on Shooman's (2014, 2016) work on the phenom-enon. We understand anti-Muslim racism in Germany as a system of dis-courses and practices in which people marked as Muslims,

> regardless of their religiousness, are racialized. That is, they are constructed as a homogeneous, [static,] quasi-natural group. This group is positioned in binary opposition to white Christian/Atheist Germans or Europeans and ascribed certain collective characteristics from a dominant social position. (Shooman 2014, 64–65, authors' translation)

The two groups that emerge appear as mutually exclusive and are implicitly or explicitly put into a hierarchical order at the expense of the Muslim collective (Shooman 2014, 62). In that context, all social behavior of the racialized is considered to result from their group affiliation and its supposed characteristics (Shooman 2014, 58–59). In other words, Muslims are considered to behave a certain way because they are Muslim. Anti-Muslim racism typically mixes cultural, religious, ethnic, and somatic factors regarded as indicative of a "foreign background" (Shooman 2014, 66). For instance, black hair, Muslim-sounding names, or religious clothing may function as markers of group affiliation and thus become stigmas (Shooman 2014, 68; cf. Goffman 1963).

Drawing on the work of Jenkins (2008) as well as Lamont and Molnár (2002), we defined Muslim identities as the idea of being Muslim that people who identify as Muslim have. Our interest lies specifically with the construction of Muslim identities in their respective social contexts. Biskamp identifies three relevant lines of research on the matter: one that may be called an individual-situational perspective, one that draws on discursive traditions within Islam, and a third that focuses on the societal debates on Muslims and Islam (2016, 203ff.). We argue that research on Muslim identities has to take all these factors into account, establish how they intertwine, and identify mechanisms of the specific inside-outside dialectic of Muslim identity construction.

We chose "Muslim" as a category to be able to analyze experiences and perceptions of anti-Muslim racism and their impact on identity construction. We explicitly did not use certain criteria—for instance, piety—to define "Muslim." Rather, we wanted this category to reflect the participants' self-definitions, leaving it open to the myriad of different reasons why people identify as Muslim, including being marked as such by others. We chose "Non-Muslim" as the counter-category as our research question addresses the construction of identities in the face of anti-Muslim debates, where the dichotomy of Muslim and Non-Muslim is central (cf. Attia 2009; Foroutan 2012; Shooman 2014).

We found our participants partly through a call for participation via email addressed to all *Humboldt-Universität* students, and partly through personal contacts. In total, we had four participants in each group, two male and two female on each side. They were born between 1972 and 1995. Six were students and two were not. One of the Muslim participants explicitly identified as a *white* convert. The Imitation Game was conducted in German. We interpreted the data, using Mayring's (2014) approach of qualitative content analysis.

Our analysis focuses on Muslim identity construction in the face of ascriptions by non-Muslims and anti-Muslim debates. We found three components of Muslim identity construction that all of the Muslim participants referred to, to a certain extent: a political, an ethnic-cultural, and a religious component.[7] Below we focus on the political component.

The Muslim participants of the Imitation Game are aware of anti-Muslim discourses and reference them. Debates on Muslims in Germany and reflections on collective experiences of racism are at the core of the political component of their Muslim identities. They take on the category assigned to them (Muslim) and redefine it with regard to racist ascriptions. Being Muslim thus becomes a social rather than a religious affiliation. What is important is the collective nature of this component. Muslim participants refer to anti-Muslim racism as a collective experience, a public discourse that targets all Muslims or Muslims in general. Furthermore, the experience of racism is reflected on as a common or collective denominator and of course, anti-racist resistance takes on a collective form.

We have identified two mechanisms of the specific inside-outside dialectic between anti-Muslim racism and the political component of Muslim identity. First, we found what DuBois has called "double consciousness, this sense of always looking at one's self through the eyes of others, of measuring one's soul by the tape of a world that looks on in amused contempt and pity" (1903, 2–3). This experience of seeing oneself through anti-Muslim discourse, internalizing it to a certain extent and being able to see oneself as *Other* becomes apparent in the Muslim participants' contributions as *pretenders* in the Imitation Game. Asked by a Non-Muslim judge about his "experience" with Muslims, one Muslim pretender replied:

> Overall the contact [I have with Muslims] is alright, but they tend to shut themselves off, which results in exclusion because they don't want any contact. Women with headscarves seem foreign/strange to me because I simply cannot understand why they cover themselves like that. The men seem foreign/strange to me as well because I simply have no contact with them and because they are very loud and provocative. And they don't want to integrate. (Authors' translation)

The Muslim participant's use of common anti-Muslim narratives—Muslims keeping to themselves, seeming different or foreign—in his non-Muslim *performance* points to his awareness of this image of Muslims in German society.

Another mechanism of said inside-outside dialectic is what Stuart Hall called "identity politics" (1997, 52). Hall differentiates two phases of the latter. The first entails building a collective counter-identity that appropriates the racist labels and ascriptions assigned to one and redefines them in a positive manner (Hall 1997, 54). Tiesler (2006) has coined the term "Muslimness" where being Muslim is not primarily an indicator of religious affiliation, but rather a social experience that Muslims turn into a (political) statement (Eickhof 2010, 15).

While the Muslim participants consider their experience of anti-Muslim racism a common denominator, they also differentiate between *different* experiences of "being Muslim" based on gender and religious practices and thus affirm what Stuart Hall calls "identity through difference," the second phase of identity politics (Hall 1997, 57). One participant stated:

> Based on their name, especially Muslim men are often discriminated against at school, in day-to-day life, at work. If the name sounds Muslim, people assume that the person is a "religious man" and then there are certain images linked to that: terrorists, drug dealers, misogynists... etc. When it comes to women with Muslim (Arabic/Turkish) names, people are surprised when those women are modern. (Authors' translation)

This Muslim participant considers anti-Muslim racism to affect all Muslims while at the same time being aware of differences of ascriptions based on gender. It is also worth pointing out that the participant's idea of "Muslim" names are Arabic or Turkish names—something that points to the conflation of ethnicity and religious affiliation in discourses about Muslims in Germany (see research on the "Muslimization" of the German debate on migration (Spielhaus 2011, 54; Karakayalı 2012)) and the ethnic-cultural component of Muslim identity construction.

In summary, we have identified three components of Muslim identity that are constructed in the context of inner-Muslim debates as well as discourses concerning Muslims in larger society: a political, an ethnic-cultural, and a religious component. The political component, which we focused on here, refers to a process in which Muslims identify their shared experience of racism as a common denominator and create a counter-identity that seeks to redefine the (ascribed) label "Muslim" politically. The three components—however contradictory at times—represent elements that were present in all of the Muslim participants' identities to a certain extent. We argue that Muslim identities are constructed as social identities in the context of an inside-outside dialectic; *outside* referring to anti-Muslim discourses within broader society, and *inside* to the internalization and politicization of those discourses as well as hybrid self-positioning between personal needs, inner-Islamic debates, and other societal points of reference. The three components of identity construction that result from this process each refer in a specific way to those dialectics and to the boundary drawing connected to them.

10.2.3   "I Always Get Asked Where I Come From": An Analysis of the Connection Between Whiteness and Germaneness and Its Effects on Black and White Identities in Germany

Speaking of whiteness in Germany is sometimes met with refusal, often with a lack of understanding but almost always comes with a certain amount of insecurity. Due to German history being entangled with colonialism and dominated by national socialism, the idea that whiteness might still matter in terms of living conditions and opportunities seems to be too much to bear for some Germans and is therefore often pushed aside or attributed to right-wing extremists. However, while we were writing this chapter in late 2017, over 90 deputies of the far-right party *Alternative für Deutschland* (Alternative for Germany) were moving into their new offices in the German parliament, meaning that their political positions are shared or at least tolerated by at least 13 percent of this society. Their campaign was dominated by a racist rhetoric and images of how a "real German person" looks like according to them: unquestionably white. While shocking, this notion is neither new nor exceptional, but can rather be understand as a continuity, easily traced back far beyond the German citizenship law introduced in 1913. While some adjustments have been made in the intervening decades, it is still heavily based on the so-called *ius sanguinis* or blood law, meaning that a German can only be German by heritage. That heritage is constructed as white, ignoring the fact that Black people and other people of color (PoC) have been German citizens for centuries. For most of modern history, whiteness as an idea has been used to stratify the German society into two categories—those who belong to the national collective and those who do not. Regarding the current political climate, it seemed interesting to us how the idea of what it means to be German is still connected to whiteness and how this influences the identities of white and Black people in Germany.

As whiteness is considered the norm in Germany it is often unspoken or even invisible, while non-white people are seen and marked as the *Other*. Correspondingly, our main assumption is that whiteness poses as an invisible norm in Germany and is strongly connected to what is perceived as German and what is not. Further we are interested in the consequences which emerge therefrom for white and Black collective identities in Germany.

While the foundation of critical whiteness studies has already been laid in the 1990s in the USA through Black feminist authors and scholars like bell hooks, Audre Lorde, and Toni Morrison, it is budding only very cautiously in Germany. The little research published so far consists predominantly of essays, but rarely is it empirical research. This mirrors the lack of discussion about whiteness in Germany in general, as whiteness is rarely named or called out in the wider national discourse (Müller 2011). As whiteness is a construct that is in its form strongly dependent upon the context in which it is set (Garner 2007), it is of great interest to our research, especially concerning what particular form whiteness takes in Germany, how it has historically evolved, and how it is linked to other concepts specific to Germany. As the modern concepts of whiteness and German-ness both emerged in the eras of Enlightenment and colonialism, and were both used to constitute a homogenous nation state and to legitimize the violent submission of other peoples and their lands, it seemed sensible to analyze how these concepts are still linked today (Arndt 2009).

To build up a theoretical basis for our research, we focused on the few theories from the field of critical whiteness studies set in Germany. Grada Kilomba's *Plantation Memories* (2008), a psychoanalytic perspective on being a Black woman in a predominantly white society, served as a pivotal source of inspiration for this work. Additionally, we took Maisha-Eggers' (2009) Hegelian conceptions of whiteness as the normative center from which everything that is "other" is measured, and Katharina Walgenbach's (2009) thoughts on the interconnections between whiteness and German nationhood as analytical starting points. Based on Tilly and Brubaker (1993), and Hannah Arendt (1986), we understand German nationhood as a form of ethnic nationalism, where the national collective is based on heritage. In order to analyze the practice of constructing collective identities, we use Lamont and Molnár's (2002) concept of symbolic boundaries. Following this concept, identity is being constructed in a dynamic process by social actors via emphasizing on the difference of the "other." Furthermore, we follow Stuart Hall's suggestion to understand identity not as a person's essential core but as product of the continuous negotiation between the subject and society. Consequently, identity construction can be understood as a daily practice. Further, this allows the simultaneous existence of multiple identities that can be ambivalent.

In order to test our thesis, we collected qualitative data through the Imitation Game. Focusing on how Black and white identities and discourses about race and German-ness were constructed and reproduced in the written dialogues, we predominantly analyze the discursive entanglements of questions asked and answers given with specific attention to the meta-intentions stated by the participants. This allowed us to collect extensive data around which markers of race and forms of tacit knowledge are assumed and applied by Black and white Germans to identify people within and without their racial categories. The data collected in this procedural application of the Imitation Game was then structured according to deductive Qualitative Content Analysis and further analyzed according to the inductive approach of Grounded Theory.

The research was conducted with a total of 6 white and 6 Black Germans and produced about 50 pages of qualitative material systematized into 64 categories on 4 levels. The methodological approach was criticized for reproducing racist discourse and entailing elements of "blackfacing," as it partly consists of white people imitating Black identity. Taking these aspects into account throughout the research process constituted a central element of our reflexive approach. In reference to our research thesis, we were able to retrace a close and interactive connection between the concepts of whiteness and German-ness. We could identify symbolic boundaries, clearly defining a German national collective in the collected dialogues. These boundaries were drawn by white participants along aspects of culture, history, and language, which were thus explicitly understood as *white* and exclusive to those who are read as *white*. Black participants were consequently placed outside of an imagined national collective and consistently constructed as foreign. Examples from our research include the attempt to identify white and Black Germans through their knowledge of German history or their experience with typical German cuisine. Many of the Black participants shared the experience of constantly being faced with questions about their language skills and presumed countries of origins, asked by white people in everyday situations:

> People ask me quite frequently whether I speak German, I often get compliments for speaking German very well also, or people have asked me whether I speak English. Often they just started speaking English to me right away.

This practice of assuming Black people to be from somewhere else can be understood as the underlying challenge to the existence of Black people in the German context at all, and marking their bodies as "not normal" and therefore foreign.

> [W]hen I had long hair, people would touch it a lot. When I wore braids people liked to ask: "Can you even wash it? How do you get through to the skin on your head?" and so on. A man I didn't know, who was sitting behind me on a bus, just touched my hair, without even talking to me before.

This quote from one of the dialogues exemplifies the positioning of Black People outside of the norm and how they were constructed as "other" through racializing specific bodily features such as hair and skin, as well as subjecting them to processes of exoticization.

Whiteness was often shown to work as a normative yet implicit center and reference point for the definition of the deviate. Inter alia, this could be identified by the difficulties of white participants in finding questions focusing on their whiteness. This was resolved mainly through one strategy in which questions were asked about the experience of whiteness outside of the predominantly white German context (e.g. holidays in Africa or Asia). This inability to talk about whiteness as a structural phenomenon in the national context of Germany exemplifies how whiteness as an invisible norm is strongly connected to Germanness. Naturally, the exclusionary effects of the conceptualization of German-ness showed effects in the identity processes of Black Germans—the identification of Black participants predominantly took place through shared experiences of exclusion and discrimination, and their implications for various aspects of everyday life and mental health. One Black participant elaborated on the different aspects of being a Black German:

> Isolation (being the only afro-German person, e.g. in class), alienation, searching and questioning your identity, knowing even as a child that you've got to work harder to get the same recognition as other (white) people. Different strategies in reaction to marginalization and alienation: Rejecting the idea of wanting to belong, looking for identity and support outside of […] "German" culture; exaggerated adaptation or assimilation, trying not to stand out […]

This constant marginalization and a persistent questioning of their existence in German society seemed to be a reason for collective identification among Black Germans, which could offer at least some protection and understanding. *White* participants, however, did not explicitly understand themselves as part of an imaginative *white* group and even had the tendency to reject whiteness as a concept in general, which is consistent with the idea of whiteness as an invisible norm. Our results offer a perspicuous proof for the centrality of whiteness in the construction of a German national collective, the interconnectedness of these concepts, and its crucial role for all those who are being placed outside of this collect. Beyond this research, we encourage further scrutiny of the institutions of the Black German community as much as applying further research outside an academic context, both being aspects that we deem central yet could not analyze.

10.3   A Critique of the Imitation Game

As part of the student research project on identities, the implications and characteristics that mark the Imitation Game, especially regarding the use of categories, were examined. Following a constructivist approach, identities can be seen as performative, that is, they are created, rather than expressed, through social interaction (cf. Bell 1999, 3; cf. also West and Fenstermaker 1995; Butler 2006). Thus, Imitation Game research should not presuppose identities and group/category memberships but instead critically examine whether the studied groups exist at all, and which discourses/power structures foster their (dis)establishment (cf. Brubaker 2004, 17, 20f.; Hirschauer 2014, 172).

Is the Imitation Game able to provide sufficient evidence that a category does not exist or is not relevant, when the whole setup strongly encourages participants to act as their assigned category's representatives? This encouragement takes place when participants are divided into two groups, with which they do not necessarily self-identify, and are instructed to compete with the other group. Following Judith Butler, this categorization can be viewed as a form of interpellation which is likely to reproduce power imbalances. It is rather obvious, in the case of many of the students' research questions, that power imbalances tend to be a feature of most binary categorizations.

10.3.1 Categorization as Interpellation

Interpellation is the mechanism central to Louis Althusser's notion of subjectivation. He claimed that ideology does not only take the form of abstract ideas, but that it plays a crucial role in the subjectivation of individuals: Individuals become subjects by learning, and ultimately embodying and reproducing the material practices of ideology (Althusser 1971, 127–186). Interpellation refers to this (symbolical) hailing of ideology to which subjects submit by internalizing its demands.

Judith Butler took on this concept but argued that interpellation is a constant process, the success of which does not depend on the power of the hailing subject, but rather on the historicity of the discourse it taps into (Butler 1997b, 31–34). While Butler specifically looked at gender-related interpellations, generally all power-saturated, that is, hierarchical, categorizations can be enforced through interpellation.

Interpellations work as a call or a reminder of appropriate behavior, temporarily reducing the interpellated person to their (presumed) category membership (cf. Butler 1997a, 85). This is the way that the categorizations in the Imitation Game can have an important impact on the method's results. Although it is possible to subvert and resist interpellations, challenging discourse always risks social exclusion and often requires conscious effort (cf. Thiele 2015, 53; see also Butler's notion of *social death* as described in Schippers 2014, 40). The establishment and assignment of categories thus is not neutral but "itself an exercise of power" (Crenshaw 1991, 1297), the influence of which on the participants' behavior should not be neglected.

10.3.2 Binary Oppositions

The effect of this categorization into groups might be aggravated even more by the binary oppositions used in the Imitation Game. Generally, pairs of opposite concepts—including, for example, nature/culture, female/male, body/mind, private/public, object/subject, or other/self—can be said to be fundamental for Western thought (cf. Fausto-Sterling 2000, 43; Harding 2015, 97; Schmitz 2006, 331). Their effect is one of polarization and hierarchization: "[D]ualism is a process in which power forms identity, one which distorts both sides of what it splits apart [...]" (Plumwood 1993, 32; cf. Becker-Schmidt 1998, 85). Consequently, binary oppositions encourage neglect of interdependences and connections (cf. ibid., 84).

During the Imitation Game, participants have to view each other as opposite, maybe even antagonistic, which might overemphasize the respective categories: "[T]o the extent that individuals may be contrasted by their group memberships, such identifications may become more important or relevant for the interaction at hand […]" (Snyder and Stukas 2007, 375). The influence of the setting, in this case the Imitation Game, on the participants' behavior thus should not be underestimated (cf. ibid., 372–375).

10.3.3   Stereotypes and Stereotype Threat

One consequence of this act of interpellation that constitutes the Imitation Game is a heightened risk of stereotyping and stereotype threat. Stereotypes can be defined as "a set of associated beliefs" (McGarty et al. 2004, 7)—more precisely, "a specific representation of a particular group at a particular time" (7)—and they rely on previously established categories of people (Thiele 2015, 26ff.). Both researchers and participants who were interviewed mentioned the stereotyping that tends to take place during the Imitation Game. This stereotyping is no coincidence, but systematically grounded in a method which assigns categories to its participants and then asks them to guess the other players' categories. The Imitation Game constitutes a situation in which the participants, who have been made aware of their (presumed) group membership, are contrasted with the respective *other* and subsequently might act as representatives of their group. In this context, it becomes clear that researching the power relations between groups and/or categories of people is hardly possible without reproducing them—a problem that can also foster stereotype *threat*. As self-fulfilling prophecies, stereotypes, even in a very latent and abstract form,[8] negatively influence the targeted persons and impair their confidence and performance (cf. e.g. Woodcock et al. 2012, 635ff.). Stereotype threat could be seen as a movement toward interpellation, as the ongoing, often hurtful, or traumatizing discursive demand to embody the norms of a certain category. Often this stereotype threat fosters a behavior that in turn confirms these stereotypes, as "people tend to enact their stereotype of the social role in which they find themselves" (Turner 2010, 33).

Thus, there is a risk of attributing categories in the Imitation Game, because those categories can work as a form of interpellation, reducing participants to one of the two categories and potentially impairing their performance through stereotype threat. Moreover, intersectionality theory can help understand the ambiguous results stemming from a potentially oversimplified selection of participants.

10.3.4 Intersectionality

Intersectionality theory posits that categories always already exist in combination, and it is therefore not possible to isolate a single category and attempt to distill its meaning (cf. West and Fenstermaker 1995, 9; Hirschauer 2014, 175). Coined by Kimberlé Crenshaw (1991), the term intersectionality has been used to understand the experience of Black women who are discriminated against both on the basis of race and gender, and later has been expanded to include categories like class, disability, or age (cf. McCall 2005, 1771). Categories then are understood "not as distinct but as always permeated by other categories, fluid and changing, always in the process of creating and being created by dynamics of power [...]" (Cho et al. 2013, 795).

According to Leslie McCall, who mapped several research approaches regarding intersectionality theory, an intra-categorial approach to researching social groups is primarily interested in the *relationship* between them, but at the same time also explores if there are any differences or inequalities at all (McCall 2005, 1785). This comparative approach could be used during the Imitation Game but requires careful preparation regarding the recruitment of participants: "The categorical space can become very complicated with the addition of any one analytical category to the analysis because it requires an investigation of the multiple groups that constitute the category" (1786). It is nevertheless worthwhile to consider recruiting people who are similar to each other in a range of potentially relevant categories[9] but differ in the one that is central to the research question, as it could sharpen the Imitation Game's focus.

10.3.5 Conclusion Concerning the Critique

That an experimental setup reproduces and potentially reinforces the categories it relies on is by no means a critique unique to the Imitation Game. However, the very explicit binary categorization and the subsequent confrontation of groups that take place in the Imitation Game could significantly increase this risk. Therefore, both the research question and the choice of categories should be critically evaluated with regard to the discourses they reproduce and potential effects on participants.

A critical understanding of the functioning of categories and their attribution can thus improve the research process, and at the same time can help interpret some of the participants' reactions. While some confirmed their assigned category membership, others tried to subvert it by reclaiming a previously derogatory label or by reacting in unexpected ways—which was often interpreted by the judges as a special sign of authenticity. This shows that because interpellations depend on discourses that exceed the intention of the single subject, shifts in meaning are inevitable and can even be used as a means of agency and self-determination (Butler 1995, 135–138).

To summarize, it is important to consider discourses and power relations because they influence the research situation itself as well as the interpretation of results. Using powerful interpellations can have a totalizing effect on identity so that certain group/category memberships are likely to be overstated. Although the subversion of categories is possible, stereotype threat and the internalization of categorizations cannot always be consciously averted.

The final assessment of the method would be ambivalent: On the one hand, the Imitation Game reaffirms stereotypical discourses, and its use of categories might strongly influence the research results; on the other hand, it makes it possible to subvert categories and create new ideas for what authenticity can mean and what certain categories can include.

10.4   Conclusion

The seminar topic was "identity." The students were able to produce very interesting and theoretically as well as empirically based research questions showing that identity should be seen as a processual concept. Although their research questions differed widely, one can see some similarities in the overall results: In all three Imitation Games, the one group of participants which was categorized as the dominant group did not reflect on their own role as the normalized group. This was especially obvious when looking at the behavior of the white German participants who mostly *othered* the Black Germans who were acting as their counterparts in the Imitation Games. Similarly, the non-Muslim Germans mostly *othered* Muslims as not being of German descent. Muslim identity is associated with being Arabic or Turkish. This inside-outside dialectic was revealed in the Berlin identity game (see Chap. 9 of this volume)—it seems to be very easy for a newcomer to become a Berliner, as the identity of Berliners is so open und "fluid." Combined with the other projects that focused more on the national aspects of identity than on the regional aspect, the Imitation Games discussed here clearly revealed the various aspects of research on identity.

After using Imitation Games in a seminar context, we could say that this method of collecting data is *first of all* very fruitful for working with students, and *secondly* useful for research focusing on the concept of identity. The Imitation Game is a very effective tool for connecting students very quickly with their own research data. The data collection needs some time for recruiting and preparing the research group, but having done this, it is possible to produce a large amount of data that can be meaningfully analyzed in less than two hours. After this, it is possible for the students to work practically with and analyze these data. The students used qualitative content analyses for analyzing the dialogues, although a range of other methods and approaches are available. For example, observing the participants during the game could provide a lot of qualitative data; moreover, it would have been interesting to follow up the imitation game with group discussions or single interviews. All of these quantitative and qualitative methods are very strongly accepted in the canon of sociological methodology. In order to have enough time to prepare the Imitation Game, it is important for students to engage with the seminar topic and develop their research question very early on, within the first weeks of the seminar. From a didactic point of view, this is very helpful because upper level students especially benefit from a connection with the practical aspects of research. Being able to carry out research in a team is one of the most important competences students need to have in professional life. For the lecturers, it was important to reflect on the research process together with the students. If mistakes happened or research organization failed, it was quite easy to discuss this in both the small research team as well as in the large seminar group, to help others avoid making the same mistakes. As we can see in the short research reports presented here, the students were able to create, analyze, and reflect sociological research data, and the Imitation Game helped to educate them both methodologically and theoretically.

Notes

1. Patriotic Europeans against Islamization of the Occident.
2. Hooligans against Salafists.
3. vb61-12 is the name of a theatre production performed during the occupation of the Berlin theatre "Volksbühne" initiated by the collective "staubzuglitzer" that mainly organized the occupation.
4. Capital city image campaign initiated by the Berlin senate. There have been several posters, letters, and other marketing means with the slogan "be Berlin" presented in the city.
5. Value campaign. The overall aim is to save values such as tolerance, freedom, and openness (das-b.berlin).
6. For discussions of anti-Muslim racism/"Islamophobia" as a form of *racism*, see, for example, Meer (2008), Meer and Modood (2009), Moosavi (2015).
7. The ethnic-cultural component connects being Muslim to a familial migration history from a Muslim majority country and thus to the idea of ethnic or cultural heritage. The religious component builds on religious rules, practices, and knowledge as criterions to distinguish Muslims from Non-Muslims as well as to debate "correct Muslimness."
8. A study found that the "mere prospect of being in the numerical minority decreases women's sense of belonging and their desire to attend professional events in male-dominated domains […]" (Woodcock et al. 2012, 636).
9. Of course there is no definite answer to the number of categories that should be considered. Gudrun-Axeli Knapp emphasizes that the number of categories has to depend on the concrete research interest (Knapp 2013, 347).

References

Althusser, Louis. 1971. *Lenin and Philosophy and Other Essays.* New York and London: Monthly Review Press.
Arendt, Hannah. 1986. *Elemente Und Ursprünge Totaler Herrschaft: Antisemitismus, Imperialismus, Totale Herrschaft.* 9th ed. München: Piper.
Arndt, Susan. 2009. Weißsein. Die Verkannte Strukturkategorie Europas Und Deutschlands. In *Mythen, Masken Und Subjekte*, 24–30. Münster: UNRAST Verlag.
Attia, I. 2009. *Die "westliche Kultur" und ihr Anderes. Zur Dekonstruktion von Orientalismus und antimuslimischem Rassismus.* Bielefeld: Transcript Verlag.
Balibar, Etienne. 1991. Is There a 'Neo-Racism'? In *Race, Nation, Class: Ambiguous Identities*, ed. E. Balibar and I.M. Wallerstein, 17–28. London: Verso.
Bayraklı, E., and F. Hafez. 2015. *Islamophobia Report.* Istanbul: SETA.
Becker-Schmidt, Regina. 1998. Zum feministischen Umgang mit Dichotomien. In *Kurskorrekturen. Feminismus zwischen kritischer Theorie und Postmoderne*, ed. Gudrun-Axeli Knapp, 84–125. Frankfurt and New York: Campus Verlag.

Bell, Vikki. 1999. Performativity and Belonging. An Introduction. *Theory, Culture & Society* 16 (2): 1–10.

Bhabha, Homi K. 1994. *The Location of Culture.* London: Routledge.

Biskamp, F. 2016. Muslimische Identitäten im Konflikt. Identifikationsprozesse zwischen islamischem Diskurs und Islamdiskurs. In *Religiöse Identitäten in politischen Konflikten*, ed. I.-J. Werkner and O. Hidalgo, 193–210. Wiesbaden: Springer Fachmedien.

Brubaker, Rogers. 2004. *Ethnicity Without Groups.* Cambridge, MA and London: Harvard University Press.

Butler, Judith. 1995. For a Careful Reading. In *Feminist Contentions. A Philosophical Exchange*, ed. Seyla Benhabib, Judith Butler, Drucilla Cornell, and Nancy Fraser, 127–143. New York and London: Routledge.

———. 1997a. *The Psychic Life of Power. Theories in Subjection.* Stanford: Stanford University Press.

———. 1997b. *Excitable Speech. A Politics of the Performative.* New York: Routledge.

———. 2006. *Gender Trouble. Feminism and the Subversion of Identity.* London: Routledge.

Cho, Sumi, Kimberlie Crenshaw, and Leslie McCall. 2013. Toward a Field of Intersectionality Studies. Theory, Applications, and Praxis. *Signs. Journal of Women in Culture and Society* 38 (4): 785–810.

Collins, Harry, and Robert Evans. 2010. *Tacit and Explicit Knowledge.* Chicago: The University of Chicago Press.

Collins, Harry, Robert Evans, Martin Weinel, Jennifer Lyttleton-Smith, Bartlett Andrew, and Martin Hall. 2015. The Imitation Game and the Nature of Mixed Methods. *Journal of Mixed Methods Research.* https://doi.org/10.1177 %2F1558689815619824.

Crenshaw, Kimberlé. 1991. Mapping the Margins. Intersectionality, Identity, Politics, and Violence against Women of Color. *Stanford Law Review* 43 (6): 1241–1299.

Du Bois, W.E.B. 1903. *The Souls of Black Folk.* Newburyport: Dover Publications (Dover Thrift Editions).

Eggers, Maureen Maisha. 2009. Rassifizierte Machtdifferenz als Deutungsperspektive in der Kritischen Weißseinsforschung in Deutschland. In *Mythen, Masken und Subjekte. Kritische Weißseinsforschung in Deutschland*, ed. Maureen Maisha Eggers, Grada Kilomba, and Peggy Piesche, 56–72. Münster: UNRAST Verlag.

Eickhof, I. 2010. *Antimuslimischer Rassismus in Deutschland. Theoretische Überlegungen.* Berlin: wvb Wiss. Verlag.

Fausto-Sterling, Anne. 2000. Sich mit Dualismen duellieren. In *Wie natürlich ist Geschlecht? Gender und die Konstruktion von Natur und Technik*, ed. Ursula Pasero and Anja Gottburgsen, 17–64. Wiesbaden: Westdeutscher Verlag.

Foroutan, Naika. 2012. *Muslimbilder in Deutschland. Wahrnehmungen und Ausgrenzungen in der Integrationsdebatte*. Bonn: Abteilung Wirtschafts- und Sozialpolitik der Friedrich-Ebert-Stiftung (Gesprächskreis Migration und Integration, 2012, November).

Garner, Steven. 2007. *Whiteness – An Introduction*. London: Routledge.

Goffman, Erving. 1963. *Stigma: Notes on the Management of Spoiled Identity*. Englewood Cliffs: Prentice Hall.

Hall, Stuart. 1997. Old and New Identities, Old and New Ethnicities. In *Culture, Globalization, and the World-System: Contemporary Conditions for the Representation of Identity*, ed. A.D. King, 41–68. Minneapolis: University of Minnesota Press.

Harding, Sandra. 2015. *Objectivity and Diversity. Another Logic of Scientific Research*. Chicago: University of Chicago Press.

Hirschauer, Stefan. 2014. (Un)Doing Differences. Die Kontingenz sozialer Zugehörigkeiten. *Zeitschrift für Soziologie* 43 (3): 170–191.

Jenkins, Richard. 2008. *Social Identity*. London and New York: Routledge.

Karakayalı, Serhat. 2012. Zur "Islamisierung" der Einwanderungsdebatte. In *Die Rolle der Religion im Integrationsprozess. Die Deutsche Islamdebatte*, ed. B. Ucar, 173–184. Frankfurt: Peter Lang.

Kilomba, Grada. 2008. *Plantation Memories: Episodes of Everyday Racism*. Münster: UNRAST Verlag.

Knapp, Gudrun-Axeli. 2013. Zur Bestimmung und Abgrenzung von "Intersektionalität". Überlegungen zu Interferenzen von "Geschlecht", "Klasse" und anderen Kategorien sozialer Teilung. *Erwägen Wissen Ethik* 3: 341–354.

Lamont, Michèle. 1992. *Money, Morals, and Manners. The Culture of the French and American Upper-Middle Class*. Chicago: University of Chicago Press (Morality and Society).

Lamont, Michèle, and Virág Molnár. 2002. The Study of Boundaries in the Social Sciences. *Annual Review of Sociology* 28 (1): 167–195.

———. 2017b. *Das B*. Accessed November 13, 2017. http://das-b.berlin/.

Mayring, Philipp. 2014. *Qualitative Content Analysis: Theoretical Foundation, Basic Procedures and Software Solution*. Klagenfurt: Beltz Verlag.

McCall, Leslie. 2005. The Complexity of Intersectionality. *Signs* 30 (3): 1771–1800.

McGarty, Craig, Vincent Y. Yzerbyt, and Russel Spears. 2004. Social, Cultural and Cognitive Factors in Stereotype Formation. In *Stereotypes as Explanations. The Formation of Meaningful Beliefs About Social Groups*, ed. Craig McGarty, Vincent Y. Yzerbyt, and Russe Spears, 1–15. Cambridge: Cambridge University Press.

Meer, Nasar. 2008. The Politics of Voluntary and Involuntary Identities. Are Muslims in Britain an Ethnic, Racial or Religious Minority? *Patterns of Prejudice* 42 (1): 61–81.

Meer, Nasar, and Tariq Modood. 2009. Refutations of Racism in the 'Muslim Question'. *Patterns of Prejudice* 43 (3-4): 335–354.

Moosavi, Leon. 2015. The Racialization of Muslim Converts in Britain and Their Experiences of Islamophobia. *Critical Sociology* 41 (1): 41–56.

Müller, Ulrike Anne. 2011. Far Away So Close: Race, Whiteness, and German Identity. *Identities* 18 (6): 620–645. https://doi.org/10.1080/10702 89X.2011.672863.

Plumwood, Val. 1993. *Feminism and the Mastery of Nature*. New York and London: Routledge.

Said, Edward W. 2003. *Orientalism*. New York: Vintage Books.

Savage, Mike, Gaynor Bagnall, and Brian Longhurst. 2005. *Globalization and Belonging*. London: SAGE Publications.

Schippers, Birgit. 2014. *The Political Philosophy of Judith Butler*. New York and London: Routledge.

Schmitz, Sigrid. 2006. Entweder – Oder? Zum Umgang mit binären Kategorien. In *Geschlechterforschung und Naturwissenschaften. Einführung in ein komplexes Wechselspiel*, ed. Smilla Ebeling and Sigrid Schmitz, 331–346. Wiesbaden: VS Verlag für Sozialwissenschaften.

Shooman, Yasemin. 2014. *"...weil ihre Kultur so ist." Narrative des antimuslimischen Rassismus*. Bielefeld and Berlin: Transcript Verlag.

———. 2016. Between Everyday Racism and Conspiracy Theories. Islamophobia on the German-Language Internet. In *Media and Minorities: Questions on Representation from an International Perspective*, ed. G. Ruhrmann, Y. Shooman, and P. Widmann, 136–155. Göttingen: Vandenhoeck & Ruprecht.

Snyder, Mark, and Arthur Stukas. 2007. Interpersonal Processes in Context: Understanding the Influence of Settings and Situations on Social Interaction. In *Social Communication*, ed. Klaus Fiedler, 363–388. New York: Psychology Press.

Spielhaus, Riem. 2011. *Wer ist hier Muslim? Die Entwicklung eines islamischen Bewusstseins in Deutschland zwischen Selbstidentifikation und Fremdzuschreibung*. Würzburg: Ergon-Verlag.

Thiele, Martina. 2015. *Medien und Stereotype. Konturen eines Forschungsfeldes*. Bielefeld: Transcript.

Tiesler, Nina. 2006. *Muslime in Europa: Religion und Identitätspolitiken unter veränderten gesellschaftlichen Verhältnissen*. Berlin: LIT.

Tilly, Charles, and Roger Brubaker. 1993. Citizenship and Nationhood in France and Germany. *Contemporary Sociology* 22 (4): 501–502. https://doi.org/10.2307/2074376.

Turner, John C. 2010. Towards a Cognitive Redefinition of the Social Group. In *Social Identity and Intergroup Relations*, ed. Henri Tajfel, 15–40. Cambridge: Cambridge University Press.

Walgenbach, Katharina. 2009. Weißsein und Deutschsein – Historische Interdependenzen. In *Mythen, Masken und Subjekte. Kritische Weissseinsforschung in Deutschland*, ed. Maureen Maisha Eggers, Grada Kilomba, and Peggy Piesche, 377–394. Münster: UNRAST Verlag.

West, Candace, and Sarah Fenstermaker. 1995. Doing Difference. *Gender and Society* 9 (1): 8–37.

Woodcock, Anna, Paul R. Hernandez, Mica Estrada, and P. Wesley Schultz. 2012. The Consequences of Chronic Stereotype Threat: Domain Disidentification and Abandonment. *Journal of Personality and Social Psychology* 103 (4): 635–646.

Zick, Andreas, Beate Küpper, and Andreas Hövermann. 2011. *Die Abwertung der Anderen. Eine europäische Zustandsbeschreibung zu Intoleranz, Vorurteilen und Diskriminierung*. Berlin: Friedrich-Ebert-Stiftung.

Zick, Andreas, Beate Küpper, and Daniela Krause. 2016. *Gespaltene Mitte – Feindselige Zustände. Rechtsextreme Einstellungen in Deutschland 2016* (edited for the Friedrich-Ebert-Foundation by Ralf Melzer). Bonn: Dietz Verlag.

Interactional Expertise

Shannon N. Conley

1.1   INTRODUCTION TO PART III

Interactional Expertise is a central concept of interest to those in the Studies of Expertise and Experience community. It originates from the seminal work of Harry Collins, in which he posits that a non-practitioner (non-contributory expert) can achieve a certain level of linguistic fluency in order to pass a Turing-like test and thereby "pass" as an expert, on a linguistic basis alone. Much of this insight emerged from Collins's own experience interacting with gravitational wave physicists—living among them, becoming a part of their community, and learning their expert language. In order to achieve Interactional Expertise, the non-practitioner has to be immersed within a community of practice to the extent that they achieve linguistic fluency, but do not participate in hands-on contributory practices. Collins calls this learning via immersion within a community of practice "linguistic socialization"—it enables one to obtain "informal and tacit knowledge pertaining to the language even if one does not have the practical skills to pass as a fully competent member of the form of life once we move beyond language" (Collins 2004, 127). One need not participate in the material culture of a domain in order to obtain linguistic fluency—to understand the tacit knowledge and "inside jokes" of a particular domain, one only needs to spend enough time living within an expert community, participating in its linguistic practices, in order to pick up such elements. Ultimately, Interactional Expertise and Contributory Expertise are similar—in both forms of expertise, one must be linguistically fluent, but it is only in contributory expertise that one must be competent in the sense of also being able to expertly "do" or contribute in a hands-on manner. This part explores the notion of Interactional Expertise in a number of diverse ways, examining it experimentally, conceptually, and, in some cases, from the perspectives of scholars who have been immersed in groups of experts with competencies substantially different from their own.

In Chap. 11, "The Test of Ubiquitous Through Real or Interactional Expertise (TURINEX) and Veganism as Expertise," Berardy and Seager posit that Interactional Expertise is instrumental for interdisciplinary research and education as it enables collaborators to efficiently communicate across disciplinary silos. Berardy and Seager illuminate a challenge associated with the Imitation Game (IG), an approach which has been documented earlier in this volume, insofar as it places individuals into binaries—one either has Interactional Expertise or does not. The limitation of the IG, they argue, is that since it operates in binaries, it is limited in examining one's *progression* toward Interactional Expertise. Like Conley and Fisher (Chap. 13, in this volume), Berardy and Seager argue for an intermediate category known as *interactional competence*. Berardy and Seager developed a software program aimed at assessing the intermediate stage of interactional competence. The TURINEX web-enabled software platform tests for three levels of communicative competence, and was applied to a case study exploring veganism as an expertise for proof of concept testing. The TURINEX approach provides an important step in IG modifications, examining the development of interactional competence prior to the Interactional Expertise acquisition phase.

In Chap. 12, "Why They've Immersed: A Framework for Understanding and Attending to Motivational Differences Among Interactional Experts," Kennedy explores the motivation of those who choose to pursue Interactional Expertise. Kennedy notes that there are significant case studies that emerged prior to the Interactional Expertise term being formalized, such as the work of Wynne and Epstein, and raise questions about the roles and perspectives of those who do not neatly fall into categories of "expert" or "possessing expert knowledge." Kennedy argues that such cases demonstrate epistemic diversity, which can enable a fuller appreciation of the array of approaches, backgrounds, skills, and experiences embodied within a "rich variety of interactional experts." Following a review of case studies that represent a diverse array of motivations regarding the acquisition of Interactional Expertise, Kennedy proposes a framework for understanding four different motivations for the acquisition of Interactional

Expertise, arguing that these motivations are characterized by different types of relationships between interactional and contributory experts. Kennedy's work in highlighting and analyzing a diversity of special Interactional Expertises provides an excellent springboard for scholars interested in pursuing in-depth investigation of Interactional Expertise.

In Chap. 13, "Developing a Theoretical Scaffolding for Interactional Competence: A Conceptual and Empirical Investigation into Competence versus Expertise," Conley and Fisher contextualize Interactional Expertise within the Socio-technical Integration Research (STIR) program. The STIR program embeds social scientists and humanities scholars, known as "embedded humanists," within science and engineering laboratories in order to collaborate with scientists and explore capacities for responsible innovation within the laboratory context. Specifically, Conley and Fisher argue that the term "Interactional Expertise" has been used more loosely than Collins may have originally intended, and in contexts where it might not be exactly applicable—such as the STIR program; for example, where time frames of immersion (usually three months) tend not to be long enough to gain full linguistic fluency. Instead, based on an auto-ethnographic account of Conley's STIR study, in which she gained a modest level of linguistic fluency but also engaged in hands-on contributory activities, Conley and Fisher argue for new terminology to better encompass cases in which linguistic fluency has not occurred (i.e., one could not pass a Turing-like test), even as contributory activities and collaborations are occurring. They term this new category "interactional competence," and provide theoretical and empirical evidence to support inclusion of this category within the SEE (Studies in Expertise and Experience) community.

In Chap. 14, "Collaboration Among Apparently Incommensurable Expertises: A Case Study of Combining Expertises and Perspectives to Manage Climate Change in Costal Virginia," Gorman, Zhang, Fauss, and Bowes use ethnographic and auto-ethnographic approaches to compare the acquisition of Interactional Expertise and T-shaped expertise. Gorman and colleagues approach the acquisition of Interactional Expertise and T-shaped expertise in tandem, arguing that both are necessary (in order to effectively collaborate across diverse disciplinary terrains) if "wicked problems" such as climate change are to be effectively dealt with. Gorman et al.'s chapter specifically grapples with the problem of "incommensurable" divides between expertises, and integrates auto-ethnographic reflections from the co-authors regarding their own experiences developing trading zones with various collaborators as they honed their interactional and "T-shaped" expertises—T-shaped expertise refers having both a depth (stem of the "T") and breadth (top of the "T") of expertises. Gorman et al. distinguish between T-shaped and Interactional Expertise, insofar as (1) T-shaped expertise adds experience and expertise in different systems, and is comprised of a suite of both verbal and non-verbal skillsets that transcend different systems, while (2) Interactional Expertise is the ability to "have a deep conversation with a native expert" that demonstrates deep knowledge of the subject matter and expertise community. Gorman et al. examine and explore the utility of these frameworks within an interdisciplinary collaboration of different experts that is modeling the impacts of climate change in coastal Virginia.

In sum, the contributions in this part offer a diverse set of perspectives on Interactional Expertise, and span from the experimental (Berardy and Seager), to the conceptual (Kennedy), to the auto-ethnographic (Conley and Fisher and Gorman et al.). Although the contributions are rich and diverse in their perspectives and approaches, a strong and primary thread holding them together is a desire to explore the capacities, limitations, and new conceptual horizons for Interactional Expertise.

Reference

Collins, H. 2004. Interactional Expertise as a Third Kind of Knowledge. *Phenomenology and Cognitive Sciences* 3 (2): 125–143.

CHAPTER 11

The Test of Ubiquitous Through Real or Interactional Expertise (TURINEX) and Veganism as Expertise

Andrew Berardy and Thomas Seager

11.1   INTRODUCTION

11.1.1   *Interactional Expertise*

Expertise is formed over time through education, experiences, social inter-actions, and the acquisition of both tacit and explicit knowledge. People gain information, then knowledge, and then wisdom, and eventually may become an expert in certain disciplines or practices. One step along this path of development is that of *interactional expertise* (IE). IE is the result of extensive linguistic socialization imparting sufficient tacit knowledge to enable communication across domains without the necessity of becoming a "subject matter expert" or creating new terminology (Collins et al. 2007). A person with IE can "converse expertly about a practical skill or expertise, but without being able to practice it, learned through linguistic socialization among the practitioners" (Collins 2004, 125). Therefore, IE

A. Berardy (✉) • T. Seager
Arizona State University, Tempe, AZ, USA
e-mail: Thomas.Seager@asu.edu

© The Author(s) 2019
D. S. Caudill et al. (eds.), *The Third Wave in Science and Technology Studies*, https://doi.org/10.1007/978-3-030-14335-0_11

is essential in interdisciplinary efforts because these require people from different disciplines working together or synthesizing methods across disciplines. Genuine interdisciplinary collaborations require IE to be successful (Seager et al. 2011).

11.1.2   Interdisciplinary Research

Interdisciplinary research and education requires effective communication across disciplinary boundaries. IE is instrumental for this, but also for managers of large scientific organizations, scholars working in sustainability, critics, and journalists (Berardy et al. 2011). All of these professions share the expectation that one will be able to communicate well outside one's own area of expertise, which is exactly what IE enables.

11.1.3   Imitation Game

A person with IE should have the linguistic capability to pass as a member of a discipline or as having had certain experiences, which can be tested using the Imitation Game (IG) (Collins et al. 2006). The IG is run with three participants. An expert judge asks questions, intended to test tacit knowledge in the target expertise, to an expert and non-expert (the two respondents) in the given topic. The judge must attempt to guess whether each respondent has expertise in the topic or not. If the judge determines that the non-expert has expertise, then the non-expert has IE, even though they are not a *contributory* expert (Collins et al. 2006). Questions that are most effective at testing tacit knowledge are those that reflect a person's experience more so than their explicit knowledge. Interactional experts are typically able to provide expert critique, tell jokes only experts would understand, play devil's advocate, and make context-specific judgments (Berardy et al. 2011). Judges for the IG have to decide whether they think each respondent is an expert or not, meaning that there is no intermediate determination. According to IG results, a person either has IE or they do not.

11.1.4   Expertise Development

It is logical and accepted that expertise does not form instantaneously after a sufficient period of learning and practice. Rather, expertise exists along a continuum and people advance through stages along the path. The "Five-Stage Model of Adult Skill Acquisition" consists of five levels of expertise acquisition that can be differentiated based on the actions of the person being evaluated, which include novice, advanced beginner, competence, proficiency, and expertise (Dreyfus 2004). In "Three Dimensions of Expertise," Harry Collins argues that expertise can be represented as progress along a three-dimensional space representing esotericity, exposure to tacit knowledge of the domain, and individual or group accomplishment (Collins 2011). Rather than refuting the progression model put forward by Dreyfus, Collins adds two other elements of progression, noting that the level of expertise grows with the degree of exposure to tacit knowledge and the esotericity of the expertise (Collins 2011). One consistent characteristic of theories of acquisition of expertise is that it develops over time and is not an instantaneous switch from non-expert to expert.

11.1.5 Intermediate Expertise

Unfortunately, the IG results in a binary determination of non-expert or expert and cannot capture the *development* of expertise. The definition of IE itself requires that a judge cannot tell the difference between what are termed a "contributory expert" and an "interactional expert," and for the purposes of communication, these two experts are in fact identical. The definition states that an interactional expert is so "well socialized in the language of a specialist group" that they are "indistinguishable from those with full blown practical socialization but distinguishable from those who are not well socialized" (Collins et al. 2006, 656). This type of expertise assessment is useful for sociological understanding and large-scale experimentation across cultures and over time, but not for testing individual level progression toward IE. Despite this limitation of IE and the IG, there must be tests to identify an intermediate level of expertise.

11.1.6 Need for Intermediate Judgment

Understanding the stages of expertise development is useful in improving education efforts to improve tacit knowledge in a given discipline. Many modern higher education programs stress the importance of multidisciplinary collaboration and integrative education, both of which benefit from instilling higher levels of tacit knowledge in students. It is unreasonable to expect a single semester of work to impart sufficient tacit knowledge to gain full IE, so it is difficult to evaluate the effectiveness of such programs in training students to function as effective collaborators outside their primary discipline. There is a need for a methodology which can make an intermediate determination as well so that the program can be evaluated on the basis of whether it imparted a sufficient level of tacit knowledge, without needing to have created full interactional experts.

11.1.7   *Interactional Competence*

Andrew Berardy collaborated with Dr. Thomas Seager and Dr. Evan Selinger to examine the problems and potential advances related to IE, the IG, and the development of intermediate expertise. The team chose *interactional competence* (IC) as the name to describe the level of expertise between no expertise and IE. Several authors utilize the term competence to describe the nature of interactions expected from those possessing IC. Dreyfus' model describes competence as the stage at which someone must plan or acquire perspective to determine what aspects of a situation are important, but despite easier decision-making than earlier stages, there is an emotional investment added to the risks involved if a decision turns out to be wrong, and more responsibility for the consequences of the decision (Dreyfus 2004). A person with competence will not contribute new knowledge to a domain, but rather will show that they understand the foundation of the domain knowledge in a cohesive manner (Alexander 2003). Research regarding education for expertise development found that competence is a stage where a person has higher technical skills and organizational capacity, additional responsibility and ability to handle familiar complex situations (but not unfamiliar situations), more responsibility, and a realization that colleagues are fallible (Dunphy and Williamson 2004). We defined IC as a cohesive understanding of domain knowledge, which promotes easier decision-making and confidence, coupled with the fallibility of experts. As a linguistic ability, it excludes aspects such as organizational ability, technical skills, and emotional investment in choices, because those are within the domain of practice rather than socialization. However, a person with IC will still be able to understand and portray some of these aspects in dialogue, such as emotional investment, even if they do not experience them personally.

11.2   TURINEX Development

The team developed TURINEX with the programming assistance of Russel Uhl to address the gap in assessment by providing an intermediate option—that is, IC—missing from the IG. TURINEX is a web-enabled

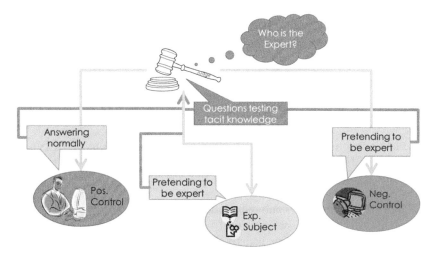

Fig. 11.1 TURINEX structure

software platform created for the purpose of testing three levels of communicative competence (Berardy et al. 2013). Figure 11.1 shows the structure of TURINEX testing, which requires four participants.

As Fig. 11.1 illustrates, TURINEX requires one judge and three respondents. Two of these participants (the judge and positive control) must be experts in the target expertise. One can be a non-expert and act as the negative control. Finally, the last respondent is the experimental subject. The expert judge asks questions based on their experience that they believe will test tacit knowledge of the respondents. The expert positive control answers normally as they would in any typical conversation. The two remaining respondents (experimental subject and negative control) answer in the way they would expect an expert to answer, which reveals their beliefs regarding the nature of the target expertise. The TURINEX platform requires all three respondents to answer the judge's question before the responses are sent to the judge. This eliminates potential bias across respondents based on the speed with which they answer a question. However, it also requires a significant time commitment for participants. Participants must wait while judges devise questions and then evaluate responses to those questions. Judges must wait while all three participants respond to each question, and if one participant takes longer to answer, it delays the entire process. Judges are also discouraged from asking questions that could easily be looked up online, have a definite correct answer, or require utilization of domain-specific skills, such as asking a complex mathematical question to test mathematics expertise. Rather, questions that get at tacit knowledge are based more on the lived experience of an expert.

11.2.1   TURINEX 2.0

The first version of the TURINEX platform required all four participants to be logged on simultaneously. Implementation of TURINEX testing therefore had a significant time burden and was especially difficult to coordinate across time zones. Early applications of TURINEX were implemented across time zones and included respondents with unreliable access to the internet. Sessions were not set up to allow pausing and resuming, so some TURINEX testing had to be restarted when connection issues caused interference. In response to these difficulties and to address other programming flaws, a second version was developed—TURINEX 2.0. The primary change made was to allow asynchronous testing. This would allow judges and respondents to log in and out as they desired, and limit the time commitment to complete an action such as asking or responding to a question or judging a response. Spreading the test across multiple sessions did not change the nature of the dialogue, as participants were never restricted from accessing the internet during testing. It did however allow additional time for thought and reflection without the pressure of knowing others were waiting for a response or question. As a result, asynchronous TURINEX sessions lasted much longer than early TURINEX sessions, and yet demanded far less of the participants' time. Another improvement in TURINEX 2.0 was the addition of a transcript that recorded the judges' questions and respondents' answers, which the judges could refer to in order to help them keep track of the dialogue, including previous exchanges so that they could build upon them with subsequent questions.

11.2.2   Veganism Expertise

TURINEX 2.0 was applied to a case study in veganism as an expertise to serve as a proof of concept, to examine the notion of IC, and to ensure that the new software was stable and appropriate for testing. Recruitment for participants used snowball sampling and targeted advertisements. Each

TURINEX test required two vegans, one vegetarian, and one omnivore. One vegan would act as the judge, while another vegan would serve as the positive control. The omnivore provided the negative control while the vegetarian acted as the experimental subject. The vegan judge was instructed to ask questions intended to test tacit knowledge regarding veganism. The vegan respondent was instructed to answer honestly because it is expected that they have expertise in veganism. The other two respondents were instructed to answer the way that they thought a vegan would, or to pretend to be vegan. Demographic data was collected before testing, which included participants' dietary preferences, exposure to veganism, other dietary restrictions, and potentially confounding factors. The research was considered exempt by the Institutional Review Board.

11.2.3   TURIENX Veganism Hypothesis

TURINEX testing was used to investigate two hypotheses. First, judges would be able to consistently differentiate between vegans, vegetarians, and omnivores using the TURINEX platform. This would provide evidence that veganism was an expertise with its own associated tacit knowledge. It would also serve as a proof of concept that TURINEX was effective in differentiating between levels of expertise in respondents with one testing session. Second, increased levels of exposure to veganism and related practices would increase the likelihood that a person would pass as a vegan in the TURINEX test. Three corollaries are proposed for this hypothesis. First, the actual vegans would be most likely to pass as vegans in TURINEX testing. Second, those non-vegan respondents with vegan friends or family have the second highest likelihood of passing as vegans after actual vegans due to frequent conversations and exposure to vegan practices. Third, vegetarians would have the third highest likelihood of passing as vegans due to having some shared practices and experiences with vegans. As a result, omnivores without vegetarian or vegan friends or family would have the lowest likelihood of passing as vegans in the TURINEX test for veganism. The null hypothesis was that there would be no correlation between the level of exposure to veganism, and the likelihood of a participant being judged as a vegan. This would be the case if judges could not make accurate determinations of diet for respondents between vegans, vegetarians, and omnivores, or if judges found that vegetarians or omnivores without significant exposure to veganism or vegan practices demonstrated better linguistic expertise and communicative competence than actual vegans.

11.2.4   TURINEX Veganism Results

The hypotheses were supported by the results found through TURINEX testing, although the sample size was limited (Fig. 11.2). First, as expected, despite some errors easily explained by collected demographic data, judges overall consistently identified vegans, vegetarians, and omnivores in their correct category. One outlier was an omnivore who passed as a vegan due to an exceptionally high tacit knowledge of veganism owing to a long-term exposure to a vegan relative. This result is consistent with the expectation that a respondent with vegan family members would have higher tacit knowledge of veganism and be more likely to pass as a vegan. Their interactions with a vegan family member made the omnivore an interactional expert in veganism, allowing them to sound like a vegan to the judge. Another outlier was a vegetarian Indian respondent who was judged as an omnivore due to a lack of knowledge regarding vegan products available in the United States. Both of these outliers are easily explained based

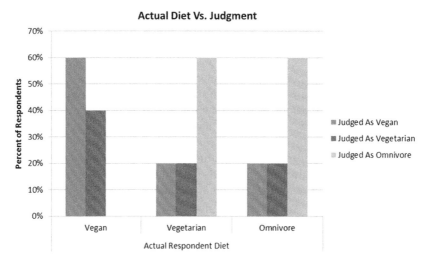

Fig. 11.2   Results of TURINEX veganism testing. $n = 20$ participants over 5 sessions

on existing theories of tacit knowledge and IE (Collins et al. 2006; Collins 2004). There was not a large enough sample size for statistical analysis, but within the sessions that were performed, no vegans were mistaken for omnivores and the only omnivore judged as a vegan was explained as an interactional expert due to high tacit knowledge acquired from a vegan relative. Therefore, the null hypothesis was not supported by the results. Although expertise rankings were the same for vegetarians and omnivores across judgment categories, demographic data is again useful in explaining the differences. Correcting for confounding variables supports the idea that the three categories of diet can be differentiated across levels of expertise in veganism. Judgments also have high confidence ratings that indicate the judge's level of certainty regarding respondent expertise levels. Potential evidence to support the null hypothesis is that 8 out of 15 respondents were judged incorrectly, but again at least 2 of these can be explained by confounding variables influencing tacit knowledge that were captured in the demographic data.

11.3   DISCUSSION

The empirical results of TURINEX veganism testing support the hypotheses regarding actual vegans, tacit knowledge exposure, and shared practices across vegetarians and vegans. Other dietary restrictions do not appear to play an important role in expertise judgment. There is potentially less overlap between vegetarians and vegans in terms of expertise and shared experience than expected, but the sample size is insufficient to make definite conclusions in this regard. A much larger sample size is needed to make conclusive statements regarding the nature of veganism itself, especially in relation to omnivores and vegetarians.

One TURINEX judge had a session with perfect judgment. In this session, the judge focused on interactions with omnivores, relationships, and social situations, as well as food choices and health. One TURINEX judge had a session with all three judgments wrong. In this session, the judge focused on food choices, with only a couple questions about health and interacting with omnivores in social situations. Differences in the nature of the questions could help explain why some judges were better than others in differentiating between respondents, despite every judge being an "expert" vegan. Perhaps one reason for this was that a focus on food missed other aspects of the lived vegan experience, which are captured by questions about relationships and social situations. Despite being the most commonly asked type of question, this focus on food provides less of an opportunity to evaluate tacit knowledge in a wide variety of categories that can better capture the vegan experience and reveal disconnects between what pretender respondents believe and what reality is for vegans.

11.4   Conclusion

Expertise development occurs along a continuum and tacit knowledge is necessary for its advancement. Despite the knowledge that expertise develops in stages, the IG cannot capture development within an individual between no expertise and IE. The creation of TURINEX fills this gap in assessment methodology by allowing researchers to test for the development of tacit knowledge before the stage of IE. This intermediate stage, called IC, is useful because it is the stage where a person understands the concepts, terminology, and tacit elements of a domain without having to be an expert or interactional expert in the domain. It is more feasible to gain IC in several domains than it is to gain expertise or IE in those domains, reducing the demands on education for sustainability or any other interdisciplinary endeavor. A case study in veganism used as a proof of concept for TURINEX found that vegans typically exhibit higher tacit knowledge in veganism than both vegetarians and omnivores. Demographic data was useful in explaining anomalies where an omnivore was judged as a vegan and a vegetarian was judged as an omnivore. These exceptions demonstrated the successful transfer of tacit knowledge and the importance of understanding cultural differences in an otherwise identical expertise category.

TURINEX has significant potential outside of veganism assessment in applications including supporting sustainable consumption through the examination of other groups that exhibit desirable behaviors. TURINEX as a methodology may also support the assessment of educational efforts through the evaluation of linguistic expertise. Finally, TURINEX assessment can help identify the most effective methods for advancing tacit knowledge without the necessity that the training imparts IE.

References

Alexander, Patricia. 2003. The Development of Expertise: The Journey from Acclimation to Proficiency. *Educational Researcher* 32 (8): 10–14. https://doi.org/10.3102/0013189X032008010.

Berardy, Andrew, Thomas Seager, and Evan Selinger. 2011. Developing a Pedagogy of Interactional Expertise for Sustainability Education. *Proceedings of the 2011 IEEE International Symposium on Sustainable Systems and Technology*, May. IEEE, 1–4. https://doi.org/10.1109/ISSST.2011.5936891.

Berardy, Andrew, Thomas Seager, Evan Selinger, and Russel Uhl. 2013. TURINEX: A Social Science Tool to Help Understand and Predict Sustainable Consumption. *Proceedings of the International Symposium on Sustainable Systems & Technologies*, Cincinnati. http://figshare.com/articles/TURINEX_A_Social_Science_Tool_To_Help_Understand_and_Predict_Sustainable_Consumption/715918.

Collins, Harry. 2004. Interactional Expertise as a Third Kind of Knowledge. *Phenomenology and the Cognitive Sciences* 3. Springer, pp. 125–143. http://www.springerlink.com/index/T108471556145810.pdf.

———. 2011. Three Dimensions of Expertise. *Phenomenology and the Cognitive Sciences* 12 (2): 253–273. https://doi.org/10.1007/s11097-011-9203-5.

Collins, Harry, Robert Evans, Rodrigo Ribeiro, and Martin Hall. 2006. Experiments with Interactional Expertise. *Studies in History and Philosophy of Science Part A* 37 (4): 656–674. https://doi.org/10.1016/j.shpsa.2006.09.005.

Collins, Harry, Robert Evans, and Mike Gorman. 2007. Trading Zones and Interactional Expertise. *Studies in History and Philosophy of Science Part A* 38 (4): 657–666. https://doi.org/10.1016/j.shpsa.2007.09.003.

Dreyfus, Stuart E. 2004. The Five-Stage Model of Adult Skill Acquisition. *Bulletin of Science, Technology and Society* 24 (3): 177–181. https://doi.org/10.1177/0270467604264992.

Dunphy, Bruce, and Stacey Williamson. 2004. In Pursuit of Expertise. *Advances in Health Sciences Education* 9: 107–127. https://doi.org/10.1023/B:AHSE.0000027436.17220.9c.

Seager, Thomas, Evan Selinger, and Arnim Wiek. 2011. Sustainable Engineering Science for Resolving Wicked Problems. *Journal of Agricultural and Environmental Ethics* 25 (4): 467–484. https://doi.org/10.1007/s10806-011-9342-2.

Why They've Immersed: A Framework for Understanding and Attending to Motivational Differences Among Interactional Experts

Eric B. Kennedy

12.1 Introduction

The study of interactional expertise (hereinafter "IE"), as initially proposed by sociologists Harry Collins and Robert Evans, provides a unique framework for understanding nontraditional instantiations of expert behavior. At the most basic level, interactional experts (hereinafter "IEs") are those who are able to speak the language of a specialization without being able to practice the physical skills associated with it—this linguistic expertise having been gained through prolonged engagement with "contributory experts" within the specialization (Collins and Evans 2002; Evans and Collins 2007; Collins et al. 2006; Collins 2011). Over the past decade, theoretical development and case studies alike have provided first glimpses at the variety of practices that might be included under the IE

E. B. Kennedy (✉)
York University, Toronto, ON, Canada
e-mail: ebk@yorku.ca

© The Author(s) 2019
D. S. Caudill et al. (eds.), *The Third Wave in Science and Technology Studies*, https://doi.org/10.1007/978-3-030-14335-0_12

umbrella, ranging from individual sociologists (like Collins' experience becoming immersed in the gravitational wave physics (GWP) community) to large groups (such as comparisons drawn between IE and the experiences of Steven Epstein's AIDS activists, or calls for interdisciplinary mediators in situations of public-scientist conflict) (Evans and Collins 2007; Epstein 1995; Whyte and Crease 2010). Yet, despite the many and varied examples that have been considered within this body of literature, there remains room to reflect upon what these numerous case studies may reveal about IE as a concept.

Moreover, while studying IE provides an interesting location for considering the influence of epistemic diversity, it is just one case study within a broader project of attending to epistemic situatedness, which is vital to discussions of expertise, collaboration, and socio-technical integration more generally. Examples of contesting and assessing credibility and expertise like Wynne (1989) and Epstein (1995)—which predate interactional expertise as a theory—raise questions about the exclusion of epistemic perspectives and individuals that do not fit traditional conceptions of "expert" or "expert knowledge." There are substantial reasons to believe that this is an important area of reflection—not only to better appreciate the diversity, skills, and experiences embodied within the rich variety of IEs, but also to ensure that future examples of varying incarnations of expertise are not overlooked. In this chapter, I suggest that by attending to the plurality of motivations that can compel an individual to develop IE, we can gain a better understanding of some of the diversity present among IEs. In particular, I propose that four common examples cited within the IE literature represent four different potential categories of motivation for developing IE: learners, challengers, collaborators, and facilitators (see preliminary discussion in Plaisance and Kennedy 2014).

To develop this proposal, I begin with a brief account of the concept of IE, with a focus on its initially broad conception and subsequent refinements. From there, I will introduce and consider four accounts of IE—Collins himself, Epstein's AIDS activists, Kathryn Plaisance's discussion of philosophers of science, and Brian Wynne's Cumbrian sheep farmers—to highlight the subtle differences in the experiences of each interactional expert group. I will then offer a proposed framework for understanding four different motivations for IE and suggest that each profile is characterized by a different and asymmetrical exchange of knowledge and influence between the interactional and contributory experts. Finally, I will briefly explore a few of the reasons why this project is important, namely by offering the further development and appreciation of diversity within expertise as an important goal for Studies in Expertise and Experience (SEE), the subject of this volume. In doing so, I hope to call attention to some of the diversity revealed by the concept of IE, suggest that it offers a fertile area for further IE research and studies of expertise more broadly, and sketch possibilities for future consideration in the field.

12.2 Four Narratives of Interactional Expertise

According to Collins and Evans, IE is a form of expertise that allows someone to speak the language of a specialism at an expert level in the absence of the ability to practice the discipline's tangible skills. This linguistic immersion is acquired through prolonged enculturation within the expert community and depends for its maintenance on ongoing contact with the traditional "contributory" experts within the specialization. Importantly, knowing the language is seen as more than just memorizing definitions, but rather fully grasping the tacit subtleties about the language of the discipline. In their first article on the subject (2002), Collins and Evans focus on the ability of IEs to "interact interestingly" with the contributory experts, usually for the purpose of performing a sociological analysis of a domain. The IEs may be capable of raising interesting new points after a great deal of enculturation, but their contribution—as people who are "able to convey the scientific thoughts and activities of others"—is only recognized and implemented by the contributory experts. In other words, IE is (at least in early 2002–2004 conceptions) dependent on deep linguistic enculturation and, at most, makes contributions through astute observations shared with the contributory experts.[1]

Note that recent publications have allowed for a different perspective on the role of IEs. In particular, a 2011 article by Collins entitled "Language and Practice" acknowledges the central role of linguistic exchange in many domains of practice. Accordingly, the demarcation between contributory and interactional experts is recast, primarily because of the fact that contributory experts do indeed possess IE. Contributory experts are those who gain their IE in the "normal way," by making contributions and gaining access to specialist domains. By contrast, the newly labeled "special interactional experts" gain their IE despite the disadvantage of lacking the traditional routes to a "valued embodied skill." Special IEs, then, must take a different route to acquire their linguistic expertise and specialist immersion. While the proposed taxonomy of four quintessential IE narratives is therefore particularly salient for these special interactional experts (who have gained their expertise through nontraditional routes), the varied experiences also resonate with the diversity of experience among contributory experts.

As part of a pair of 2015 responses to this author (Collins and Evans 2015; Collins et al. 2016), Collins and Evans shed light on the history of the concept via their "privilege [as authors as having] special access to the origins of the ideas." Four streams—which they refer to as the philosophical, sociological, imitation game, and sociology and policy "tributaries"— fed into the development of the concept. Special interactional experts are separated from those with ubiquitous interactional expertise, the former including those who have IE within a particular domain (e.g., a sociologist of a discipline, an advanced journalist, or a non-player who has become an effective sports coach) and the latter consisting of IE in a more general population phenomenon (e.g., women who are able to gain IE in the linguistic patterns of men) (Collins and Evans 2015).[2] They also lay out an argument against "softening" IE to be excessively inclusive, with which I agree for purposes of this chapter. My aim is not to broaden the inclusion criteria by orders of magnitude, but rather to argue for more careful attention to (a) the epistemic and motivational diversity among already recognized IEs, and (b) to be sensitive to (a likely small number of) boundary cases of potential IEs who may be excluded *if* the imitation game were to be seen incorrectly as a definitional, demarcating test of interactional expertise at an individual level.

One particularly seminal instantiation of IE is that of Harry Collins himself, namely his experience of becoming an interactional expert in gravitational wave physics (hereinafter, "GWP"). Beginning in 1972, Collins developed IE in GWP through spending a great deal of time interacting with the physicist community. As he explains in *Rethinking Expertise*, an interactional expert (presumably like himself and drawing on his experiences) progresses "from 'interview' to 'discussion' to 'conversation' as more and more of the science is understood" (Evans and Collins 2007, 33). Thanks to this development, the quality and relevance of questions improve, language is used more naturally and appropriately, and the interactional expert becomes a more active participant in the exchange. Through this enculturation, Collins found that he was indeed able to pass the imitation game, a key marker of the successful acquisition of IE.[3] Note that Collins is a sociologist of science, a discipline that leverages IE to study and analyze the domain in question. His extensive publications in sociology journals related to GWP evidence his sociological motivations for becoming an interactional expert and maintaining IE.

Another example cited early in the development of IE is that of the AIDS treatment activists in the United States who learned the language of the medical community to take an active role in critiquing the dominant existing forms of clinical trials. Originally studied by Steven Epstein, these activists challenged the established protocols for trials by engaging directly with the medical community. This was an incredibly diverse group of actors, including those with and without (1) the disease, (2) formal medical training, or (3) existing scientific experience, and stratifying an incredible range of social, political, and economic classes. Among all these differences, however, was a shared commitment to the cause of, and connectedness and solidarity with, AIDS patients, and a desire to see specific changes to the testing protocols. Notable for their tendency to "speak in their own voice," they still managed to earn a right to talk and a place at the table, thanks to dedicated study of the issues and prolonged and persistent immersion in the medical community (Epstein 1995).

In contrast to the experiences of Collins and Evans as sociologists, one emerging example in the IE literature is that of philosopher of science Kathryn Plaisance and the other philosophers she discusses in her work. An interactional expert in behavioral genetics, Plaisance originally began to acquire IE for similar purposes of analysis to that of Collins (albeit philosophical rather than sociological). This disciplinary situatedness, however, made a substantial difference—by focusing on critiquing and clarifying concepts essential to active research within behavioral genetics, opportunities emerged to share these critiques with the behavioral geneticists themselves. One such example involved equivocation of the terms *shared* and *non-shared environments*, which led to epistemic problems in the research and practice of the discipline. This direct engagement with behavioral geneticists—even though her work and contributions are strictly at a theoretical level—has led to ongoing engagement with the scientific community. Although her initial experiences aligned well with the interview-to-discussion-to-conversation model present in Collins' experience, her IE has developed in a markedly distinct way compared to the researcher analyzing the discipline from afar (Plaisance 2006).

A final example present in Collins' account of IE is that of the Cumbrian sheep farmers, initially popularized by Brian Wynne (Wynne 1989). Following the Chernobyl meltdown, scientists in the United Kingdom were tasked with setting emergency regulations surrounding sheep farming. They failed, however, to consult with local farmers and accordingly were unable to include the great deal of local, agricultural, and ecological knowledge possessed by the farmers. This resulted in both ineffective regulation and increased distrust between the parties. While Collins emphasizes the role IE acquired by the farmers or scientists could play in this situation, Kyle Whyte and Robert Crease (2010) suggest that an important role could exist for a "trusted mediator" who maintains IE in both disciplines. The trusted mediator would play an active role in facilitating epistemic and collaborative connections between groups involved to constructively manage and challenge distrust that may exist. An interactional expert, according to their analysis, could have avoided what they dub an "unrecognized contributor case," where a great deal of legitimate expertise was disregarded because of exclusion, disengagement, or inability to communicate.

12.3   Motivations for Developing Interactional Expertise

As these four brief cases illustrate, there are many commonalities to be found between the various accounts of IE cited by Collins and Evans and present in the IE literature. At the same time, however, I would suggest that these accounts are, in fact, telling slightly different stories about IE, the people who hold it, and their rationales for acquiring it in the first place. To illustrate this, I propose examining one feature of each case study—the *motivation* of the interactional expert for pursuing and maintaining their IE—and some of the ways it might impact what I term their "IE profile." Each case study can be mapped onto one of four proposed profiles of IE to provide a rough tangible example of some of these attributes: the interactional expert as "learner" (Collins as sociologist), "challenger" (Epstein's AIDS activists), "collaborator" (Plaisance as philosopher), and "mediator" (Whyte and Crease's proposed trusted mediators). Following an introduction of each type, I offer a table summarizing some of the key comparisons between the prototypical forms of each.

As with the development of any skill, it is unsurprising that prospective IEs have a multitude of reasons for gaining that skill. For nearly all IEs, for instance, similar themes could likely be found in the motivations that drive their pursuit of IE: the desire to gain new knowledge and skills, the need to earn the trust of an expert community, and the desire to gain exposure for their ideas or to a new community. Yet, the motivations that I am interested in considering lie a layer deeper—*why* they pursue that knowledge and skills, *why* they wish to earn a new community's trust, and *why* they want to share ideas or experiences. This can be profoundly shaped by one's role and context—working under a formal facilitation capacity or mandate, for instance, or among a group of colleagues that are deeply collaborative (or, alternatively, radically competitive and focused on individual outputs). At the same time, these motivations are deeply personal and tied to individual identities, aptitudes, and personalities, similar to the "interactive ability" proposed by Evans and Collins (2007), but wider in scope. These underlying motivations require attention precisely because they are core to how one frames, understands, and pursues one's acquisition of IE.

Learner IEs represent the most paradigmatic form of IE as described by Collins and Evans. Generally, these IEs are motivated by a desire to learn, analyze, or understand a specialist domain, whether for internal (e.g., an autodidact seeking to learn a new discipline outside of their background) or external (e.g., a sociologist seeking to better understand and conduct research on a community) reasons. Accordingly, the quintessential learners typically become IEs along the most traditional path described by Collins and Evans—progressing from interviews to discussions to conversation—as they seek to develop a highly accurate, representative knowledge of the target community. This emphasis on precise understanding doesn't preclude a critical awareness. In fact, learners are ideally well positioned to offer informed analysis and critique of the target community because of their commitment to listening and learning first.

For the most prototypical learners, this focus on accurately understanding the target domain continues to impact their IE well after its initial development. The learner embodies the observer role, asking questions for clarification, but often simultaneously being weary of playing too active a part and "going native." Learners may be driven to intensive and detailed study of the discipline because of their goals of complete understanding (particularly when later compared to challengers or mediators seeking to simply "know enough" to fulfill their goals). At the same time, however, because the learner's motivations may be highly project-oriented (e.g., gain the IE in order to complete a study), there could be little incentive to continue enculturation following the achievement of these initial goals. Alternatively, intentional steps will be required to maintain sufficient linguistic enculturation, lest they risk losing their tacit understandings. This aligns well with Collins and Evans' notion that ongoing enculturation is required—if they as sociologists completed their immersive project and stopped "hanging out" with the expert community, there would likely be little incentive or ability to organically maintain their linguistic and tacit proficiency.

By contrast, the quintessential challenger IEs (as exemplified by members of the AIDS activist community profiled by Epstein) are not necessarily motivated by a desire to learn about a discipline, but rather by strong ambitions to change something about that domain. Similar to learners, the linguistic enculturation serves as a means to an end, although the goal is being able to effectively challenge experts rather than understand and study them. To some degree, this goal may be predetermined, although it can vary from generalities (e.g., "we want to see clinical trials done differently") to very specific ambitions (e.g., "we want you to adopt our proposed methodology"). Although there are other, more confrontational methods to challenging a group of experts, the prototypical challengers believe that by gaining linguistic and tacit understanding of the expertise (and perhaps through the process of proving that ability alongside the existing experts) they will have a more effective voice amid expert discussions. The acquisition of IE for a challenger, then, is characterized by attaining *enough* expertise to be able to fulfill these ambitions, rather than focusing on capturing a precisely accurate or complete understanding of the experts' language and culture. The severity of the disagreement undoubtedly affects the journey toward enculturation, ranging from fairly positive interactions akin to those of learners, to an emphasis on book learning, self-study, or consulting with allied experts to avoid having to learn the basics from conversation, and to be able to assert some linguistic competence even in early interactions.

As with learners, the ongoing experiences with IE for challengers will be shaped by their motivations as well. Their understandings of language, for instance, might be more adversarial (such as in framing terms by emphasizing perceived flaws), or their immersion may be constrained by an urgency imposed by what they seek to challenge (e.g., learning enough language to challenge contributory experts on a contemporary and time-sensitive issue). Challengers may also strive to pick up the language as more of a "mask" to be worn when advantageous for advancing their agenda, rather than for the purposes of studying the field and its terminology as a learner. Much like some learners might be afraid of "going native," challengers too may try to maintain an independent identity from the expert community, only blending in or impressing when beneficial.[4] It is also important to note that these goals can certainly evolve as exposure to the expert community changes, both in terms of radical changes like understanding why something is done the way it is, and in more nuanced developments like learning how to articulate or pursue certain goals more effectively. This exposure to the field may include opportunities to more closely examine ideas held by the experts (e.g., having a revelatory conversation or having their feedback taken seriously) or even getting to know the experts themselves (e.g., humanizing an expert community they may have previously demonized). This exposure can be mutually reshaping as well, affecting both the challengers' perceptions of experts and expert ideas, and the experts' perceptions of the challengers and the challengers' ideas. Finally, although the word "challenge" often carries connotations of confrontation, challengers are not restricted to being forceful or set in their positions. The defining characteristic of the challenger, as for the AIDS activists, is the desire to gain IE as a way of influencing or changing something about the established expert community.

For collaborator IEs, gaining IE is both intrinsically worthwhile and a means to an end. In their most prototypical form, collaborators are substantially motivated by the process of learning and working across disciplinary boundaries, and further driven by the potential outcomes of such cross-boundary work. The end goal could be predefined (e.g., collaborating to solve a specific problem in a relatively understood and typical way) or could be fairly open ended (e.g., tackling a complex problem or creatively exploring new possibilities). In important respects, this end is usually collaboratively defined and open to change over time, based on the co-creation of work with partners from other communities.

Accordingly, collaborator IEs experience different enculturation and maintenance of linguistic and tacit proficiency than learners or challengers. Rather than focusing on the language itself, many collaborations may initially center on the problem or project to be solved together. Initial phases of collaboration—like many experienced by the author—can be characterized by mutual discovery of misunderstandings and linguistic assumptions. Learning the language of the other expertise, then, becomes part of resolving these challenges and attending to the target problem, rather than explicitly focusing on trying to learn the language. A collaborator's language acquisition is likely to be heavily influenced by making connections to one's own expertise (e.g., "this concept sounds like a concept I know, but with these differences"). Finally, relative to the learner, the projects at hand provide a more natural reason to maintain ongoing linguistic and tacit knowledge (contrast "I work with many French-speaking friends, giving me good reason and easy opportunity to keep up this second language" with "I want to keep up this language, so I need to make sure to hang out with French speakers often enough").

Finally, mediator IEs have a goal of facilitating communication between two groups, whether disciplinary, linguistic, cultural, social, or otherwise. Mediators may be motivated by the end of resolving a conflict or facilitating communication, by the experience of learning about each group, or by the process of helping bridge these boundaries. Their enculturation process can range drastically in length, from mediators who have (purposefully or unintentionally) spent their lives immersed in multiple communities to those who have only a short period of time to prepare to facilitate an acute conflict resolution between two groups. Accordingly, their enculturation process depends heavily on interactive and reflective abilities, and is characterized by empathy, understanding, seeking common ground between parties, identifying potential misunderstandings, and a high degree of metacognition about the process of enculturation and communication. Much like learners, emphasis is placed on the importance of accurately understanding language, perspectives, and tacit knowledge. For mediators, however, the accuracy facilitates the capacity to explain and moderate these inter-community dialogues, rather than being attained for its own sake (Evans and Collins 2007).

Having already considered the three other motivations, it is possible to view the mediator's use of IE as a blend of the other strategies. In addition to being like a learner in their focus on accuracy, the mediator is also similar in potentially facing an uphill battle in maintaining their IE after the goal (resolving the conflict) is complete, unless relationships with the communities are maintained. Although the mediators work closely with the parties involved to determine their desired outcome, just as challengers wish to see some sort of change, mediators come in with a predetermined lean toward resolving misunderstandings and disputes. This may very well affect how they frame the language and tacit knowledge they acquire, as they are specifically attuned to potential points of controversy or confusion. Finally, like a collaborator, mediators use their acquired linguistic skills for mutual benefit; working toward a mutually defined emerging goal. This profile is highly inspired by Whyte and Crease's call for the use of "trusted mediators" who are capable of developing interactive expertise to be able to resolve unrecognized contributor cases and other situations. In a case, for instance, where scientists and policy makers over-look local farmer expertise in the development of agricultural regulations, a trusted mediator could identify distrust, highlight salient knowledge, and facilitate more collaborative engagement processes (Whyte and Crease 2010).

With these four motivations in mind, it is worth taking a moment to sum-marize some of the basic hypotheses about their profiles. In Table 12.1, I highlight some of the distinctions that separate each profile of expert, rang-ing from the origin of the goals to the views on expertise. While it is beyond the scope of this chapter, I would also propose that an interactional expert's profile consists of many factors, including the way IE is motivated, devel-oped, maintained, used, self-understood, and perceived/tested by others.

When the four ideal types are placed into this sort of 2×2 matrix, it is tempting to form a quadrant space where the x and y axis represent different attributes, and each type falls into a corner. The role of voice, for instance, could serve as the vertical access if Table 12.1 were converted to a sort of graph representation. In the positive y space (above the x axis), challengers and collaborators place a higher degree of importance on their individual voices being heard in the process, while learners and mediators below the x axis emphasize maintaining a professional distance, avoiding inserting their own voice too heavily, and empowering the expert voices involved. The x axis, then, could represent predetermined versus emerging goals, with challengers and learners bringing more predetermined agendas than mediators and col-laborators, whose desires are intentionally left open to change and influence.

Yet, while this arrangement helps to elucidate certain comparisons, it also flattens the number of variables involved and the heterogeneity within the examples. For one, there are simply too many dimensions in play to be

Table 12.1 Key attributes of each profile of IE

Challenger	Collaborator
• Predetermined goals (make a change)	• Emerging goals (work together)
• Gain sufficient IE as means to an end	• IE as byproduct and collaborative tool
• Exert influence on experts	• Co-create as mutual experts
• Maintain own voice and identity	• Equality and sharing of views
Learner	**Mediator**
• Predetermined goals (analyze or learn)	• Emerging goals (help facilitate)
• Linear progression to IE is desired end	• IE as tool for facilitating conversation
• Accurately understand expert voice	• Facilitate expert conversation
• Maintain proper distance	• Empower existing voices

convinced that any two axes capture the essential differences between the types. Furthermore, it does not seem as though the challenger and mediator are necessarily more "opposite" than learner and mediator, leading to difficulty in placing the elements. Most importantly, each motivation above is meant to sketch out at most an ideal type. I intentionally do not set demarcation criteria for what ought or ought not count as a "true" example of each type. Rather, my aim here is to illustrate that there is variance between interactional experts and that this diversity is noticeable and important. Indeed, instead of undermining the theory that there are a diverse set of IEs, the challenges revealed in trying to distinguish them precisely simply lend credence to an underlying commonality between them—their interactional expertise. This framework is not intended to create debates about which IE ought to be classified precisely where, but rather to indicate that any given interactional expert is uniquely shaped by a number of variables in his or her profile.

It is also important to make a few general notes about these varying motivations for acquiring expertise. Perhaps most importantly, none of the motivations are intended as superior to others—I suggest a plurality of conceptions of IE, not a hierarchy. Because their purposes are so varied, each offers substantial benefits and value for its own goal, and none are without potential trouble spots. The degree of intentionality in each motivation is also highly variable, ranging from very intentional acquisition (like the four examples developed here) to almost coincidental development of IE (such as enculturation in a different culture by virtue of where one lives). Similarly, not only are the motivations open to interpretation, but they are also nonexclusive and dynamic. Nonexclusivity indicates that an interactional expert can hold several motivations simultaneously (e.g., a mediator can desire to learn, and a challenger can desire to collaborate). Their dynamic nature highlights how motivations and manifestations of a particular interactional expert might change over time (e.g., Plaisance moved from learner to collaborator and even at times mediator or challenger depending on context). Because they are dynamic, it is also difficult to discern the difference between an accurate account of motivations (that may very well be unarticulated or subconscious at the time) and post hoc explanations that downplay the nuances of motivations that change over time. Indeed, these observations indicate that further substantial empirical work is needed to develop methodologies for assessing these motivations and their impacts on the acquisition of IE.

12.4 Varying Interactional Expertise Profiles and Asymmetrical Knowledge Flow

Before concluding this brief introduction to IE, one more observation should be made about the four types. In addition to the differences in motivation, development, and use of IE, it may be instructive to consider the ways in which information flow varies within the prototypical examples of each type. Table 12.2 offers a visual representation of this variety between profiles.

As discussed in Sect. 12.3, each profile has a different set of motivations for attaining and maintaining IE, which results in manifestly different realizations of the role. One key variation is the quintessential direction of knowledge transfer experienced between different groups when interacting with varying IEs. The learner (Collins and Evans' quintessential, sociologist-like IE) follows the most typically conceived model for IEs. The interactional expert is the one in the learner role, absorbing tacit, explicit, and linguistic knowledge from the established experts as part of the learning process. As Collins describes, these types of IEs make contributions primarily through comments that spur on contributory experts to realize new perspectives or ideas about their specialties. In Collins (2004, 128–129), he suggests that IEs can make contributions to disciplines not on their own, but by causing contributory experts to say "I never thought of it that way." This asymmetrical flow is largely due to the priority on understanding and analyzing, and the reduced desire (i.e., "why would I want to?") or willingness (i.e., "it's not appropriate to go native") to make direct contributions.

The challengers, however, attempt to drive knowledge flow in the opposite direction. Just as insightful perspectives can flow from learner IEs to the expert community, challengers do obtain a great deal of tacit and linguistic knowledge from their enculturation process. The thrust of their

Table 12.2 Asymmetric knowledge flows between IEs

Challenger		Collaborator	
Established experts ⬅	Interactional experts	Established experts ⬅➡	Interactional experts
Learner		**Mediator**	
Established experts ➡	Interactional experts	Interactional experts Established experts ⬅⬆	Established experts

motivation, however, comes from a desire to advocate for a new position and cause the experts to see something in a new way. In this sense, the challenger hopes to exert influence in the other direction, instead compelling the established experts to change their position through persuasion and knowledge-sharing. For challengers, their linguistic abilities achieved through IE become the vehicle for allowing this communication with the expert community.

The quintessential collaborators, by comparison, experience a bi-directional knowledge flow. While collaboration could be entirely one-directional (i.e., one participant learns the language in order to collaborate with several contributory experts within the same field), the enculturation process could also be characterized by a multi-directional immersion, where each party is learning to communicate with one another. The enculturation is likely also characterized by frequent attempts to draw connections and parallels between the backgrounds of the participants, both individually and collectively. Plaisance's collaborative work with behavioral geneticists typifies many elements of this instantiation of IE—a type of IE that is certainly heavily motivated and shaped by learning, but also willing and aspiring to make contributions of significance thanks to the combination of unique perspectives and immersed experience (Fehr and Plaisance 2010).

Finally, the mediator IEs add additional dimensions to this conversation. The expert groups (perhaps two, perhaps more) they are helping to mediate provide a powerful knowledge transfer of tacit and linguistic information toward them, much as the learners seek to acquire an accurate understanding. Yet at the same time, the mediator IEs end up playing an important role in connecting and facilitating the mutual exchange between two expert parties, as evidenced by the bi-directional arrow between each of those involved.

Again, much like the earlier typologies of each profile developed, these knowledge flows are not absolute. Instead, they offer a rough sketch of how different priorities on learning, teaching, influence, and knowledge transfer can, and do, arise in exemplars of IE. Accordingly, they call on us to recognize and attend to the diversity that we see, while recognizing the deep commonalities between each form of IE that validate the concept as a whole. I now turn briefly to understanding the importance of attending to this diversity among IEs.

12.5   Importance of Understanding Diversity Among Interactional Experts

At the most basic level, it is important to acknowledge the existence of this diversity among the many varied IEs who are already regarded as exemplars of the concept. Such an acknowledgement ensures descriptive accuracy, namely identifying a potentially significant characteristic so that we do not overlook salient variables within IE. If motivations for IE do indeed vary, it may be that different motivations lead to individual IEs manifesting their expertise in different ways (Plaisance and Kennedy 2014). Furthermore, it opens new avenues for better understanding the skills (including, but not limited to, interactive and reflective abilities introduced by Collins and Evans) required to become an IE and the ways they might vary in importance and instantiation depending on one's motivations. The acquisition, framing, use, and importance of linguistic enculturation might also vary between motivations and instantiations of IE. Learners, for instance, may seek to understand the current language of a discipline as authentically and precisely as possible, while challengers may attempt to replace or circumvent existing terms. Finally, it may also be that different motivations lead to different profiles if individuals were subjected to an imitation game.[5] A challenger might be quite obvious thanks to atypical examples or phrasings, or even flat out refusal to see the game as a valid way of testing for expertise (since the established experts may be perceived as intentionally excluding them), while a collaborator might give atypically interdisciplinary answers.[6] Understanding these varied motivations therefore helps develop a better theoretical account of IE.

Acknowledging and appreciating this diversity among IEs is also important, however, for reasons of justice and inclusion. By acknowledging the diversity present within IEs, we are more likely to be able to recognize IE in new—and perhaps currently overlooked—settings. Having a broadened conception of IE, for example, might be particularly valuable for marginalized groups attempting to articulate the work they have done to learn about a discipline before challenging it, or to see the value in implementing the suggested trusted mediators in situations excluding nontraditional experts. This is not to suggest that the definition of IE ought to be "softened," as Collins, Evans, and Weinel worry (Collins et al. 2016, 1); rather, it is to acknowledge that there may be a relatively small number of boundary cases that are wrongly excluded or go unacknowledged if our conception of a special interactional expert subconsciously looks more like a sociologist/philosopher of science, rather than a community facilitator, patient activist, or artistic collaborator. These pragmatic reasons speak to ways in which the IE literature, and Studies in Expertise and Experience, can be effectively used to improve policy and governance on a wide variety of issues.

12.6   Conclusion

Having such a rich variety of examples of IEs over the past decade has played an invaluable role in developing our theoretical understanding of IE. Yet, the diversity of special IEs remains unexplored, leading to a similarly fertile set of future research for those interested in IE. On the question of motivations alone, for instance, many avenues remain: Do IEs generally fit into these four categories, or are there others? Do these motivations indeed lead to different individual manifestations of IE, and are they generalizable or highly individual? How is each developed, and can skills and training be targeted to the type of IE trying to be achieved? Should this diversity affect our concept of IE as a whole, and perhaps serve to broaden what it includes? Perhaps most importantly, how does this diversity of motivation and profile manifest in studies of expertise and collaboration beyond IE?

In this chapter, I have suggested that when we consider case studies of IEs, we are in fact telling subtly different stories about the nature of each case. I have argued that by examining the motivations of those who become individual IEs, we can see four general motivations that emerge: learner, challenger, collaborator, and mediator. I have provided a framework of ideal types for each profile, not to create strict demarcations between each type, but to sketch out a realm of possible diversity among the many examples of IE already cited and in those yet to be discovered. Furthermore, I have introduced the concept of asymmetric knowledge exchange, suggesting that each type of IE relates differently to the experts with whom they interact. This offers support for the idea that IEs do indeed have unique "profiles." Attending more closely to these varied motivations not only allows us to develop a more grounded theoretical understanding of IE but also allows IE to continue to become a more practically valuable and empowering concept.

NOTES

1. Most of this perspective on IE remains similar throughout papers from 2002 to 2007. Earlier work (2002) provides the source of broader conceptions of IE (e.g., the ability to "interact interestingly" with experts), while later publications emphasize the importance of the imitation game and enculturation process to a higher degree.
2. In this chapter, I am focused on recognizing epistemic diversity among special interactional experts.
3. In short, the imitation game requires a judge to question two other participants about the specialized area and assess their anonymized replies. One participant is a contributory expert, while the other is a candidate interactional expert. According to Collins et al. (2006), if the IE is able to convincingly reply as an expert in the field, their replies will be identified at only a chance rate, and they will "pass" the imitation game.
4. Note that it is not always the case that challengers wish to avoid being seen as knowing the language. In the case of Epstein's AIDS activists, for instance, the ability to acquire linguistic expertise was positively linked with achieving the desired change and feeling increasingly empowered.
5. The imitation game, described in note 3 above, relies on the transmission of blinded text replies to questions posed by a judge. While identifying information like names are removed from the replies and each is delivered simultaneously to account for speeds of reply, I suggest that the blinding process may not remove idiosyncratic examples, references to experience, or particular phrasings in the replies that become more salient and prominent when this diversity is acknowledged.
6. In Plaisance and Kennedy 2014, we raise the concerns that recent citations of Collins and Evans seem to take the imitation game to be a test to be applied in individual cases (e.g., can a prospective interactional expert pass this test to validate their status, yes or no?) and that early formulations of IE seem to leave open this possibility. In their response, Collins and Evans (2015) clarify that the imitation game is not a test to be applied in individual cases. The point about how an individual would react to a prospective imitation game, however, is still salient, as it reveals the different priorities, concerns, and inclusion/exclusion. Some prospective IEs, for instance, would be entirely unfazed by such a request or opportunity; others would take it as an affront, have serious concerns with the language of "passing," or see it as indicative of problematic power dynamics overall.

REFERENCES

Collins, Harry. 2004. Interactional Expertise as a Third Kind of Knowledge. *Phenomenology and the Cognitive Sciences* 3 (2): 125–143.

———. 2011. Language and Practice. *Social Studies of Science* 41 (2): 271–300.

Collins, Harry, and Robert Evans. 2002. The Third Wave of Science Studies: Studies of Expertise and Experience. *Social Studies of Science* 32 (2): 235–296.

———. 2015. Expertise Revisited, Part I – Interactional Expertise. *Studies in History and Philosophy of Science Part A* 54: 113–123.

Collins, Harry, Rob Evans, Rodrigo Ribeiro, and Martin Hall. 2006. Experiments with Interactional Expertise. *Studies in History and Philosophy of Science Part A* 37 (4): 656–674.

Collins, Harry, Robert Evans, and Martin Weinel. 2016. Expertise Revisited, Part II: Contributory Expertise. *Studies in History and Philosophy of Science Part A* 56: 103–110.

Epstein, Steven. 1995. The Construction of Lay Expertise: AIDS Activism and the Forging of Credibility in the Reform of Clinical Trials. *Science, Technology, & Human Values* 20 (4): 408–437.

Evans, Robert, and Harry Collins. 2007. *Rethinking Expertise*. Chicago: University of Chicago Press.

Fehr, Carla, and Kathryn Plaisance. 2010. Making Philosophy of Science More Socially Relevant [Special Issue]. *Synthese* 177 (2).

Plaisance, Kathryn. 2006. *Behavioral Genetics and the Environment: The Generation and Exportation of Scientific Claims*. Minneapolis: University of Minnesota.

Plaisance, Kathryn, and Eric B. Kennedy. 2014. A Pluralistic Approach to Interactional Expertise. *Studies in History and Philosophy of Science Part A* 47: 60–68.

Whyte, Kyle Powys, and Robert P. Crease. 2010. Trust, Expertise, and the Philosophy of Science. *Synthese* 177 (3): 411–425.

Wynne, Brian. 1989. Sheep Farming After Chernobyl: A Case Study in Communicating Scientific Information. *Environment Science and Policy for Sustainable Development* 31 (2): 10–39.

CHAPTER 13

Developing a Theoretical Scaffolding for Interactional Competence: A Conceptual and Empirical Investigation into Competence Versus Expertise

Shannon N. Conley and Erik Fisher

13.1 INTRODUCTION

The chapter begins with a conceptual overview of existing frameworks for expertise, followed by an introduction to the proposed notion of *interactional competence*. We focus on examples from the Socio-technical Integration Research ("STIR") program, in which "embedded humanists" spend time within a laboratory context, collaborating, engaging, and

This material is based on work supported by the US National Science Foundation under grant numbers 0849101 and 0531194.

S. N. Conley (✉)
James Madison University, Harrisonburg, VA, USA
e-mail: conleysn@jmu.edu

E. Fisher
Arizona State University, Tempe, AZ, USA
e-mail: efisher1@asu.edu

© The Author(s) 2019
D. S. Caudill et al. (eds.), *The Third Wave in Science and Technology Studies*, https://doi.org/10.1007/978-3-030-14335-0_13

235

participating in laboratory practices with the goal of both understanding and enhancing laboratory reflexivity. We argue that the bar that is set for having obtained Interactional Expertise (IE) is a different bar than what is needed to characterize what is obtained both in the STIR context and in the case of other similar roles. Instead, we argue for Interactional Competence (IC) as a more appropriate lens for understanding productively engaged collaborative contexts, where the goal is not to become an interactional expert in a particular field but to instead become conversational and knowledgeable to the extent of being able to ask effective questions, engage in ongoing, in-depth conversation with experts, and gain legitimacy in the laboratory setting in order to facilitate impactful socioethical reflection. We then share empirical examples from Conley's STIR studies, during a time when she was embedded as a social scientist in reproductive genetics laboratories collaborating with scientists and simultaneously reflecting upon her own acquisition of interactional competence. Through analysis of these examples, we posit that interactional competence is potentially a useful concept for both thinking about and more effectively developing the abilities that critical outsiders develop in such collaborative contexts.

13.2   THE INTERACTIONAL EXPERT

The notion of the interactional expert, the individual who has become so immersed within a field outside of their own expertise that they can actually "pass" as an expert in that outside field, is synonymous with Harry Collins's own canonical example of working as a sociologist among gravitational wave physicists. While he did not consider himself a contributory expert, someone who contributes to technical papers and does calculations, he did consider himself an interactional expert—someone who could, in his words "understand the field to the point of being able to make reasonable technical judgments" (Collins 2017, 314). The notion of interactional expertise has enjoyed widespread use, largely because it helps open up discussions around the nature and acquisition of the knowledge and skills that scholars, managers, and other "outsiders" need to acquire in order to perform in certain roles.

Collins explicitly stated that the linguistic accomplishment of interactional expertise contrasts with the practical accomplishment of contributory expertise. More than a linguistic accomplishment, contributory expertise is "the ability to contribute to an area of practical accomplishment" (Collins et al. 2016, 104). Unlike interactional expertise, contributory expertise requires the ability to perform a skill, not just talk about it. If an interactional expert were able to make such a contribution, Collins and colleagues would most likely categorize this person instead as a contributory expert. As we will argue, neither of these two terms accurately captures the knowledge and skills cultivated by collaboratively engaged social scientists and humanities scholars who facilitate the kind of reflection that leads to changes in the material and epistemic practice of the engaged experts.

13.3   EXPERTISE VERSUS COMPETENCE

In order to further unpack the difference between interactional expertise and contributory expertise, and to open up space for a third category, we move beyond expertise and consider competence. Although the two terms are closely related, and are often used as synonyms (Evans and Collins 2010, 54), there are also differences between them (Collins and Evans 2002, 288 n. 4) that can be helpfully explored. Expertise is defined by the Oxford Living English Dictionary as "expert skill or knowledge in a particular field." Competence can be defined as the "ability to do something successfully or efficiently." There are a few key differences between these simple definitions, specifically the association of a particular set of *skills or knowledges* related to a *particular field* in the expertise definition versus the orientation toward ability in the definition of competence. In terms of the expertise definition, the skills could be linguistic in nature, in line with interactional expertise, or could be both linguistic and material in nature, in line with the notion of contributory expertise. This is in opposition to the competence definition, which, although it too can arguable embody linguistic and/or material accomplishments, does not require the same field-specificity. In short, abilities can be broadly applied across multiple specialized and non-specialized domains, whereas an expertise is a very specific set of skills applicable only to a specialized knowledge domain. As such, expertise is far more limited in scope and, we suggest, in its ability to explain the ability of individuals and groups of experts to do the kinds of things they typically do.

13.4   EXPLORING CONTRIBUTORY COMPETENCE

We now explore the utility of distinguishing between these two different ideas, expertise and competence, in an empirical setting, drawing from selected vignettes from Conley's STIR experience. To operationalize these concepts, we understand expertise to consist of knowledge or skills that pertain to a specialized knowledge domain, whereas we operationalize competence as abilities to construct, align resources around, and effectively resolve problems. At the time of her immersion in two genetics laboratories, Conley was certain that she was either gaining, or on the cusp of gaining, interactional expertise. However, upon further reflection on these experiences, we argue that interactional expertise is not the appropriate lens for understanding what occurred as a result of her collaborative engagements.

Conley was certainly honing her collaborative abilities and gaining knowledge and hands-on experience in genetics, but could not have linguistically "passed" as an expert in a rigorous way. Superficially, she could have "passed" to an observer, or maybe even an expert, since one could often find her in the laboratory participating in material practices, wearing a white lab coat, but it was never her goal to pass as an expert.

In Conley's case, ignorance was an asset, and we argue that one does not have to become an interactional expert in order to engage in STIR. But one does need to become interactionally competent by developing a suite of *abilities* that enable them to become engagement agents who can move fluidly among the discourses and terrains of scientific, industrial, and political activities. These individuals should be able to incorporate social, ethical, and political considerations into a problem-solving approach.

13.5   Socio-technical Integration Research

STIR is a platform for interdisciplinary collaboration that is designed to enhance specialized expert capacities for more reflexive and socially responsive research and innovation. The process includes real-time, collaborative description of expert decisions in order to facilitate reflection on problem framing, recognition of values, exploration of alternatives, and possibilities for integrating broader societal considerations into routine expert cognitive, affective, and behavioral practices (Schuurbiers and Fisher 2009, 424–427). The goal of integration research is to assess the responsive capacity of laboratories to reflect on societal concerns associated with research and development (R&D) activity, by means of feeding societal concerns back into scientific practices at the level of the laboratory. Responsive capacities allow scientists and engineers to more explicitly engage and thereby broaden their routine practices and processes with respect to broader socio-ethical dimensions. Integration *work* attempts to expand the considerations that scientists take into account while in the

R&D phase, while integration *research* attempts to understand the conditions for such work. Integration activities are located within the midstream of scientific research, *after* public research goals and mandates have been set, but before research results are published and products enter the market (Fisher et al. 2006).

After initial pilot studies (Fisher 2007, 2010), STIR was employed in 30 science and engineering laboratories across North America, Europe, and Asia as part of an NSF-funded study designed to assess laboratory capacities for reflection and action regarding the social implications of scientific and engineering research (Schuurbiers and Fisher 2009; Fisher and Schuurbiers 2013). Since then, the approach has been applied in some two-dozen additional sites in the form of individual studies (McTiernan et al. 2016) and in larger projects that coordinate multiple studies in the US (Richter et al. 2017), Europe (van Oudheusden and Fisher 2018), and South-Eastern Europe (Lukovics and Fisher 2017).

13.6   THE RELEVANCE OF SEE WORK

Like Collins and others who have conducted laboratory ethnographies, STIR researchers observe scientists in action; however, integration work requires researchers to go beyond observation and actively perturb the system using a suite of tools and methods, including a decision protocol and a midstream modulation framework (Fisher and Schuurbiers 2013) that structure their "laboratory engagement studies" (Fisher 2007).

In order to fully immerse themselves in the laboratory environment, embedded researchers (building on Fisher's work) engage in an "extended" form of ethnography, using a decision-making protocol that explores the various considerations that scientific researchers currently integrate and could integrate into their research. Such considerations can range from material considerations, to social considerations, to legal considerations. Weekly interviews serve as a venue for the social scientist to provide constant feedback to researchers, focusing on researchers' decisions, and how the considerations taken into account for material, social, and political practices might be broadened and productively reshaped.

The interview protocol used by STIR researchers and their collaborators is fairly open-ended, and one could think of it as a collaborative brainstorming worksheet. It is centered around four basic questions: What are we doing? Why are we doing it? How else can we do it? And who might care? The broad open-endedness of these questions allows for the STIR researcher and their scientist collaborator to facilitate an in-depth conversation, as opposed to simply answering a rigid interview protocol. Interviews serve as a unique opportunity for social scientists and natural scientists to think together about social, legal, and/or ethical considerations, with the social scientist serving as a reflexive tool for thinking more deeply about such issues.

13.7   STIR INVESTIGATORS AS INTERACTIONAL EXPERTS

Collins defines interactional expertise as the "ability to converse expertly about a practical skill or expertise, but without being able to practice it, learned through linguistic socialization among the practitioners." At a specific point along the way, in many of the STIR studies that have been conducted (e.g., Fisher 2007; Flipse et al. 2013, 2014; Schuurbiers 2011), a shift can be observed from conversing with the researchers about their experiments to actively participating in their material practices alongside them. Collins (2004, 128) saliently highlights this transition, from the "painful period" of ignorance, to being able to "join in" and even transfer knowledge among scientists, to the point where the social scientist can coherently engage with his or her scientist collaborators.

13.8   UNDERSTANDING LABORATORY PRACTICES

The material used here is drawn from two studies conducted by Conley as part of the original coordinated series of STIR studies. She was embedded in two laboratories, primarily focusing on genetics and human reproduction. In the summer of 2009, she was embedded in a laboratory in Canada, and in the fall and winter of 2009 she was embedded in a laboratory in the UK. Each study was three months long.

During the first two weeks of the Canadian laboratory engagement, Conley despaired ever coming to a real understanding of what the researchers did in their daily practices. She would stare, mystified, at the large machines that surrounded my workspace. She would hear conversations regarding "snips." *What is a snip?* She desperately scanned the Internet in an effort to find answers. However, she was not able to find a clue to the mysterious "snip," S-N-I-P, an entity that seemed to be so popular in laboratory discussions.

Conley decided that, despite the potential embarrassment it might cause her, she would broach the topic of the "snip" in her interviews with the researchers. Her weekly interviews with laboratory members Joy and Zhi, two PhD student researchers, served as a primary source of information for her, particularly when it came to learning the language of genetics. The primary reason that she could not solve the mystery of the "snip" is that although the term is pronounced as "snip" it is actually an acronym: "SNP," which stands for "single nucleotide polymorphism." These SNPs occur when one "letter" (the nucleotides represented by the letters A, C, T, and G) in the genetic code gets switched out for another letter. Depending on where these SNPs occur, they can be either harmless or considered a genetic mutation, having a dramatic impact on human development and health.

Although conducting interviews and spending time in the laboratory was important in establishing rapport and trust relationships, spending time, in and of itself, does not necessarily translate to gaining competence or understanding. Each day spent at the laboratory meant being surrounded by strange equipment that Conley only vaguely recognized as being important for DNA analysis from forensic television programs. Researchers would spend hours hunched over their benches, using slender instruments to draw liquid from one set of tubes and deposit it into other sets of tubes. This ritual was simultaneously hypnotizing and perplexing.

13.9   DISCOURSE DIVORCED FROM PRACTICE

During Conley's weekly interviews with Joy and Zhi, terms such as "PCR," "sequencing," and "SNP" were used quite frequently, and she was coming to have a nebulous grasp of what the terms meant; yet the discourse, at this point, was far divorced from an understanding of practice. She could engage in conversation about scientific practices, and could even string the words "polymerase chain reaction" together, yet she could not connect the concept with the practice. Discussing SNPs and PCRs was akin to talking about fairytales and swords in stones. She could attempt to imagine them situated in scientific practice, but had never witnessed or experienced them firsthand. She could have a conversation about a PCR, but still could not understand how it was actually done. Conley and her collaborators might talk about ethedium bromide agarose gel in multiple conversations, yet she could not connect the idea of the gel to the actual practices of the laboratory. The researchers would patiently explain concepts to Conley in their interviews, but without an understanding of material, physical practices that she could anchor them to, the concepts continued to remain empty and meaningless to her. Understanding the concept was not enough; she needed to understand how the concept operated in practice.

13.10   FROM LINGUISTIC TO MATERIAL ENGAGEMENT

The opportunity to move from engaging linguistically with the concept to engaging materially with the technique came in Conley's interactions with Frank, the post-doctoral researcher in the laboratory. Her work area was right next to his workbench. Frank's hands were constantly busy preparing and executing experiments. While working, he typically carried on one or more conversations on a wide array of topics with Conley and his lab mates, topics ranging from music to food to science. Approximately three weeks into the project, she asked Frank if she could watch him "do a PCR." That same day, she reflects, "my bench-side friend transformed into my key informant." Conley's guide readily agreed to let her watch him "do the PCR," but he actually did much more than just let her watch. Having taught courses at his former university, he pulled up the PowerPoint slides (which were in Spanish) and began the process of teaching Conley about genetics. He realized that they would have to start with the basics when he asked Conley if she knew what a PCR was. Rather than pretend to know something she did not, she admitted that she hardly understood it, with only a vague understanding from popular television shows such as CSI.

13.11   LEARNING PCR

Frank described to Conley how all genetics research depends on DNA amplification. For a geneticist to study a particular gene or region of DNA, the tiny fragment must be amplified. The PCR, or as she came to learn, "polymerase chain reaction," is both a process and an entity, which explained some of her earlier confusion. The process includes putting together a complex combination of liquids to create a reaction. The reaction only happens under a series of intense heat exposures, which are carried out in a PCR machine. So when a researcher says that he or she "has to go do a PCR," the expression encompasses both the PCR process of mixing liquids and the machine itself. Put simply, the purpose of the PCR is to amplify particular regions of DNA. The regions to be amplified depend on what the researcher wants to study, and he or she will put together a specific and customized mixture of primers, enzyme, and nucleotides that will bind to and amplify the specific regions to be studied. The "chain reaction," the process of DNA amplification, only happens when specific temperatures are applied to the mixture inside of the PCR machine. Conley was struck by how simple the process was—there was basically no difference between PCR and cooking: one must add the proper ingredients and use the proper temperatures to achieve the desired product. However, like cooking, a good PCR requires both experience and skill. A novice can stumble through, but the old adage that "practice makes perfect" holds true for PCRs; the steady hand and experienced eye of a veteran typically results in a more consistent PCR reaction.

13.12   DOING PCR: TRANSITIONING FROM OUTSIDER TO LABORATORY MENTOR

About nine weeks into the project, laboratory members and Conley were regularly engaging in lab social events, such as lunch, coffee, and after-work outings. Around this time, Frank showed Conley that he had redesigned the laboratory member's pictures and biographies on the door to include her picture and blurb. Laboratory members and Conley were also connected on social media. On social media, Conley signaled her intention to audit a molecular genetics course in order to deepen her understanding of some of the laboratory's experiments. She was confronted by Zhi, who had learned of her expressed interest. "Why would you want to do that?" he demanded. After Conley explained her motives, Frank, also present, asked if she had "done a PCR." When she responded that she had not, Conley's collaborators immediately suggested that she try her hand at one. Within a matter of days, donning a lab coat and rubber gloves, and armed with a pipette, Conley was doing her own PCR, no longer "benchside," but at the bench itself. The researchers found it novel and exciting that Conley was rolling up her sleeves and engaging in the physical, material aspects of their work. When Pearl, the technician, saw Conley working, she exclaimed, "Wow, I can't believe my eyes!" Pearl and some of the other researchers excitedly snapped pictures of Conley holding a tray of samples and using a pipette.

13.13   INSIGHT INTO MATERIAL PRACTICE

The experience was a vital learning exercise, providing Conley with insight into scientific practice that she would not have had otherwise. For example, when pipetting PCR product into the ethedium bromide agarose gel wells, she realized that her blood sugar had dropped quite low (she had not eaten that morning), since her hands were shaking, and she was beginning to feel slightly lightheaded. When she expressed how unsteady her hands had suddenly become, the undergraduate student, Tsai, showed Conley a way to hold the pipette with both hands that helped her steady her grip. If she had not been performing the delicate pipetting task, she would never have noticed that something as seemingly trivial as skipping breakfast could have on the physical aspects of a scientist's work. Knowing that she would be doing more work with Frank, she changed her eating habits and began to eat breakfast. Despite her shaky hands, she managed to successfully pipette the rest of the PCR product into the wells, and a few hours later, after the completed gel electrophoresis, Frank found the PCR results to be so exemplary that he ran to the copy machine and made a copy, to use as an example of a "good PCR result" in his future lectures on the topic.

13.14   GAINING INTERACTIONAL COMPETENCE

The process of gaining interactional competence while also participating in the material practices of the laboratory culture poses what some scholars might perceive as serious risks to the integrity of ethnographic research. The transitional experiences from laboratory outsider to laboratory insider highlight an important aspect of ethnographic research, that is, the risks associated with "going native," of blurring the distinction between the observer and the observed, of participating *too much* in the culture that one is observing. Ethnographers are warned that feeling too "at home" is a danger. While there is the risk that the ethnographer might lose his or her objective ethnographic gaze by actively breaking down the boundaries between the "Self" and the "Other," there are also advantages to conscientiously going native. In the case of Conley's STIR studies, going native by engaging in material and other cultural practices of the laboratory served as a strategy to foster diverse modes of engagement and discourse, and hone her collaborative abilities and disposition.

13.15   UK: Hitting the Ground Running

In the UK, following the completion of the Canadian study, Conley "hit the ground running," and shortly after her arrival, began participating in material practices on an almost daily basis. Unless they already knew of Conley as the "Jones laboratory's American social scientist," other researchers at the UK research facility assumed that she was also a geneticist, based on her growing capacity to fluently converse with them, and also empathize with their day-to-day challenges. If their PCR was not turning out, or they were feeling overwhelmed by the amount of pipetting they had to do, Conley could empathize, and even offer advice in some circumstances. She was able to empathize with the struggles of the doctoral student, Sonny, and help him identify a specific issue in terms of how he was recording his PCRs and identify something that might help him by transferring the Canadian lab's PCR protocol over to him. Sonny was willing to take Conley's advice and attempt doing things differently because she could not only dialogue about PCRs with him, she was able to show him an artifact (the PCR sheet and pictures of a successful PCR) of her firsthand experience that served as evidence of competence in the domain.

13.16   Transferring Material and Knowledge Practices

Before Conley met Sonny, she learned about his PCR challenges in her first conversation with Edward Jones, the laboratory's director. Part of the conversation between Conley and Jones centered around trying to understand each other's "cultures." When Edward expressed to Conley that he understood only about "one-tenth" of what she did, she told him that she was still trying to understand his world as well. She explained that she had been engaging in some material practices in her last laboratory engagement and had some basic understanding of genetics from a practitioner's perspective, but that there was still a great deal to learn. She showed him results from the PCR that she had done in the Canadian laboratory. Edward stated: "You are probably equal to or farther along in your understanding of genetics as Sonny is, who has been here for months, and still can't manage to do a PCR."

Edward's comment, that Conley was equally competent or surpassing in understanding material practices as one of his doctoral students, was an unanticipated acknowledgment of her increasing capacities for material competence and understanding. The day following her conversation with Edward, Sonny and Conley were casually chatting in the lab, and he expressed his frustration with his PCRs to date. They sat down at his workspace, and Sonny showed Conley his PCR notebook. Most of the researchers in the laboratory used large red notebooks to record their experiments and notes. The sturdy red covers ensured that they could withstand wear and tear, and could be referred to years later. Despite spending hours at his bench preparing his PCRs, they always ended in failure. The bands signifying the presence or absence of specific DNA mutations were non-existent, or very faint at best. The ability to complete a PCR is a basic skill in which a geneticist must attain competence before he or she can do anything else, and Sonny's futile attempts, after four months of trying, were preventing him from going any further in his research endeavors.

Disconcerted at Sonny's distress, Conley reached for her folder containing her notes and PCR results from the Canadian laboratory. "Maybe we could compare PCRs," she said. She pulled out the PCR sheet and results that she had completed in my last laboratory engagement.

"Where did you get this?" Sonny asked.
"It's from my laboratory engagement this past summer," Conley said. "This is one of the PCRs that I did."
"*You* did this?" Sonny asked.

Conley responded that it was her very first attempt at a PCR. Sonny commented that he was very impressed that it was her first try. "The bands look so nice!" he exclaimed. "Bloody good. Goes to show that you don't need a scientific background to do a PCR." Sonny then took a closer look at the PCR "sheet," a rubric that Frank, the post-doc in the Canadian lab, had designed. The sheet listed all of the basic ingredients for a PCR, and allowed the researcher to fill in all the specific amounts of the necessary materials. It was a useful tool for both seasoned veterans and new researchers to keep track of precisely what was going into their PCR solution. Sonny found the PCR sheet design to be both elegant and useful. He had been writing everything down in his notebook, and he noted that without the PCR sheet, it is more likely that the researcher could omit something or make an error. Sonny asked if Conley could provide him with a copy of the PCR sheet so he could use it and employ some of its characteristics in his own note-taking and PCR practices. She contacted Frank from the

Canadian lab and asked him if Sonny could have a digital copy of his PCR sheet design. Frank was happy to oblige and was excited that someone was interested in using his PCR sheet.

13.17   Linguistic and Material Engagement

The vignettes above demonstrate how an embedded social scientist in order to interface with scientists in a critical and collaborative manner must gain both linguistic and material abilities. Te Kulve and Rip (2011) call for "engagement agents"—individuals who can traverse the multiple "streams" and "work at more than one level" of innovation processes. Such actors can serve as "linking pins" among the multiple levels that comprise a particular scientific and policy domain. Integration work presents one way of developing interactionally competent engagement agents. The trading zones (Collins et al. 2007) that embedded social scientists develop with their scientist collaborators within the context of the laboratory are not necessarily confined to the four walls of the laboratory. Rather, as the collaboration strengthens over time, and the social scientist becomes more familiar with the technical aspects of the scientists' work, and also becomes more comfortable asking questions at the confluence of the socio-technical, they can take their newfound perspectives, knowledge, and critical insight to other levels, or streams, within the innovation system.

The poet, Alfred, Lord Tennyson (n.d.), in recounting the journeys of Odysseus, writes, "I am a part of all that I have met." Similarly, the embedded social scientist carries his or her experiences both inside and outside of the laboratory with them, moving between the laboratory and other domains of scientific, policy, and socio-cultural practices. The embedded social scientist becomes a mobile trading zone, in a sense, capable of directly engaging with laboratory cultural and material practices, while also being able to dialogue and provide critical insight into those same practices in which she actively participates.

13.18   Interactional Expertise
Versus Interactional Competence as Analytic Tools

According to Collins's framework for interactional expertise, "one can acquire the language of a domain without engaging in the wider practices of a domain" (Collins 2004, 130). Collins is clear in distinguishing the linguistic learning from participating in the material culture of a domain:

Being able to speak a language is a social skill, but the new point is that it is not the same social skill as being able to practice the corresponding physical activities; crucially, the latter is not necessary for the former. What you get from immersing yourself in the linguistic culture pertaining to a practical domain rather than the practice itself is what I call "interactional expertise." This is opposed to "contributory expertise"—which is what you have if you immerse yourself in the culture in a full-blown way. (Collins 2004, 127)

The focus of IE on language, and not on the contributory role of participating in material practices, contrasts with Conley's experiences within her studies, in which her interlocutors engaged her in the learning of the *language* by guiding her through hands-on *material practices*. Given the three-month period of each of the studies, it would be hard to imagine Conley going from a naive novice to a completely linguistically savvy interactional expert in the relatively short period of time. For Conley, the material and the linguistic were inextricably interlinked. However, by Conley routinely engaging in material practices by assisting with and conducting her own laboratory experiments, she was afforded the opportunity to establish a bench-side trading zone and the development of a professional camaraderie in which both parties were invested in helping the other learn the "lingo" of their respective disciplines. Collins notes that it is a massive undertaking and investment to gain interactional expertise, stating that "[d]eveloping interactional expertise is the job of months or years of interaction" (Collins 2004, 129). While Conley's studies spanned a total of six months embedded in laboratories and collaborating with scientists, she never gained perfect fluency in the linguistics, often relying on the trading zones and creole she had developed with her collaborators in order to have productive, and challenging, interactions regarding topics social, ethical, and technical in nature. Despite not having achieved the high level of linguistic fluency needed for interactional expertise, Conley's experiences interacting with her collaborators, especially as the relationships developed and she became more immersed in laboratory practices and culture, becoming a reliable and respected collaborator, resonate saliently with an aspect of interactional expertise that Collins highlights:

When the sociologist becomes really good at the work it becomes possible to take a devil's advocate position in respect of some scientific controversy and maintain it well enough to make the conversational partner think hard about the science. This asking of new questions that the scientists might not have thought about, conveying of information, embellished in a way that makes it clear to the recipient that it is reliable, and making the real-time creative moves that are needed to maintain a devil's advocate position in the face of determined opposition, are discursive skills, not a matter of selection from an assembly of discrete propositions. (Collins 2004, 129)

There were a number of instances where Conley was able to play the devil's advocate and facilitate eye-opening conversations on a various socio-technical topics, and challenge her collaborator to reconsider their position, such as when, in conversation, she challenged her collaborator regarding the implications of his research on autism genetics, highlighting that research outcomes could be applied in unanticipated ways, such as in the context of pre-implantation genetic diagnosis, effectively removing embryos with those genetic traits from being implanted in the womb. Her collaborator's immediate response was "I had never thought about it that way before. That's certainly not how I would like this research to be applied."

Perhaps one of the major distinctions between Collins's desire to gain interactional expertise and Conley's experiences is that Collins sought to acquire interactional expertise in order to better and more fully engage in a study of the sociology of scientific knowledge:

A question that has been with the sociology of scientific knowledge from the beginning is "How much scientific knowledge do you need to have in order to do the sociology of a scientific domain?" We now have three decades of experience of case studies and can give an answer: you need quite a lot of scientific knowledge but not as much as a practitioner. (Collins 2004, 127)

While integration work has some methodological overlaps with studies in the sociology of scientific knowledge, it diverges in a number of ways, in particular with regards to an essential emphasis on building rapport and emphasizing that laboratory members are not solely objects of study to be scrutinized but collaborators in jointly producing reflexive, socially robust science. Thus, this different approach, with different aims, requires a different set of skills than a pure sociology of scientific knowledge study might entail. In particular, it requires the integration researcher to possess or develop key *dispositional traits*.

Table 13.1 highlights some of the key overlaps and distinctions in interactional expertise and interactional competence. Language plays an impor-

Table 13.1 Comparative table of interactional expertise and interactional competence

Elements	Interactional expertise	Interactional competence
Role of language	Depends on linguistic fluency	Depends on development of trading zones/creole
Temporal	Requires months to years to acquire via immersion in linguistic practices	Requires months to acquire via immersion in linguistic, material, and cultural practices
Role of material practices	No participating in material practices	Participation in material practices assists in learning and development of collaborative relationships
Role of cultural practices	Participation in lab meetings, social outings, etc., assists with acquisition of tacit knowledge	Participation in lab meetings, social outings, etc., assists acquisition of tacit knowledge and fosters collaborative relationship development
Role of ignorance	Ignorance is a detriment	Ignorance can be an asset
Focus of attention	Focused on one sphere/discipline	Boundary spanning (i.e., focused on multiple domains, such as laboratory and policy spheres)
Dispositional traits	Unknown	Requires development of: collaborative skills, humility, and empathy
Role of relationship development/rapport	Important, but specifics unknown	Highly important

tant role in each, but in different ways. Interactional expertise requires the attainment of a high level of linguistic fluency, so much so that one with interactional expertise could "pass" as an expert. Interactional competence, on the other hand, in the absence of a high level of linguistic fluency, necessitates the development of shared trading zones and a collaborative creole. While an understanding of key vernacular and concepts is important, one does necessarily need to know enough to "pass" as an expert, but needs to be conversant enough to engage with scientist collaborators, as was the case with Conley, whose primary objective was not to study the sociology of scientific knowledge, like Collins, but to explore collaboration via socio-technical integration and investigate capacities for reflexive governance within the laboratory setting. There is some overlap in the temporal aspect of each—both interactional expertise and interactional competence take time to acquire. Interactional expertise, due to its focus on linguistic fluency, requires months to years; Collins's example demonstrates that it takes many years, while IC can be obtained over a shorter period of time—months, as opposed to years, as demonstrated by Conley's studies.

Participating in laboratory cultural practices, such as laboratory meetings and social events, has been demonstrated to be of importance to the development of both interactional expertise and interactional competence, allowing Collins and Conley to both build rapport and gain tacit knowledge in their respective studies. While participating in such cultural practices enabled Collins to demonstrate his increasing fluency in the language of gravitational wave physics, Conley "had to be comfortable with and vulnerable about my ignorance with my collaborators." Conley learned quickly that her collaborative personality, willingness to be vulnerable, and desire to be a "team player" enabled her to break through the initial distrust and hesitation of her collaborators. Indeed, while the literature is not specific regarding the role of disposition and affective qualities of those gaining IE, we would posit that a collaborative disposition is a prerequisite and important first building block for gaining IC and critical for building rapport and developing relationships.

13.19   FOSTERING INTERACTIONAL COMPETENCE

With new modes of engagement come new ways of understanding. Just as integration equips natural scientists with new tools for thinking about the broader context of their research, integration also furnishes the embedded social scientist with new perspectives and understandings cultivated through bench-side dialogue, and even, in some cases, participating firsthand in material practices. During this period, the embedded social scientist is honing their interactional competence—a suite of cap*abilities* including the ability to move between micro and macro contexts (such as the laboratory and policy spheres); humility, which includes the ability to admit ignorance and ask questions; and empathy, which requires "stepping into the shoes" of one's collaborator. Taken together, these traits provide the building blocks for interactional competence.

REFERENCES

Alfred, Lord Tennyson. n.d. *Ulysses by Alfred, Lord Tennyson.* Poetry Foundation. Accessed July 31, 2018. https://www.poetryfoundation.org/poems/45392/ulysses.

Collins, Harry. 2004. Interactional Expertise as a Third Kind of Knowledge. *Phenomenology and the Cognitive Sciences* 3 (2): 125–143.

———. 2017. *Gravity's Kiss: The Detection of Gravitational Waves.* Cambridge, MA: MIT Press.

Collins, H.M., and Robert Evans. 2002. The Third Wave of Science Studies: Studies of Expertise and Experience. *Social Studies of Science* 32 (2): 235–296.

Collins, Harry, Robert Evans, and Mike Gorman. 2007. Trading Zones and Interactional Expertise. *Studies in History and Philosophy of Science Part A* 38 (4): 657–666.

Collins, Harry, Robert Evans, and Martin Weinel. 2016. Expertise Revisited, Part II: Contributory Expertise. *Studies in History and Philosophy of Science Part A* 56: 103–110.

"Definition of Competence in English by Oxford Dictionaries." Oxford English Dictionaries. Accessed July 31, 2018. https://en.oxforddictionaries.com/definition/competence.

"Definition of Expertise in English by Oxford Dictionaries." Oxford English Dictionaries. Accessed July 31, 2018. https://en.oxforddictionaries.com/definition/expertise.

Evans, Robert, and Harry Collins. 2010. Interactional Expertise and the Imitation Game. In *Trading Zones and Interactional Expertise: Creating New Kinds of Collaboration*, ed. Michael Gorman, 53–70. Cambridge, MA: MIT Press.

Fisher, Erik. 2007. Ethnographic Invention: Probing the Capacity of Laboratory Decisions. *NanoEthics* 1 (2): 155–165.

———. 2010. Integration. In *Encyclopedia of Nanoscience and Society*, ed. D.H. Guston, 344–345. Thousand Oaks, CA: SAGE Publications, Inc.

Fisher, Erik, and Daan Schuurbiers. 2013. Socio-technical Integration Research: Collaborative Inquiry at the Midstream of Research and Development. In *Early Engagement and New Technologies: Opening up the Laboratory*, 97–110. Dordrecht: Springer.

Fisher, Erik, Roop L. Mahajan, and Carl Mitcham. 2006. Midstream Modulation of Technology: Governance from Within. *Bulletin of Science, Technology & Society* 26 (6): 485–496.

Flipse, Steven M., Maarten C.A. van der Sanden, and Patricia Osseweijer. 2013. Midstream Modulation in Biotechnology Industry: Redefining What Is 'Part of the Job' of Researchers in Industry. *Science and Engineering Ethics* 19 (3): 1141–1164.

———. 2014. Setting up Spaces for Collaboration in Industry between Researchers from the Natural and Social Sciences. *Science and Engineering Ethics* 20 (1): 7–22.

Lukovics, Miklós, and Erik Fisher. 2017. Socio-technical Integration Research in an Eastern European Setting: Distinct Features, Challenges and Opportunities. *Society and Economy* 39 (4): 501–528.

McTiernan, Kaylie, Brian Polagye, Erik Fisher, and L. Jenkins June. 2016. *Integrating Sociotechnical Research with Future Visions for Tidal Energy.* http:// cspo.org/wp-content/uploads/2016/07/STIRandFutureVisions_KM_BP_ EF_KJ.pdf.

Richter, Jennifer A., Abraham S.D. Tidwell, Erik Fisher, and Thaddeus R. Miller. 2017. STIRring the Grid: Engaging Energy Systems Design and Planning in the Context of Urban Sociotechnical Imaginaries. *Innovation: The European Journal of Social Science Research* 30 (3): 365–384.

Schuurbiers, Daan. 2011. What Happens in the Lab: Applying Midstream Modulation to Enhance Critical Reflection in the Laboratory. *Science and Engineering Ethics* 17 (4): 769–788.

Schuurbiers, Daan, and Erik Fisher. 2009. Lab-scale Intervention. *EMBO Reports* 10 (5): 424–427.

Te Kulve, Haico, and Arie Rip. 2011. Constructing Productive Engagement: Pre-engagement Tools for Emerging Technologies. *Science and Engineering Ethics* 17 (4): 699–714.

Van Oudheusden, Michiel, and Erik Fisher. 2018. *'Stirring up' TERRITORIES: Integrating Social and Ethical Considerations into Radioecology.* Paper given at Social Sciences and Humanities in Ionising Radiation Research, International conference: RICOMET 2018. Antwerp, June 13–15, 2018, University Antwerp, Belgium.

CHAPTER 14

Collaboration Among Apparently Incommensurable Expertises: A Case Study of Combining Expertises and Perspectives to Manage Climate Change in Coastal Virginia

Michael E. Gorman, Zihao Zhang, Kristina D. Fauss,
and Benjamin D. Bowes

14.1　Introduction: T-Shaped and Interactional Expertise in the Context of Hampton Roads

In this chapter, we trace the evolution of a collaboration from submission of a grant proposal through the first year of research, focusing on the kinds of expertise both shared and gained by the members of a team Gorman

M. E. Gorman (✉)
University of Virginia, Charlottesville, VA, USA
e-mail: meg3c@virginia.edu

Z. Zhang • K. D. Fauss • B. D. Bowes
School of Engineering & Applied Science, University of Virginia,
Charlottesville, VA, USA
e-mail: zz3ub@virginia.edu; kdf3we@virginia.edu; bdb3m@virginia.edu

© The Author(s) 2019　　　　　　　　　　　　　　　　　　255
D. S. Caudill et al. (eds.), *The Third Wave in Science and Technology Studies*, https://doi.org/10.1007/978-3-030-14335-0_14

gradually formed with the goal of gaining sufficient T-shaped and interactional expertise to understand whether and how sensors, models, and platforms for sharing information could collectively improve shared management of this system across a range of stakeholders. In particular, we analyze the experiences of Gorman and Fauss in acquiring T-shaped skills in the field, and Zhang's experience as an "outsider" architecture scholar foraying into the "incommensurable" world of the engineering school, and there pursuing collaborations with civil engineers. This chapter will explore the utility of interactional and T-shaped expertise for understanding the collaboration among an interdisciplinary team in the University of Virginia (UVA) that is modeling the effects of incidental and recurrent flooding and land subsidence in Hampton Roads, a metropolitan area in southeast Virginia that consists of ten cities and six counties with a total area of 7500 km^2. Interactional expertise is the ability to have a deep conversation with a native expert that shows not only knowledge of the nature of the expertise but also of the expertise community; T-shaped expertise adds experience and expertise in different systems. The capital "T" of the T-shaped concept represents the depth (stem of the T) and breadth (horizontal bar of the T) of expertise that one gains in becoming T-shaped (see Fig. 14.1 below). Interactional expertise is gained verbally. T-shaped experience in different systems can be both verbal and non-verbal because aspects of the system that will be salient to an expert will not be noticed by a novice; for example, an expert can recognize invasive plants encroaching upon a shoreline that looks healthy to a novice. To become T-shaped, the novice would have to be able to recognize another occurrence of the same combination of plant and shoreline and know that it constituted an

Fig. 14.1 T-shaped expertise illustrated

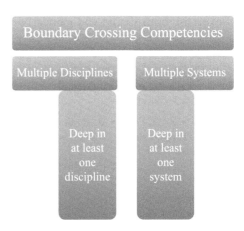

invasive situation, but would not have the expert's knowledge of the cause or understand the options for remediation in that specific situation.

The Hampton Roads area sits on a low-lying coastal plain at the south of the Chesapeake Bay watershed. It is home to the East Coast's largest naval base, the fifth-largest container port in the United States, and many other heavy industries such as the largest coal trans-loading facility of Norfolk Southern Railway, which exports coal from Virginia, West Virginia, Kentucky, and Pennsylvania to the world. Over 1.7 million people live in its dense urban cores and lower density suburban sprawls. The confluence of three rivers—James, Nansemond, and Elizabeth—and the Chesapeake Bay sustains amazingly diverse ecosystems, from wetlands and saltwater marshes to bald cypress swamps, which provide habitats for countless wildlife species.

Like many coastal regions, Hampton Roads is experiencing the effects of climate change,[1] which not only produces a rise in sea levels but also an increase in the variance in weather events and flooding—which means the system becomes less predictable, making mental models developed from past experience with the system gradually obsolete, thereby undermining both the tacit knowledge of experts in the system who were able to anticipate changes in flooding based on years of experience and also the quantitative models based on past data.

The effects of climate change on the Hampton Roads area exemplifies what Allenby (2012) calls coupled socio-technical-environmental systems, where a change in the environment will affect both the social and the technical, and the effects may be "wicked," that is, a small effect in any of the three dimensions might be enough to shift the system into a new state from which it will be hard to recover. These kinds of systems require that the experts studying and managing them have sufficient interactional and T-shaped expertise to collaborate with each other and also with stakeholders.

14.2   Expertise and Coastal Environment Management: An Overview and Analysis of Gorman's Experience in Cultivating Trading Zones and Becoming T-Shaped

Gorman joined a team that included two Civil Engineers and two Computer Scientists who submitted a funding proposal focused on the challenges facing Hampton Roads program to an NSF program whose acronym was CRISP (Critical Interdependent Resilience Infrastructure

Systems and Processes).[2] One goal of this NSF solicitation was to "foster an interdisciplinary research community of engineers and social, behavioral, and economic (SBE) scientists who work synergistically together for innovation in the design and management of infrastructures as processes and services."[3] The solicitation, with its emphasis on synergy, was calling for deep collaboration, not just a division of labor, and it required social science expertise.

The method used to study and facilitate the **Data-driven Management for Interdependent Stormwater and Transportation Systems** (dMIST) collaboration is socio-technical engagement (Fisher et al. 2015) which involves learning about expertise cultures by engaging in projects with them while continuously reflecting on how the collaboration is working.

Gorman's status as a collaborator was greatly helped by the fact that he is in the Engineering School at UVA, part of a department called Engineering and Society that includes social scientists and humanists who teach undergraduate engineering courses and collaborate with engineers on a variety of projects. This made the engineers his colleagues, even though their expertises were very different from Gorman's.[4] In the CRISP project, Gorman not only had to become an interactional expert in the expertises represented by the engineers, he also had to become a contributory expert because his background in social psychology and cognitive science were relevant to understanding how key organizations and individual stakeholders worked together to manage traffic and flooding in the Hampton Roads area and therefore what models would be most useful to them. Therefore, Gorman was not just observing whether the research team formed a kind of trading zone, he was in a position to see if one was needed and if so to catalyze it.

Collins, Gorman, and Evans (Chap. 15 in this volume) developed an evolutionary model of trading zones (see Fig. 15.1 in that chapter). Writing the proposal could be described as a fractionated heterogeneous trading zone, which appears in the collaboration row in that figure. The initial boundary object was the proposal itself, the content and goals of which were represented differently by the members of this nascent trading zone. Each of the co-principal investigators (co-PIs) contributed by adding sections reflecting her or his expertise, and the PI, Jon Goodall, ensured final coherence in constant online dialogue with the co-PIs. Trades revolved around the amount of space devoted to different expertises as part of the proposal and also being aware of how each part fit into a larger whole. The Interdependent Stormwater and Transportation Systems management goals required interactional expertise across disciplines and among stakeholders.

After the proposal was funded, the PI established a series of weekly meetings. To improve his understanding, Gorman appointed himself note-taker at these meetings and uploaded his notes on each meeting in a shared file, asking members of the team to correct any errors and misconceptions. The graduate students were expected to make presentations at the meetings, talking about their current research project, which allowed the faculty to ask questions and provide direction—they were learning modeling methods and also how to obtain and transform data. Gorman's typical questions sought to clarify the method each student was using and why it fit the problem, which is an appropriate question for a graduate student; indeed, in cases where Gorman did not raise it, others did.

The environment in which the meetings were conducted favored the development of interactional expertise; we met in the Engineering School's new Link Lab, a renovated floor of a building where the offices and conference rooms had glass doors so anyone could see into them. Our team met in one of the conference rooms, which had the capability to bring in others online. The Lab had desks for graduate students in an open area. Some faculty had offices with glass doors so anyone could see in. Gorman did not have an office, but he was happy to be out in the open space where he could see the flow of activity and offer advice.

What was unusual was the absence of laboratory equipment except for a track where one researcher and his students tested toy-sized autonomous vehicles. The Link Lab felt more a kind of market or trading space for ideas than a true laboratory—a good space for developing interactional expertise. It also had a kind of elite status—members were selected by the initial core faculty, and members could then bring in students. The Lab itself was an experiment in creating collaborations.

14.3   Collaboration Between Incommensurable Disciplines: The Experience of Zhang and Fauss— Incommensurability Between Two Schools?

Zihao Zhang is a PhD student in the Constructed Environment, which is a rather new PhD program in the School of Architecture at UVA. Before his PhD, Zhang has received a master's in Landscape Architecture from the same school. He took Gorman's Robotics Ethics seminar because the environmental design disciplines—architecture, landscape architecture, urban design, and so on—are interested in adopting advanced digital technologies such as sensing, artificial intelligence, and robotics to the design of environments such as cities and landscapes. Zhang learned about the dMIST project and expressed interest in working with Gorman on it. Zhang's own research focuses on the idea of cybernetic urbanism and considers complex socio-technical-environmental systems faced by today's design disciplines and looks for ways to better understand these systems from a design perspective. He has to gain interactional expertise in order to conduct his research successfully.

In order to better understand Zhang's involvement as an "outsider" in the dMIST, one should look more closely into the school-level collaborations and disciplinary incommensurability among humanities, sciences, and engineering. The collaborations between the two schools—architecture and engineering—have not been easy. There are jointly hired professorships in both architecture and engineering schools; there are also NSF-funded projects that have co-PIs from both schools; faculties and students from both schools form teams to apply for pan-university funding (i.e., funding intended to stimulate creative collaborations across disciplines) thanks to the top-down university policies and incentives to promote interdisciplinary studies.

But the collaborations are made difficult because they span incommensurable paradigms. Scholars in architecture have built a discourse that is heavily influenced by postmodernism[5] that rejects top-down approaches and comprehensive planning and promotes (but also romanticizes) informality and self-organization of urban spaces. Architecture and landscape architecture are disciplines that tend to adopt philosophical ideas outside the discipline to enrich their own considerations. For example, in a Landscape Theory class, students were asked to read passages such as Donna Haraway's *Cyborg Manifesto* (1991) and Bruno Latour's *We Have Never Been Modern* (1993). In general, there is an unstated skepticism in the community toward scientific and engineering approaches that assume a total control over systems. The Landscape Architecture department states plainly in their program introduction that "[a]s a department, we develop critical perspectives on issues that affect landscapes across a broad range of scales, including issues of *technology, social* and *environmental justice, ecology, and design culture*."[6] Moreover, concerns about social and environmental justice distinguish this program from others in the United States and draw people sharing the same concerns to the program.

Kristina Fauss, a civil engineering undergraduate and collaborator recruited by Gorman to join dMIST, is primarily involved in the engineering department of UVA through class and work with engineering design teams. However, much of her design work involves direct interaction with the Architecture School. She started as an engineer and is most exposed to the engineering perspective, but has initiated and participated in interactions between engineers and architects. She draws on this experience to reflect on the distinct approaches to design of students and faculty of the two schools. She has observed that the Engineering community places an emphasis on data-driven design. Civil Engineers distinguish themselves from Architects by prioritizing structural integrity and function over aesthetics; this engineering paradigm is captured in the phrase "form follows function." They are open to collaboration and curious about the architectural design style, but they maintain their opinion of the superiority of more linear design methods as more practical and efficient. Maintaining this distinction is a way of reinforcing the superiority of one's own disciplinary culture, a dynamic which can create friction between architecture and engineering scholars and students, complicating collaboration.

Building on Harman's (2018) observation and argument on "actual knowledge," we suggest that the incommensurability between the two schools is mostly an epistemological one for they have different understandings of what constitute evidence and knowledge. This epistemological incommensurability leads to a methodological difference between the two schools even when approaching the same subject during collaborations. Two false caricatures were produced in both communities about the other: in the engineering community, architecture and landscape design is reduced to style and aesthetics, leaving their social, technical, and environmental considerations outside the scope; in the architecture community, all types of engineering are reduced to practice of optimization, and their complex systems thinking was unjustly overlooked. Collaboration would give each discipline a chance to gain a more sophisticated understanding of the other.

14.4 Development of T-Shaped Expertise: Analysis of Fauss' Acquisition of T-Shaped Skills

Gorman wanted his research team to focus on the central issue in the proposal. There are two coupled parts to management of traffic and flooding: emergency response when a traffic jam and flood occurs, and long-term planning for infrastructure and policies that will reduce the impact of floods. The dMIST team is focused on cyberinfrastructure, including both improving sensor networks and making better use of existing sensors to provide the data necessary for predictive modeling and machine learning as the system changes.

Fauss took Gorman's Earth Systems Engineering & Management course, which focused on coupled socio-technical-environmental systems, and served as a teaching assistant on the next two iterations of the course (Allenby 2012). As a member of dMIST, she was embedded in the Hampton Roads area with Bethany Gordon, a graduate student who worked with Leidy Klotz, a Link Lab member whose expertise spanned civil engineering and architecture, showing that these two broad areas of expertise do not have to be incommensurable. Gorman and Klotz were already collaborating, so it made sense to invite Gordon to work with Fauss on interviewing stakeholders in the system.

Fauss spent a week in the Norfolk region to interview a variety of stakeholders and system managers with Gordon. Gorman joined when possible. The goal of the interviews was to stimulate a conversation that would give us an understanding of expert/stakeholder perspectives on the existing system, what parts ought to be preserved, which parts would have to change and why. The interview protocol was to explain our project, then begin with a series of broad, standard questions concerning, for example, the informant's background, and with what other experts and stakeholders he or she regularly interacted, and then find out more about his or her perspective on the future of the system. The interviewer took notes on each interview and sent them to the informant for review, so that the informant could review what we thought he or she said, and correct or redact anything in our notes. The notes would be the only record of each interview and were password-protected. We plan on sharing this and other publications with any informants listed in it, and obtain their consent for using their materials.

Whenever possible, the research team went to meetings that included multiple stakeholders and experts, to see how they explained their visions of the system to each other. Gordon, Gorman, and Fauss attended the Eastern Shore of Virginia Climate Adaptation Working Group (CAWG), a meeting of experts and stakeholders in the region who were working to affect change in their localities. The primary topics of the meeting were local adaptation and shoreline management. The team participated in as well as observed these meetings, consistent with the methodology, which involves active engagement with stakeholders—telling them about the project and its purpose and making suggestions about their work. During breakout sessions, small groups of these leaders and experts, and members of the dMIST research team, developed mock grant applications to meet at least some needs of each member of the breakout group. All participants chose projects from mock proposals to create a package with maximum benefits and competitiveness. The meeting concluded with a roundtable discussion of the proposals. Some stakeholders left with actionable plans, intending to apply them in their community. One of the best ways to understand a project is to make a suggestion to improve it. If the suggestion was plausible, that meant the team was developing an accurate understanding of the system and interactions among its stakeholders and managers. If it was orthogonal to the project, the team realized we did not understand the goals of the project and were often corrected, adding to our understanding.

The students were gaining expertise in Civil Engineering through their education at the university; this project gave them a chance to learn how to conduct interviews with stakeholders, which meant they gained methodological expertise in one of the methodologies associated with Science and Technology Studies (STS). Fauss developed a set of STS skills to support her development of interactional expertise around the issues of coastal flooding in the Hampton Roads region. Through repetition and active reflection, Fauss developed functional skills that allowed her to accelerate her own understanding of the studied system. Learning and expanding her STS methodological expertise allowed her to interact with interviewees on a deeper level than she had initially. She expanded on the initial note-taking and return strategy, adding a step of review, where she read her own notes and those of her team before returning them to the interviewee and then read any returned notes or corrections. She actively sought her own mistakes, identifying gaps in understanding post-interview and reflecting on what could be changed during the next cycle to avoid such mistakes.

At the beginning of the process, she noticed that she was asked simple questions and received simple responses. She worked to conduct the interview as a conversation, and largely succeeded, but focused too much on the prewritten set of questions. Sean Corson and Andrew Larkin from the National Oceanic and Atmospheric Administration (NOAA) were the first to be interviewed by Fauss and the team. Fauss felt unsure of her experience and decided to ask few questions and listen as Gorman and Gordon led the conversation. She asked few questions, and on reflection, they felt shallow. She received answers to her questions, but compared to later interviews, the resulting notes lacked detail. She received dry details on the organizational structure of NOAA. The primary office of the NOAA in the region is the Chesapeake Bay and NOAA Restoration Center, which is primarily focused on restoring coastal habitat and works with local communities to achieve its goals.

While this information is key to understanding the purpose of NOAA and its function in the region, it lacked depth. It did not reveal the story of NOAA and the Restoration Center and how these local groups interacted with the system in its living complexity. Gorman's targeted prompting revealed more of this complexity. The discussion with Corson and Larkin covered the Chesapeake Bay Program, an EPA-led federal and state consortium that combines expertise of academic organizations, nonprofits, localities, and state and federal agencies to lead restoration of the Chesapeake Bay watershed across state lines and jurisdictions. NOAA works to concentrate its impact on areas of intersection between NOAA goals and community goals. It emphasizes community input through its Collective Impact Approach, where it works with people who live in the region to identify the most pressing issues threatening the community. Fauss observed that the question-answer format often does not reveal the full reasoning of the interviewee; it leaves gaps in logic and fails to capture the big picture. For the dMIST project, it was important to have a detailed understanding from each perspective of each of the diverse interviewees. To correct this, Fauss began to use the question set less and focus on the flow of the conversation. If the interviewee became excited about a particular issue or talking point, she asked questions to continue the conversation on that point. She applied this alteration to her technique in the interview with John Parkinson and David Pryor of the design firm Clark Nexen. Clark Nexen has experience with restoration work. Fauss was prepared to discuss a well- documented project that the firm led in Colley Bay. As the conversation progressed, discussion on Colley Bay evolved to include interesting details on the process of construction. Clark Nexen typically oversees construction and hires contractors to build. Colley Bay was unique as citizens primarily staffed construction. Clark Nexen and other consulting firms are able to access volunteers to do light construction work through coordination with the city, which then connects the firm with volunteer organizations. This was new information to Fauss. She could not have known to ask a question concerning project staffing. Allowing the conversation to evolve naturally revealed a unique nexus where private firms, city organization, and volunteer groups interact. Such overlapping interactions are relevant to this project, which examines how stakeholders and management groups interact to cope with rising sea levels, flooding, and associated problems.

If the interviewee had specialized expertise outside of what was expected from the description of her organization and position, Fauss shifted the focus to include her niche expertise. By the end of the process, Fauss still used the question set, but it had become more of a checklist. She returned to it at the end of the conversation to ensure that all critical points were discussed, but the skills she had learned from observing Gorman's interview strategy resulted in much more detailed and varied information than required by the questions.

Fauss developed STS skills much in the way an apprentice might master a new art. Gorman presented an initial structure and made suggestions on interview strategy, but Fauss could not fully understand how to conduct an interview effectively until she began the process herself. She observed how Gorman and the interviewee interacted, and then applied that observation to her own experiences in the interview process. Through observation and self-reflection, she eventually developed a custom strategy and skill set to allow her to effectively interact with interviewees, to connect with them and develop enough understanding of the system and how the stakeholders understood it, and to begin to flesh out her own interactional expertise.

She learned how to pace an interview and how to listen for when there might be more information behind a seemingly succinct statement. Over time, it became easier for Fauss to recall and reference previous conversations where they may add to the interview. By the end of the week, Fauss could recognize names of people and locations, and common themes. She began to recognize discourse, where one stakeholder presented an argument that contradicted another's, and could enter into discussion on either side of such discourse when appropriate to gain a broader understanding of the problem. She gradually developed increased interactional expertise such that she could have robust discussion on the problems facing the system.

Throughout the interview process, the best interviews were conducted in spaces and places where the team could begin to see parts of the system as stakeholders saw it, thereby gaining T-shaped expertise. Immersion in the system was critical to gaining an interactional level of understanding. Interactional expertise requires that the researcher come to a level of understanding similar to those who exist inside the system. This understanding is more easily developed when the researcher may observe an insider to the system interacting with the environment. For example, Kyle Spencer, Deputy Resilience Officer for the City of Norfolk, took us to a place called the Hague where expensive housing close to the ocean surrounds an estuarial channel that terminates in a one-way valve which prevents water from flowing out of the channel at high tide or during a storm, but allows it to drain from the houses and streets when the tide is low. There is an abandoned Unitarian Church near the coast. Kyle showed us a neighborhood where houses are being raised, sometimes over the objections of neighbors—which is why a comprehensive plan is needed. He also showed us attempts to restore a living shoreline using native plants. At the Virginia Institute of Marine Science, we saw adaptive management experiments on the best ways to restore shorelines. Oysters are often part of this restoration; they not only shore up the banks, but they also filter the water. One unanticipated problem is that raccoons will climb down the banks and eat the oysters!

A key component of T-shaped expertise is experience in the system. The students were learning a lot about the system from their analyses of data from sensors and Waze traffic reports and other sources of digital information. Seeing parts of the system alongside an expert reveals elements that would help the students have mental models of the situations represented by the data. Gorman took students from the project team to key locations in Hampton Roads where they could see management strategies being implemented in different neighborhoods and along estuaries.[7]

14.5   Is the DMist Collaboration Becoming a Trading Zone?

According to Galison (2010), the first stage in a creole is developing a shared jargon, or common meanings for terms familiar to one expertise community in the trading zone but not to others. At this stage in the collaboration, we are developing shared meanings for concepts such as machine learning and modeling, the latter exemplified by the EPA's Storm Water Management Model (SWMM), which is the standard for simulating different conditions that affect runoff in urban areas. Machine learning involves the evolution of algorithms that learn to make predictions based on input data in a "black box" fashion with respect to human understanding of how they work. In the case of climate change, where the rise in global temperature increases local variance of weather conditions, machine learning can potentially make predictions using patterns that would not be obvious to human decision-makers. Unlike machine learning techniques, the physics-based SWMM is transparent to the expert user. SWMM allows the user to predict and simulate different conditions affecting water flow based on physical processes (e.g., infiltration of rain, overland flow of excess rain, and the flow of stormwater through pipes). Given the increase in variance that comes along with climate change, it makes sense to use both SWMM and machine learning, because the data-driven predictions made by the latter may lead to revisions in the former.

To help develop a creole, Gorman felt it was essential to have one of the engineering graduate students work both with his team and on an engineered component of the project. Benjamin Bowes, a PhD student in the Civil and Environmental Engineering department under the direction of the PI, volunteered. Bowes has a degree in Environmental Science and expertise in hydrology and environmental modeling; his work involves using neural networks, a type of machine learning, to forecast the level of the groundwater table in Norfolk during storms. This is an important part of creating more accurate predictions of flood severity, a key part of the dMIST project, and will continue to become increasingly important as sea level rises.

The modeling work conducted by Bowes and others in the dMIST project is done in part to extend cognition through detection, verification, and comparison of observed patterns in the environmental system. Experts and residents in coastal systems often have intuition about how the system should behave based on past experience. Modeling provides a check on that intuition, but can also reveal patterns in the system behavior that are not obvious even to experts. In the case of Bowes' groundwater forecasting, for example, local decision-makers may know that the groundwater table is shallow, but there is no easily accessible product to show them how storms will change the groundwater table level and the impact that may have on flood severity.

Because such model results need to be interpretable by non-subject matter experts, such as city managers, Bowes, and the other modelers on the project have welcomed the increased perspective and insight provided by the social psychologist (Gorman) and the landscape architect (Zhang). Having these researchers on the project has also made apparent the need to address incommensurabilities between the interdisciplinary collaborators involved by developing a creole. For example, the models developed by Bowes involve jargon that is unfamiliar to non-subject matter experts (e.g., neural networks, hidden layers, hyperparameters). While model results can be used without understanding such terms, interdisciplinary collaborators need to be proficient with them to make meaningful contributions to the modeling.

Do terms such as machine learning and the SWMM model represent shared jargon that eventually leads to a creole? Most of the team seemed familiar with both these concepts, though it was clear that one graduate student was the expert on SWMM and one faculty member the expert on machine learning. Both Gorman and Zhang were familiar with the strengths and weaknesses of machine learning and both had heard of SWMM but knew very little about it. So these started as jargon and are becoming terms that can be used with creole proficiency. It is important that interdisciplinary collaborators such as Gorman and Zhang understand the trade-offs in using particular kinds of models and algorithms, just as Collins learned how to discuss the pros and cons of different kinds of detectors with experts. One solution is to have Bowes on our team while he continues his modeling work. By presenting his modeling work at the weekly meetings, Bowes has been able to both develop more effective skills to communicate technical results and share disciplinary terms that contribute to a creole and interactional expertise.

14.6   Conclusions and Suggestions for Future Research

This engagement study follows the development of a research group that uses concepts from the Third Wave of STS (Collins et al. 2007) and architecture to collaborate with engineers and computer scientists in research designed to improve the management of a coupled techno-social-environmental system. Gorman's situation is unique because he was a social scientist who for many years had been embedded in the Engineering School at UVA and therefore he was not an outsider in terms of culture: he reported to the same Dean, served on the Engineering School's Promotion and Tenure committee, was involved in hiring decisions, and therefore had the kind of camaraderie and trust that emerge from frequent interactions with his engineering colleagues—and that includes being able to tell insider jokes only someone else in the School would understand. Gorman and Zhang bring referred expertise from their own expertise communities to the project, and gained interactional expertise with each other and with the computer scientists and civil engineers because those who live in the system have to be intimately involved in the process of understanding it and changing parts of it. Fauss is taking the lead on interviewing stakeholders and groups in the system to try to see the problems and possible solutions as each group sees them, gaining at least some interactional expertise. Whenever possible, members of our team go to parts of the system with the stakeholders, so we can learn what features are salient to them, thereby gaining some T-shaped expertise.

Our team is trying to identify trading zones in the system already that link groups and interests and managers. For example, Mike King at the Norfolk Naval Shipyard is working with the city of Norfolk on joint flood and storm maintenance. The city has people trained to respond to flooding and snow, so why not have them perform a similar function on the base? The base already depends on the city to keep the roads open so sailors living in the area can get to and from their work. Such a system will require a trading zone to coevolve the details of the management of roads and water and make continuous improvements over time.

14.6.1 Analysis of Expertises

To what extent were Gorman and the members of his research group becoming interactional and/or T-shaped experts? The canonical example of interactional expertise is how Collins achieved it in gravitational wave physics by embedding himself in the gravitational wave physics community. He gained sufficient interactional expertise so he could discuss issues on the cutting edge of the field with experts, including the debates over the designs of detectors, why some research groups had more credibility than others, and so on. Judging from his book *Gravity's Shadow* (2004), he may also have developed good mental models of how various gravitational wave detectors worked.

Collins gained his interactional expertise by engaging with gravitational wave physicists via constant discussion about their work. Gorman was gaining his interactional expertise through a collaboration in which his own expertise in STS, social psychology and cognitive science played a role—so others had the opportunity to gain a bit of interactional expertise from him. Gorman had to follow arguments about different ways of modeling the system, what were desirable characteristics of sensors and other highly technical topics. He did not have to be a contributory expert in these areas—he would not have to do the coding to create or modify a model. But he did have to understand the trade-offs and limitations of different approaches. In that sense, he was learning to master parts of esoteric expertise languages. He was helped by the fact that the graduate students were learning some of this also and by the fact that his "why" questions were tolerated, even welcomed. Having Ben Bowes participate in Gorman's research team created the opportunity to gain interactional expertise in at least some modeling approaches, and begin to see where and how they might add value to our study of the system.

Collins was identified as an expert in gravitational waves in an imitation game based on the Turing Test. It would be harder to create an imitation game that would capture Gorman's situation, because he needs interactional expertise sufficient to interact with this specific team, not with the larger communities of civil engineers and computer scientists and architects. Gorman would have to be able to give a coherent account of the research conducted by our the team and why we chose these certain and other methods and tools were favored and would have to be a collaborator on most of the deliverables. Gorman therefore had to gain at least some interactional expertise in traffic management, machine learning, the EPA's SWMM model and other aspects of the project. Like expertise, interactional expertise may be a continuous function rather than a binary one—there may be degrees of interactional expertise.

Gorman also had to become T-shaped by spending time in the system, learning as much as he could about how various stakeholders view their parts of the system. Reading articles about or written by stakeholders and even literary accounts can help get a feel for stakeholder mental models.

Gorman's team had to learn enough about each other's expertises to develop a transactive memory (Gorman 2002) within the team, of the system across the team, where transactive means knowing which team members know and are able to do specific things, like Zhang's ability to see the system from an architectural perspective, Bowes' ability to develop models and therefore understand their potential roles and limitations in management, and Fauss' growing T-shaped expertise in the system, developed from looking at parts of the system from different stakeholder perspectives. One way of sharing this knowledge and thereby building more interactional expertise is to collaborate on this paper, which itself serves initially as a boundary object, but the goal is to have every author understand enough of the paper so any of us can carry on a productive discussion about the ongoing work, and bring suggestions back to the rest of the team.

14.6.2 Refinement of Theory and Future Research

The trading zones and interactional expertise framework needs further development. There are different kinds of trading zones, depending on how equal or unequal the partners are, in terms of their ability to influence one another (Collins et al. 2007). Right now, the dMIST group is a fractionated trading zone, in which individuals are gaining interactional expertise in each other's specializations sufficient to coordinate research. If this trading zone continues and expands, the result might be a new creole, or interlanguage, that allows a larger community to expand this kind of collaborative work into new situations. Closer analysis of exchanges of information, resources, and time among groups in this system might reveal other types of cooperative arrangements that do not fit into the trading zone category.

NOTES

1. See, e.g., https://www.ucsusa.org/global-warming/global-warming-impacts/sea-level-rise-chronic-floods-and-us-coastal-real-estate-implications#.W1GZidhKjrI.
2. CBET CRISP Type 2: dMIST: Data-driven Management for Interdependent Stormwater and Transportation Systems. NSF CBET ($2,499,238.00) With Jon Goodall (PI), Madhur Behl, Donna Chen, Kamin Whitehouse. Material in this chapter reflects the views of the author and not the National Science Foundation.
3. https://www.nsf.gov/funding/pgm_summ.jsp?pims_id=505277.
4. Concurrent with Gorman's work on CRISP he was on a search committee for faculty in a combined Systems/Civil department and also participated in evaluating candidates for the new Link Lab, which he was invited to join after the team received funding for this project.
5. The use of the term "postmodernism" in its broadest sense includes approaches found in feminist theory, deconstruction, structuralism and post-structuralism, etc.
6. See https://www.arch.virginia.edu/programs/landscape-architecture, emphasis added.
7. The graduate students joined a field trip that Gorman had arranged for his undergraduate class in Earth Systems Technology and Management.

REFERENCES

Allenby, Braden R. 2012. *The Theory and Practice of Sustainable Engineering.* Upper Saddle River, NJ: Pearson Prentice Hall. https://search.lib.virginia.edu/catalog/u5519290.

Collins, Harry. 2004. *Gravity's Shadow: The Search for Gravitational Waves.* Chicago: University of Chicago Press. https://search.lib.virginia.edu/catalog/u4075156.

Collins, Harry, Robert Evans, and Michael E. Gorman. 2007. Trading Zones and Interactional Expertise. *Studies in History and Philosophy of Science Part A, Case Studies of Expertise and Experience* 38 (4): 657–666. https://doi.org/10.1016/j.shpsa.2007.09.003.

Fisher, Erik, Michael O'Rourke, Robert Evans, Eric B. Kennedy, Michael E. Gorman, and Thomas P. Seager. 2015. Mapping the Integrative Field: Taking Stock of Socio-Technical Collaborations. *Journal of Responsible Innovation* 2 (1): 39–61. https://doi.org/10.1080/23299460.2014.1001671.

Galison, Peter. 2010. Trading with the Enemy. In *Trading Zones and International Expertise: Creating New Kinds of Collaboration*, ed. Michael E. Gorman, 25–52. Cambridge: The MIT Press.

Gorman, M.E. 2002. Types of knowledge and their roles in technology transfer. *The Journal of Technology Transfer* 27 (3): 219–231.

Haraway, Donna. 1991. A Cyborg Manifesto: Science, Technology, and Socialist-Feminism in the Late Twentieth Century. In *Simians, Cyborgs and Women: The Reinvention of Nature*, 148–181. New York: Routledge.

Harman, Graham. 2018. *Object-Oriented Ontology: A New Theory of Everything.* London: Penguin.

Latour, Bruno. 1993. *We Have Never Been Modern.* Translated by Catherine Porter. Cambridge, MA: Harvard University Press. http://search.lib.virginia.edu/catalog/u2338434.

Conceptual and Theoretical Developments

Michael E. Gorman and Shannon N. Conley

INTRODUCTION TO PART IV

This part provides a sampling of new conceptual and empirical directions for Third Wave scholarship, including Collins, Evan, and Gorman, who begin this part by refining and improving the concepts of trading zones and interactional expertise in light of new theoretical and empirical work. Part IV also includes Third Wave scholars Schilhab and Dasgupta; the former provides a rigorous analytic reflection on interactional expertise and cognition, while the latter ventures into new temporal and geographic domains with an analysis of the expertise involved in Maya blue.

In Chap. 15, "Trading Zones Revisited," Collins, Evans and Gorman continue their work of (1) refining Galison's concept of trading zones (as a means by which experts can collaborate across apparently incommensurable expertises), and (2) linking that concept to Collins and Evans' notion of interactional expertise, which is the capability to understand enough of the language of another expertise to talk intelligently with those experts. Galison's paradigmatic example would be the formation of new fields like biomedical engineering, the name of which indicates that at least three expertise groups had to develop enough of a shared jargon to begin collaborating, and then this jargon became its own specialized language. The paradigmatic case for interactional expertise is how Collins himself embedded in the gravitational wave physics community to the point where he could talk in the language of the "natives" without being able to perform their practices, for example, designing and troubleshooting the detectors, and collecting and interpreting the data. Collins et al. propose two new types of interactional expertise: an *ambassador* who gains sufficient inter-actional expertise in another community to be able to represent that expertise to her original core group, and a *referred expert* who joins another expertise community, adding her own expertise to their work.

In Chap. 16, "Interactional Expertise as Primer of Abstract Thought," Schilhab links language learning to the way parents and others co-present objects or experiences while they are saying the words that label these experiences, for example, "you are riding a bike" to a child mastering the language and the skill at the same time. After the initial connections among actual objects, processes and words are established, someone learn-ing the language can then imagine or mentally model a set of activities in response to words. Schilhab refers to this response as embodied cognition, and argues that later in the development of language capability, the acqui-sition of interactional expertise supplements embodied cognition.

In Chap. 17, "A Scientific Research Program at the US-Mexico Borderland Region: The Search for the Recipe of Maya Blue," Deepanwita Dasgupta proposes that trading zones can span both time and culture. Her case study focuses on chemists at the University of Texas at El Paso (UTEP) who reverse-engineered how a Mayan pigment was created, and then translated that knowledge into the language and methods of current chemistry, such that the Maya pigment could be made again using modern techniques. Here, the UTEP chemists played the role of brokers or agents of the trade, translating ancient cultural practice into modern chemical language and disseminating it to the scientific community. These chemists have now founded a company, Maya Blue, Inc., which will presumably translate ancient knowledge into modern products.

The scholars in this part demonstrate the creative ways in which Third Wave concepts are being interrogated and developed in an array of fresh empirical and theoretical domains. The editors of this volume hope that other scholars will be inspired to try the Third Wave approach on other case studies that promise to challenge and improve the framework.

CHAPTER 15

Trading Zones Revisited

Harry Collins, Robert Evans, and Michael E. Gorman

15.1   Introduction

In Collins, Evans and Gorman's 2007 paper—"Trading Zones and Interactional Expertise" (Collins et al. 2007)—interactions between separate linguistic communities, often known as "trading zones," were shown to work in variety of different ways. The term "trading zone" was introduced by Peter Galison as a supposed resolution of the problem caused by Kuhn's notion of "paradigm incommensurability." Under paradigm incommensurability, the concepts belonging to one paradigm cannot be translated into those of another paradigm. We tend to agree with Kuhn's characterisation of the problem, but apply it far more generally to "forms of life" which vary hugely in scale and are embedded within one another.[1] We refer to all cases in which there is tension caused by problems of translation between forms of life as trading zones; we note that where there is no problem of translation, there is merely unproblematic "trade." Galison's supposed resolution to the general problem was to posit the existence of in-between languages—creoles and pidgins—which developed to enable

H. Collins (✉) • R. Evans
Cardiff University, Cardiff, UK
e-mail: CollinsHM@cardiff.ac.uk; EvansRJ1@cardiff.ac.uk

M. E. Gorman
University of Virginia, Charlottesville, VA, USA
e-mail: meg3c@virginia.edu

© The Author(s) 2019
D. S. Caudill et al. (eds.), *The Third Wave in Science and Technology Studies*, https://doi.org/10.1007/978-3-030-14335-0_15

"trade" to happen between communities with radically different languages. His paradigm case was the invention of biochemistry, which grew out of the invention of a new language which captured the appropriate parts of the language of chemistry and the language of biology. Galison's resolution seems to work well for this and similar cases, but we argued (Collins et al. 2007) that this is just one way in which the problems of trading zones are resolved and there are many others. These *many different ways* were represented in a 2 × 2 table in Collins et al. 2007, which original table is reproduced as the shaded part in Fig. 15.1 below.

As can be seen, one dimension of the 2 × 2 table is the final degree of melding, or homogeneity, of the communities (high in the case of biochemistry, and lower where the cooperation takes place around a boundary object or by the deployment of interactional expertise), while the other dimension is the degree of coercion used to bring about the cooperation (low in the case of biochemistry). Biochemistry is just one example among others found in the top left-hand cell and representing "inter-language" trading zones. Examples of coercion include sheer physical and institutional ways of forcing people to cooperate in a mechanical way, even when they do not understand what they are doing, and the cultural coercion of the "McDonaldization" type where a dominant society infuses their view of the world into a subservient society without physical force. For the complete explication of this scheme, readers should consult the original 2007 paper.

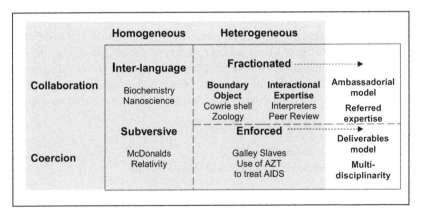

Fig. 15.1 Original model of trading zones (*shaded*) with additional categories (*unshaded*)

15.2   SOME ADDITIONS TO THE ORIGINAL MODEL

Here we make four additions to the scheme just described; these are shown in the right-hand unshaded column of Fig. 15.1. The dashed lines and arrows indicate that the additions belong in the two right-hand cells of the original table. We believe that with these additions, the scheme better represents the full range of different ways in which cross-linguistic-community communication takes place in practice.

In the top right hand, relatively voluntary, "fractionated trading zone," cell (as well as the enforced cell below it), the parties to a cross-disciplinary interaction, rather than attempting a merger, continue to maintain the difference between their forms of life even while they cooperate; this is in contrast to the "inter-language cell." Joint work in the fractionated cell is achieved by the parties sharing only a fraction of their respective forms of life. The left-most method in this cell is sharing a "boundary object," but here we extend the right-most method, interactional expertise, when the fraction that is shared is the "practice language" with no attempt being made to share practices.[2] In other words, parties try to learn the linguistic discourse of those with whom they wish to work without trying to engage in the same activities. The first extension to this cell is the "ambassadorial model."

15.2.1   Ambassadorial Model

In the original 2007 paper, it was assumed that the working of the interactional expertise method depended on every member of each community learning the other party's language. But another important method is the ambassadorial model. Here, rather than all members trying to learn the new practice language, one or more individuals from the "home group" are selected to spend enough time with the "away group" to master the target interactional expertise. They can then *represent* the thinking of the other group within the home group. *Representing* is not the same as translating; translation is always incomplete if not impossible across deep cultural divides.

An example of the ambassadorial model at work can be seen in gravitational wave physics research.[3] In this research it is vital that potential detections are promulgated to the regular astronomical community, so that they can point their telescopes in hope of seeing light or radio signals that correspond to a putative gravitational wave signal. Such a signal might be caused by the coalescence of two binary stars, but probably not by the coalescence of two black holes—this is a matter of astrophysics. Members of the gravitational wave community are sent to spend time with the astronomical and astrophysical communities to learn their ways of thinking, and these ambassadors can represent the astronomers and astrophysicists in the gravitational wave group as the protocols for joint observation are worked out—they can say such things as "this is how the astronomers will think or react to that suggestion and this is what they would prefer." Here is an example of such a phrase from an email circulated to the gravitational wave physics community on December 24, 2016:

> I concur with XXXX et al. that our EM partners would prefer we send out more triggers than less. ['EM' stands for 'electromagnetic' and refers to regular astronomers who mostly look for electromagnetic signals rather than gravitational wave signals.]

Ambassadors could also be sent the other way—from astronomy and from astrophysics to the gravitational wave community.

15.2.2   Referred Expertise Model

A second, closely related, addition to this cell is the referred expertise model. Here one-time astrophysicists (more likely than astronomers) will become members of the gravitational wave community, bringing their expertise with them. We call this an example of "fractionated" cooperation because we are thinking of the recruited astrophysicists as *representing* their old community and fitting in via their newly learned *interactional expertise* in gravitational wave physics. This constitutes the astrophysicists acting like emissaries, rather than continuing to practise their old expertises within the new community. The difference is that the referred experts learn their trade in their home community before travelling, whereas in the case of the ambassadorial model, the ambassadors undertake an expedition to someone else's community to learn a new trade. It is worth noting, however, that in gravitational wave physics, both the ambassadorial and the referred expertise models are temporary phenomena—they apply only to the pre-detection era when astrophysics and astronomy were clearly distinct from gravitational wave physics. In that era, gravitational wave detection was *physics*—something that gave rise to much bad feeling with the first large interferometric detectors referred to themselves as

"LIGO," standing for "Laser Interferometer Gravitational-Wave Observatory"; astronomers complained that it was not an observatory but a physics experiment. Now that gravitational waves have been detected, however, and with many more observations expected shortly, LIGO *has* become an observatory, and the distinction between the detection of gravitational waves, on the one hand, and astronomy and astrophysics, on the other, is disappearing. Gravitational wave physics is becoming part of astronomy and astrophysics, and one can already see the first signs of the two communities merging and the cultures becoming unified (Collins 2017). It will soon cease to be correct to think of there being a trading zone, or even *trade*, linking the enterprises, as there will be no enterprises, only an enterprise.

15.2.3   Deliverables Model

With "deliverables" thought of as a means of communication, we move away from the fractionated trading zone cell to the bottom right "enforced" cell. Specified deliverables follow the same cognitive model as the galley slaves, discussed in Collins et al. 2007, who might not even know that they are propelling a ship so long as they pull on a pole in response to the slave master's punishments and rewards. The analogy is brutal, but it is useful because it makes the cognitive model of deliverables clear—the only people doing any of the understanding required to meld the deliverables into the home activity are the home group. Of course, payment for services rendered is not as brutal as slavery, but in both cases the provider of services—slave or consultant—need have no idea what they are doing so long as they deliver the specified object.

In the gravitational wave field, the task required might be something like this: "install a seismometer of sensitivity such-and-such at such and such a location with readout that can be fed into a computer." The seismometer installer need not know that the location is close to a scientific instrument, need not know that the instrument is an interferometer, need not know that the interferometer is part of a network of gravitational wave detectors and need not know that the readings will be used to "veto" stretches of potential signal that are contaminated by seismic noise.

It is probable that many difficulties emerge from confusing short-term referred expertise with deliverables. For example, we, the Cardiff expertise group, employed a software firm to build a programme to run our Imitation Game experiments.[4] We assumed that the firm would make adjustments in response to its growing understanding of our needs—using its expertise in our context. We found, however, that the firm interpreted its job as doing only what we could formally specify in advance, with any departures that came with growing understanding of the task in its context being rejected except on pain of extra charges. In research, it is impossible to specify everything in advance, so what we really needed was referred expertise, not specified deliverables, and we have consequently employed our own programmer to finish the job—that programmer has become part of our research team. There is a useful lesson here for the relationship between software houses and customers, and for all such contractual arrangements. Wherever the desired expertise is less than completely specifiable at the outset, it should be *absorbed* in one way or another rather than purchased.

15.2.4   *Multidisciplinary Model*

Multidisciplinarity is an extension of the specified deliverable model. It differs from *inter*disciplinarity because there is no attempt at common understanding by either home group or foreign group—indeed, it is not clear if there is a "home" group. Under *multi*disciplinarity, many deliverers or groups of deliverers are brought together to contribute their skills to some project, without understanding the overall goal or their contribution to it. There is no real trading zone. Mass slave labour is the cognitive model. Once more, someone has to understand how all the deliverables fit together if such projects are to work—which often they do not. Since none of the cooperating parties understand the other parties at any deep level, the "slave-master"—the manager who is holding the whole project together—will have to be a person of remarkable abilities, with at least interactional expertise in every separate discipline represented. Tragically, multidisciplinary projects are usually funded and organised on the assumption that the contributions of all the separate disciplines will slot together automatically like the pieces of a jigsaw puzzle. This is hardly ever going to be the case.

15.3   Conclusion

In this chapter we have elaborated and improved upon the model of trading zones first presented in Collins et al. 2007. We believe this expanded version of the model includes some very important but previously overlooked ways for separate language communities to communicate. We have found examples that fit three out of the four additional cases, and have offered some insights into how to avoid at least one kind of failure, but we are pessimistic about the likelihood of success of the fourth model.

NOTES

1. The sources for forms of life are Winch 1958, and Wittgenstein 1953. Discussion of the "fractal model" of forms of life, in which they are embedded within one another and overlap, can be found in Collins 2011.
2. The term "boundary object" is often used rather loosely and care should be taken to make sure that real explanatory work is being done when the term is invoked.
3. For gravitational wave physics see, for example, Collins 2004, 2017.
4. For Imitation Games see, for example, Collins and Evans 2014.

REFERENCES

Collins, H.M. 2004. *Gravity's Shadow: The Search for Gravitational Waves.* Chicago: University of Chicago Press.

———. 2011. Language and Practice. *Social Studies of Science* 41 (2): 271–300. https://doi.org/10.1177/0306312711399665.

——— 2017. *Gravity's Kiss: The Detection of Gravitational Waves.* Cambridge, MA: MIT Press.

Collins, H.M., and R.J. Evans. 2014. Quantifying the Tacit: The Imitation Game and Social Fluency. *Sociology* 48 (1): 3–19. https://doi.org/10.1177/0038038512455735.

Collins, H.M., R.J. Evans, and M. Gorman. 2007. Trading Zones and Interactional Expertise. *Studies in History and Philosophy of Science Part A. Case Studies of Expertise and Experience: Special Issue* 38 (4): 657–666.

Winch, P.G. 1958. *The Idea of a Social Science.* London: Routledge and Kegan Paul.

Wittgenstein, L. 1953. *Philosophical Investigations.* Oxford: Blackwell.

CHAPTER 16

Interactional Expertise as Primer of Abstract Thought

Theresa Schilhab

16.1   Introduction[1]

Harry Collins concedes that while "there could be no Lionese without zebra-ripping," that does not imply that everyone who is fluent in Lionese "has to be a zebra-ripper"—

> Lionese is the collective property of lions and their "form-of-life" but that does not stop non-lions from acquiring it if they put enough effort into it. To acquire a language in this way is not a trivial accomplishment—which is why it remains true that if a lion could speak most of us would not understand him—but one or two of us who had put in the effort that it takes to become fluent in Lionese could understand him even though we have no claws or ripping-teeth. (Collins 2012, 226)

Although language mirrors the "form-of-life" of a community, this in no way implies that for the individual language user to become fluent, he or she must have direct experiences with every aspect of that form-of-life (Collins 2011). Thus, knowledge about a subject area is acquired either as

T. Schilhab (✉)
Danish School of Education, Aarhus University, Copenhagen, Denmark
e-mail: tsc@edu.au.dk

© The Author(s) 2019
D. S. Caudill et al. (eds.), *The Third Wave in Science and Technology Studies*, https://doi.org/10.1007/978-3-030-14335-0_16

"interactional knowledge" achieved exclusively through *prolonged social-ization* in a language community or as "contributory knowledge" acquired also through *direct experience*. The former are exemplified by popular science writers and sociologists and the latter by gravitational wave physicists (Collins 2004; Collins and Evans 2007). In "Imitation Games," examining linguistic knowledge as it occurs in conversations, interactional experts—who "only" possess linguistic experiences—have proven insignificantly different from contributory experts. Sociologists can express themselves like gravitational wave physicists, and midwives who have not given birth can express themselves as if they really had (Collins et al. 2006; Schilhab et al. 2010). Hence, we are able to acquire knowledge about direct experiences without being physically involved with them.

What in language grounds the ability to transfer knowledge of phenomena, occurrences or events with which we have no direct experiences as if we actually did have them in the same way as contributory experts? The question becomes all the more important given the fact that numerous studies in contemporary neuroscience strongly suggest that conceptual understanding is based on embodied cognition (Schilhab et al. 2010; Schilhab 2017). Following Barsalou et al. (2003, 84), "[r]esearchers report that re-enactments of states in modality-specific systems underlie conceptual processing [and] empirical research and theoretical analyses implicate modality-specific systems in the representation and use of conceptual knowledge" (Glenberg et al. 2008; Barsalou 2008; Chatterjee 2010).

Accordingly, sensory-motor experiences are significant to the individual's development of concepts and language use (Gallese and Lakoff 2005; Calvo and Gomila 2008; Pulvermüller 2013). As infants, when acquiring language, we have simultaneous perceptual access to the concrete phenomena and events to which the language refers along with "traditional" linguistic processes such as sounds, articulation and so on (Pulvermüller 2005, 2013 Pulvermüller et al., 2009; Glenberg et al. 2008). In this "Linguification Process" (Schilhab 2013, 2017), external and internal stimulations in the present are combined with prior experiences to form new lasting neural combinations sustaining language (Gallese 2003; Hesslow 2002).

This process is "business as usual." Crudely put, when riding a bicycle, the neural correlate combines the present rich experience of the landscape, the felt sensation of, say, pedalling, with the memory of a former ride (Sheckley and Bell 2006; Barrett 2009). If daddy adds the linguistic overlay to the ongoing scenario by pointing verbally to "bicycling," language becomes associated and thereby enriched with fully fledged bicycle experiences.

What are the mechanisms corroborating this perceptual enrichment? In infancy, when acquiring the expression "banana," small children are typically repeatedly exposed to and therefore perceptually engaged with real bananas (Glenberg et al. 2008; Pecher et al. 2011). After the co-wiring of neural circuits for the perceptual experiences in the present, later in life "banana" articulated (or heard) in conversation also activates through co-wiring sensory-motor areas (González et al. 2006; Schilhab 2015a). Support for this interpretation appears, for instance, in studies in which the meaning of a sentence is assessed—thus testing linguistic knowledge. Such tasks seem to involve "simulations" of perceived situations categorized linguistically during the experience concerned (Zwaan et al. 2002; Barsalou et al. 2003; Boulenger et al. 2009; Barsalou 2009; Hesslow 2012).

How does the embodiment claim harmonize with the idea of interactional expertise? If we learn language from direct experiences, how can "one or two of us who had put in the effort that it takes to become fluent in Lionese understand him even though we have no claws or ripping-teeth?"

However, a reconciliation between the embodiment and interactional expertise studies is possible. Learning without direct experiences occurs if language acquisition takes place in scaffolding stages. Then the early mastering of language would be concerned with directly experienced phenomena (the concrete stage) (Schilhab 2011b, 2015a, b, 2017), and this stage could ultimately pave the way for mastering language without concomitant direct experiences (the abstract stage) found in, for instance, interactional expertise. Language has exactly this property and it is the embodied cognition in the first stage that seems to be key. (While I focus in this chapter on the child when discussing the social embedding of language acquisition, I suggest that much of our childhood acquisition of advanced, abstract language is comparable to the acquisition of interactional expertise in adult life.)

The notion that embodied experiences also inform language at an advanced linguistic level is not new (Lakoff and Johnson 1980). Williams et al. (2009, 1257) introduce the concept of scaffolding as "a process through which humans readily integrate incoming information with extant knowledge structures." Scaffolding is then

> the passive, natural process through which new concepts are formed, especially in early childhood. Features of abstract or less understood concepts are mapped onto existing and well-understood concepts, such that the structure of the developmentally earlier, primary concept is retained in the newly constructed concept. This structure imbues the newer concept with meaning. (Williams et al. 2009, 1257)

However, to my knowledge, the actual mechanism by which such scaffolding is accomplished has only been clarified by the use of contemporary neuroscience principles in what I have referred to as "derived embodiment" (Schilhab 2012b, 2017).

Derived embodiment is, in the absence of experiences of any real referents of the concepts achieved, to use words imaginatively to simulate experiences. A concept (and even more encompassing language games) without concomitant direct experiences achieves its meaningfulness from prior experiences. In short, derived embodiment emerges when language re-enacts states in modality-specific systems that now become associated with new conceptual understandings.

In derived embodiment, intangible items with which one has had no prior direct contact become tangible because of their borrowing of corporeality from direct experiences with real objects. Knowledge of what has not been perceived becomes perceptible. Knowledge that borrows the material context is then upgraded to "original" knowledge corroborated by perceptual experiences despite the complete absence of relevant perceptual grounding (Schilhab 2017).

Naturally, the individual's ability to engage in internally directed attention to maintain imagery is then fundamental to attain abstract knowledge. Surprisingly, however, so are the cognitive capabilities of conversational partners. True, midwives without direct birth experiences may adopt these by observation and embodied simulating (Schilhab 2007a; Schilhab et al. 2010). Sociologists learning from gravitational wave physicists may, however, attain gravitational wave physics knowledge entirely through conversations. In the following paragraphs, I will expand on the role played by the conversational partner in language acquisition at the concrete and abstract levels.

16.2   The Role of the Conversational Partner

Schilhab (2011b, 2012b, 2015b, c, d, 2017) proposed that interactional expertise, although indirectly achieved by the process of derived embodiment, depends on direct experiences, apparently giving rise to two linguistic acquisition stages: concrete and abstract. When the referent to which the knowledge applies changes from the concrete to the abstract stage, the function of the conversational partner also changes. In the concrete phase, the conversational partner, say the mother serving bananas, or the father riding the bicycle, is basically responsible for the concurrent presentation of objects, scenarios and concepts to support the association of sensory and conceptual representations in the language learner. Therefore, the conversational partner often concretely arranges the scene of conversation. He or she uses "cues" in the form of the interest of the child (i.e., direction of gaze) to organize a scene believed to lead to learning. Thus, the success of the linguistic exchange between the language learner and the conversational partner lies predominantly in the hands of the interlocutor who, in this case, is also the linguistic expert. He or she furnishes the concrete world to pave the way for the language learner to easily acquire word-object relations (Pulvermüller 2011). If the child points to the family dog, the expert decodes this interest and establishes a scene by interacting with the dog, calling its name, patting its head or pointing in its direction. Dealings with the real world involve practical arrangements and overt preparations of the location for the conversation, such as the positioning of objects in connection with other objects, saliency in the behavioural response and amplified articulation of phrases; for example, "See, a dog" or "Where is the bicycle?"

The repetitive presentation of online objects, scenarios and expressions gradually prepares the language learner to accomplish language skills at the concrete stage. One could argue that when undertaking such scene-construction, conversational partners make use of so-called material anchors, since they might alleviate the cognitive task of acquiring language (Hutchins 2005; Wilson 2002). Hutchins (2005, 1574) claims that

> [t]he fact that some of the task relevant structure is crystallized in a material artifact may reduce the demands on memory. Computing on complex mental images that have material anchors permits people to substitute robust and fast perceptual processes for slow and vulnerable conceptual processes. Since conceptual models work by embodying constraints among conceptual elements, both memory and processing loads can be reduced if the constraints of the task can be built into the physical structure of a material device.

From the aspect of materiality, this stage has important similarities with how language acquisition is thought to evolve in the *contributory* expert who speaks fluent Lionese because he or she is also a zebra-ripper.

Using material anchors when learning conceptually is cognitively important. Concrete phenomena guide attention to external stimuli while also displacing irrelevant thoughts. In addition, when concrete objects are involved in the process, as posited by neuroscience studies on the anchoring of infant language, thinking becomes bodily and multifaceted, so that it can more easily attract joint attention and mutual direct interaction with others (Borghi and Cimatti 2010; Barrett 2014; Granito et al. 2015). Kirsh (2010, 446) writes:

> Things in the world behave differently than things in the mind. For example, external representations are extended in space, not just in time. They can be operated on in different ways; they can be manually duplicated, and rearranged. They can be shared with other people. Tools can be applied to them. These differences between internal and external representations are incredibly significant.

16.3   Conversational Partner in the Abstract Stage

When the learner masters everyday concepts such as food items, basic tools and artificial and natural objects as well as everyday phrases on requests, greetings and, to some extent, subjective experiences, the learner might well have acquired a level of linguistic competence needed to enter phase two, the abstract stage.

The ability to process language without leaning too much on external representations is likely to mature with age (Wetzel et al. 2006). According to Vigliocco et al. (2013, 1), the age of acquisition of given word categories differ:

> [O]nly 10% of 3-year-olds' vocabulary is abstract, rising to 25% in 5-year-olds. Acquisition of abstract concepts then increases steadily: >60% of 11-year-olds' vocabulary is abstract.

The presentation of stages in linguistic acquisition that reflects the transition from concrete to more abstract understanding, though not meticulously reflecting developmental ages, nevertheless helps disentangle the processes involved in abstract knowledge acquisition and ultimately the emergence of the kind of knowledge interactional expertise represents (Schilhab 2017). In conversation between the language learner and the interlocutor, unknown expressions, supposed or desired to be understood, are impediments to normal understanding. Typically, one pauses and ponders about such expressions to crack them open.

Obviously, if understanding is not immediate, the learner repeatedly poses questions to improve the pictures he or she is about to get. He or she will probably also ask the expert interlocutor to refine (or simplify) his or her explanation to facilitate understanding (Schilhab 2011b). At this stage, language usage elicits re-enactments of previous experiences in the sense that perceptual qualities associated with language learning at the concrete level are co-activated and add to meaning attribution of linguistic expressions (Schilhab 2011a). This does not exclude the contribution of mechanisms for abstract learning from other sources. To Collins, learning a language is in itself a practical skill (2011, 280):

> Children learning their first language acquire the knowledge of where to put the verb only tacitly, however. The child learns verb placement by learning to perform the language. The child learns where to place the verb just as the child learns to ride a bicycle—by doing it. To that extent and more, language speaking is a practice. Having acquired verb placement, the child then "knows" how to do something, even though they usually cannot say what they know, nor do they even "know" that they know it.

Obviously, as soon as we begin acquisition of language, simultaneously we start establishing short cuts to create internal scenarios (Schilhab 2017). At the same time, words are tagged to and become part of complex representations. As proposed by neuroscience studies, in the early years, these tags (words or sentences) are primarily of concrete objects, events and phenomena with which we are perceptually familiar.

When these words occur later in life they elicit re-enactments, which are representations that now exist independently of convergence with external conditions (Schilhab 2017). In the words of Scorolli and Borghi (2008, 11):

> the word "glass" should reactivate the experiences of our previous interactions with glasses. So it leads to the activation of auditory, visual, and tactile information, for example the smoothness of a glass of wine, its sound banging into the dish, its shape and size, that surprisingly do affect the smell and the taste of the wine. The same word re-activates also proprioceptive and kinesthetic information, for example hand/arm feedback, whereas bringing a glass to our mouth as well as information on its affordance.

The linguistic establishing of imagery, that is, the ability of language to elicit simulations with a perceptual feel to them, renders language into an unmatched tool for learning without any relevant direct experiences.

And although the conversational partner still furnishes the world of the learner, there is no need for involvement of real items. In fact, the part played by the interlocutor is to compensate for the lack of perceptual corroboration in this advanced phase of language acquisition. Thus, for the language acquisition of abstract concepts to succeed, the role of the interlocutor is to replace the perceptual cues provided by the real world at the concrete level.

The task is challenging since the furnishing happens in a non-existent room created by the individual imaginations of the adult interlocutor and the learner. Such virtual spaces might be sparsely decorated compared to the space in real life (the living room, the kitchen, the landscape) and since the existence of the imaginative space is entirely dependent on the linguistic web spawned in the conversation between the interlocutor and the language learner, the construction is fragile (Schilhab 2017). What generates the virtual space and what enables its continued existence?

The imaginative space seems to emerge as a result of the deliberate use of expressions by the conversational partner, thus initiating the process of derived embodiment. Just as in the case of the previous level, the adult interlocutor is responsible for inhabiting the space (now virtual), while he or she helps the novice expand his or her vocabulary. In the abstract phase, however, concrete scenarios that involve real and therefore perceivable objects have been replaced by pure linguistic constructs supplied by behavioural signs and intonations (Schilhab 2012a). There is no material anchoring and perceptual common ground informing the conversation like the multimodal perception of bananas and bicycles in the concrete phase.

Thus, the feasibility of the arrangements unavoidably builds on the ability of the adult interlocutor to gauge the level of comprehensibility in the language learner. As such, the interlocutor appears to be a serious determinant of what re-enactments occur, since the learner is directed by the choices made. For abstract understanding via derived embodiment to be consolidated, the interlocutor will need to establish metaphors that immediately capture the concrete meaning of the unknown expression to mediate the desired learning. Hence, he or she must seek mutual comprehensibility and make mental tableaus that are thought to match the understanding of the learner.

When does this description of a conversation ever apply? For children, it often happens when they are taught desired knowledge at school. Imagine how impaired children are in making sense of prehistoric dinosaurs—or were at least until *Jurassic Park* became a cultural meme (Schilhab 2007b).

We will never get to pat a *Tyrannosaurus rex*. This means that we cannot get quite the same sense of such knowledge through sensing the impact on our own body. In such cases, we have to try to make sense of the thing by associating the kind of knowledge with something else that makes sense to us. We could try to understand *T. rex* by imagining a giant lizard as tall as the second floor with a tiger's taste for meat. Using language, we re-enact emotions and sensations, such as lizards or chameleons from the zoo; we imagine the distance from the ground level up to the second floor to represent the idea of *T. rex,* which would otherwise lack corporeal sensations because no concrete experience is involved (Williams et al. 2009). At the concrete level, along with the re-enactments produced by the expressions chosen by the adult interlocutor, the language learner also makes use of his or her individual perceptual experiences to form appropriate interpretations and associations. For instance, the fact that the cake is actually on the table helps the child make sense of the sentence.

Hence, the public availability of material and perceptual qualities clearly dissociates the concrete from the abstract stage. Koening, Clément and Harris (2004, 694) posit:

> [W]hen young children have well-established knowledge of a given fact— for example, they know what an object is called, they know what color it is, or they know the properties of the class to which it belongs—they do not accept statements that contradict those known facts. They correct speakers who make false statements and refuse these statements as bases for subsequent reasoning.

At the abstract level, however, the associations used to corroborate the emerging understanding of the new concept (derived embodiment) depend on what representations are *chosen* by the interlocutor. His or her ability to select appropriate representations will be decisive of the quality and degree of understanding achieved by the learner. *T. rex* is imagined differently if we re-enact experiences with a common lizard instead of a Comodo dragon. If the interlocutor is less skilled at probing the level of understanding, he or she will have difficulties in the process of selecting the appropriate words to obtain the desired clarity. The interlocutor's own insight to how language matches the world (the word to world reference) also determines whether the information conveyed to the language learner is appropriate. This of course shows that among interlocutors, individual components of language competence might differ. A competent (contributory) language user might pass as competent even if he or she fails at the task of furnishing the virtual world of the conversational partner, the novice. To probe the level of understanding and to present the learning interlocutor with comprehensible conversation relies on sensitivity and the ability to take on the viewpoint of the other. To quote Kierkegaard (opening paragraph to Chapter A2, 1998):

> If one is truly to succeed in leading a person to a specific place, one must first and foremost take care to find him where he is and begin there. This is the secret in the entire art of helping. Anyone who cannot do this is himself under a delusion if he thinks he is able to help someone else. In order truly to help someone else, I must understand more than he–but certainly first and foremost understand what he understands. If I do not do that, then my greater understanding does not help him at all. If I nevertheless want to assert my greater understanding, then it is because I am vain or proud, then basically instead of benefiting him I really want to be admired by him. But all true helping begins with a humbling.

16.4   Concluding Remarks

The concept of derived embodiment forces us to rethink how language works, what linguistic transfer is and what the connection is between actual experiences and the linguistic retelling.

When we discuss the fundamentals of language acquisition in the concrete phase, we may satisfactorily explain it at the level of the individual. Here, the concrete and the perceptual processes seem to spur the process. However, later on when scaffolding processes set in, the table is turned. Now, language acquisition becomes increasingly social, demonstrated in its most extreme form in the formation of interactional expertise. To explain exchanges of ideas in common conversations in which all of us engage on a daily basis, we need to supply the embodied cognition framework with the concept of interactional expertise and derived embodiment.

Note

1. The argument in this chapter is a condensed version of Schilhab (2017).

References

Barrett, Lisa F. 2009. The Future of Psychology. *Perspectives on Psychological Science* 4 (4): 326–339.

———. 2014. The Conceptual Act Theory: A Précis. *Emotion Review* 6 (4): 292–297.

Barsalou, Lawrence W. 2008. Grounded Cognition. *Annual Review of Psychology* 59: 617–645.

———. 2009. Simulation, Situated Conceptualization, and Prediction. *Philosophical Transactions of the Royal Society B* 364: 1281–1289.

Barsalou, Lawrence W., W. Kyle Simmons, Aron K. Barbey, and Christine D. Wilson. 2003. Grounding Conceptual Knowledge in Modality-Specific systems. *Trends in Cognitive Sciences* 7 (2): 84–91.

Borghi, Anna M., and Felice Cimatti. 2010. Embodied Cognition and Beyond: Acting and Sensing the Body. *Neuropsychologia* 48: 763–773.

Boulenger, Véronique, Olaf Hauk, and Friedemann Pulvermüller. 2009. Grasping Ideas with the Motor system: Semantic Somatotopy in Idiom Comprehension. *Cerebral Cortex* 19 (8): 1905–1914.

Calvo, Paco, and Toni Gomila, eds. 2008. *Handbook of Cognitive Science. An Embodied Approach.* San Diego, CA: Elsevier.

Chatterjee, Anjan. 2010. Disembodying Cognition. *Language and Cognition* 2 (1): 79–116.

Collins, Harry. 2004. Interactional Expertise as a Third Kind of Knowledge. *Phenomenology and the Cognitive Sciences* 3: 125–143.

———. 2011. Language and Practice. *Social Studies of Science* 41 (2): 271–300.

———. 2012. Language as a Repository of Tacit Knowledge. In *The Symbolic Species Evolved*, ed. Theresa Schilhab, Frederik Stjernfelt, and Terrence Deacon, 225–239. Dordrecht: Springer.

Collins, Harry, and Robert Evans. 2007. *Rethinking Expertise.* Chicago, IL: University of Chicago Press.

Collins, Harry, Robert Evans, Rodrigo Ribeiro, and Martin Hall. 2006. Experiments with Interactional Expertise. *Studies in History and Philosophy of Science* 37 (a): 656–674.

Gallese, Vittorio. 2003. The Manifold Nature of Interpersonal Relations: The Quest for a Common Mechanism. *Philosophical Transactions of the Royal Society* 358: 517–528.

Gallese, Vittorio, and George Lakoff. 2005. The Brain's Concepts: The Role of the Sensory-Motor System in Conceptual Knowledge. *Cognitive Neuropsychology* 22 (3/4): 455–479.

Glenberg, Arthur M., Marc Sato, Luigi Cattaneo, Lucia Riggio, Daniele Palumbo, and Giovanni Buccino. 2008. Processing Abstract Language Modulates Motor System Activity. *The Quarterly Journal of Experimental Psychology* 61 (6): 905–919.

González, Julio, Alfonso Barros-Loscertales, Friedemann Pulvermüller, Vanessa Meseguer, Ana Sanjuán, Vicente Belloch, and César Ávila. 2006. Reading Cinnamon Activates Olfactory Brain Regions. *Neuroimage* 32 (2): 906–912.

Granito, Carmen, Claudia Scorolli, and Anna Maria Borghi. 2015. Naming a Lego World. The Role of Language in the Acquisition of Abstract Concepts. *PloS one* 10 (1): e0114615.

Hesslow, Germund. 2002. Conscious Thought as Simulation of Behaviour and Perception. *Trends in Cognitive Sciences* 6: 242–247.

———. 2012. Current Status of the Simulation Theory of Cognition. *Brain Research* 1428: 71–79.

Hutchins, Edwin. 2005. Material Anchors for Conceptual Blends. *Journal of Pragmatics* 37: 1555–1577.

Kierkegaard, Søren. 1998. *The Point of View*. Edited and translated by Howard V. Hong and Edna H. Hong. Princeton, NJ: Princeton University Press.

Kirsh, David. 2010. Thinking with External Representations. *AI & Society* 25 (4): 441–454.

Koenig, Melissa A., Fabrice Clément, and Paul L. Harris. 2004. Trust in Testimony. *Psychological Science* 15 (10): 694–698.

Lakoff, George, and Mark Johnson. 1980. *Metaphors We Live by*. Chicago, IL: University of Chicago Press.

Pecher, Diane, Inge Boot, and Saskia Van Dantzig. 2011. Abstract Concepts: Sensory-Motor Grounding, Metaphors, and Beyond. In *The Psychology of Learning and Motivation*, ed. Brian Ross, 217–248. Burlington: Academic Press.

Pulvermüller, Friedemann. 2005. Brain Mechanism Linking Language and Action. *Nature* 6 (7): 576–582.

———. 2011. Meaning and the Brain: The Neurosemantics of Referential, Interactive and Combinatorial Knowledge. *Journal of Neurolinguistics* 25 (5): 423–459.

———. 2013. Semantic Embodiment, Disembodiment or Misembodiment? In Search of Meaning in Modules and Neuron Circuits. *Brain & Language* 127 (1): 86–103.

Pulvermüller, Friedemann, Yury Shtyrov, and Olaf Hauk. 2009. Understanding in an Instant: Neurophysiological Evidence for Mechanistic Language Circuits in the Brain. *Brain & Language* 110: 81–94.

Schilhab, Theresa. 2007a. Interactional Expertise Through the Looking Glass: A Peek at Mirror Neurons. *Studies in History and Philosophy of Science A* 38: 741–747.

———. 2007b. Knowledge for Real - On Implicit and Explicit Representations. *Scandinavian Journal of Education* 51 (3): 223–238.

———. 2011a. Neural Perspectives on 'Interactional Expertise': The Plasticity of Language. *Journal of Consciousness Studies* 18 (7–8): 99–116.

———. 2011b. Derived Embodiment and Imaginative Capacities in Interactional Expertise. *Phenomenology and the Cognitive Sciences* 12 (2): 309–325.

———. 2012a. Levels of Embodiment. In *The Symbolic Species Evolved*, ed. Theresa Schilhab, Frederik Stjernfelt, and Terrence Deacon, 241–251. Dordrecht: Springer Verlag.

———. 2012b. On Derived Embodiment: A Response to Collins. *Phenomenology and the Cognitive Sciences* 12 (2): 423–425.

———. 2013. Derived Embodiment and Imaginative Capacities in Interactional Expertise. *Phenomenology and the Cognitive Sciences* 12 (2): 309–325.

———. 2015a. Re-live and Learn–Interlocutor-Induced Elicitation of Phenomenal Experiences in Learning Offline. *Progress in Biophysics and Molecular Biology* 119 (3): 649–660.

———. 2015b. Doubletalk–the Biological and Social Acquisition of Language. *Biologically Inspired Cognitive Architectures* 13: 1–8.

———. 2015c. Words as Cultivators of Others Minds. *Frontiers in Psychology* 6: 1690.

———. 2015d. Why Animals Are Not Robots. *Phenomenology and the Cognitive Sciences* 14 (3): 599–611.

———. 2017. *Derived Embodiment in Abstract Language*. Cham: Springer.

Schilhab, Theresa, Gudlaug Fridgeirsdottir, and Peter Allerup. 2010. The Midwife Case: Do They 'Walk the Talk'? *Phenomenology and the Cognitive Sciences* 9 (1): 1–13.

Scorolli, Claudia, and Anna M. Borghi. 2008. Language and Embodiment. *Anthropology and Philosophy* 9 (1–2): 7–23.

Sheckley, Barry G., and Sandy Bell. 2006. Experience, Consciousness, and Learning: Implications for Instruction. *New Directions for Adult and Continuing Education* 110: 43–52.

Vigliocco, Gabriella, Stavroula-Thaleia Kousta, Pasquale Anthony Della Rosa, David P. Vinson, Marco Tettamanti, Joseph T. Devlin, and Stefano F. Cappa. 2013. The Neural Representation of Abstract Words: The Role of Emotion. *Cerebral Cortex* 24 (7): 1767–1777.

Wetzel, Nicole, Andreas Widmann, Stefan Berti, and Erich Schröger. 2006. The Development of Involuntary and Voluntary Attention from Childhood to Adulthood: A Combined Behavioral and Event-Related Potential Study. *Clinical Neurophysiology* 117 (10): 2191–2203.

Williams, Lawrence E., Julie Y. Huang, and John A. Bargh. 2009. The Scaffolded Mind: Higher Mental Processes Are Grounded in Early Experience of the Physical World. *European Journal of Social Psychology* 39 (7): 1257–1267.

Wilson, M. 2002. Six Views on Embodied Cognition. *Psychonomic Bulletin & Review* 9 (4): 625–635.

Zwaan, Rolf A., Robert A. Stanfield, and Richard H. Yaxley. 2002. Language Comprehenders Mentally Represent the Shapes of Objects. *Psychological Science* 13 (2): 168–171.

CHAPTER 17

A Scientific Research Program at the US-Mexico Borderland Region: The Search for the Recipe of Maya Blue

Deepanwita Dasgupta

17.1 INTRODUCTION

The concept of a trading zone has been one of the main tools to study scientific and technological expertise from both the social and the cognitive points of view. Introduced by Peter Galison in the 1990s (Galison 1997), and subsequently refined and developed further by Harry Collins, Robert Evans, and Michael Gorman in the next decade (Collins et al. 2007; Gorman 2005, 2010), this concept has undergone several revisions since its inception, all aiming to show how scientific communities negotiate among a variety of people, expertise, and paradigms, and yet avoid collapsing into a Tower of Babel, more formally known as the problem of incommensurability.

However, what have so far been (mostly) explored are cases where such trades occur between two parties that are set in contemporary zones of space and time. But could such trading zones also occur in a more spread-out fashion, involving more than two parties, involving the present as well as the past? If so, how would such complex trades affect (and perhaps also

D. Dasgupta (✉)
The University of Texas at El Paso, El Paso, TX, USA

297
D. S. Caudill et al. (eds.), *The Third Wave in Science and Technology Studies*, https://doi.org/10.1007/978-3-030-14335-0_17

enrich) the research programs of a particular scientific community, and what would be its dynamics? In this chapter, I shall attempt to envision whether such a scenario is at all possible, present a case study in its favor, and finally consider how attempts like this can potentially open doors to hybrid sorts of research programs—perhaps making science a crucial partner in the work of preserving and recovering various lost cultural heritages. This vision of a hybrid practice formed via trading zones may also give us a quick glimpse of the possible diverse nature of the twenty-first-century science.

Speaking of trading zones, it is of course generally well-known that trades of all sorts have always immensely enriched human endeavors,[1] so the same might be true of science. Regarding the structure of such trades and how they affect (and enrich) our scientific practices, we may perhaps put the matter as follows, borrowing some terminology from Imre Lakatos. If the heart of a scientific practice consists of producing chains of research programs, then trading relationships might afford us with ways of extending (or even re-designing) those programs by surrounding them with varieties of heuristics. Such trades and such heuristics would of course be born from the proximity to, and cultural ties of, a scientific community.

To highlight the importance of this proximity factor further, in this chapter I shall also make use of the notion of a borderland, that is, those places that straddle two communities, countries, and cultures, and which can thus provide us with good settings for new trading zones. Scientific communities that exist (and function) in such hybrid spaces might therefore act as pioneers in setting up different kinds of novel trades, and those might, in turn, give rise to different forms of hybrid research practices. In the sections that follow, I shall explore a research program born of a trading zone undertaken by a group of material chemists at my home university, the University of Texas at El Paso. I shall give an account of the significance of their project, and its possible role in the task of the preservation of heritages and traditions. The results, when seen through the prisms of a trading zone, can be quite rewarding. Science has often been accused of destroying cultural heritages and traditional practices—but it can be, as I try to show below, also fully capable of rendering an enormous service in the task of preserving it.

17.2   THE MYSTERY OF THE MAYA BLUE

In 2000, at a workshop titled *Synchrotron Radiation in Art and Archeology*, held in Palo Alto, California, a group of material chemists from the Department of Chemistry at the University of Texas at El Paso (UTEP), led by Russell Chianelli, presented an interesting piece of research.[2] This presentation was focused on re-creating the long-lost recipe for a historic pigment known as Maya blue. This beautiful pigment deserves some introduction because of its rather exceptional history. Known as Maya blue or *Azul Maya*, this brilliant blue pigment is seen on various Maya mural paintings as well as on potteries all over the Maya Yucatan region (and in several other parts of Central America). The wide dispersion of this pigment suggests that not only did the ancient Maya develop their products after long periods of exploration and variation, but they were also quite capable of maintaining a robust level of quality in their production (Figs. 17.1 and 17.2). After nine hundred years, not only does the pigment still retain its brilliant blue hue—even though all other colors on those walls have faded long ago—the pigment shows an exceptional stability in the face of acid, alkali, and all other similar harsh chemical solvents, showing none of the bio-degradations that one would expect to see under such tropical climatic conditions. More important than even the stability factor, Maya blue contains none of the traces of heavy metals, such as Co-phthalocyanine, which are routinely used today in making different

Azul Maya

Fig. 17.1 Maya blue murals (Reprinted with permission from Russell Chianelli)

Mayan Pigments

Pigments produced by the Mayas, show colors of various hues, ranging from a purple to a greenish blue

Mayan Pigments are extremely stable: it can resist the attack of boiling, concentrated nitric acid, alkali and organic solvents.

Fig. 17.2 Maya blue murals (Reprinted with permission from Russell Chianelli)

kinds of pigments. Neither does the pigment contain the traditional old staples for making blue color, for example, ground lapis lazuli, which was once used widely in medieval Europe. Since Maya blue is free from all the standard heavy chemicals routinely used in the modern pigment industry, and since it remains exceptionally stable in the face of all chemical and environmental degradations, there arises the very interesting possibility that this material—if only it could be resurrected—may provide us with an array of heavy metal-free and environment-friendly paints. The attention that was bestowed on this classic material, and the serious attempts that followed in resurrecting it, thus come from the practical concerns of a modern day research program, and an awareness that perhaps those ancient masters still have something left to teach us.

17.3 Reviving a Forgotten Research Program

The legendary Maya blue has of course received its share of artistic and scientific attention over the last 40 years, with various sorts of attempts to bring it back into existence. It has been cited in *the Encyclopedia of Nanoscience and Society* as an ancient case of nanotechnology (Guston 2010), and it has also been the subject of numerous books dealing with the artistic contributions of the Maya culture (Berke 2007; Berrie 2012; Houston 2014). More recently, a study has been published by a group of Portuguese researchers who sought to use a physical model of the Maya blue made of some beads and LEDs as an important teaching tool in their classroom (Leitão et al. 2013). Thus, when Russell Chianelli's group picked up the Maya blue research program, they were stepping into a long-standing artistic/scientific concern, hoping to give it some form of a definite conclusion. Additionally, there was a personal motivation factor involved in the game. The group leader, Russell Chianelli, had come from a background where he has had considerable exposure to various art forms and artists, and he had been living in the US-Mexico borderland region for well over 30 years.

A detailed version of their research was eventually published in the *Journal of Inorganic Biochemistry* (Polette et al. 2000; Polette-Niewold et al. 2007), which I shall mostly follow here to give an account of their research practices. Collaborating with their counterparts across the US-Mexico border at the National Autonomous University of Mexico (UNAM) for electron microscopy and x-ray diffraction (XRD) images, the material chemists at UTEP hoped to find the long-lost recipe for Maya blue and to harness it in the service of their current research program.

17.4   Taking Things Apart

The efforts of Chianelli's group began with obtaining samples of the ancient Maya blue from different murals and then examining those samples with synchrotron XRD technique, a standard form of material analysis. Their express aim was to harvest new products—materials and pigments— from this old technology. Note that from the very beginning, the structure of this interaction had the nature of a three-way trade, involving more than two traditional parties. Not only did the UTEP chemists have to source something from the remote past, and re-create it with sufficient precision, they also had to introduce this new synthetic product to the present-day scientific community, assuring them of its relevance for current problems. Over the course of the next six to seven years, this work led to two important results. The first was the production of a range of samples, visually very similar that of the classic Maya blue, which under a battery of tests revealed properties similar to that of the original material. But more importantly—and this is what I wish to highlight here—they also forged a strong bond with an ancient set of expertise, embedding it in their own research and thus saving that old expertise from oblivion and extinction. The whole effort thus had structure of a trade between the old and the new.

Chianelli's group began their research program with a two-pronged approach. Their first attempts were designed to come up with a recipe for creating synthetic Maya blue in their lab. But soon their efforts began to converge around understanding the structural reasons for the stability of the pigment, which they explored with a battery of techniques, such as scanning electron microscopy (SEM), high-resolution transmission electron microscopy (HRTEM), and infra-red (IR) and Raman spectroscopy. Those tests helped them to visualize the nature of the surface bonds that held the organic/inorganic material together. In the course of this research, they came to the conclusion that the stability of Maya blue arises from the nature of the molecular bonds that are forged between the organic/inorganic compounds as a result of heating. It is those bonds which protect the hue from all kinds of degradation. This investigation also showed them how to introduce new organic ingredients in the process, thereby essentially opening doors to a world of new materials and pigments. Thus, Maya blue—and all other similarly wonderful technologies of the ancient world (e.g., Damascus steel)—are all ancient examples of nanotechnology, the precursors of many other such hybrid materials that we are trying to develop today. Examples of such historic expertise can well inform our current day research programs as well as opening doors to a new form of cultural and context-sensitive science.

17.5   SYNTHESIZING THE MAYA BLUE

In trying to re-create this classic pigment, the researchers first had to locate its main ingredients. The first ingredient in Maya blue turned out to be indigo, an ancient plant dye that once dominated the world, and is still used today for dyeing denims and other kinds of textiles. The second element in the pigment turned out to be a kind of fibrous clay, called palygorskite. However, since neither of the elements display any of the stabilities of classic Maya blue, the secret lies in finding out just how the two materials were combined together, and then recovering the details of that process.

17.5.1   Three Methods of Reverse Engineering

The modern chemical structure of the indigo was formulated by the German chemist Adolf von Baeyer in 1883. Since indigo is practically insoluble in water or in any other solvent, the traditional technique of indigo dyeing had always been to first reduce it to its oxygen molecule-less equivalent, called leuco-indigo, a yellowish-white liquid. Skeins of yarn are then dipped into this leuco-indigo solution, and then exposed to the air. Once exposed to the air, the yarn picks up the lost oxygen molecules from air, thus quickly turning into the familiar deep shades of indigo blue.

The group's first attempts at synthesizing Maya blue thus began with reducing indigo to leuco-indigo. Once the leuco-indigo was obtained, it was poured over 5 gm of palygorskite clay. The resulting product was then heated in the oven at 125 °C for four days. This technique produced a result that was sufficiently similar in appearance to that of classic Maya blue, even though the color samples appeared to be somewhat lighter and of less intensity. In their second attempt, the researchers did away with the reduction process and used the technique of wet grinding instead. Various concentrations of indigo were mixed with 5 gm of palygorskite clay and blended with de-ionized water. To determine whether the pH of the system was making any contribution to the final color of the product, samples were prepared both with a basic or acidic solution at various pH levels (4, 7, 9, and 11). The resulting solution was once again placed in the oven for four days at 125 °C. The researchers found that using a ≥2% indigo, they obtained the closest possible look to the classic Maya blue. Visually speaking, their best results were obtained when the solution were either neutral or close to an acidic pH.

The third and final method that they used was that of dry grinding. This time the mixtures were not blended with water—instead, palygorskite clay was directly mixed onto thioindigo, a reddish dye similar in chemical structure to indigo at room temperatures. One gram of this mixture was kept in a vial as a control sample. The rest of the mixture was then heated at 100 °C for 24 hours, at which point another sample was extracted, and the rest of the mixture was returned for an additional 24 hours of heating. The samples taken out at different stages tracked the (gradual) color changes in the mixture. Upon heating, the reddish mixture first turned purple, then greenish blue, and then with more heating, it finally assumed the typical deep shades of the classic Maya blue (Figs. 17.3 and 17.4).

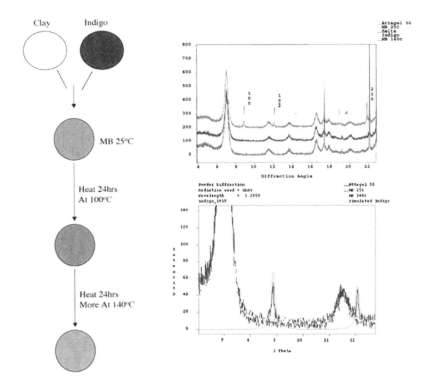

Fig. 17.3 Change of colors (Reprinted with permission from Russell Chianelli)

17.5.2   Similarity, Stability, and Structure: The Indigo-Palygorskite Bonds in Maya Blue

But how to determine if those synthesized samples are indeed proper counterparts of the real Maya blue? This decision turned on three factors—*similarity, stability, and structure*. While the samples looked visually quite similar to those of the original Maya blue, and thus satisfied the similarity criterion, these products had to be tested for stability. To test the stability of the synthetic material then, the researchers applied Gettens' test, that is, keeping those samples in nitric acid, aqua regia, and other similar harsh reactants for 24 hours—generally waiting to see if any change of color or fading shows up in their synthetic product.[3] For most of the specimens, there were no such significant color changes, thus showing

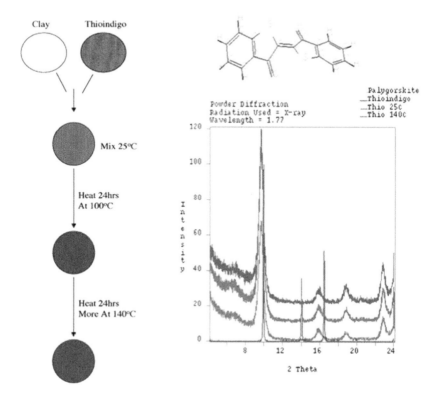

Fig. 17.4   Change of colors (Reprinted with permission from Russell Chianelli)

that both the wet and the dry grinding techniques can produce equally good results. Additionally, the samples were washed and extracted by dimethyl sulfoxide (DMSO) until the clay once again turned nearly white. This established that it was indeed the chemical reaction between the clay and the organic indigo that was causing the typical blue color.

The chemists now asked the most important question: *If the pigment remains stable under all kinds of harsh testing, just where does its stability come from?* It was therefore necessary to investigate how the indigo binds onto the palygorskite clay, the exact nature of those bonds, and whether such binding were good counterparts of the traditional samples of Maya blue. The second part of their task thus consisted of exploring the nature of the chemical interactions between the inorganic clay and the organic indigo molecules. Both the heated and the unheated samples of Indigo-palygorskite complex were exposed to synchrotron XRD techniques. While the unheated mixtures of indigo and palygorskite complex showed clear diffraction peaks in indigo crystals, those peaks disappeared in the heated samples of the synthetic Maya blue, thus showing that the crystal structures of indigo have been disrupted because of its bonding with the clay. The super-lattice structure of the palygorskite clay, however, appeared quite undisturbed, which suggests that the stability of Maya blue does not arise from the indigo entering the nano-sized channels in the clay. Instead, the stability seems to arise from the formation of *an organic/inorganic complex* upon the surface of those channels.

The resistance to chemical degradation, the striking color changes, and the disappearance of the indigo diffraction peaks under XRD all suggested that upon direct heating, the two organic/inorganic ingredients get fused to produce a surface complex, the organic molecules of indigo covering the surfaces of the fibrous clay material but also (sometimes) entering into the open ends of those channels. This possibility of the formation of such a stable surface complex made of organic/inorganic material was further supported by high-resolution transmission electron microscopy (HRTEM). While normally the palygorskite clay shows itself to be quite unstable under electron beams, quickly leading to a collapse of its channels because of rapid water evaporation, after the indigo was allowed to bind onto those channels, the ensemble appeared to be quite stable, producing clear lattice images under HRTEM. This suggested that the indigo molecules are now tightly bound onto the channel ends as well as on to the exposed channel surfaces, thus preventing the usual kind of collapse. Differential thermal analysis (DTA) also showed that the bonding between indigo and the clay surface is stronger than a normal hydrogen bond. The palygorskite clay can thus be thought of as affording a cylindrical surface upon which the indigo binds very tightly after heating, occasionally even filling up the exposed ends of the nano-sized channels (Fig. 17.5).

To this general picture of an organic/inorganic surface complex, the IR and Raman spectrography (applied both to the indigo-palygorskite and the indigo-thioindigo samples) added new bits of information. While the spectra from the palygorskite-indigo mixture, with 6 percent and 16 percent indigo concentration, resembled the spectra from the original Maya blue, the indigo-thioindigo mixture showed the possibility of making new types of organic/inorganic complexes, which were unknown to the Maya,

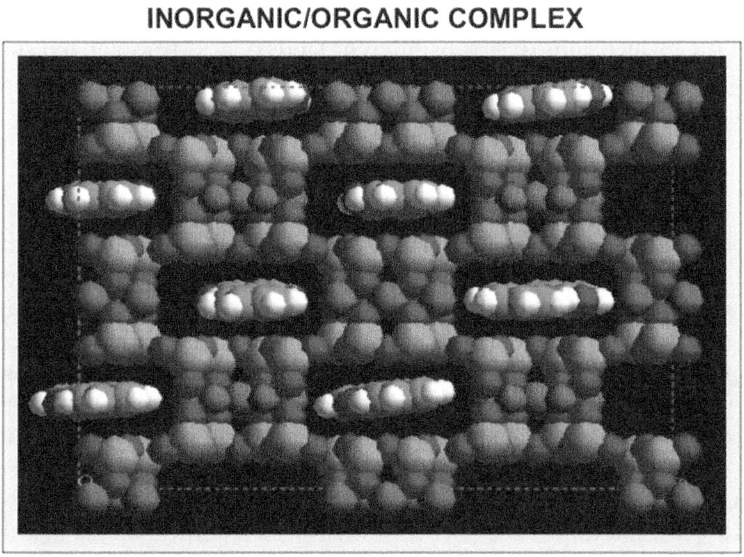

INORGANIC/ORGANIC COMPLEX

Fig. 17.5 The hybrid bonds (Reprinted with permission from Russell Chianelli)

but which could be brought into existence in our day, by replacing the indigo with other numerous kinds of organic dyes. A proper understanding of the hybrid organic/inorganic surface complexes formed via Maya blue thus throws new light upon our current understanding of the range of such possible organic/inorganic materials, showing us how to revise this process at will, indeed opening doors to a whole world of new materials. Stated very briefly, the path of the interaction between the indigo and the palygorskite clay goes as follows. The palygorskite clay consists of ribbons of tetrahedral structure that carry silicon-oxygen-silicon and silicon-oxygen-(hydrogen-aluminum and magnesium). As the nitrogen loses a proton, bonding occurs onto the exposed surfaces, which causes a change in their electronic structure, thus naturally changing the color of the substance. This understanding leads us to conceive several new possibilities. First, the organic indigo could be replaced by other kinds of organic materials, essentially promising new kinds of useful and environmentally safe products for the paint and the pigment industry, perhaps eventually extending those things even to possible biomedical usage.[4] At the end of this project, the researchers ambitiously founded a company called Maya Blue Inc., which aims to supply different kinds of acid-resistant and stable paints for the plastic, concrete, and cement.

17.6   FROM AN OLD TECHNOLOGY TO A DIVERSE SCIENCE: A THREE-WAY TRADE

Hybrid organic-inorganic materials are now opening a world of possibilities, giving rise to ranges of functional nano-materials that could be of immense interest to chemists, physicists, and certainly material scientists. The search for the recipe of Maya blue, its hopeful conclusion with a set of samples, a potential line of new pigments, and a budding understanding of many new hybrid materials of various physical and chemical properties that could be now made in the lab, tell us that often a scientific community may gain remarkable insights into its own research program via its trade with a historic predecessor, even when the predecessor no longer exists in actual space and time. Yet evidence of their work and the material that they have left behind might prompt or inspire such a search, causing the beginnings of a three-way trade, and with it perhaps the possibility of new lines of discovery. Consistent with the idea with which I began this chapter, I consider such interchanges cases of three-way trading zones. Notice that instead of the usual two parties, here we have a multitude of partners present from the very beginning. The material chemists at UTEP picked up their program from the ancient Maya heritage, but having concluded their project, they must now enter upon a new set of trade with the larger scientific community in order to receive its consensus. Thus, the whole interaction spans the present as well as that of the past, involving multiple communities in the give-and-take. Following Michael Gorman, I consider trading zones as spaces where an interaction between different parties give rise to new outcomes that neither of them could have achieved alone. Like all other trading zones, these kinds of zones also serve various kinds of purposes. In my present example, it linked a community of modern chemists with a group of historic predecessors, thus guaranteeing the inclusion of this ancient knowledge into the stock of expertise of a modern scientific community. Out of this exchange emerged the fruitful extension of a current research program, and an interesting possibility that this ancient tradition might now be able to inspire various other kinds of trades. The expertise of those ancient masters, once lost, can now be re-inserted into

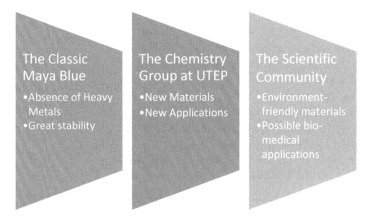

Fig. 17.6 Structure of the 3-way trade in Maya Blue

our present stock of knowledge, thereby saving, on the one hand, the old knowledge from extinction, and giving the new knowledge an unexpected boost in the arm. Research programs like this could give rise to a very context and culture-sensitive science, where the old and new are bonded together to create a diverse range of new outcomes (Fig. 17.6).

17.7 ENRICHMENT OF A RESEARCH PROGRAM VIA POSITIVE HEURISTICS

The notion of a research program was introduced by Imre Lakatos, Karl Popper's student as well as his critic, who tried to provide a reply to Thomas Kuhn's problematic notion of a paradigm. Trying to develop a language that would capture the dynamics of day-to-day scientific practice, and yet somehow remain amenable to a set of rational standards, Lakatos proposed the more nuanced notion of a research program via which science makes progress (or sometime degenerates). A research program consists of a sequence of several historically associated theories within a particular domain (Lakatos 1978). The business of science then, according to Lakatos, consists of working on numerous auxiliary hypotheses that surround a program's hard core. Thus, instead of simply trying to confirm or falsify a single theory, scientists are usually engaged with chains of research programs that may either flourish (or die) in the course of their practice.

This work of extension or modification is carried out by what Lakatos calls heuristics, that is, sets of prescriptions that surround the "hard core"—the non-negotiable parts of a research program. A core is thus always surrounded by a large class of protective hypotheses, upon which a scientist applies his or her heuristics. It is this kind of work which constitutes the day-to-day life of a scientist. The question of the progressive nature of science thus boils down to the question of how these research programs are rendered progressive by means of the various kinds of heuristics used by the scientific communities.

If we apply this intuitive analysis on how research programs are born and evolve in the hands of the working scientists via their heuristics, we can quite clearly see the anatomy of the Maya blue research program with its conspicuous trading zones. What Chianelli's group undertook was to develop sets of positive heuristics around the search for environment-friendly materials and this heuristic quickly led them onto the Maya blue project, and its eventual synthesis. This project was born via their trade with an ancient culture and its stock of expertise. Trying to wed the two traditions, they next produced samples of an organic/inorganic hybrid compound, and developed a battery of tests through which those samples could be examined. These positive heuristics were born in the context of a fertile cultural borderland, receptive to all kinds of influences from the two countries, two cultures, and two heritages. Their training as chemists allowed them to meld all these complex influences into a coherent form of research program. Through this process, they gained a glimpse of a world of possible new materials, and even formed a sort of transnational community with the UNAM researchers across the border because of their shared collaborations.

17.8   Fertile Contexts of Science: Borderlands and Peripheries

While our general analysis of science looks mostly to the contexts of a few resource-rich communities and their outputs, I have argued elsewhere that the various constrained circumstances of science can also allow us equally beautiful windows onto the processes of scientific discovery and its creativity (Dasgupta 2012). My earlier studies were about scientific practices in the peripheries, that is, settings where someone who is largely self-trained works mostly alone in the absence of communities or mentors, and yet still manages to attain some kind of a fundamental breakthrough. To this original concept, I now add the notion of a borderland as another such fertile context of science. A borderland, briefly speaking, is a context where people (in this case, the UTEP researchers) are surrounded by multiple kinds of influences. This condition, far from diminishing the strength and the focus of a scientific research program, might actually lend it a sharper creative edge, allowing the protagonists to marry old things with the new, and devise novel heuristics for their research programs. Looking into the details of such a scientific practice when science is carried out under such conditions might allow us to grasp the processes of creativity in various new contexts. Of course, statements like this will be accepted easily in their general format, but there exists a serious dearth of case studies that show us the fine-grained structure of such possible practices. This chapter seeks to fill this conspicuous gap as well as to invite other similar case studies.

The complex concept of a three-way trade that I have developed here can be used to formulate visions of a diverse science, suitable for our twenty-first century, where old stocks of knowledge might be combined and married with the new in order to solve complex current problems. To give another quick example of this sort of trade, consider the interesting case of what is called gravity lights, a very simple way of producing illumination for daily use by means of the rather well-known medieval technology of falling weights. Such falling weights can power a generator for the space of 20–30 minutes (after which of course it must be re-adjusted by hand). Not only can such lights be very effective in different resource-poor conditions, bypassing the need for a sophisticated infrastructure, but it can also replace the more expensive (and the more polluting) use of other light sources, such as kerosene lamps, thus solving at once whole hosts of economic problems as well as preventing potential health hazards. Hence, such contexts of science, for example, contexts in which science is practiced under a variety of conditions such as peripherality or that of borderlands, might actually afford us with new opportunities for scientific creativity. Additionally, such hybrid practices may now allow scientists to use those things as valuable teaching tools and even maintain and preserve cultural identities. In the Maya blue study, for example, the ancient masters who were the originators of this technology must now be accorded a place as contributors in our expert knowledge, thus giving them a place of respect in the tradition of scientific expertise.

17.9   CONCLUSION

The Maya Blue case study is an excellent example of how a complex three-way trade can inspire and enrich existing research programs of a scientific community, giving scientists an expanded vision of their task as well as suggesting new places where they might direct their future efforts. To recap my study, I presented here the case of a scientific community that took up its work on Maya blue with the goal of integrating that ancient expertise into their modern day research programs. In my earlier work, I have pointed out that while reconstructing the image of a scientific practice, we mostly tend to think of science as a great concentrated center in the shape of a few key communities (Dasgupta 2012). In this mental image, all epistemic authority and all innovativeness are concentrated in the hands of a few central players, and it is their efforts that we endlessly discuss and celebrate. In its place, I suggest that we should now think of science more as an extended epistemic landscape, dotted by places such as borderlands and peripheries. This incorporation of a cluster motif into the models of science would be useful to show how different kinds of scientific practices may be born of different forms of trades. While the research programs pursued by a few central communities might become very well-known, yet, from spaces such as peripheries or borderlands, there might arise very innovative new ideas, thus affording the scientific community further epistemic opportunities.

The ability to move back and forth between those different frameworks, and trade the results of one system with the other, can give rise to fertile new forms of research programs. The very business of recovering the recipe for Maya blue shows the implicit creative potential of such trades. The location of the UTEP material chemists on a borderland, situated in the midst of two countries, two cultures, and two languages gave them a keener eye and a motivation to pursue such trades with an ancient culture. But trades like this can indeed be repeated multiple times in the future. Reclaiming a piece of knowledge from the past, and building bridges with an ancient brand of expertise, might usher in different forms of research programs. Such newly emerging contexts of science will perhaps be one of its most productive and most innovative contexts, and an old research program extracted from history can sometimes serve as a springboard for new ideas, in its wake setting up a dialogue with the past.

NOTES

1. And conversely, trading has given rise to many forms of exploitation.
2. This 2000 workshop titled *Application of Synchrotron Techniques to Materials Issues in Art and Archeology* was organized by Nick Pingitore, Russell Chianelli, and Herman Winick. Other equally attractive presentations in this workshop included synchrotron studies of the Tyrian purple dye as well as the manufacture of cosmetics in ancient Egypt. A good portion of this workshop was thus devoted to explore various kinds of old technologies, obviously intending to use them as spring boards for a variety of new research programs.
3. Gettens' test is a test for chemical stability, which consists of applying various harsh reactants, such as hydrochloric, sulfuric acids, etc., at room temperatures and then heating the mixture to test its final stability.
4. In October 2013, Russell Chianelli and his students presented a poster in the UTEP biomedical symposium, titled, "Novel Mayan Treatments for Cancer Treatment."

REFERENCES

Berke, Heinz. 2007. The Invention of Blue and Purple Pigments in Ancient Times. *Chemical Society Reviews* 36: 15–30.

Berrie, Barbara H. 2012. Rethinking the History of Artists' Pigments Through Chemical Analysis. *Annual Review of Analytical Chemistry* 5: 441–459.

Collins, Harry M., R. Evans, and M. Gorman. 2007. Trading Zones and Interactional Expertise. *In Case Studies of Expertise and Experience: Special Issue of Studies in the History and Philosophy of Science* 38 (4): 657–666.

Dasgupta, D. 2012. Creating a Peripheral Trading Zone: Satyendra Nath Bose and Bose-Einstein Statistics, Doing Science in the Role of an Outsider. *International Studies in the Philosophy of Science* 26 (3): 259–287.

Galison, Peter. 1997. *Image and Logic: A Material Culture of Microphysics.* Chicago, IL: University of Chicago Press.

Gorman, Michael. 2005. Levels of Expertise and Trading Zones: Combining Cognitive and Social Approaches to Technology Studies. In *Scientific and Technological Thinking*, ed. Michael Gorman, David Gooding, and Alexandra Kincannon. Mahwah, NJ: Lawrence Erlbaum Associates.

———, ed. 2010. *Trading Zones and Interactional Expertise: Creating New Kinds of Collaborations.* Cambridge, MA: The MIT Press.

Guston, David H., ed. 2010. *Encyclopedia of Nano-sciences and Society.* 1st ed. London: Sage Publications.

Houston, Stephen. 2014. *The Life Within: Classic Maya and the Matter of Permanence.* New Haven, CT: Yale University Press.

Lakatos, Imre. 1978. *The Methodology of Scientific Research Programmes.* Cambridge: Cambridge University Press.

Leitão, Inês M.V., and J. Sergio Sexas de Melo. 2013. Maya Blue, an Ancient Guest–Host Pigment: Synthesis and Models. *Journal of Chemical Education* 90 (11): 1493–1497.

Lori Polette, Norma Ugarte, Russell Chianelli, et al. 2000. *In-Situ Identification of Palygorskite in Maya Blue Samples Using Synchrotron X-ray Powder Diffraction.* Presentation at the 18th Workshop on Synchrotron Radiation in Art and Archaeology (Stanford Synchrotron Radiation Lightsource).

Polette-Niewold, Lori Ann, Felicia Manciu, Brenda Torres, Manuel Alvarado Jr., and Russell Chianelli. 2007. Organic/Inorganic Complex Pigments: Ancient Colors Maya Blue. *Journal of Inorganic Biochemistry* 101: 1958–1173.

CHAPTER 18

Conclusion

David S. Caudill

The editors of, and contributors to, this volume hope that the foregoing studies demonstrate the analytical potential of the "Third Wave" in science and technology studies. Collins and Evans' work on expertise over the last two decades has resonated with and inspired numerous scholars throughout the world and across many disciplinary boundaries. Indeed, the chapters in this volume represent only a minor selection from the papers presented (and often thereafter, published) at the annual Studies in Expertise and Experience workshops (SEESHOPs) held since 2007 in Cardiff and occasionally elsewhere.

It is also hoped that the studies in this volume not only explore and elucidate the theoretical and practical aspects of the "Third Wave," but also inspire others to adopt and/or critically reflect upon, and improve, the analytical frameworks associated with Collins and Evans' categories of expertise and their Imitation Games project. The success of this volume will initially be measured by increasing the understanding and the applications of "Third Wave" methodologies, but in the long run our goal is to help maintain a critical discourse, within the inter-discipline of science and technology studies, concerning expertise and experience as bases for decision-making in various social, political, scientific, legal, and business contexts.

D. S. Caudill (✉)
Villanova University, Villanova, PA, USA
e-mail: caudill@law.villanova.edu

© The Author(s) 2019
D. S. Caudill et al. (eds.), *The Third Wave in Science and Technology Studies*, https://doi.org/10.1007/978-3-030-14335-0_18

INDEX[1]

[1] Note: Page numbers followed by 'n' refer to notes.